THE RISE OF ALCHEMY IN FOURTEENTH-CENTURY ENGLAND

The Rise of Alchemy in Fourteenth-Century England

Plantagenet Kings and the Search for the Philosopher's Stone

Jonathan Hughes

continuum

Continuum International Publishing Group
The Tower Building 11 York Road, London SE1 7NX
80 Maiden Lane, Suite 704, New York, NY 10038

www.continuumbooks.com

First published 2012

British Library Cataloguing-in-Publication Data
A catalogue record for this book is available from the British Library.

ISBN: HB: 978-1-4411-7804-6
PB: 978-1-4411-8183-1

Library of Congress Cataloging-in-Publication Data
A catalog record for this book is available from the Library of Congress.

Typeset by Newgen Imaging Systems Pvt Ltd, Chennai, India
Printed and bound in India

White is specially employed in the celebration of the Passion of our Lord; though in the vision of St. John, white robes are given to the redeemed, and the four-and-twenty elders stand clothed in white before the great white throne, and the Holy One that sitteth there white like wool; yet for all these accumulated associations, with whatever is sweet, and honourable and sublime, there yet lurks an elusive something in the innermost idea of this hue, which strikes more of panic to the soul than that redness which affrights in blood. (Herman Melville, 'The Whiteness of the Whale', in Moby Dick)

Contents

Illustrations

Acknowledgements

In the early stages of this book, while attempting to gain funding, I received much help in formulating research proposals from Peregrine Horden of Royal Holloway, London and Jeremy Catto of Oriel College, Oxford. They have both been kind enough to read and comment on the final text. The British Academy has helped me with the expenses involved in consulting manuscripts with study grants. I also wish to thank the staff of The Bodleian Library, Oxford, the British Library, London and Cambridge University Library. I also wish to thank my parents, Robert Owen and Barbara Hughes. Their decision to emigrate to New Zealand exposed me to foreign travel at an early age, and while they may have transported me from the medieval influences of my infancy, Cuddington, Delamere Forest and Chester, this move would ultimately expose me to the inspiration of the late Valerie Flint at Auckland University.

Unlike my two previous books, which were written in some difficult circumstances, this one has been conceived and completed in a very happy and fulfilled environment, and for this I am very grateful to my wife who has supported me throughout all the research and writing. We met at a conference on alchemy organized by myself at the Wellcome Unit in the University of East Anglia in March 2002 and from that moment she has been a constant inspiration. Together we have travelled to many of the places associated with alchemy and the occult and she has shared all my enthusiasms and excitement as we visited the red and white springs at Glastonbury; the site of Merlin's vision of the red and white dragons in Snowdonia; the *Wilton Diptych* in the National Gallery; the Cosmati pavements at Westminster Abbey, St Cecilia, Trastavere, Maria Maggiore, Rome and Hagia Sophia, Istanbul; the Grail sites in Languedoc; the treasury in San Marco, Venice; the Golden Lane and alchemical furnace at Prague Castle; and places associated with the birth of alchemy in the Nile Valley and with Muslim alchemy in Morocco. In addition she has carefully read the manuscript and made many valuable suggestions. This book is dedicated to her and to our son, Alexander, and to my children Venetia and Timothy who has helped me through many an ICT crisis.

Foreword

Com sir Palomydes, the good knight, folowyng the questynge beste that had in shap lyke
a serpentis hede and a body lyk a lybud (leopard), buttocked lyke a lyon and footed lyke
an hart. And in hys body there was such a noyse as hit had bene twenty couple of houn-
dys questynge, and such a noyse that beste made wheresoever he wente. And thys beste
evermore sir Palomydes followed, for he was called hys queste

Sir Thomas Malory, *Morte d' Arthur* [1]

The origins of this book lie in my childhood, the first five years of which were
spent in a council estate called Sandiway, near the medieval village of Cuddington,
on the edge of Delamere Forest in Cheshire. The forest seemed to be ruled by a
great beast, the steam engine that crossed the forest on the mid-Cheshire railway
line east-west on its way from Manchester to Chester. We regularly travelled to
Chester from Cuddington station and my earliest memories are of this frightening
and fascinating monster announcing its approach with a tremendous roar. As the
sleek, black trunk of the engine and the serpentine tail of red and white carriages
glided alongside the platform a momentous interplay of the four elements would
take place in the form of steam (air and water), fire and coal. My walks through the
forest with my parents were accompanied by the distinctive smell of burning coal
and steam and the bellowing of this fire-breathing beast, whose shrill cries
resounded through the trees.

The steam trains are long gone but there is another beast that ruled the forest
for much longer, the great stag, reminders of which can be seen in the image of
the white hart found on many pubs in the area, especially in Chester. Delamere
Forest is a remnant of the forests of Mara and Mondrew which covered 60 square
miles in the eleventh century; and even in the fourteenth century the northern
part of Mara, which covered an area from the River Mersey to the River Weaver,
was a royal forest preserved since 1268 for hunting. Richard II was passionately
fond of hunting and he quested in this forest after a session of the Shrewsbury
parliament of January 1398. His closest friend, Robert de Vere, the earl of Oxford,
was killed while hunting in Louvain in 1391, and the one who came closest to De
Vere in the king's affections, Edward of Norwich, the duke of York and first duke
of Aumale (according to the French chronicler Jean Creton 'there was no man in
the world whom Richard loved better') wrote a treatise on hunting called the

Master of the Game, which reflects his experiences hunting with the king.[2]
The work was partly a translation of *Livre de Chasse*, written by Gaston Phoebus,
Count of Foix (who was also killed while hunting a bear in 1391), but with original passages and five additional chapters added by the duke of York while he was
in prison after his arrest for his involvement in a plot to release the captive King
Richard on the Feast of Epiphany, 1400. Much of the work, especially the additional chapters provided by York, is concerned with the nature of the hart, the
term given for a stag when it reached the age of ten, and how to hunt it.[3] The hart
was regarded by York as the monarch of the forest: it could be identified by its
long antlers, 'well-pearled' with royals (the tines near the antlers). It was supposed to live to be a hundred years of age and myths about its ability to renew
itself by eating the venom of a serpent suggested parallels with the durability of
the monarchy. Because of its kingly qualities the hart was seen as the natural
focus of the king's hunt; it was the ultimate test of the hunter: 'It is fair to hunt the
hart, for it is a fair thing to seek well a hart, and a fair thing well to harbour him –
I hold that it is the fairest hunting that any man may hunt after.'[4] The hunting
season for the hart lasted from the 3 May to 14 of September and Richard hunted
in royal forests like Delamere every summer. He would be stationed with his
queen in a clearing in the forest under the shelter of an awning of green branches
made by yeomen, either waiting with his bow for the hart to approach after being
roused from its lair or pursuing the tracked hart with his hart hounds, greyhounds led by his Irish wolfhound, Mathis.[5] With every hunt Richard's identification with this king of the forest intensified; a legend commemorated on a stone
near Bagshot records that Richard II was attacked by a wounded stag while hunting and was apparently saved by a white hart that came between them. In grati-
tude he set up four hostelries with the white hart in the area. Richard made an
albino hart his personal badge and by 1391 the white hart was being distributed
to his followers. In 1393 he passed an act making it compulsory for inns in London to have this insignia in order to identify them to the official ale taster and the
white hart was soon displayed on inns throughout the country. In particular in
Chester and the towns and villages around Delamere forest the badge of the white
hart became a prominent icon. This was the heart of Richard's kingdom and centre of his loyal support. All his followers were required to wear the badge of the
white hart. By 1396 Richard chose to portray himself on the outside of his portable altar (known as the *Wilton Diptych*) as a crowned white hart with the pearled
antlers described in the *Master of the Game*.

But Richard's identification with the hart went beyond his seeing it as an embodiment of his own power and authority. Although the white hart on the *Wilton
Diptych* is crowned, it is also chained to suggest the beast harboured (the term given
for the refuge chosen by the stag) by the hunters. York's description of the pursuit
of the hart by the greyhounds, and the creature's attempts to avoid inevitable

capture by beating up rivers and brooks, hiding in coverts or disguising his scent by going back over his droppings before eventually turning his head and standing at bay as every man and his hound draws near, evokes the last days of Richard's reign as his options dwindled and Henry Bolingbroke's forces closed in on him. The hart's death is heralded and mourned as if it is the death of a king. As it is stabbed behind the shoulder through to the heart, all the hunters gather around and blow the animal's death with their horns, and their blowing continues until they meet with the lord of the hunt.[6] Richard's deposition, capture and death were similarly evoked in hunting terms. It was widely reported that his hitherto faithful hound, Mathis, deserted him and went to Bolingbroke's side and slept on his bed (lymerer's dogs, which hunted by scent, would sleep with their lords). Bolingboke's badge was the greyhound (the hound used to hunt the hart) and chroniclers described how the harts were driven out of England by the greyhounds. Sir Thomas Malory may even have offered an oblique commentary on Richard's fate in 1471 in his *Morte d'Arthur* in his description of Sir Gawain's quest when he was charged to recover the white hart: 'Then Sir Gawayne and Gaherys followed after the white herte, and lete slyppe at the hert thre couple of greyhounds. And so they chace the herte into a castel, and in the chyef place of the castel they slet the hert.'[7]

There was more to this royal preoccupation with the hart than seeing in the animal a reflection of the themes of power, authority and mutability; at the heart of Richard's obsession with the hunting of this great beast was a preoccupation with something mystical, powerful and divine. York's account of the pursuit of the fierce great bull stag in the medieval forest, which had something of the depth and mystery of the ocean, evinces the sort of fascination and awe for the primeval creature of the id shown in Captain Ahab's pursuit of the great, white whale, Moby Dick. The hunt of the hart was described by York as if it were a religious quest, preceded by an acute sense of anticipation. The trials and joys of the hunter were thought to make him a better person and brought about his salvation: he was able to see the sunrise, listen to the birds singing and see the dew glistening on the leaves and shining on the grass and this was believed to bring him great joy as he sets out on his quest to meet the hart: 'It is a great joy and liking to the hunter.'[8] The evening before a royal hunt for the hart the master of the game gathers the sergeant of the office, the yeomen, berners and lymerers (those who help the huntsmen harbour the deer and have the hounds on a leash) and they choose a meeting place, 'a fair mead surrounded by green trees beside a running brook.'[9] Officials bring towels, broad cloths and set out diverse foods; this space is where the lord of the hunt (or the king) and the master of the game and all the officials will gather to form an assembly. On this vigil before the hunt the master of the game will assign different tasks to the yeomen, berners and lymerers, and establish which of them will attempt to harbour the hart. They arrange to meet at sunrise at an appointed place in the forest with all the yeomen, grooms and the relays of hounds.

On the 'grey dawning' they seek out the signs of the great stag in his droppings, or in broken boughs which denote his entry into his lair; and the finders hurry back to the gathering of officials headed by the lord (or the king) and the master of the game, bringing the broken boughs and droppings stuffed in their hunting horns and stopped with grass. The assembly will examine these traces to ascertain if it is the great stag they seek and every man shall shout: 'Lo here is a great hart and deer of high meating or pasturing; go we and move him; . . . then one can say the hunter has great joy.'[10] What Foix and York convey is a growing sense of awe and joy the hunter feels as he approaches the great hart and what amounts to a religious ecstasy when the hart is spotted: 'when all the hounds have passed before him then shall he ride after them and shall round and blow as loud as he may with great joy and pleasure – wherefore I say that hunters go into paradise when they die and live in this world more joyfully than any other man'.[11]

As the hunt proceeds through the forest following the beast's trace, the hunters watch for the signs of hoof marks, or the clawing of the earth, which they announce with peals on their horns 'Cy-va-cy-va-cy-va', while they listen for the sound of the great bellowing of the bull stag, 'who either stoops with his muzzle towards the earth, a token of an old and malicious hart, or stretches his muzzle out before him, the bellow of a great younger hart'.[12] The feelings aroused by this quest for the great bull of the forest are ambivalent. The hart is seen as cunning: 'there was no hunter in the world that can think of the tricks a hart can do'; elusive: 'the harts be the lightest (swiftest) of beasts and strongest and of marvellous great cunning'; and malicious and dangerous: 'And they be wonderfully perilous beasts, for with great pain shall a man revive that is hurt by a hart and therefore men say in old sais after the boar the leech and after the hart the bier.' Primitive, powerful, dangerous and even evil, this beast with its great pearled antlers is also like the great, white whale, somehow divine. This is borne out in York's description of the slaying of the hart and the division of his flesh, which takes on the aura of a religious ceremony. After the hunters had divided the body, in the same way that they would divide and consume the host on the midsummer feast of Corpus Christi, there would be drinking of wine and exchange of tales of the quest. This killing of a beast seen as more powerful and cunning than man is a religious sacrifice. The hart, with its 32 tines and regenerating velvet, was seen as a figure of Christ: it was killed and consumed by men, and York's account of the hunting of the hart provides an allegory of Richard II's kingship, his sense of messianic destiny, martyrdom and betrayal.

Something much older also lurked behind these hunting rituals. The stag in Celtic mythology was the sacred, horned beast or man of the forest (*cernunnos*), represented on bowls as a god with stag's horns, worshipped for its regenerative qualities, the lord of the hunt who becomes the hunted, sacrificial victim. This much is implied in the rituals surrounding the slaying of the hart announced by peals of the hunters' horns which continued as the master of the game and the lord placed the head on two poles and took it up by the antlers on either side, and every hunter blew the death in a procession to the assembly where after the division of the body every man would cry 'devour'.[13] However the hunting metaphor not only leads us into the world of pagan, occult mysteries; it is central to the development of late fourteenth-century science through the rise of alchemy. The notion conveyed in York's hunting treatise is of a dangerous, cunning and elusive beast that in its primeval power represents something profoundly evil and good, even divine, and this explains why the fugitive stag represented for late medieval alchemists the primal substance of mercury. Mercury and the hart were seen to share much in common: both were elusive, potent tricksters. The capture, or fixing, of mercury, an elusive, omnipotent and dangerous substance that existed before the creation, was at the heart of the alchemist's quest, and like the hunter he pursued his quarry with self-discipline and dedication. When captured, mercury, like the hart, was tortured: its power was harnessed and it was made to serve mankind, becoming in its earthly incarnation a symbol of Christ. Richard II, like the white hart in the *Wilton Diptych* is bounded, captured in a golden chain, and his followers, the wearers of the white hart, were seen as the disciples of a king who was also to be betrayed and martyred, a sacrificial Christ figure; a fate fulfilled when Richard was deposed and murdered at the turn of the century. Richard II's identification with the white hart introduces us into the world of late fourteenth-century alchemy, its popularization and deployment in political and cultural life.

The pursuit of the white hart in the forests of medieval England takes one into a different mental world. The cultural and intellectual life of the late fourteenth century has been extensively studied by Bruce McFarlane, Jeremy Catto, Maurice Keen and the present author in terms of a flourishing code of chivalry and the growth of devotional enthusiasms among the clerical and lay nobility.[14] However modern historians have paid little attention to the development of a scientific curiosity about the workings of the natural world among the educated elite of late medieval England. The emerging popular awareness of alchemy and the insights it could provide into the hidden forces within the earth adds a new dimension to understanding the literature of the Plantagenet court and especially the works of the two great geniuses of the late fourteenth century, Geoffrey Chaucer and the poet known as The Gawain Poet. *The Canterbury Tales*, *Sir Gawain and the Green Knight* and *Pearl* have been extensively studied within the context of Christian and chivalric values but a consideration of their occult, alchemical themes and symbolism can add a new dimension to understanding the richness of these texts. The politics of the reigns of Edward III and Richard II have been evaluated according to the same chivalric and religious values: Edward III has been regarded as a king of average intelligence whose successes have been attributed to his normality and his adherence to the chivalric conventions of the baronial class. Richard II's enigmatic personality and spectacular fall have been attributed to his immaturity and unwillingness to endorse the same martial values adopted by his grandfather. But such explanations do not do justice to the intelligence and complexity of both men and fail to consider their cultural sophistication and the fascination they had for ceremony and ritual. Above all, it is their involvement in, and patronage of, alchemy and related occult arts that explains their successes and failures.

Part 1

Alchemy and the Occult in English Cultural and Political Life

1

Introduction: Alchemy and the Occult in England

Merlin cared deeply for Uther Pendragon and – spoke to him privately saying 'I ought to reveal to you some of my deepest secrets now that this land is fully in your hands. Because of my love for you I shall conceal nothing'

Boron's Book of Merlin [1]

The term occult, derived from the Latin *occultus* (hidden), refers to the secret super-natural or divine forces to be found in the terrestrial sphere beneath the moon. [2] The belief in such powers was based on the notion that everything within the earth emanated from the same divine force that governed the heavens and that nothing corporeal could ever be lost but remained in a constant state of flux and would ultimately be restored to its original divine purity. The scientific understanding of the workings of nature was the key to the occult wisdom imparted to the late medi-eval art of alchemy, which attempted to understand the growth of metals in the earth and to transmute them to the primal state of perfection found in gold. The alchemist was privy in his laboratory to the awesome powers described in the *Book of Genesis*: 'In the beginning God created heaven and earth, the earth was without form and void, with darkness over the face of the abyss and the spirit of God hover-ing over the surface of the world, and God said, "let there be light" and there was light, and God saw the light was good and he separated light from darkness.' Besides witnessing the distilling and sublimating that formed the world, the alchemist con-tinued to attempt to harness the transformative powers of the sun and moon. Occult knowledge of the dynamic interplay between the four elements was seen as a key to knowledge of the workings of natural forces and the destinies of individu-als and nations (all products of the earth) and even of the origins and ultimate fate of all life on earth. The purpose of this book is to explore the origins of alchemy in the fourteenth century when it was considered to be a respectable form of scientific enquiry into the natural world, and alchemists were less likely to be viewed with suspicion or derision or associated with diabolic practises or superstition.

Since the Renaissance Britain had been the source of scientific and industrial revolutions that laid the foundations for an overseas empire and the modern age. This has helped to perpetuate the myth that the British are a supremely rational and pragmatic people. The national church established in the Reformation was

Protestant with a Calvinistic ethos: its members envisaged a remote divinity and his predestined elect as the instruments of an inscrutable providence unfolding through human ingenuity and reason in the fields of science and politics.[3] This 'Protestant work ethic' was supposedly the basis for national achievements in science, law and politics. In the face of this perceived rise of empirical science in the seventeenth and eighteenth centuries the role of magic in people's lives was perceived to have inevitably declined. Such generalizations overlook the important place that a belief in the workings of supernatural, occult forces occupied in the minds of the intelligentsia in the fields of religion, science, politics and literature. The key to an understanding of these forces is the art of alchemy.

Throughout the sixteenth to the eighteenth centuries, when popular belief in magic was supposed to be declining, some of the nation's leading scientists and natural philosophers were involved in the study of alchemy. Many within the established Protestant church were of an Arminian persuasion and believed in God's imminence in the physical world. John Milton, the author of the Protestant epic *Paradise Lost*, told a story of the friends of truth searching for the mangled body of Osiris.[4] Although the 39 articles denied transubstantiation, the priest, when he uttered the words of the consecration, became in effect an alchemist presiding over a miracle of transubstantiation, the manifestation of the divine: Christ's presence in the bread on the high altar at the moment of communion testified to the possibility of transmutation, the ultimate goal of alchemy. Francis Bacon, the leading proponent of empirical science during the reign of James I, took alchemy seriously enough for the service it could provide to natural philosophy and experimental science. He collected the alchemical works of the fifteenth-century alchemist George Ripley and was interested in the first seeds and menstrue of minerals. Robert Boyle, the father of modern chemistry and pioneer of experimental science, regarded alchemy as a tool for analysing nature and saw transmutation as a possibility. Although he insisted on conducting alchemical research in a controlled laboratory environment, he also embraced the magical side of alchemy and possibly communicated with the spirit world.[5] The physician Thomas Browne was a leading proponent of experimental science, a rational scientist who claimed he valued Harvey's discovery of the circulation of blood above Columbus's voyages of discovery. Browne, a friend of fellow Norwich resident and physician, Arthur Dee, physician to Charles I (1635–40), and son of John Dee, took alchemy seriously as a way of approaching natural philosophy and experimental science and believed in the possibility of transmutation.[6] Browne saw evidence of God's power throughout nature and believed in the realization of the invisible, numinous world of Platonic teaching. Alchemy for Browne was a way of learning about the mysterious operation of the soul in the body during its three stages of existence prior to and following physical birth and death. For him the life death and rebirth of metals, played out in the alchemical process and the exaltation of gold, was a model for the spirit's transformation and regeneration and the resurrection of the putrefied body on the last day. This could be demonstrated experimentally by the dispersion and subsequent fusion of droplets of mercury (quicksilver) into a coherent ball (like a pearl).[7] The sale of Sir Isaac Newton's papers in 1936 even showed that the founder of modern science and discoverer of the mechanistic universe spent most of his life gaining inspiration for his theories of the laws of light and gravity from a lifelong study of alchemy. Newton conducted alchemical experiments in his laboratory and closely studied the allegorical texts of such English alchemists as George Ripley, believing that the key to all scientific wisdom lay in obscure alchemical texts and in the wisdom of the ancients. Isaac Newton saw the Last Judgement in terms of the conclusion of an alchemical opus. Alchemy provided the bridge enabling him to unify all his scientific and religious interests.

The political importance of alchemy in Spain has recently been studied. The court of Madrid was a meeting place for alchemists and natural philosophers and Philip II financed expeditions to discover the treasures of his overseas possessions. An Irishman Richard Stanyhuirst, the natural philosopher, was employed at the Escorial to experiment in alchemical distillation to find a medicinal essence to treat the ailing monarch. It is possible that the broadening imperial concerns of the Tudor court resulted in an interest in the acquisition of alchemical remedies. Sir Henry Platt in *The Jewell House of Art and Nature* in 1597 wrote with a sense of wonder at the potential for exploring the earth for remedies to reverse the effects of the fall.[8] John Dee and his alchemical associate, Edmund Kelly, were employed in the court of Philip II's nephew, Rudolph II, who shared his uncle's alchemical interests.[9] Dee was engaged in memorials pertaining to the art of navigation, the first part of which was published as *Pety Navy Royal* in 1577 and the fourth part as a treatise urging the need for overseas enterprise.[10] Queen Elizabeth I sought astrological advice from Dr John Dee on her accession day ceremonies, and her minister, William Cecil, Lord Burghley (1521–98), owned a collection of alchemical works, including those of George Ripley.[11] The political life of Britain from the end of the Middle Ages was frequently understood in terms of hermetic philosophy. The politics of the English Civil War and the interregnum took on a hermetic alchemical significance for commentators such as Thomas Vaughan (1622–66), the alchemist and twin brother of poet Henry Vaughan,[12] and Thomas and William Habington,[13] for whom the disintegration of the kingship had obvious parallels with the torture and dismemberment suffered by precious metals in the alchemist's furnace; the restoration of the monarchy in 1660 was accordingly seen in terms of the resurrection of the dead king and his body politic to the original purity of gold. It was partly to underline this point that Charles II maintained his own alchemical laboratories.

Occult, alchemical themes also pervaded English literature from the time of the Renaissance. The nation's leading poet and dramatist, William Shakespeare, chose as the theme of *The Tempest*, his last complete play (and the only one containing a plot of his own invention), the retirement of a magus, Prospero, who was partly modelled on John Dee but also on Shakespeare himself, who, like a creative artist, has the power to create illusions, open graves and invoke the dead and explore the mysteries of nature and the human personality. The characters of Prospero, Caliban and Ariel were used to analyse the relationship between the soul, body and spirit and the limited possibilities of the transmutation of human nature. The Dean of St Paul's, John Donne, drew on the notion of Christ's blood as a tincture for the purification of souls, and his fellow poet, George Herbert, used alchemical images to write about his religious alchemy in which he worked on the dross of his free will, transmuting his own poetic will into the gold of divine will through the elixir of Christly presence.[14] The poetry of Henry Vaughan is concerned with the potentiality of nature: the sense that everything is in a state of movement and flux with a latent possibility of the transformation of various states of existence to a return to a state of primal perfection, a new life of immortality after the Last Judgement.[15]

Despite this interest in alchemy in such refined circles there has been, since the Renaissance, a history of tension concerning the relationship between alchemy and other intellectual pursuits. The Enlightenment, ironically identified with such figures as Isaac Newton, was a cultural movement that maintained a belief in a rational, mechanistic universe and a rational philosophy and experimental science that disproved theories of magical correspondences and material transformation and dismantled the network of myths and legends that wove a line from Hermes Trismegistus to Moses and Merlin; this in turn encouraged a polarizing of opinions between those who maintained an Aristotelian, materialistic view of the universe and those who held to a Platonist, hermetic philosophy. This tension between the occult and science continued to be reflected in intellectual life in the nineteenth century as Romantic poets like William Blake reacted against what they perceived to be Newton's Godless universe by asserting the mysterious, irrational forces within nature and man himself. In the twentieth century the debate took different forms in the field of psychiatry. A sceptical, rational and mechanistic model of human behaviour was propounded by Pavlovian analysts and cognitive therapists and it was the occult, and alchemy in particular, that inspired the articulation of opposite views. The visions and myths of alchemists from the sixteenth to eighteenth centuries provided the Swiss psychiatrist Carl Jung with his model for the collective unconscious, a dark primeval natural force that he maintained (in the tradition of the Romantics) defined human personality and behaviour.[16] What was missing from Jung's comprehensive, pioneering analysis of the alchemical writings of Western Europe was a sense of historical and geographical perspective. He gave little consideration to the national identities and dates of the writers he discussed and, with the exception of George Ripley, he referred sparingly to alchemical writers of the late Middle Ages and the circumstances and influences under which they were writing.

However, such omissions are not unusual in the modern age. Alchemy is a much studied subject, but its origins in Western Europe in the late Middle Ages are relatively neglected. Most university courses on alchemy and the occult tend to start from the Renaissance. However in the seventeenth century the reputation of late medieval English occult learning was such that Elias Ashmole compiled his *Theatrum Chemicum Britannicum,* which he defined as an ark salvaging the alchemical treasures of the English nation which had a special reputation as a repository of occult learning.[17] The French were so jealous of this reputation and the status enjoyed by such late medieval English alchemists as George Ripley that an elaborate hoax was perpetuated in the seventeenth century in which alchemical works and a colourful autobiography were foisted on to a late-fourteenth-century wealthy bookseller by the name of Nicholas Flamel.[18] The purpose of this book is to look at the occult in England in the period just before the Renaissance, when the tensions between alchemy, which was becoming increasingly mythologized, and religion were beginning to appear. This was a period when the conflict between science, religion and the occult had not been articulated and alchemy was at the centre of English scientific, cultural and political life. A study of alchemy in the fourteenth century may help to explain a number of anomalies. The British nation that exported to its vast overseas empire the scientific and industrial revolutions that laid the foundations for the modern world also incorporated onto its flag an occult symbol, the Red Cross on a white background that, as we shall see, has strong alchemical associations. King James I, under whom the realms of England and Scotland were united, adopted the lion and the unicorn as the royal coat of arms, and by the sixteenth century this was a common alchemical motif with its roots in the late Middle Ages. Even the national saint, St George (d. 303), who was probably martyred in Syria during the persecutions of Diocletian, and whose cult established itself in the eastern Mediterranean around a Byzantine soldier saint[19] is remembered for his association with the dragon (also a key symbol for the alchemists); and there is an occult dimension to the myth of the founding of the British nation under King Arthur, for Arthur's destiny was believed to have been guided by the magician/alchemist Merlin. The explanation for the emergence of these symbols does not lie in the Dark Ages of Arthurian myth, or in the time when the Saviour was supposed to have walked upon 'this green and pleasant land', but in the late Middle Ages when the alchemical, scientific learning of the Muslim world penetrated learned circles and even popular culture in England.

During the Renaissance the emergence of empirical, scientific method was beginning to open a widening rift between scientific method and the occult. The practice of magic was deemed to be an illicit attempt to harness supernatural powers that occurred outside the sphere of respectable intellectual enquiry sanctioned by the universities and the church. The appearance of the *Malificius malificarum* (*The Hammer of the Witches*) in 1481 encouraged the notion that involvement in occult activities implied entering into a diabolic pact with the forces of darkness. The Renaissance magus drew on the possibility of *exaltacio* and the deification of man, the power of sacred white magic and an ambition to communicate with the creator after whose image man was forged. But interest in such ambition brought the danger of *hubris* and falling into the clutches of God's adversary. By the late sixteenth century such tensions were being mythologized in the Faust legend, the story of a man prepared to manipulate occult powers in such practices as necromancy in pursuit of nature's secrets, and the concept of service to Satan began to appear in portrayals of alchemists and magicians in Greene's *Friar Bacon and Bungay* and Marlowe's *Doctor Faustus* who were depicted as corrupted scholars who had strayed beyond the realms of orthodox intellectual enquiry and fallen into the clutches of the powerful adversary of man. Dr John Dee, Queen Elizabeth I's foremost scientist, mathematician, astrologer and natural philosopher, whose navigational skills were employed in attempting to find a North West passage to Cathay and whose imperial designs encouraged the expansion of the Elizabethan empire,[20] was regarded as such a Faust figure. Described by the alchemist Heinrich Khunrath as England's Hermes,[21] Dee spent 30 years of his life trying to harness the hidden powers in the earth. He attempted to communicate with angels by looking into a stone mirror,[22] strove to achieve alchemical transmutation in his alchemical stills at his home in Mortlake, and studied the manuscripts of the fifteenth-century alchemist George Ripley. Dee also owned a fourteenth-century manuscript of the *Tabula Smaragdina* (*The Emerald Table*) attributed to Hermes which was illustrated in the margin with the alchemical symbol of the dragon.[23] His Faustian pact occurred when he was involved with Edward Kelly in séances and discourses with angels which involved an infamous incident of cross-hatching where Dee and Kelly were instructed by a spirit called Madini to exchange their wives.[24] Alchemists in this period, however intellectually distinguished, were viewed with suspicion by monarchs and their advisers. Although Dee was visited by Elizabeth I, who consulted him on astrological matters, he ended his last days in poverty and his library was sacked by a mob. Another distinguished alchemist, Thomas Charnock, was unable to secure crown patronage and his writings were never published.[25] When alchemists were employed by crown officials they were required to use specific scientific skills: Dee provided maps and navigation charts to facilitate voyages of exploration. There was no general endorsement of occult philosophy and no evidence of any real alliance between politics and the occult in the sixteenth century.

The premise of this book is that such an alliance and acceptance of the broader principles of occult philosophy, and alchemy in particular, did exist in the late Middle Ages. Keith Thomas, in *Religion and the Decline of Magic*, suggests that in this period the operation of learned magic was largely the prerogative of the church, a repository of occult power.[26] Medieval kings did utilize ecclesiastical powers: coronation rituals were performed by clergy who bestowed on kings a quasi-priestly power, and Henry III made full use of the powers invested in holy relics in establishing Westminster Abbey as a focal point of royal authority. The alliance between crown and church was however an uneasy one, borne out by the crown's implication in the killings of Thomas Becket, the archbishop of Canterbury, and Richard Scrope, the archbishop of York, which resulted in the churches of Canterbury and York being turned into shrines where the power of ecclesiastical relics became a challenge to royal authority. However sources of occult power were not confined to sanctified ground and knowledge of such arcane matters was not restricted to a clerical elite: it was part of the mainstream of intellectual and spiritual life. One fundamental difference between the late Middle Ages and the Renaissance was the lack in the earlier period of any divide between science and magic. For a thousand years Christianity had been grafted onto traditions of cyclic renewal of the seasons and myths about the fertility and regeneration of the wasteland (which may be a motif of Arabian origin brought back by early crusaders believing the deserts to be punishment for the loss of the Holy Land to the Muslims) and which were expressed in the Grail legends and in Arthurian romances written in the twelfth, thirteenth and fourteenth centuries.

The fundamental principle of the occult philosophy of the Grail legends and myths of Arthur and his tutor Merlin was the wisdom and sanctity of nature.[27] By the mid-twelfth century, Latin translations of classical and Muslim natural philosophy texts included alchemical works. The close connection between nature and the occult was given a scientific dimension with the arrival from Catalonia and Majorca in the thirteenth century of treatises by Islamic scholars on astrology, geomancy, physiognomy and, above all, alchemy. These included: the *Turba philosophorum*; the treatises ascribed to the mythic sage, Hermes Trismegistus; the pseudo Geber's *Summa perfectii magisterii*;[28] and the *Secreta secretorum* (which is relatively well known as a regimen but surprisingly its occult alchemical content has been passed over). English scholars soon responded. Roger Bacon (1220–90) went to Spain and studied the works of Jabir. He was one of the first Europeans to discuss the healing powers of potable gold and to use the Arab derived work elixir. Bacon defined alchemy as a science in his *Epistola de secretis operibus artis et naturae* (*Letter on the Secret Works of Art and Nature*, 1249–52), which suggested the philosopher's stone was the integration of the four elements. Bacon adapted Galenic humoral medicine for alchemical purposes in the *Opus maius* (*Great Work*, 1266–68), *Opus minus* (*Small Work*, 1367) and *Speculum Alkymie* and *In libro sex scientiarum in 3 gradu sapientie* (*In the Book of the Six Sciences in the Third Grade of Wisdom*).[29]The survival in Britain of nearly 3,500 fourteenth-, fifteenth- and sixteenth-century manuscripts of Latin translations of these Arabic treatises and the Latin alchemical treatises of the thirteenth-century English alchemists is testimony to the significance of alchemy in the later Middle Ages.[30] In the thirteenth and fourteenth centuries the universities were developing enquiry into the natural world through the disciplines of natural philosophy and medicine; Aristotelian texts in natural philosophy were at the centre of curriculums.[31] The struggle to comprehend and manipulate nature was not confined to the universities. Unlike medicine, natural philosophy, astronomy and astrology, alchemy never gained an official place in the university curriculum, even if many of its practitioners were university trained and spent time in Oxford and Cambridge; it remained a closely guarded secret but drew many of its principles from university disciplines and shared the assumptions of Oxford and Cambridge scholars about the structure of the natural world. The most impressive evidence of the increasing importance of alchemy in the fourteenth century is the original composition of alchemical texts in Latin. These alchemical texts indicate an interchange of ideas between university scholars, physicians and alchemists. Alchemists were not a lunatic fringe but hard-headed scientists in touch with the intellectual currents of their time. They conducted practical experiments with matter and, influenced by Aristotelian ideas about nature, they theorized on such abstract subjects as creation and provided medical expertise on blood and humours. Although the teaching of alchemy was imparted from master to disciple in secretive circumstances the pedagogical nature of the texts, written in the form of dialogues, provides insights into the ways alchemists acquired their practical and theoretical knowledge. The occult in the fourteenth century can be defined as the investigation into the hidden forces of nature: the operation of magic was seen as merely the marvellous workings of nature.

The basis of the occult philosophy of fourteenth-century alchemists was the sulphur mercury theory of the origin of creation and the evolution of gold. Mercury occurred in pearl droplets in rocks and was extracted in furnaces from its ore cinnabar (mercury sulphide coloured red and white). In the process the pure silver white mercury was separated from the red sulphur and in this pure form it was found in Egyptian tombs from 1500 BC, and the alchemical symbol for mercury, two horns on a circle, is at least 3,000 years old. By 500 BC it was used to make amalgams with other metals. This precious substance (identified with the moon) was deemed to be the origin of all matter and the origin of pure gold. It was seen as the philosopher's stone, incorruptible and eternal; the divine presence in a fallen world; the manifestation of Christ understood in scientific terms. The sulphur from which mercury was extracted was identified with the corporeal forces of nature and especially the heat of the sun. It possessed its own natural mineral heat by which it could digest all substance and was related to mercury as the male to the female. Such ideas about the occult forces in the earth and heavens the regenerative power of the sun, the holistic interplay of man and his social, political environment and the capacity of nature to renew itself through the manifestation of the eternal mercury in the cyclical renewal of the seasons had obvious intellectual excitement. The circulation of alchemical theories coincides with the emergence of a vernacular literature during the reign of Richard II. Court writers: Geoffrey Chaucer, John Gower, and the author of *Sir Gawain and the Green Knight, Pearl, Patience* and *Purity* (known as the Gawain poet) were incorporating, alongside standard medical teaching, heliocentric and regenerative themes and symbols that have their basis in alchemical literature. In the case of the Gawain poet this has hitherto gone unnoticed. The appearance of occult themes in the literature of the Gawain poet and Chaucer will be investigated.

There was also a political dimension to occult traditions in England. Central to the fertility of the land was the well being of the king. And the mythology of English kingship was dominated by the figure of the alchemist/magician Merlin, who guided the fortunes of the dynasties of the rulers of Britain to oversee the emergence of King Arthur, the inspiration of many late medieval kings including Henry II, Edward I and Edward III. The occult sciences arriving from Islamic countries encouraged the exploration of the mysteries of nature and were therefore of interest to physicians, and this had wider political implications offering kings and their advisers the opportunity to treat the ills of the body politic and its head, the king. The English monarchy was in a state of malaise in the early fourteenth century. When Edward II's son, Edward of Woodstock, seized power in 1327 he and his advisers sought to rejuvenate the monarchy and the body politic through the therapeutic application of alchemical medicine. Between 1327 and 1334 alchemical texts were written for Edward III, his mother, Isabella, and his queen, Philippa. They included: the Majorcan *Testamentum*, a comprehensive philosophy of alchemy and practical compendium of the 'secrets of nature' that included recipes, medicines and accounts of distillation; and the *Secreta secteto-rum* and the writings of the English alchemist, John Dastin. A close relationship existed between the specific advice in these texts and the king's political decisions. Advice on occult knowledge, alchemical remedies, humoral balance and heroic visions of redemptive kingship can be considered in relation to the healing of the body politic. These texts offer the possibility of a more comprehensive explanation of Edward III's political actions, his policies of foreign conquest, and his revival of Arthurian ceremony in terms of the pursuit of heroic ideals recommended by alchemists such as Dastin.

The claims of the alchemist to hold the key to eternal youth and purity in his understanding and manufacture of the mysterious mercury, the first principle of all matter, may have been intellectually exciting; but it also aroused the interest of those in the pursuit of political power and especially Edward III's successor, Richard II who, in the course of this 22-year reign, made a less successful attempt to rejuvenate his kingdom through the application of alchemical medicine. Indeed a dependence on the occult is given as one of the reasons for his deposition. The perception that Richard II was steeped in alchemy and the occult is the fundamental premise of this book. Claims were made by the Benedictine monk who wrote the Chronicle of the Abbey of Evesham covering the years 1214–1418; by Thomas Walsingham (d. 1422) the Benedictine author of *Historia Anglicana* covering the period 1272–1422;[32] and the Welsh chronicler, Adam of Usk (c. 1352–1430) that the king kept secret occult writings, consulted prophets and advisers intent on extending the royal prerogative who were especially notorious practitioners in the black arts. The decisions and public persona of this enigmatic king have been explained in conventional political terms but an alternative explanation can be found in alchemical/medical manuscripts that were written and circulated in the court and were especially relevant between 1370 and 1399. The body politic was again sick; there were military reversals and social unrest culminating in the Peasant's Revolt; the Black Prince was mortally ill, and a once great king was senile. Richard II owned occult tests. John Doubelay's *Stella alchemiae* was dedicated to the king in 1384,[33] and in 1391 a compendium of occult learning (Bodleian 581) containing extracts from the *Secreta secretorum* (referred to by Doubelay)[34] relating to the art of physiognomy,[35] an account of the interpretation of dreams,[36] and a book of geomancy was commissioned by him. Richard's decisions can be related to his book of geomancy, which provides answers to questions about medical diagnosis and treatment, and about choosing friends and times of travel.[37] The origin of Richard's identification with the three kings, Solomon and the redemptive Christ child and his obsession with asserting the royal prerogative may be found in these alchemical texts. And, while others have seen his deployment of such symbols as the lamb, the pearl the sun and the white hart differently, I shall explore the possibility of an additional resonance in alchemical literature. A debate about the political uses of the occult focussed on Richard II's kingship and this explains why Richard's attempts to establish a strong, autocratic kinship in the face of baronial opposition (which must have accorded with the desires and expectations of many of his subjects) caused such controversy. Failure to appreciate that Richard's obsession with the royal prerogative was linked with his preoccupation with occult sources of power has contributed to a lack of any clear understanding of a king who has been alternatively condemned as neurotic, immature, narcissistic and tyrannical. Shakespeare pointed the way to a proper appreciation of Richard in late medieval terns in his depiction of a flawed man who was resolutely convinced that the dignity of his office placed him above mere mortals.

The occult science of alchemy emerged in the fourteenth century as a popular intellectual and political force and it is extraordinary that it has never been studied. An understanding of Richard II's failure to harness successfully the powerful and unstable forces represented by sulphur and mercury to the service of his dynasty helps to appreciate how this was successfully achieved in the following century by the Yorkist and Tudor monarchs. Alchemical theories about creating gold by extracting impure sulphur from mercury thereby creating a pure sulphur conjoined with white mercury to produce pure gold were exploited for political purposes in the fourteenth and fifteenth centuries. Besides promising to deliver gold to their royal patrons, alchemists encouraged kings to identify themselves with the life-giving and regenerative powers of the sun (the planet of gold) and with the end product of transmutation: the state of perfection represented by this most highly evolved of metals. Alchemists also applied healing and therapy to the body politic.

The fruits of their meditation – political, medical and intellectual insights – were of profound importance for kings, courtiers and the ruling aristocracy, especially during the 1450s when the king of England, Henry VI, was insane. One of the most influential alchemical writers in the sixteenth and seventeenth centuries was George Ripley, a fifteenth-century monk. For Ripley exaltation was more than a term representing the creation of gold: it involved the exaltation of the flesh to spirit and the removal of the distance between body and soul. Ripley's strongly symbolical and allegorical writings were used by the house of York to justify Edward IV's seizure of power in 1461 and his recapture of the throne in 1471. Alchemists in the service of Edward earl of March meditated on genealogical rolls and the political forces that shaped royal lineages. Kings refined in the furnace of history were subjected to the same processes as metals in the alchemist's athenor. The sun of March, Edward IV was the alchemical gold, the fruition of years of struggle that was seen in chemical terms in the conflict between mercury and sulphur, the white and red roses. The emergence of a single nation from the disparate baronial factions in the Wars of the Roses was celebrated in alchemical terms as the emergence of alchemical gold from the chaos of civil war in the form of the sacred rose of alchemy combining the red and white roses of York and Lancaster. It can be argued that Henry VII, when he founded the Tudor dynasty, capitalized on the alchemical significance of this conjunction of the warring opposites of sulphur and mercury when he adopted the red and white Tudor rose as the symbol of his dynasty and anticipated the future national symbol of the red and white flag of St George. The political application of occult symbols in the fifteenth century has been extensively studied by the present author; but we now must turn to the fourteenth century when these myths and images constituted a much more powerful, disturbing and unpredictable brew.

The Origins of English Alchemy and Sources for the Study of Alchemy in Fourteenth-Century England

Ask him to tell you truly where his heart is directing him, and he will tell you that he intends to go unto the west, to the vales of Avalon

Merlin and the Grail[1]

ALCHEMICAL MYTHS AND THE IMPACT OF ISLAMIC ALCHEMY 700–1250

Alchemy is best defined as the attempt to understand and master the hidden powers within the earth. Although these powers were influenced by the heavenly forces exerted by the seven planets, the example of the Muslim alchemist from Baghdad, Al Razi (Rhazes) (865–925), who defined alchemy as 'the astrology of the lower world'[2] will be followed and this investigation of the occult will be confined to alchemy and such related arts as geomancy. The most obvious manifestation of occult forces within the earth was a belief in the slow, organic growth of the six metals in the bowels of the earth towards the state of perfection achieved by the seventh metal, gold, and the possibility that this could be accelerated and replicated. This involved a philosophical search for a perfect balance between the four elements that existed in a mysterious fifth substance from which all the elements were believed to be derived, the quintessence. The most comprehensive theory defining this quintessence was the assertion that all metals derived from mercury and sulphur. Mercury was the female, cool and moist; and sulphur the male, hot and dry. Mercury is found in silver, pearl-like droplets in rocks and is extracted by smelting cinnabar, and sulphur can be found in its natural state in volcanoes. These two substances were seen as opposites (like the Yin and Yang water and fire principles that form the foundations of Chinese alchemy) that could, in a Manichean sense, represent the forces of light and darkness, good and evil, that form the basic principle of life.[3] The quest of the alchemist was to find the original *prima materia*, the pure form of mercury, the original water of creation, which could be obtained by removing from mercury all impure sulphur. This pure mercury was believed to be the one unchanging substance that was the origin of all life, the manifestation of God in matter which constituted the philosopher's stone. Pure mercury could be discovered through practical, scientific experimentation: a combination of heating, melting and colouring metals and above all by the process of distillation. These secretive procedures were expounded in allegorical, symbolic language and mythological narratives that combined practical experimentation and scientific investigation with a degree of religious fervour.

During the sixteenth and seventeenth centuries a mythology developed that alchemy had evolved in England. Elias Ashmole contended that no nation had written more or better on alchemy, and he conceived his *Theatrum Chemicum Britannicum* to be an ark in which he could save the alchemical treasures of this land. The nation's identity, commemorated in the flag of St George, could be interpreted as an allusion to the union of sulphur and mercury. These two forces and the fixation of the elusive, pure, original mercury or the philosopher's stone, was a phenomenon that was believed to have sprung within the English earth itself at Glastonbury. The Elizabethan alchemist, Dr John Dee, claimed to have found the alchemical red and white powders of St Dunstan in the grounds of the Benedictine abbey of Glastonbury.[4] By the time of Dee's visit, the tradition that St Dunstan, a tenth-century abbot of the abbey, was an alchemist was so strong that a number of alchemical treatises were ascribed to him in sixteenth-century manuscripts. According to legend this abbot had diverted a red and white spring from Chalice street into the abbey grounds, and this spring rose at the foot of Chalice Hill from the spot where (according to the Glastonbury monk, John of Glastonbury, in a chronicle written in 1342) Joseph of Arimathea, arriving from Palestine, deposited a pair of cruets containing the blood and sweat of Christ, (the myth of Christ sweating on the cross derives from Luke 22:43 where Jesus dispersed his blood outside his body in the form of sweat).[5] This event was recorded c. 1475 in a stained glass window of St John's Church, Glastonbury, showing the cruets emblazoned on the arms of St Joseph between a cross composed of green hawthorns. Descending onto the cruets is heavenly dew, a distillation of these red and white elixirs. The source of this alchemical symbolism is a prophecy of sixth-century Welsh bard and contemporary of Merlin, Melkin (perhaps identical with the Welsh bard Maelgwyn of Gwynedid d. 547 and possibly invented by John of Glastonbury), who was incorporated into the *Glastonbury Chronicle* in 1342 which claims Joseph was buried in a south corner of the original wattle church with two silver vessels filled with the sweat and blood of Jesus. The prophet predicts that neither water nor heavenly dew (*ros coeli*) will be lacking for the inhabitants of this holy isle.[6]

This vision of alchemical regeneration had wider ramifications. Glastonbury was the legendary site of the burial of King Arthur and of his anticipated return. In 1192 the grave of Arthur and Guinevere in the abbey grounds was opened in the presence of King Henry II and the remains were translated to a raised, green marble tomb before the high altar in the abbey church. This tomb (illustrated in a fifteenth-century copy of Lydgate's *Fall of Princes*[7] and visited by Kings Edward I

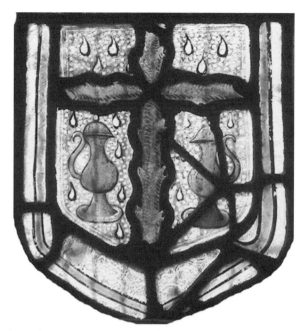

The Glastonbury thorn. Cruets and the heavenly dew. St John's Church,
Glastonbury

and Edward III) was destroyed in the Reformation. The man believed to be behind
this vision of a united Great Britain, the home of the Holy Grail, and expectations
of a return to these days of greatness was Merlin, a magician steeped in occult arts
who was reputed to be born of a virgin and who was also reportedly the son of the
devil. In Robert de Boron's *Estoire de Merlin,* written in the 1190s and incorporated into the Vulgate cycle c. 1215–35, Merlin decides to reveal some of his deepest secrets to King Uther Pendragon: 'You must understand sire that I have
knowledge of all things both word and deed inherited from the enemy. But our
Lord omnipotent gave me knowledge of things to come and now you know the
source of my power.'[8] Merlin's special knowledge, allowing him mastery and
understanding of the forces of nature, was believed in the later Middle Ages to be
the science of alchemy. One alchemical text, written in the form of a dialogue
from master to disciple, or father and son, promises to impart the blessed knowledge of the 'verity of the whiteness', the fixing of mercury, after a process involving
40 days burial and several distillations which will produce pure, cleansing spirit,
described as the 'joyful whiteness of the moon shining above the earth' and which
it is claimed is as eternal as the Trinity.[9] This work, surviving in many fifteenth-
century manuscripts, was known as *Liber Merlin.*[10] Another work of alchemy, the
Gemma salutaris or *Laudabilis sanctum,* describing the wedding of the white
woman to the red man, a nuptial marked by the shining of a golden rose[11] and

sometimes attributed to Hermes Trismegistus, was in most later medieval copies attributed to Merlin.[12] The fifteenth-century alchemist, Thomas Norton, referred to Merlin as an alchemical authority, and by the sixteenth century Merlin's reputation as an alchemist ensured that he was described as a founder of British alchemy in a list of British alchemists in *The Lookeing Glass of Illiterate Alchymists*.[13] In Robert de Boron's *Book of Merlin,* Merlin is identified with the forces of nature; and by the fifteenth century he came to represent for alchemists a more scientific outlook, the forbidden knowledge that had been the devil's gift to his son. Merlin himself was identified with the alchemical process. His unnatural conception linked him with the artificially created *homunculus*. He was also seen as an unpredictable and powerful agent in the birth of Britain, fulfilling the function of the volatile mercury in the gestation of the philosopher's stone. Like mercury Merlin was an elusive shape shifter, an amoral reconciler of opposites including good and evil, and he, like mercury, was eventually imprisoned in matter either in glass or a rock, symbolic of the trapped energy of the primal substance.

Merlin's greatest feat of alchemical conjunction was to bring together Uther Pendragon and Igraine to beget Arthur, under whom Britain would attain its identity. Geoffrey of Monmouth, in his *Historia Regum Britannicum,* described how Merlin witnessed the failed attempts of Vortigern to build a tower on Mount Snowdon to resist the advancing Saxons. His castle was being continually swallowed by the ground and Merlin pointed out that there was a pool underneath the foundations in which two dragons were sleeping. Merlin ordered the pool to be drained to expose the warring red and white dragons subverting the foundations of the tower. He delivered a prophecy that would reverberate through to the fifteenth century. According to Merlin, the red and white dragons represented the struggle between the Celtic Britons and the invading Saxons, and he prophesized the defeat of the red dragon by the white, which represented the Saxon conquest of Britain and the eventual triumph of the red dragon or revival of the Celtic kingdom of Britain.[14]

By the fifteenth century copyists of alchemical texts were associating these texts with romance and prophetic works featuring King Arthur.[15] Merlin had become the alchemist and prophet who had supervised and orchestrated the birth of Great Britain under Arthur: with his unparalleled knowledge of the past and future he held the key to the redemption of Great Britain from foreign, Saxon invaders under a second Arthur, a Welsh, British king. This was conceived in terms of an alchemical drama; a conflict between two dragons, red sulphur and white mercury, and the point was reinforced in the alchemical texts attributed to Merlin in the fifteenth century which described the reconciliation of these fighting opposites. *Laudam sanctabile* described an alchemical conjunction concluded when:

The white woman beth then is wedded to the red man

A kniteth so that two become one.

The end result of the experiment is an evolution from white to red then gold, achieved when 'a rare colour shall shine'.[16] In the *Book of Merlin,* Merlin is informed by his master (described as father): 'In early things accord will be' and is taught how to achieve an end 'that will make many men thy friend'. This will occur when the white and the red are brought to conjunction, resulting in the transmutation of the white work, which will shine as clear as crystal and as bright as gold. Merlin was therefore a powerful archetype in the later Middle Ages, a man of science with an understanding of history who sees a way to use conflict, civil war and foreign defeat to bring about the birth of the philosopher's stone, which was the nation. This was symbolized by the Round Table. In the Cistercian *Queste le Saint Graal,* part of the Vulgate cycle composed by Cistercian monks between 1215 and 1235, an instrument of renewal (the Round Table) 'was devised by Merlin to embody a very subtle meaning, for in its name it mirrors the roundness of the earth, the concentric spheres of the planets and of the elements in the firmament; and in these heavenly spheres we see the stars and many things besides, whence it follows that the Round Table is a true epitome of the universe'.[17]

Another of the myths about Merlin was that he was instructed by Islamic alchemists. There is a tradition that the Muslim physician Rhazes (Abu Bakr ibn Zakariya al-Razi) took Merlin as his disciple. As late as the seventeenth century Ashmole, in his *Prologemon* to the *Theatrum Chemicum Britannicum,* noted that Merlin was a contemporary of Rhazes. The instructions imparted from Rhazes to Merlin (his son and heir in an alchemical sense) were recorded in the *Liber Merlin* which was widely circulated in the fifteenth century. In the popular imagination such Muslim wisdom could be seen as diabolic and may have contributed to the belief that Merlin was the son of the devil. However because England's national identity was bound up with the alchemical myth that the nation was born out of a resolution of a conflict between sulphur and mercury in the sixth century, especial emphasis was placed on the holiness of England and especially Glastonbury, because the sweat and blood of the Saviour had been brought here soon after the Crucifixion. This event contained a 'secret within a secret' believed to have been closely guarded by such alchemists and holy men as Joseph of Arimathea, the prophet Melkin, Merlin, and St Dunstan the first abbot of Glastonbury; not only did the sweat and blood signify the sulphur and mercury which was the origin of all matter, it also symbolized the mystery of the philosopher's stone or holy grail: mercury was also the original *prima materia* representing the humanity of Christ and his divinity, the presence of God within matter. England (and Glastonbury in particular) were therefore regarded as holy places where the presence of God was manifest.

In fact English alchemical myths probably date back to no further than the twelfth century. The prophet Melkin was probably a thirteenth-century invention or a fabrication by the fourteenth-century chronicler, John of Glastonbury.

There is no contemporary evidence that St Dunstan was an alchemist. The myths about Merlin and the red and white dragons go no further back than 1120 and Geoffrey of Monmouth's *Historia Regum Britannicum*. However if there is one place where the true origin of such symbolism can be seen it is in the Islamic kingdom of Al Andalusia and its capital Cordoba. The dome of the great mosque of La Mezquita Mesque (784–86) is buttressed by a forest of horseshoe arches decorated with white and red colours, and in the tenth-century palace of Medinat az Zahara, just outside Cordoba, the same white and red arches occur before a fountain of flowing mercury, a liquid mirror. The symbolism of red sulphur and white mercury emerged in England at the same time that Islamic science was making its first impression on English scholars visiting Islamic territories in Spain and Southern Italy.[18]

The Muslim Arab Empire that developed from the deserts of Arabia at the end of the seventh century covered an area from Syria in the East to Morocco in the West and included the cities of Fez, Alexandria, Baghdad and Damascus, all important centres of alchemy. The cradle of alchemy within this vast empire was the Nile valley. The name alchemy is derived by prefixing the Arabic definite article al to chemia (the preparation of silver and gold) which may be derived from Khem, an ancient name for Egypt. Even during the time of the Pharaohs Egypt was regarded as an ancient, holy land: it had witnessed the emergence of the primeval hill from the all encompassing waters and the birth and burial of the gods themselves. The ancient Egyptians had their equivalent of sulphur and mercury in the form of Ra, the sun god, identified with light and consciousness, and his counsellor, Thoth, the moon god of the old kingdom, identified with the underworld and the unconscious. The origins of the symbolism of the red and white and their conjunction may derive from the ancient tradition that the white crown of Upper (southern) Egypt and the red crown of Lower (northern) Egypt were united by King Narmer (Menes) c. 2925 BCE. Thoth, the source of all occult power and the lord of science acquired the role in the drama of creation of the demiurge who called all things into being when he laid the cosmic egg. The Greeks who settled in Egypt after the conquest of Alexander the Great identified Thoth with Hermes, the mercurial messenger of the gods, the trickster patron of medicine. The Arab conquerors of Egypt believed Hermes lived before the flood, built the pyramids and was the first alchemist, who bestowed on humanity the seeds of ancient pre-lapsarian wisdom. The allegories and symbolism of alchemy with their emphasis on death and rebirth may owe much to the Pharonic religion of the Nile valley with its emphasis on the cult of the dismemberment and reintegration of the God Osiris; the worship of the sun God, Ra (represented by the alchemical sign for gold); and the advanced techniques in gold making and mummification of bodies.[19] In the north wall of the chamber of Tuthmosis III at Thebes there is a large serpent, the oldest known representation of the alchemical ouroboros.[20] Although knowledge

Hermes Trismegistus (Siena Cathedral)

of the traditions of this land were hidden during most of the Middle Ages because of the Arab occupation, there was by the fourteenth and fifteenth centuries some acknowledgement that Egypt was the true home of the occult. During this period the corrosive acid salt petre, derived from camel dung, was imported from Egypt. Hermes Trismegistus was credited with the authorship of a collection of Neo-Platonic hermetic writings that included the *Corpus Hermetica* and the Latin *Asclepius*, originally written in Greek in fourth-century Alexandria. In 1486 the nave of Siena Cathedral was dedicated to Hermes Trismegistus, shown with Moses above an inscription saying: 'Take up the laws of Egypt'.

The Greek origins of alchemy are also rooted in fact. Aristotle outlined the principles of the origin of minerals and metals from exhalations and secretions in the earth and the four fundamental properties of hot, moist, cold and dry, and the four elements of fire, water, air and earth borne by all bodies. Alexander the Great conquered Egypt in 332 BC and it was from the marriage of Greek and Egyptian culture, especially at Alexandria, that the science of alchemy flourished. Here there were small communities of Egyptians, Greeks and Syrians involved in the practical arts of metallurgy, dyeing and glassmaking and absorbing the theoretical, contemplative doctrines of Babylonian and Greek philosophers. The earliest surviving descriptions of Greco-Egyptian alchemical craft recipes for artificial pearls, gold and silver and dyeing date from papyri around 300 BC found in a cemetery in Upper Egypt and they are based on older models.[21] The Royal Library at Alexandria would have been the repository of occult wisdom of these two great cultures, most of which vanished when the library was destroyed, perhaps by Julius Caesar during the Roman occupation of Egypt in 48 BC, and by the decree of Theopolis, bishop of Alexandria AD 391. Only a few papyri and alchemical texts survive from this period. One name to emerge was Zosimus (c. 350–AD 420), a native of Ahkmin in Upper Egypt, who employed an enigmatic and aphoristic style that would characterize later alchemical texts.[22]

When the Arabs conquered Egypt (Alexandria fell in AD 641) they became the heirs to the alchemical traditions of the Egyptians and Greeks. The sources for Arabic alchemy were such authors as Hermes, Cleopatra and Mary, who came from Egypt, and while their works were possibly works of pseudo Arabic authors it is also possible that they were written before Islam. From Aristotle Arab scholars derived the elemental principle that the elements changed from one to another in a circular motion and that changing the proportion and combination of these elements could make a different body. Arab alchemists perpetuated a myth of a recovery of original alchemical knowledge from the ancient Egyptians (the alchemical symbol for gold is identical to the ancient Egyptian symbol of the sun god Ra) and they were drawn to what they perceived to be the occult mysteries underlying the pyramids, temples and the hieroglyphic inscriptions of the Nile valley.[23] Muhammad Ibn Umail (900–60), the alchemist connected with Andalusia and Egypt, recorded a visit to Busir al Sidir in Egypt to ancient temples the statue of Hermes and tablets showing the stages of the alchemical process. In his *Tabula Chemica*, Umail claims to have seen in a subterranean chamber of a pyramid hieroglyphic signs carved onto the marble slabs resting on a statue of Hermes and wall paintings (subsequently copied) depicting two birds holding one another to form a circle (an early symbolic representation of the dragon biting its tail or uroboros representing the coupling of the sun and moon, the union of sulphur and mercury).[24] The tenth-century Arab scholar, An Nadir, called Hermes the inventor of alchemy and claimed his tomb was in the Great Pyramid and that the temples were built for grinding, dissolving and distilling.

The fusion of Egyptian and Greek influences on which Arab alchemy was founded may have originated in Alexandria but the advancement of metallurgical techniques, the use of corrosive acids and the refinement of the theory that all metals and indeed life itself merged from sulphur and mercury developed in cities in the heart of the Islamic empire in the seventh and eighth centuries in Baghdad and Damascus. It was in this environment that distillation techniques were employed in such inventions as the alembic to produce such essences as rosewater and where chemical retorts and cucurbits were first used to melt metals with the use of nitric and sulphuric acids.[25] The earliest known Muslim alchemist in Damascus was Khalid ibn Yazis (660–704) who was made Caliph; but like Shakespeare's Prospero he retired from court to study alchemy under a hermit, Maryanus, a follower of the Melkite Byzantine Greek church. Khalid was the supposed author of a *Testament of Alchemy* written in the form of a dialogue to his son.[26] From about 750 Baghdad became the centre of the Muslim world. In the Middle Ages there was a trinity of revered alchemists revered as forerunners of hermetic art. One of the earliest practitioners in Baghdad was Jabir ibn Hayyan (b. 721 in Tus, Persia and d. 815 in Kufa, Iraq). Jabir studied alchemy under a monk who had been a pupil of Maryanus, tutor of Khalid and he was employed as an alchemist at the court of the Abbasid Caliph, Harin al Rashid. Regarded with Boyle as the father of modern chemistry, Jabir achieved fame through a corpus of works on alchemy, chemistry, medicine, physics and philosophy, compiled between the eighth and tenth centuries. The most important works attributed to him are the collections of 112 books dedicated to the viziers of Caliph and containing the Arabic version of the *Emerald Table*, and the 70 books, most of which were translated into Latin in the Middle Ages and known as the Septuaginta. The Arabic originals of some of these writings were missing until the first two decades of the twentieth century. There are also at least seven Latin treatises carrying the name of Geber (Jabir's Latin name) for which the Arabic originals have not yet been identified, giving rise to the assumption that they were the product of pseudo Latin authors.[27] One of the most influential of these works was the *Summa perfectionis magisterii* (actually written by Paul of Tarento in the late thirteenth or early fourteenth century). The Jabirian corpus of ninth- and tenth-century works defined the philosopher's stone as a transmuted elixir that could transform any metal into gold and introduced the use of chemical agents such as sal ammonia and saltpetre. Jabir may be the originator of the sulphur mercury theory of the generation of metals: for fourteenth-century alchemical writers like Petrus Bonus he was the authority who defined the active principle of metals as sulphur and the form of metals as mercury. Jabir was also preoccupied with the tincture that turns metals to gold and the necessity of carrying out experiments. Abu Baki Al Razi, known in the West as Rases, was a physician, poet and philosopher who studied in Baghdad. Eight alchemical works were attributed to him, the most important were the *Book of the Secret of Secrets*, a work of practical experiments and a book concerning alums and salts.[28] Ibn Wahisha or Ibn Umayl (900–60) known in the West by his Latin name, Senior Zadith filius Hammel, was interested in the allegorical, spiritual and philosophical side of alchemy and composed poems on alchemy. *Risalat al-shami ila al-hlal* (*The Message of the Sun to the Crescent Moon*) was translated into Latin as *Epistola Solis ad Lunam*. This poem was explained by the author in a treatise known as *The Silvery Water in the Starry Earth*, known in Latin as *Tabula Chemica*. Senior expounded in these works the sulphur mercury theory of the origin of matter in an allegory of a union between the sun and the moon. Abu Mashama al-Majariti, from Madrid in al-Andalus, was the author in the first half of the eleventh century of *Chayat al hakim (The Goal of the Sage)*, a work on magic, alchemy and astrology which was translated into Spanish and Latin under the title of *Picatrix*.[29] Abu Ali ibn Sina (980–c. 1036) known in the West as Avicenna, was a physician and commentator on Aristotle whose canon of medical writings became one of the great authorities of the Middle Ages. But Avicenna also had alchemical treatises ascribed to him.

The other most influential Islamic alchemical works of the late Middle Ages were of mythic origins. The basic creed of medieval alchemy embracing the philosophy of the interdependence of the macrocosm and microcosm manifested in the procedures of distillation and evaporation was summarized in *Tabula smaragdina (The Emerald Table)*: 'That which is above is that which is below.' This text, the Mosaic tablet for medieval alchemists, was believed to have been found in the hands of Hermes Trismegistus in his tomb in the Great Pyramid of Cheops by the conqueror of Egypt, Alexander the Great. The Alexandrine legends of the table's origins can be attributed to its composition in Egypt, probably Alexandria. It was subsequently translated into Syriac and Arabic, possibly by the eighth-century Arab, Balinus. Latin versions probably first appeared in Europe in versions of the *Secreta secretorum* and in the fourteenth century Ortolanus (or Hortulanus) wrote a commentary on the table which survives in many fifteenth-century manuscripts. *The Emerald Table* was only known in Medieval Latin versions until 1923 when Holmyard discovered an abridged text in the *Second Book of the Elements of the Foundations* attributed to Jabir and dating from the eighth century AD.[30] Another work of mythic origins was the *Secreta secretorum*, a compendium of occult and alchemical knowledge supposedly provided by Aristotle in a letter intended to help Alexander the Great on his Persian campaign. It was claimed that this work was discovered at an oratory of the sun and translated at the request of a great prince from Greek to Chaldean to Arabic to be used by Muslim scholars as a basis for their alchemy, and then 'this precious margarite'[31] was rediscovered at Antioch and translated into Latin and made available to the West again; but the *Secreta secretorum* was actually originally written in Arabic in Syria in the seventh century as *Kitab sirr al-asrar (Book of the Science of Government, on the Good Orders of Statecraft)*.[32] The *Turba Philosophorum* (known as *Assembly of the Philosophers*), a dialogue between 12 philosophers meeting Hermes to discuss the nature of alchemy and the changes between the four elements was of Arabic origin and often attributed to Jabir. It was possibly written c. 900 by Utha ibn Sumaid of Kkh in Egypt.

Alchemy was practised throughout the Islamic world and especially in Syria, Egypt and Persia; but was unknown in Western Europe. This would change when

Berber tribesmen from Morocco invaded Spain across the Straits of Gibraltar in
July 711; and when they completed the conquest of the kingdom of Al Andalusia
by 718 they prepared the way for the introduction of Islamic knowledge of the
natural world into Western Europe and the circulation and adaptation of alchemical texts. Under Abdul Rashan Cordoba became the largest city in Europe with
over 70 libraries and the fountainhead of knowledge of science, astrology and
medicine. By 912, under Caliph Abdul Rashan III, Cordoba had become the centre
of the Islamic world. The collapse of the Abdul dynasty in Cordoba in 1095 and
the start of the crusade movement prefigured the fragmentation of the kingdom
of Al Andalus, and for the next 200 years there was civil war between Christian and
Muslim Spaniards. The Christian kings who seized the Muslim cities of Toledo in
1085, Cordoba in 1236 and Seville in 1248, were respectful of Islamic culture, and
Christians and Muslims lived side by side exchanging ideas. The fall of Toledo to
the Christians had the same cultural resonance as the fall of Alexandria to the
Arabs and Constantinople to the Turks. A school of translation was established
and Muslim scientific knowledge, based on the copying, translating and commen-
tating on Greek scientific, philosophic texts, especially the canon of Aristotle,
founder of the principles of the exercise of reason and investigative curiosity of the
natural world, became available to Christian travellers. The Italian tour as the
completion of the education of scholars and noblemen was not just a phenomenon of the eighteenth century. English monks, cathedral clergy and university
scholars were drawn to the medical schools and courts of Southern Italy and Sicily
which had been under Moorish control from AD 828 and had been beneficiaries
of Islamic scientific, medical and alchemical knowledge. When these areas reverted
to the control of Christian kings (the process was complete by 1300) scholars came
from all parts of North West Europe to learn about the occult. Frederick II (1194–
1250) the Holy Roman emperor and king of Sicily, a patron of science and the arts
in his court in Palermo, was hospitable to Islamic learning, founded a university at
Naples and supported a hospital at Salerno.

The Islamic world of Southern Europe, especially the Iberian Peninsula,
offered English scholars insights into the hidden powers of the heavens and the
earth and the technical means to investigate nature. Arabic numbers and navigational instruments such as the astrolabe were just some of the scientific innova-
tions arriving from Muslim Spain. The English scientist Adelard of Bath
(c. 1080–c. 1152), who studied in Tours and Salerno in Southern Italy, besides
tutoring the future Henry II, was an early interpreter of Arabic scientific knowledge: he translated Arabic astronomical tables and passed onto his nephew in
the *Natural Questions* what he learned from the Arabs and his sense of the amaz-
ing natural beauty of the universe. Robert of Ketton (c. 1110?–1160?) who was
from a village near Stamford, settled, after travels in the crusader states and
Damascus, in Northern Spain in the kingdom of Navarre, where he translated

Arabic scientific texts; and in 1143 he made the first translation into a European language (Latin) of the *Quran*. Alchemy as an important source of knowledge and manipulation of the natural world was an attraction for many of these scholars. Cordoba and Toledo in particular became important centres for the study of alchemy once they were under Christian control.[33] The earliest known Latin translation of an Arabic alchemical text was made around 1130 in Toledo by John of Seville, a translator of medical treatises interspersed with alchemy, who translated the *Secreta secretorum* and dedicated it to a queen T (probably Queen Tarasia, daughter of Sancho I of Portugal and wife of Alfonso IX of Leon). Robert of Chester (fl. 1150) travelled to Toledo to learn Arabic; his translated works in Segovia in Spain included the *Liber de Compositione Alchemiae de Morienus* in 1144; this is a dialogue between the hermit, Maryanus, and the Islamic alchemist, Khalid, beginning with Maryanus's promise that he will elucidate and define the meaning of the philosopher's stone for the benefit of those who do not know about alchemy. Daniel Morley (c. 1140–c. 1210), an English scientist educated at Oxford, came to Toledo in the late 1100s in search of the scientific wisdom of the Arabs and worked at the translation school before returning to England to write a treatise on the four elements and the fifth quintessence. Michael the Scott (1175–1232?), born in Scotland and educated at the Durham Cathedral school and Oxford, worked at the Arabic translation centre at Toledo before finding employment at the Palermo court of the Holy Roman emperor Frederick II, an enthusiastic student of science and sympathizer of Islam, translating the works of Aristotle from Arabic into Latin. Scott's alchemical works included *De sole et Luna* and he established a reputation as a wizard and alchemist for which he was entered by Dante into one of the circles of Hell.[34] In 1256 Alfonso X King of Castile and Leon (who was born in Toledo) ordered the translation into Catalan of a work called *The Final Form of the Wise* by the Cordovan alchemist Abu'l Quasin Mastinel ibi Ahr (d. 1001), which became known in the Latin version as the *Picatrix*. Hugh of Santalla, who was born in northwest Spain, translated from Arabic into Latin The *Emerald Table* attributed to Hermes in the first half of the twelfth century.

Other related occult arts were also studied in Al Andalus. Geomancy, the art of divination through the making of random marks in an attempt to harness the hidden powers within the earth and the self, originated from Arab sand divination and arrived in Europe through the translating activities of scholars at Cordoba and Toledo. The first geomancy was translated from Arabic into Latin in the first half of the twelfth century and was called *Ars geomancia* by an alchemist, Hugh of Santalla, and another translation was made by Plato of Barcelona from 1134 to 1145.[35] The activities of these translators at Toledo, Cordoba, Palermo and Naples paved the way for the flowering of alchemy in Western Europe and England in particular from the second half of the thirteenth century. The period of cooperation between Muslims and Christians ended in the fifteenth century with the expulsion of Muslims from Castile; many of the scientific and alchemical texts in the libraries of Cordoba and Toledo were destroyed when the Muslim kingdom of Granada fell in 1492 and all Muslims were driven out of the Iberian Peninsula. But during this period of cooperation between Muslim and Christian scholars in the twelfth and thirteenth centuries, Arabic alchemical and scientific texts were translated by Western scholars and Englishmen were especially prominent in this process.[36]

The reception of Islamic alchemy in England in the late Middle Ages was testified by the survival of copies of texts attributed to Islamic authors. Fourteenth-century manuscripts survive of the dialogue between Khalid and Morienus;[37] Jabir's *Summa Perfecti Magisteri*;[38] Rhazes's *Lumen Luminum*;[39] *Tabula Smaragdina* (Emerald Table);[40] *Turba philosophorum*;[41] and the *Secreta secretorum*.[42] By the thirteenth century scholars in Western Europe were beginning to bring to their study of alchemy and the occult their own ideas. This period is marked by the emergence of centres for the study of the occult, the patronage of alchemists in royal courts outside Spain and Southern Italy, and the appearance of original composition of works of alchemy.

Centres for the study of medicine and alchemy were emerging near the borders of the old Islamic empire such as the medical schools of Salerno in Southern Italy, founded by Frederick II, and Montpellier in Languedoc, within reach of the Pyrenees, the gateway to the old kingdom of Al Andalus. One of the medical teachers in Montpellier (part of the Catalan kingdom of Majorca together with the Balearic Islands and Roussillon from 1286 until the annexation by the crown of Aragon in 1343)[43] was a Catalan, Arnold of Villanova, the physician who attended James II of Aragon, Ferdinand III of Sicily and Robert of Naples. Arnold became one of the alchemical authorities revered in the late fourteenth century, and although some modern scholars are sceptical about considering him an alchemist, this may hinge on too narrow a definition of alchemy. Arnold may have been dubious about the possibility of the transmutation of metals but he shared many of the philosophical and scientific principles of Bacon, Bonus and Rupescissa. He was engaged in research into the prolongation of life and wrote a medical treatise on ageing, *De humido radicali*.[44] The study of the natural world as a means of deciphering the meaning and order of life and his belief that medical knowledge could be divinely inspired was an integral part of his programme for the reform of the spiritual ills of society. There is independent evidence from the 1340s and 1350s, when Arnold began his posthumous reputation as an alchemist, that he did practise transmutory alchemy: a witness attached to the Papal court, a lawyer Giovanni d'Andrea, remarked in his Additions to the *Speculum iudicale* of William Darant that Arnold was a 'great alchemist' who manipulated pieces of alchemical gold;[45] an alchemical work entitled the *Correctio fatuorum* claims that Arnold successfully treated a pope using alchemical gold; and Rupescissa saw Arnold as a great alchemist and prophet of the apocalypse.[46] Alchemical[47] works attributed to him included: *Perfectium magistrum*, addressed to the king of Aragon; *Flos Regis*, dedicated to the king of Naples; and his most famous work *Rosarius philosophorum*.[48] Arnold believed all ill health derived from an imbalance of humours which he applied to metals and in the *Rosarius* he endorsed the sulphur mercury theory of metals.[49] A corpus of pseudo-Arnoldian fourteenth-century alchemical works would have considerable influence on George Ripley in the fifteenth century.

In the twelfth century the cathedral schools such as Wells and Durham were important sources of scientific training, and in the thirteenth century one of the most important beneficiaries of Islamic scientific learning was the University of Oxford, which was emerging under the tutelage of Robert Grosseteste, bishop of Lincoln (c. 1175–1253), a scholastic theologian with an acute interest in the natural world, as a centre of scientific enquiry in Northern Europe.[50] An important source for the transmition of new Islamic ideas on medicine and alchemy to the emerging universities and schools of Western Europe was the Franciscan and Dominican friars. The friars as intrinsically itinerant orders were the most widely travelled scholars of the age with strong links with Italy where the mendicant orders originated. The encyclopaedias written by friars in this period acknowledged the importance of this emerging art: Vincent of Beauvais (1190–1264), a Dominican chaplain of Louis 1X, drew on Rhases's sulphur mercury theory for an account of alchemy in his *de Proprietatibus Rerum (On the Properties of Things)* declaring that mercury was the element common to all metals. Albertus Magnus (1200–80), a Dominican born in Laaingen in Swabia, Germany and empirical scientist, referred in his genuine works to magic and geomancy. Various alchemical treatises attributed to him included *Semita recta*,[51] *De Occulta naturae*,[52] and *de alchemica*; but he did compose *Meteora* and *De mineralibus*, which commented on the power of stones and contained ideas from Arab alchemical tests as well as endorsing Aristotle's theory of mineral generation and developing the notion of transmutation. Albert also introduced allegorical code names into alchemy describing sulphur as the father and mercury as the mother.[53] Albert's pupil, Thomas Aquinas (1225–74), in *Summa Theologia* also recognized the possibility of transmutation and several alchemical works were also attributed to Aquinas after his death including: *Epistolae Essentiarum* and *Aurora Consurgens*, a work which in its account of the parallels between the nigredo state in the breakdown of matter and psychological depression introduced a new visionary quality into alchemical literature. By the fourteenth century alchemical writers such as Petrus Bonus, and the authors of the pseudo Arnolian and pseudo Lullian canons were introducing a wide variety of code names drawn from the natural world and the Scriptures into their descriptions of the alchemical process. Such language was not based on university disciplines but was a cloak for a metaphorical discourse that showed how by this time alchemists considered their work incomprehensible to normal intelligent enquiry. Instead knowledge of alchemical operations required divine revelation and the art acquired supernatural import.[54]

One of Europe's leading scientists, the Franciscan Roger Bacon (1220–92), who was reputed to have had a laboratory on Folly Bridge in Oxford, is credited with the authorship of *Epistolae de potestatis artis et nature*,[55] *De Leone Viridi*[56] and *Speculum Alkymie*.[57] His alchemical theories were expounded in *Opus Maius* in 1268 which provided a new classification of science based on experience rather than argument and the principle of divine inspiration through experiment and experience; alchemy, especially in the third part of *Opus Maius*, played a vital part in this new programme. Bacon was the first alchemist in the West to introduce the concept, fundamental to Chinese alchemy, that alchemical medicines could preserve and extend human life. He had an intuitive view that all knowledge, including the disciplines of astrology, alchemy and ancient languages, were marvellously interrelated. Bacon's vision of a universal science integrating all branches of knowledge that could lead to salvation and the prolongation of life was inspired by his study in 1247 of the *Secreta secretorum* to which he also provided notes, 'for a great English patron', perhaps Henry III (1216-72).[58] This English king who was the recipient of a Latin version of a *Regimen Sanitatis* of Salerno, a dietary written for a *rex Anglorum* and given to Henry by the emperor Sigismund.[59] Bacon, at his most active in the 1260s, may have seen himself as Aristotle to King Henry III (1216–72). He was aware of the political significance of alchemical theories: in one of his notes to the *Secreta secretorum* he claimed that God inspired the wisest of alchemists with the perception that alchemy could be used for the good of the republic; another of his additional notes was a discussion of the alchemical significance of the number five and its correspondence to the cinque ports, the five coastal towns of Kent and Sussex seen to be essential to the defence of the realm.[60]

The significance of Roger Bacon in the emergence of alchemy in England during the reign of Henry III is the subject of another book. For the purposes of this study it is the emergence of Westminster Abbey as a centre for the display of alchemical symbolism during Henry's reign which indicates that by the beginning of the fourteenth century an alchemical tradition was emerging in London, and that it would no longer be necessary to travel to Cordoba or Naples to acquire alchemical wisdom. Henry's modifications to Westminster Abbey suggest that during his reign the English court was becoming the focus for the study of alchemy and the occult. In 1245 he had a throne made in the image of Solomon's described in the Bible with two leopards on either side. The connection between the English monarchy and Solomon goes back to the coronation ceremony of the tenth century which contained an antiphon celebrating the anointing of Solomon by the prophet Nathan. Henry III's tomb and that of Edward the Confessor, the last king of the house of Wessex (1042–66), and the floor of the abbey was covered in 1268, in preparation for the transfer of the body of the confessor to the abbey in 1269, in cosmati tiles (a design that came from tiles under the bishop's throne in Agnani cathedral south of Rome which also shows the seal of Solomon in a circle).[61] The patterns on the pavement, in richly coloured porphyry and glass, illustrate the way mercury approached the mystery of the Platonic ideal. On the chancel floor were depicted circles moving within circles around a gold disc with Egyptian onyx at the centre where the king was crowned. The design was intended to reveal the circular revolution of the elements in which various forms imposed on one element as it became another in a model of alchemical transmutation. The same pattern was laid on the floor of the shrine of Edward the Confessor by 1290. This shrine was destroyed in 1536 and rebuilt in the same year by Abbot Feckenham with the cosmati design reproduced in imitation of the original.[62] A similar pavement surrounding a circle on which the emperor of the East, Justinian, was crowned is in the church of Hagia Sophia in Constantinople. The Westminster pavement provided a model of the universe and the world illustrating the alchemical dictum 'that which is above is that which is below'; and a display of the working of the macrocosm and microcosm celebrating the circularity of the creator and his creation the universe as a circle within a circle, subject neither to change or disease – a *uroborus* without beginning or end and self-sufficient, the world soul of Plato's *Timaeus*. The simultaneous emergence of one of Europe's finest scientists as a practitioner of alchemy and the new design for the chancel floor, the abbey where the kings of England were crowned, is a testimony to the growing importance of the occult by the end of the thirteenth century, and was echoed in Canterbury Cathedral where a roundel on the thirteenth-century marble pavement shows Libra weighing in the scales (which represent harmony and balance) an image of the quintessence, the sun and moon. These developments are a prelude to the golden age of alchemy in fourteenth-century England.

THE EMERGENCE OF ALCHEMY IN
FOURTEENTH-CENTURY ENGLAND

By the fourteenth century the subject of magic, and in particular alchemy, had become contentious. Repeated condemnations by religious orders and papal interest stemmed from a desire to avoid the working of metals that might lead to fraudulent results and independent research that might involve heterodox religious views. Pope Clement IV had requested a copy of Bacon's *Opus maius* and Bacon sent him three of his works. Arnold of Villanova dedicated an epistle to Pope Boniface VIII, to whom he was a physician, and his *Semita* to Pope Benedict XI. Arnold maintained that the cardinals of the curia consumed potable gold regularly for their health. The late medieval papal curia was headed by elderly popes and cardinals searching desperately for the fountain of youth.[63] It was in the pontificate of the Avignon pope, John XXII (1316–34), that the subject became contentious. On 22 July 1317 John issued a bull, *Spondet*, forbidding the practice of the science of alchemy and imposing fines on counterfeiters pretending to make genuine gold and silver. The bull announced that anyone making counterfeit gold or silver would have to pay the same amount in real gold or face imprisonment and be branded with the mark of infamy.[64] Clerics engaged in alchemy would be deprived of their benefices. It was during John's pontificate, in May 1323, that the general chapter of Dominicans pronounced excommunication against all members of the order who henceforth devoted themselves to alchemy and did not burn their books on the subject within eight days. The Italian hermeticist and alchemist, Cecco d'Ascolii, professor of astrology at the University of Bologna and author of *LArebe*, an encyclopaedic poem on the natural word, was burned at the stake by the inquisition in Florence in 1327. However the decretal of John XXII was primarily directed against alchemists passing off their product as coinage and the medical and intellectual aspects of the art remained a subject of positive papal interest. In 1331 the Pope gave money to a physician, Sautre Ismod, bishop of Cavaillonn, for an alembic to make *aqua ardens* (alcohol) and for a secret work for himself.[65]

The bull of John XXII sparked a debate about alchemy which is important because it led to a series of articulate formulations of the serious philosophical principles of this art. The English monk, John Dastin, who was connected to the Papal Curia, responded to this bull in a letter that in sixteenth century copies are addressed to Pope John XXII at Avignon, *Epistola ad episcopum Johannem XXII de alchemia* explaining the real nature of an art which transferred corrupt metallic bodies into pure gold and which could make old men young again.[66] Dastin, in a letter to Cardinal Napoleon Orsini, referred to the ancient wisdom of the East which could reveal things hidden.[67] Another response to John's decretal came from the Istrian town of Pola, dominated by the signore under the house of Castropola. These overlords encouraged in these small coastal courts a cultural life and devoted themselves to financial and money-lending tricks. One prominent municipal official and physician was Petrus Bonus who wrote his *Pretiosa margarita novella* in the form of a scholastic dialogue that provided the most comprehensive defence of alchemy and its principles in the fourteenth century.[68] Writers such as Petrus Bonus and Dastin by using Christian imagery and themes to expound the chemical processes involved in alchemy were demonstrating the way Western alchemy was becoming independent from its Muslim roots.

In England alchemists, working within officially approved channels of Oxford University, continued the traditions of scientific discovery and occult investigations established by Bacon. In Merton College a group of dons devoted themselves to the study of natural science and physics, astrology and mathematics in particular. They included two victims of the 1349 Plague, the philosopher and theologian Thomas Bradwardine, and John Dumbleton, author of a number of texts dealing with natural philosophy inspired by Aristotle including: *Summa logicae et philosophiae naturalis* and *De caelo* and *de generatione et corruptione; meteorologia* and *De Anima*.[69] In this scientific unlocking of nature's secrets alchemy was to play a part. A contemporary of Bradwardine at Oxford was the Benedictine monk of Evesham, Walter Oddington,[70] who was engaged in astrological observations at Oxford in 1311. Oddington composed an alchemical treatise, *Icocedron*[71] and investigated qualitatively the primary qualities of heat, cold, humidity and aridity involved in the alchemical process. Another contemporary investigator of weather was Robert Perscrutator (fl. 1313–25) whose name was derived from his scrutiny of the hidden doctrine of secret medicine. His chief work on meteorology mentions the year 1325 and York. Robert was also the author of an alchemical treatise reiterating the Islamic sulphur mercury theory of the formulation and transmutation of metals.[72]

The main focus of alchemical experimentation and theorizing in the first half of the fourteenth century was the court of Edward III and this had been stimulated by the maritime links between the docks near the Tower of London on the Thames and the coastal towns of Naples, Montpellier and the island of Majorca, all within or near the old Islamic empire. An alchemical, *dialogue De Lapide Philosophorum et de auro potabile*, written by the Pola physician, Fabri de Dya Fabri, for the anti-Pope elected by the Council of Basel Felix V (1439–49), reproached kings for having driven alchemists to the point of desperation and extolled the attitude of Edward III as a benevolent protector of Raymund Lull, Arnold of Villanova and John Dastin, for whom he was prepared to divide his kingdom in three.[73] Although Arnold had no known connections with the English court, such links did exist with the medical school of Montpellier where he lectured. A number of physicians and pharmacists from Montpellier were at the English court including Pietro of Montpellier in 1316; and Odin the pharmacist of Queen Isabella (1328–30). The king's friend, Henry duke of Lancaster, who wrote a medical treatise *Le Livre de Seyntz Medicines* in 1354, had visited Montpellier and he had campaigned as a crusader in Granada, the former Muslim heartland of alchemy.[74]

Fabri's reference to Raymond Lull's presence at Edward III's court derives from the legend that the king imprisoned the Majorcan alchemist in the Tower until he transmuted gold nobles, and from the large number of anonymous alchemical texts attributed to Lull after 1383. Lull, a Franciscan tertiary, was neither a Muslim nor an alchemist. He was born in Palma on the island of Majorca off the South East coast of Spain. Majorca had been dominated by the Muslims from 902 to 1279 and Lull, writing in Latin, was one of the first Europeans to advocate the study of the Arabic language. His posthumous reputation as an alchemist is understandable: in his *Liber principum medicine* he saw the study and under-standing of the natural world as a way of approaching theological truths such as the relationship between complexionary equality and the paradoxes of the Trin-ity. Such analogies between nature and theology could be used to demonstrate the shared assumptions about the natural world common to all faiths and lead to the conversion of the infidel and recapture of the Holy Land.[75] The factual basis of the legend of Lull's visit to Edward's court and his alchemical corpus lay in the composition in Catalan at St Katherine's Hospital by the Tower of London between 1329 and 1332 of an alchemical work known as the *Testamentum*. This was a comprehensive account of the theory and practice of alchemy including an exposition of the theory of the sulphur mercury origin of metals, the principles of distillation and the medical benefits of the transmutation of metal which pro-duced a perfect body capable of conferring the perfection, the elixir vitae pro-duced from the transmutation of metal.[76] The third on Fabri's list, John Dastin, is significant because he represents the development of a native and highly original alchemical tradition developing in England. An obscure English monk Dastin, who corresponded with Pope John XXII and Cardinal Napoleon Orsini was a contemporary of the Majorcan author of the *Testamentum*. His familiarity with the *Secreta secretorum* is suggested in his letter to the pope in which he introduces the concept of the philosopher's stone: 'Here is the secret of secrets.' In 1328 he composed a dream vision that employed metaphors drawn from the world of Edward III's court[77] Dastin was a prolific author whose alchemical writings included: *Epistola ad episcopum Iohannem xxii, de alchemia*,[78] *Libellum Aureus*,[79] *visio super artem alchemia*.[80] Dastin's name also occurs on some copies of the *Rosarium*, usually attributed to Arnold of Villanova.[81] Just before the start of Edward's reign in 1326 the *Secreta secretorum* was being copied: an illustrated text dedicated to the king was made by Walter de Milemete.[82] By this time two other alchemists working in Latin were having an influence in England. The *Pretiosa Margarita Novella* (*The New Pearl of Great Price*) of Petrus Bonus survives in English manuscripts of the fourteenth century and was studied in the sixteenth century by readers of the *Ordinal of Alchemy* of Thomas Norton.[83] The Catalan Franciscan friar, John of Rupescissa, in 1351–52 in his *Liber de Consideratione Quinti Essentia* and in *Liber Lucis* (*The Book of Light* c. 1350) held to the Jabirian view that the philosopher's stone comprises mercury and sulphur and the initial stage of sublimation of saltpetre sulphur and mercury results in a mercury subli-mate that is 'as white as snow'.[84] Rupescissa, capitalizing on the invention of the serpente c. 1300, expounded on the medical benefits of the quintessence of alco-hol produced from multiple distillations which was supposed to remove all traces of the earthly four elements to produce the fifth heavenly element which was the basis of all life.[85]

The Western European alchemical literature emerging in the late thirteenth and early fourteenth century conveyed the separate scientific traditions from ancient Greece and the Islamic empire and added new elements. Roger Bacon articulated the Greek doctrine of the four humours derived from the four elements and the state of harmony and balance achieved in the discovery of the mysterious quintessence. The Latin writers of Catalonia, Majorca and Southern Italy, including Petrus Bonus, articulated the Arabic sulphur mercury theory of the origin of metals and all matter. Catalan writers, such as the author of the Pseudo Lullian *Testamentum* and John of Rupescissa, articulated distillation procedures. The high mortality rate associated with the Black Death of 1348–49, when at least a third of the population of Europe perished, led to changes in the practice of conventional medicine, which was ineffective against such a pandemic. The wealthy looked to alchemical medicine and such remedies as potable gold, distilled alcohol, minerals and pearls.[86] Petrus Bonus and John Dastin introduced into alchemy a mythological allegorical dimension (found also in the *Aurora Consurgens*).[87] By the second half of the fourteenth century these strands had converged to form a rich, philosophical, medical and practical occult philosophy that had a broader appeal within courts and for writers in the vernacular.

By the time of the accession of Edward III's successor, his grandson, Richard II in 1377, the alchemical visions of John Dastin and Petrus Bonus and John of Rupescissa were making an impact in English court circles. In 1384 John Dombelay dedicated to Richard II his *Stella alchemiae*. Dombelay is as shadowy figure as Dastin: he is described in a colophon to the *Stella* as a famous philosopher, and he may have taken his name from the Merton scientist John Dumbleton. He cited as influences on his work a Richard the Englishman, possibly Richard of Middleton (d. 1301), a Franciscan theologian and reputed author of *Speculum alchymiae*,[88] and *The Emerald Table*. In 1386 Dombelay wrote an exposition of the *Practica* of the alchemist Ortensius (a commentator on *The Emerald Table*) which had been written in Paris in 1356.[89] There was more to Dombelay's dedication of the *Stella alchemiae* to the king than mere flattery and search for patronage: it indicates a growing interest in alchemy in court circles reflected in a unique aspect of this period and Richard II's court in particular: the emergence of a vernacular literature dealing with occult themes. The London poet John Gower (c. 1330–1408), a friend of Geoffrey Chaucer, originally dedicated his *Confessio Amantis* to Richard in 1391, and in book seven of this work he outlined the principles of alchemy, defining the four spirits as quicksilver, sulphur, sal ammoniac and arsenic which could be refined in the alchemist's fires. Gower argued that there were three philosopher's stones: the vegetative, which could preserve a man's health until the natural end of his life, the animate, which could sustain a man's five senses, and the mineral stone which, through the virtue of the fire, could bring forth the sun and moon, the red and the white, which could be a great source of profit. Gower recognized that through a process of alchemical refinement in seven stages, metals could be restored to their original purity: that is refined to the state of gold and silver (the red and white of the sun and moon) the two extremes to which all metals desire to return. It is testimony to the way alchemy had come to the forefront of popular culture that Gower felt it necessary to warn that his was a suspect labour in which many spent more than they made. He acknowledged the authority of Hermes, Geber, Ortulanus, Morien, Plato and Avicenna on this subject, but added that few understood their books and pointed out that the way to avoid falsehood in this art was to follow the way of nature.[90] Geoffrey Chaucer issued similar warnings in his tale of a fraudulent alchemist (*The Canon's Yeoman's Tale*); but he too acknowledged the deeper mysteries of the great art and cited as his alchemical authorities pseudo Geber's *Summa perfectionis*; the *Speculum naturale* of Vincent of Beauvais, and the *Rosarium* of Arnold of Villanova.[91] Another of Chaucer's authorities was the book of the Muslim alchemist Senior, the *Epistola Sol ad Lunem Crescentem*.[92] A cleric who came from Cheshire, an area where Richard II recruited heavily for his affinity, wrote a collection of stories in a northwest dialect that have details of courtly life. They include: the Arthurian tale *Sir Gawain and the Green Knight*, *Pearl*, *Patience*, *Purity*, *Cleanness* and possibly *St Erkenwald*. All these works share a preoccupation with such occult themes as the phenomena of natural regeneration and the relationship between the spirit and flesh. They also contain alchemical symbols and themes involving transmutation and hidden knowledge.[93]

The increased profile of alchemy in this second half of the fourteenth century raises the question of what alchemists actually did. There were two kinds of alchemist: clerics, and laymen with a licence to practice. Many of the latter were employed in courts transmuting, tinting and dyeing metals. Despite the hostility of some theologically trained clergy, kings favoured alchemists because, unlike abstract theorists, they promised to yield practical results. It was probably for this purpose that Edward III in 1329 required Thomas Carey to find two escaped alchemists who he hoped would deliver the secret of this art. Much licensed activity by laymen involved counterfeiting – the subject of Pope John XXII's decree. The alchemist and physician at the court of the king of France, Charles V, Thomas of Bologna, refers in a letter to the fourteenth-century alchemist, Bernard of Treves, on the philosopher's stone to alchemists who found out how metals were falsely coloured by minerals rather than digestion.[94] Such alchemists, he asserted, were justly prohibited by written law because they were false exponents. However tinting and counterfeiting was also carried out by clergy. Geoffrey Chaucer may have taken his inspiration for the *Canon's Yeoman's Tale* after being taken in by William Shirchurch, a canon of the royal chapel of Windsor, who in 1374 had counterfeited gold pretending to multiply it from a mixture of gold, silver and sal ammoniac. In the fourteenth century there was a greater demand for alchemical gold and silver because the shortage of available gold and silver coinage reached catastrophic proportions, especially in the period between 1390 and 1415, exacerbated by the drying up of sources of Sudanese gold.[95]

Alchemy was never formally taught at universities or cathedral schools and its study and practice can only be glimpsed in religious houses and hospitals. Some monasteries, such as Glastonbury and Bridlington (the home of John Thweng, the fourteenth-century mystic and reputed author of a prophetic dream vision, and the fifteenth-century alchemist George Ripley), may have housed collections of occult texts. Hospitals, such as St Katherine's by the Tower, served as centres of alchemical experimentation in the search for distilled medicines. One fifteenth-century manuscript from a hospital library contains diagrams showing the dimensions of Solomon's temple.[96] Alchemists, through the practice of medicine, were able to secure favour at court. In 1330 Pope John XXII gave funds to his physician to set up a laboratory for a certain secret work (presumably the distillation of the *elixir vitae*).[97] Thomas of Bologna acted as physician to Charles V and appointed him on his death bed and supplied an elixir to the ailing Charles VI that included mercury and potable gold.

Shakespeare's Friar Lawrence in *Romeo and Juliet*, steeped in the knowledge of plants and powerful potions, was based on a long history of knowledge of the occult among the mendicants, and the friars were probably among the most significant collectors of occult texts. The Austin friar, John Erghome, who was associated with the Black Prince and was a regent master of the papal court near Naples in 1386, may have been a practising alchemist. Among the 220 books of his library which he donated to the Austin Friars of York, and which were catalogued in 1372 during the time Erghome was a member of this community, was a large collection of occult works.[98] Alchemical texts included: *Liber lapidum*; Albertus Magnus's *de Mineralibus*; *Secreta secretorum* from Aristotle to Alexander; *Moralis Philosophia* of Roger Bacon; *de Mirabilibus Mundi* of Alberti Magnus; *Icocedron* of Walter of Oddington; a tract on the transformation of metals; the commentary of Hortulanus on Hermes' *Emerald Table*; Bacon's *Opus maius*; *liber luminarium* of Rhazes; and Ovid's *Metamorphoses* (regarded in this period as a standard allegorical treatment of alchemical processes of transformation). Other works of a related occult nature included: *The Prophecy of St John of Bridlington*; a book on the *Interpretation of Hebrew Names*; *A Book on Antichrist*; *A Book on the Interpretation of Dreams* (attributed to Daniel but of Arabic origin); *tractatus de operibus et occultis actionibus naturalium*; *An Apocalypse*; *de Caelo et mundo* (Aristotle's cosmological treatise); *introductorium ad geomanciam docens terminus artis*; *flores coniunctionis veritatis gomancie distinctus in theoricam et practicam*;[99] *tractatus de penthagone Salomonis* (many books on magic in the Middle Ages were attributed to Solomon);[100] *tractatus ad inclusionem spiritus in*

speculo; tractatus ad habendam loquelam cum spiritu et effectum eternum (a work
of ritual magic concerned with the invocation of spirits) *opus capitis magni cum
aliis capitibus pertinencibus* (probably the Brazen Head of Friar Bacon); *Hermes de
imaginibus* (a work on astrological images),[101] *tractatus de capite Satruni; vinculum
Salomonis; liber rubeus qui aliter dicitur sapeincia nigromancie et experimentum
bonum sortis; tractatus de nominibus angelorum ordine forma et potestate et man-
sione; tractatus de nominibus angelorum et effectibus eorum; spera pythagore; tractatus de Floron* (On the demon Floron discussed by Cecco d'Ascoli, d. 1327);[102] *A
diagram for prognostications of life and death; De Radiis* (on the theory and art of
magic) by Al Kindi (an Arab philosopher (c. 800–870 CE); *forme ymaginum in
sinculis signorum faciebus; ars notoria nova completis* (*The Notary Art of Solomon*, a
thirteenth-century treatise on magic) and *multo experimentis* (presumably alchemical experiments); Erghome's occult interests anticipate those of Dr John Dee, the
Elizabethan scientist and alchemist, and his collection raises the issue of the high
rate of destruction of occult texts. This had occurred at Alexandria in 391 and at
Cordoba during the Christian reconquest in the fifteenth century and would occur
again during the English Reformation. Only four texts are known to have survived
from Erghome's catalogue. Monastic libraries such as those of the Austin friars of
York were completely destroyed and only in the case of the more orthodox standard works of theology and canon law of which multiple copies were made were the
losses replaceable. Works bearing such titles as *The Pentangle of Solomon, The
Demon Floron*, and *The Experiments in Necromancy and Conjuring Spirits* would
have aroused the particular hostility of protestant reformers. The Elizabethan
antiquary John Stow (c. 1525–1605), lamenting on the dispersal of these libraries
likened the process to the scattering of flowers in the breeze, and John Dee made
heroic attempts to collect occult texts only to have his library pillaged in 1591.[103]

Apart from the high rate of destruction of works on alchemy and natural
magic, the other problem facing the student of the occult in the late Middle Ages
is the very secrecy of the art. In 1375 the Carmelite friar, William Sedacerius,
writing in exile an alchemical work called *Sedacina*, stressed the importance in
creating the elixir vitae of having a suitable secret laboratory with trustworthy
associates that would be hidden from the uninitiated.[104] Alchemists were shadowy figures on the fringes of society with no formal standing. Petrus Bonus
described alchemy as a craft learned by observing a master: its principles and
practices of the subject were handed down from master to pupil in a secretive
manner reminiscent of the activities of the craft mysteries. Alchemists constituted a close knit clique. Benvenuto da Imola (1320?–88), a lecturer at the University of Bologna, in his commentary on Dante's *Divine Comedy*, refers to
alchemists as most chummy artificers, so much so that if there were only two in
a county they would straight away find each other and create a partnership.[105]

Despite the suspicion and hostility with which they may have been regarded in some ecclesiastical circles in the early fourteenth century their pursuit of scientific knowledge safeguarded them from serious accusations of heresy and ensured that, like hermits and anchorites, they would exert an influence on intellectual, religious and political life out of all proportion to their numbers and social position. It is through an examination of the surviving alchemical texts and the vernacular literature influenced by occult teaching that it is possible to appreciate and evaluate this impact.

Part 2

The Astrology of the Earth: The Intellectual Impact of Alchemy in Fourteenth-Century England

3

Alchemy and Science and Philosophy

In water there are many secrets – Water is the beginning of the generation of man. I do confess it to be true that the beginning of everything in the world is water. Therefore it followeth that water is the beginning of all things.

John Doubleday, *Stella Alchemiae*[1]

In the thirteenth and fourteenth centuries the study of natural philosophy, the search for material explanations for natural phenomenon, emerged as an academic discipline separate from Theology. Theologically trained scholars such as the Carmelite, John Baconthorpe, made use of Aristotle's *Nineteen Books of Animals* and medical sources such as Avicenna's canon to investigate, in his *Sentences* (c. 1325), the mysteries of God's creation, and although the goals of alchemists may have been primarily chemical and material, they too increasingly turned to the mysteries of Christian faith and especially the creation.[2] The alchemists' endeavours in the fourteenth century were dominated by the search for the original prime matter that was regarded as the origin of all life and this was known as the first water or the philosopher's mercury. From nothing God created the original chaos, an undifferentiated, formless and lifeless bulk of things all at odds; and then he sent a rain of mercurial sperm to this *massa confusa* which started the process of separating pairs of opposites (such as the sun and moon, the earth and sky) and the release of the four elements from this blind mass of things, a process which alchemists believed had been described in the opening of Ovid's *Metamorphosis* and in the beginning of the *Book of Genesis*.[3] Although these primordial events were believed to have occurred before the flood, it was thought that there were still distant echoes of these cosmic events in the presence of sulphur and mercury in all metals and of lead in the earth; lead, heavy like gold, was its dark, degenerate opposite and was known as *prima materia* or the toad by alchemists because this dull, inoperative, half poisonous and heavy waste reminded them of the original chaos, a kind of hell, a sea of impurities dominated by sulphur, the corrosive corruptor of all things; and in this wilderness the alchemist, like Noah on the flood, navigated an ocean of turbulent metals. A similar trace of these primeval, cosmic events could be discerned in the tiny pearl-like droplets of mercury found in crevices in rocks; these could inspire an alchemist to undertake a quest to find the mercurial sperm that was believed to be the origin of all life. The 'philosopher's mercury' was regarded as the divinity found within nature; in the words of John Doubelay in the *Stella alchemiae*, it was the spirit of God moving on the face of the waters at creation; the word or the light shining in the darkness. This mercury, the 'sperm' from which the seven metals and the four elements were derived, was described by Charles of Bologna in a letter of 1395 as the fifth essence, the quintessence, a special occult gift from God.[4] In his reply to this letter Bernard of Trevisa described the feminine mercury as a hermaphrodite because it also contained the masculine qualities of sulphur. The primal ocean which preceded the creation was the mercurial mother and mercury, the sperm that descended into his abyss, enacted a drama which embraced both feminine and masculine attributes. For John Doubelay, in the late fourteenth century, it was the moving force of creation that would quicken the dead, the secret of life, disguised by parables 'in words very dark' such as the toad springing from the milk of a dead mother which is then slit down the middle and fed to a cock,[5] and hidden behind an infinite number of names such

The descent of Mercurial sperm into the primal ocean of chaos.
From the *Ripley Scroll*

as: the elixir of life; the *uroboros* or dragon without beginning or end; the egg; and the philosopher's stone.[6]

However the name given to describe mercury's many qualities which would have most cultural resonance in the fourteenth century was the pearl. In the most popular occult treatise of this period, the *Secreta secretorum,* mercury or the philosopher's stone is described as 'this precious pearl' and the phrase was used in 1330 as the title of Petrus Bonus's *Pretiosa Margarita Novella,* the most influential exposition of the Muslim theories of the fundamental importance of mercury. The pearl was widely believed to mirror, in its origin and qualities, the mysterious, original mercurial force. According to medieval encyclopaedias, and Roger Bacon, pearls originated from drops of heaven's dew received into open oyster shells, whose growth was governed by the moon, which controlled the tidal movements of the sea,[7] and which, according to John Gower, was the planet particularly associated with England.[8] This process echoed the descent of the divine, mercurial sperm into the leaden waters of chaos: the pearl was the equivalent of the world egg that dissolved into the waters of the abyss to create the universe. The pearl therefore, even more than gold, represented the most spiritual and pure substance known. The dews of night descended from the heavens into the ocean into the awaiting shells of oysters in an evocation of the primal act of creation. The resulting pearl represented the primal egg in its roundness and whiteness, the divine mercury that fell from heaven; its yoke embodied the earthly incarnation of sulphur, or gold. In its perfect, white and untarnished roundness the pearl, or primal egg, was seen as symbol of the seamless eternity of nature, of purity and perfection, without end or beginning, the *uroboros* or the philosopher's stone.[9]

However this original, divine mercury, a pure spirit, was necessarily an elusive presence in the material, fallen world. It was known as *fugitivus cervus* or *fugitivus servus,* the elusive servant and the fugitive stag (possibly because of the Latin pun of *cervus/servus*).[10] Mercury was elusive precisely because it lacked body; even the impure mercury found in the earth lacked definition and evaporated at room temperature and would split and reform in apparent disregard to the laws of cause and effect. The paradox facing the alchemist was that mercury could only exist or be fixed or congealed and given form in a corporeal world by the corrupt and earthy sulphur found in all deposits of mercury. In the words of Pseudo Albertus Magnus's alchemical work, *Semita recta,* the first spirit was quicksilver, wild water from which all metals evolved, and the second was sulphur, a fatness of the earth.[11] This giving of form and body to mercury by sulphur constituted an alchemical marriage in which the spirit, the white queen, was betrothed to the body, the red king. This marriage explained the fundamental opposites in the world: the moon and sun; female and male; night and day; unconscious and conscious evil; and odd and even numbers. It also explained why the spiritual realm (represented by mercury) was compromised by the corruption and illnesses of the body (represented by sulphur). Sulphur, like mercury, was also the *prima materia*, a burning corrosive substance hostile to the matter of the stone (mercury) yet when cleansed of impurities it was the stone. Sulphur or yellow brimstone, found naturally in volcanoes, was regarded as the literal substance of hell. In its corporeal, earthly and occult power it was closely related to the dragon and its affinities with the *uroboros* made it difficult to distinguish it from mercury. According to the *Turba philosophorum* all quicksilver and sulphur were brothers and sisters with the power to kill and bring metals back to life. Sulphur's corrupting power was considered to be great: According to the *Turba philosophorum* a little sulphur powder was sufficient to consume a strong body, and sulphur was thought capable of blackening and consuming the sun with which it was closely associated (leading to the representation of sulphur as the green lion devouring the sun).[12] Sulphur was seen as the material manifestation of the spirit of Lucifer, a phosphorous light bringer manifested in the most beautiful star in the firmament down to the little bits of sulphurous tow that old men sold for lighting fires. Sulphur's association with Lucifer meant it could be seen as a source of light and regeneration as well darker forces. Sulphur's destructive energy could be seen in the use of sulphuric acids as corrosive agents, and it was also the basis for the manufacture of gunpowder, a mixture of charcoal, sulphur and saltpetre and potassium nitrate extracted from dung and lime.[13] Sulphur's corporeal earthly and occult powers identified it with the chthonic pulses of the earth, of nature, and it was represented by the dragon, a creature without beginning or end. It was also identified with the colour green, the colour of procreation and life (the green sun or green bird according to Micreris in *Tractatus Micreris suo discipulo Mimefindo*)[14] As the spirit of nature, a Lucifer fallen from heaven into earthly fate, sulphur was at the heart of all things, yearning for reconciliation with his sister mercury, to unite the head and tail and bring together the conscious and the unconscious.

Alchemy presented its practitioners with the exciting prospect of witnessing through experimental science the mysteries of creation and the eternal struggle between good and evil, God and the devil, and the spirit with nature. The conflict between mercury and sulphur was seen to be crucial to understanding the laws of nature and therefore a necessary precondition for the existence of life in the corporeal material world. Knowledge of both of these forces was believed to be necessary for the widening of consciousness. For Petrus Bonus, John Doubelay and the author of the *Secreta secretorum*[15] the key symbol that represented the importance of this marriage of two opposites as the principle of life was the egg, hatched by the bird of Hermes under the heat of the sun.[16] The egg, the origin of life, consisted of the white, watery albumen (the impure mercury) and the yellow, oily yolk (impure sulphur). Mercury, containing within itself whiteness and yellowness, was the primal egg and gold, consisting of the yellowness of sulphur and the silver whiteness of mercury, hinted at this original divine force. The primal egg, composed of these inseparable opposites, was the underlying symbol for the central dictum of alchemy from *The Emerald Table*: 'That which is within is that which is without'.

The philosopher's mercury, the original prime matter and the world egg, was the mysterious grail-like object of the alchemist's quest and it remained an elusive chimera. If the pearl represented the unsullied spirit and purity of the original heavenly mercury, the divine, then gold was the one substance that partook of the fall of nature yet evoked the original purity of mercury: in its durability it resembled the pearl or mercury and in its redness, and its gestation through fire and warmth it represented the fallen incarnate sulphur. Under the steady and profound warming influence of the sun within the womb of the earth it was believed that mercury evolved through six stages of ascending perfection, represented by the six metals of lead, iron, copper, mercury bronze and silver, to an amalgam of a more purified mercury and sulphur that created gold, a beautiful precious metal that in its purity and radiance provided a glimpse of the qualities of the divine mercury, which, if it could be procured, could be used to create gold: any metal exposed to the primal force would take the form of the original material, water, that was the philosopher's mercury. This marriage between mercury and sulphur (both sources of natural heat), which gave form to the mercury from which all life sprang, could be witnessed in nature in the interplay of night and day, the dialogue between the mercurial moon and the sulphurous sun, a daily drama of the coming to form and light of the maternal waters of creation. The *Secreta secretorum* defined the philosopher's stone as two stones, white and red, which emerged from the Mediterranean Sea and worked in tandem, mercury (the moon) sinking into the water as the sun rises, maintaining a balance and harmony of opposites. The sun (sulphur) was identified with light and the land, the moon (mercury) with darkness and the ocean; but as the ocean is vaster than the lands, so the prime mover was not the sun but the moon (mercury) whose element is water.[17] John Dastin in his dream vision celebrated a marriage between the sun (sulphur) and the moon (mercury) when during the time of Aries when the spirit of life is inspired

> The sunne that sitteth so hegh and a loft,
> His golden dew droppes still clearly raigne downe
> By mean of Mercury that nowen first made softe
> Then there shall be a glad conjuncion.[18]

Alchemy was therefore a meditation on a holistic world in which water and sun between them generated life. According to Doubelay, the marriage between mercury, the mother of all things, and the masculine sulphur, brought forth the multiplication of fruit on earth. John Doubelay in his commentary on the *Practica*, the *vera alkemia e libris Magistri Ortolani* composed in 1386 at the order of the archbishop of Trier, Conon von Falkensteyn,[19] compared the stages in the alchemical process to the four seasons and associated them with the seven planets. The author of the *Secreta secretorum*, for whom true knowledge was insight into the secrets of nature, celebrated the endless natural cycles of death and regeneration fuelled by this marriage of sulphur and mercury (which he symbolized throughout his work with references to the white and red stone). In the Spring this was manifested by the sun entering the sign of Aries accompanied by the blowing of soft winds, the melting of the winter snows, the swelling of rivers and the exhalation of moisture in the earth and trees. Under the inspiration of the sun's steadily growing power there occurred the generation of the budding and opening of the flowers, portrayed by the author as the earth receiving its garments from its spouse. This celebration of the endless cycle whereby spring emerges from the death of winter was depicted in allegorical terms as the dragon or *uroborus* constantly renewing itself. For the alchemist nothing was ever lost but in a constant process of change or transmutation.

In such a holistic view of the universe man was seen to be at the centre, mirroring the alchemical processes. In the *Rosarius*, which is also known as *Desiderabile desiderium* from its *incipit,* and was attributed to John Dastin in 22 manuscripts, the process of subjecting a hermetically sealed glass to a gentle heat, so that vapours continually ascended and descended, mirrored the constant breathing within the human body.[20] Man and the earth he inhabited were both composed of mercury and sulphur. Prolonged meditation on the course of the endless cycle of death and renewal, mirrored in the alchemical processes of distillation and evaporation, led to an acceptance of the sexual energy represented by the union of mercury and sulphur that allowed the endless cycles of death, decay and regeneration to facilitate the perpetuation of the various species in nature. By focussing on human sexuality alchemists could claim that the key to the mysterious origin of all things lay with mercurial sperm. John Doubelay in *Stella alchemiae* showed how the human body heated by the liver, fuelled by bellows of the lungs, acted as a womblike furnace in the same manner as the earth from which sulphur generated the burgeoning procreative powers of Spring.[21] In *The Withdrawing of the Accidents of Old Age* (attributed to Bacon) it was claimed that the sperm of man was derived from all the humours of the body so that it was made more subtle in nature.

If the physical make up of man mirrored that of the organic world he inhabited, the same applied to his mind and soul which were ruled by what could be termed the Gnostic principles of the opposites of mercury and sulphur and all this implied. If the physical universe was governed by the principles of day and night; male and female; light and darkness; water and fire; Man himself was regarded as a combination of body and spirit; goodness and evil (or in post-Jungian terms conscious and unconscious). The chemical processes of alchemy involved the reconciliation of opposites, especially mercury and sulphur, and the emergence from darkness of primeval, bestial sulphur to the light of pure, refined spiritual mercury. In meditative terms the philosopher's stone, the marriage of sulphur and mercury, was seen as a reconciliation of spirit and body and the evolution of human consciousness, the birth of the self and the emergence of a sense of purpose in life, a sense of having a soul symbolized by the *homunculus*.

This mirroring of the alchemical processes in the body can be seen in the fluent movement between the spheres of alchemical medicine and imagery relating to the military experiences of the nobility found in a medical treatise on uroscopy written for Richard II, an English translation of *Commentarium urinarum* of Walter of Angilon, a Frenchman of the Salerno medical school.[22] Like Henry Grosmont in his *Livre de Seyntz Medicines*, the author sees physical health in terms of alchemical balance maintained by the red and the white, sulphur and mercury, the substances that evoke the Passion of Christ and the Grail. The two friends of man are the humours of blood and phlegm (the red and the white) and these are in constant battle with the humours of choler and bile. Illness occurs when the choleric and melancholic humours escape the prisons in which they are produced, the gall and the spleen. But blood and phlegm, because they are friendly humours to man, have leave to roam the body leaving their dwellings in the liver, heart and lungs, and a battle ensues. Unless these two malevolent humours of choler and bile are driven back to their dungeons deep in the body the battle will result in the death of the body.[23]

The excitement that alchemy held for its practitioners in the fourteenth century was that it offered through scientific investigation and experimentation the possibility of coming face to face with spiritual forces manifested in the earth and possibly capturing and harnessing these powers. The ability of mercury to vaporize under a gentle heat led to speculation about its spiritual qualities and its potential relevance to the release of the spirit in the human body. Mercury after all was not just believed to be a product of gross earth, it originated in the heavens. The author of the *Testamentum* stressed the existence of a fifth element, the quintessence, a perfect balance of the four elements whose principle agent or menstrue was *noster Mercurius* (our mercury), used by God to create all things and which could be still found in the heavenly spheres and in the four elements and all bodies, and this too was derived from the original mercury. The corrosive agents sulphur dioxide and ammonium chloride, and the invention of the serpente around 1300, facilitated the process of evaporation, sublimation and distillation through gentle and controlled heating that allowed the extraction of the spiritual essence of any substance (and this was ultimately the primal mercury) from the corruptible four elements. The Franciscan, Jean de Roquetaillade (John of Rupescissa b. 1310), was introduced to the alchemical medicine *aqua vitae* (distilled alcohol) during his imprisonment at Avignon and it was during his long imprisonment, which commenced in 1346, that he wrote two alchemical works *Liber lucis* c. 1350 (*The Book of Light*) and *Liber de consideratione quinte essentie* 1351–52 (*The Book on the Consideration of the Quintessence of all Things*), in which he explained his fascination at the prospect of distilling the quintessence. Rupescissa recommended the use of a furnace known as the horse's belly (known as such because it used slow burning fuels such as horses' dung) or the placing of an inverted, stopped, sealed amphora in dung to allow the grosser elements to settle and the higher, including the quintessence, to rise to the bottom of the vessel. This was further alluded to in Rupescissa's recipe for the distillation of human blood, which, according to Doubelay in *Stella alchemiae*, produced an essence that was the origin of all things because man was the highest of all creations. The Franciscan alchemist recommended obtaining blood from babies or young sanguine men from the barbers when they let blood, and mixing it with salt and placing the mixture in a glass amphora in horses dung and fermenting it for 40 days. The resulting white powder was then ground on marble and distilled many times until the quintessence was achieved. What Rupescissa was describing, which involved a process of torture and humiliation, amounted to a version of the Passion.[25] The circulation of the red and white substances in the limbeck that accompanied the distillation of blood offered the possibility that the mysterious white mercury and red sulphur (the quintessence of all substances, the material of heaven, the holy grail itself) could be found within man himself and redemption of matter could be realized.

The alchemist's goal, therefore, was to use science to understand and imitate the natural world which was animated with the spirit of God. There was a spiritual, transcendent aspect to the theory and practice of alchemy, and the models of the Passion and the Redemption of flesh were applied to the quest to recover the divine mercury. For Rupescissa vitriol (sulphuric acid, a corrosive agent made from sulphur dioxide) and sal ammonia chloride (a salt of ammonia gathered in Egypt from soot formed from dung fuel and exported to Venice) were powerful corrosive agents that could make fire without coal and worked the way the fires of Hell were seen to work. Such agents, which could disintegrate metals and convert them to liquid vapour, offered alchemists the possibility of controlling the four elements, converting one element into another and taking these elements back to a primitive, primeval state (the crow's head or *nigredo*) in which it was possible to find the original philosopher's mercury, used, according to the author of the *Testamentum*, by God to create the planets, stars and four elements. This process of dividing substances offered fourteenth-century scientists the sort of hypothetical power that in the twentieth century would accompany the splitting of the atom, and in both cases the scientist who unlocked nature's secrets was believed to be coming face to face with divine powers.

The quest for the philosopher's stone, the original primal matter, the divine mercury, could be followed in this fallen world by attempting to refine corrupt sulphur through a process of distillation and heating in which mercury (the fugitive stag, identified with Christ through the legend that the Saviour appeared before the disciples in the form of a white stag, and from the stag's ability to shed and grow new antlers and supposedly renew itself)[26] was subjected to various tortures, which allowed it to realize bodily form in all its purity in refined sulphur. This was a scientific process that mirrored in a strikingly symbolic fashion the mysteries of the Incarnation of Christ, human consciousness and the origins of the soul and the Resurrection. John Dastin, in a letter derived from the writings of Arnold of Villanova, observed that most alchemists fail to find the philosopher's quicksilver or mercury because they believe it resides in all bodies, pure and impure. They attach what they believe to be a perfect body, mercury, to an impure body and expect to find what is good and pure in an impure body attach itself to a perfect body; they then become disillusioned when this does not take place. Dastin goes on to argue that all impure bodies in their experiments end with quicksilver disappearing and the impure body remaining. Most practitioners of alchemy fail to realize that the spirit (mercury) can only be joined to the body through the medium of the soul which is the third part of the alchemist's trinity. This involves the changing of metals back to their original primal state of mercury, the seed of all metals: 'all that is born, grown and multiplies comes from this one grain'. The separation of bodies into the four elements and their reduction into the original water from which they came is followed by a process of sublimation, creating ashes at the bottom of the alembic: 'the diadem of your heart the final goal'. The feather-like ashes denote the beating wings of the bird of Hermes, the birth of the phoenix from its ashes, the quickening into life of the soul born through pain and suffering, an incarnation in which the sun and moon, sulphur (body) and mercury (spirit), are joined to form the ferment or the soul. Just as the sun and moon rule the rest of the planets so these two bodies rule all other bodies and this ferment is alone capable of creating new life from death, bestowing life on inert matter.[27]

Such a vivid, scientific demonstration of the mysteries at the heart of Christian religion and this chemical vision of the Passion was the closely guarded secret of secrets of the alchemists, a claim that the most precious mysteries of the *New Testament*: the Immaculate Conception, the Incarnation of the Divinity in human flesh, and his Crucifixion, could be demonstrated in the material world. When Petrus Bonus first pointed out in around 1330 the parallels between the torture and redemption of metals and the Passion of Christ and redemption of mankind, he gave a specifically Christian interpretation to the sulphur and mercury theories of the Muslim alchemists, marking the new independence of the Latin, Western alchemists, and his lead was enthusiastically followed by such English alchemists as John Dastin and John Doubelay. According to Bonus, the manifestation of the philosopher's stone, the Divine Christ as mercury within the tortured and purified body of sulphur, had been known by *Old Testament* prophets who belonged to the select group of alchemists who understood the natural and divine aspects of the lapis and, operating with reason and faith, who were able to predict the coming of Christ. It was believed that the biblical prophets Moses, Solomon and John the Evangelist, were also magicians, heirs to Adam's knowledge of all natural things that was lost at the fall, and this included alchemy. Moses, 'learned in all the wisdom of Egypt', was portrayed as a sorcerer in two medieval mystery plays. These holy men of antiquity were believed to be the possessors of powers through various instruments, such as Moses' rod and Solomon's ring. Even the classical poets Homer, Virgil and Ovid were believed to have expressed hermetic, alchemical truths in their writings. The secret they all held and communicated in veiled allegories was that Christ himself, the Redeemer, continued to manifest himself in the material world in the form of the golden spirit of mercury, trapped in matter. This secret was, according to Bonus, transmitted to an elect group of initiates in veiled allegories such as the myths of Jason and the Golden Fleece and the Minotaur in the Cretan labyrinth,[28] many of which expressed the torture of metals and the Passion of mercury. Bonus even compared the death and rebirth of the *lapis* to the martyrdom and beautification of the saints. In the writings of Dastin and Doubelay the slaying of the dragon, or the hunting and capture of the fugitive servant or stag, conveyed the fixing of mercury that would be of incalculable benefit to mankind. These were seen as powerful secrets of the hidden powers in the earth that could be abused and therefore needed to be expressed 'parabolically', because this science had to be hidden 'from wicked men'.[29] Alchemical allegories of incest, expressing the phenomenon of the *lapis*, or mercury that conceives and impregnates itself so that father and son are one, and compose an indissoluble unity with the spirit (the maternal mercury) were seen as intimations of the workings of the Holy Trinity.

The realization of the divine presence of pure mercury within matter led alchemists to claim that they could scientifically demonstrate the truths of the resurrection in alchemical terms as the transmutation of lead into gold. The subjection of mercury to a process involving dismemberment, burial and decomposition into a state described as the *nigredo* mirrored the physical processes of death and decay. Dastin's vision described a leprous king (representing gold or debased mercury) instructed by his mother (the elemental mother or primal mercury) to encounter the dragon (or sulphur), an encounter that will result in his death and rebirth into pure gold. In a letter to Pope John XXII beginning 'Here is the secret of secrets' describing the congealing of mercury, he claims that it is through the marriage of sulphur and mercury that the purest gold is produced.[30] Doubelay also used the language of the Passion and Resurrection to describe the making of gold: mercury and sulphur are placed in a heated glass and reduced to ash from which tears are drawn and this residue is placed in a grave for three days, after which the figures of sun and moon (gold and silver) appear and the philosopher's stone quickens into life for the good of all mankind. The alchemical process of purifying sulphur and mercury represented more than the Resurrection of Christ; it also symbolized the resurrection of all mankind. The purified mercury and sulphur, obtained through various procedures of evaporation and distillation, represented the spirit, reconciled with the body which was described by Bonus in terms of a resurrection in which the dead and decayed body was reunited with its spirit in a purified and eternal state. During a mortal life the soul lay dead and buried in its bodily filth, the corrupt sulphur. Death was seen as an alchemical conjunction in which the soul, released through the purification of sulphur, is united with its pure body.[31] The resurrection meant the transfiguration of the body, its subtilization into an incorruptible substance. The philosopher's stone decomposed into a powder, like a man in his grave, and then the *lapis* becomes a soul beautified and united with its original body, represented by the pearl. For Bonus the spirit or mercury was a brilliantly white fugitive, hunted stag and the man who could overtake him was blessed: 'for mercury's nature adapted itself to all things'.[32] Mercury, killed and mortified by its body (sulphur) and buried with its body as in a prison until death, achieves the culmination of a glorious conjunction when the spirit, through the purification of sulphur through the process of death and putrefaction, is united with the clear, purified body it has always sought and in which it will live forever.

The concern of late medieval alchemists with the mystery of the Resurrection of Christ and all his followers led them to focus beyond the death of the individual to the alchemical transmutation that would occur towards the end of time at the general resurrection after the Last Judgement. Roger Bacon anticipated that with the help of alchemical medicine and close study of the elements and weather, it would be possible to anticipate and prepare for the approach of Antichrist by restoring men to their natural prelapsarian state of health and longevity. Arnold of Villanova, under the patronage of Frederick III of Sicily (1296–1337), whom he recognized as an apocalyptic, God elected king, espoused a programme of spiritual and societal reform in preparation for the world's last age in which the scientific study of the natural world and divinely inspired medical knowledge could be used to treat the spiritual ills of society. The author of the *Testamentum*, influenced by Bacon and the Arnoldian corpus, saw the end of the world as a vast alchemical conflagration: at the end of time all terrestrial elements would burn but a bit of the true incorruptible virgin element that remains in all matter would withstand the fire of the last days.[33] The most radical assertion of the role that alchemical knowledge could play in the drama of the last end was proposed by John of Rupescissa, who joined the Franciscan order in 1332. Rupescissa proclaimed to a hearing in the Papal curia in 1354 that he had undergone an alchemical process during his imprisonment in which he had been cooked, purged and transmuted, and this inspired his apocalyptic visions. In his most popular apocalyptic and prophetic work, *Vade mecum in tribulatione*, written in 1356 and surviving in 40 extant manuscripts, he expressed his conviction that his own age, which was witnessing the upheavals of the famines between 1315 and 1322 and the onset of the Hundred Years' War (the outbreak of which had been predicted by Rupescissa in 1335), the popular uprising in France in 1358 known as the

Jacquerie, and the Babylonian captivity of the papacy in Avignon, were signs that the social order was being inverted in what amounted to an alchemical process of the disintegration of the body politic to a state of *nigredo*, the apocalypse. For Rupescissa alchemy was more than a metaphor for the ultimate disintegration of the flesh and the world: alchemical medicine and the scientific study of the natural world allowed humans to accurately predict the coming of Antichrist, whom he had seen in a vision in the form of a young man in Fujon province in China, an event that he claimed would occur between 1365 and 1370, and the means to defeat the enemy of mankind through powerful medicines such as *aqua vitae* and distilled gold which contained within them the essence of heaven, a divine power and which could be used to extend the lifespan of the elect evangelical poor Franciscans who would survive the apocalypse to usher in a golden thousand year millennium.[34] Rupescissa predicted in his *Vade Mecum in Tribulacione* many disasters, wars and plagues for the years 1360–65 and the appearance of an Antichrist before the end of the world. Although the anticipated apocalypse did not arrive, Rupescissa's prophecies were still popular, known by Froissart and Le Bel, and enjoying increasing vogue because of such subsequent events as the Papal schism in 1378 and the Peasants' Revolt of 1381. At one point his apocalyptic prophecies were removed from the libraries of Oxford and Salisbury so they would not be accessible to Lollard dissenters who admired them.[35]

A more orthodox, alchemical interpretation of the Day of Judgment and the end of the world was provided by Petrus Bonus who maintained that the alchemical opus would be concluded when each soul is reunited with its body and each glorified body is changed and becomes the possessor of an incorruptible brightness and unbelievable subtlety. This event, he believed, was anticipated by Hermes, Moses, Aristotle, Homer and Plato, who understood that the philosopher's stone was manifested when God becomes man on the Last Day and begetter and begotten become one.[36] For the alchemist the *alpha et omega*, the slaying of the dragon, the creature with no end or beginning, symbolized the conclusion of the Great Work – the Resurrection of the body and the Last Judgement. This recognition of the existence of a link between the Great Work of alchemy, the process of destruction, decay and regeneration, and the destruction and rebirth of the world, gave a prophetic, apocalyptic dimension to alchemical writings in the fourteenth century, which claimed to find signs of the end of the world in an apocalyptic struggle between good and evil and the coming of Antichrist, an event that Arnold of Villanova predicted would occur in 1378, for which prediction he was arrested in the mid-fourteenth century. These events were expressed in chemical, scientific terms as the transmutation of base metal into gold.[37] The divine mercury (like Christ) was able to transform sick metals into gold. The philosopher's gold that emerged, purified and radiant, from the fires of time and mortality in a union of mercury and purified sulphur, was a manifestation of that state of heavenly bliss

when the world will be destroyed and (according to Bonus) reborn with the uniting of heaven and earth and the bodies and spirits of all the dead in a general resurrection that would witness the birth of the twelve-gated heavenly Jerusalem.

This belief in the presence of divine primal matter with an ability to effect
transmutation of metals led alchemists of this period to claim that they had
resolved the key intellectual conflict of the Middle Ages: this was the claim made
by Platonists, in the face of the scepticism of empirical Aristotelians, concerning
the reality of the presence of universals (divine ideas). For Bonus, Plato's philosophy represented the most sophisticated aspect of the alchemist's art: his doctrine
of supernatural ideas and forms corresponded to the primal matter of mercury in
Bonus's alchemical philosophy. Bonus, employing the scholastic, rhetorical techniques of academic debate, refuted the nominalist scholastic philosophers' objections to the principles of alchemy, especially transmutation, by first outlining the
sceptical and empirical views expressed in Aristotle's *Metaphysics* which implied
that there was no divine essence in this material world, and that alchemy was
therefore based on a false premise because it only effected a superficial change in
metals through dyeing and tincturing; their essence remained unchanged.[38] The
younger Aristotle, according to Bonus, maintained that one can only know the
qualitative properties of something by its accidents, not its substance, and this
depended on sensory perception.[39] This substantial form was therefore nothing
but an intellectual abstraction and judgements could only be formed on the basis
of practical manifestations of accidents, and this applied to the investigation of
metals. If something exhibited the qualities of gold it was gold. The claims of
alchemy appear miraculous and above the ordinary course of nature, and the
alchemist was merely a sorcerer claiming to work with signs and wonders. Bonus
then attempted to invalidate these claims by appropriating this formidable empirical opponent as an apologist for alchemy by maintaining that Aristotle was also
the author of the *Secreta secretorum.* Bonus anticipated objections that there was
no evidence for the Greek philosopher's authorship of a work totally different in
style and philosophy to his other writings by suggesting that the *Secreta secretorum*
was a work of Aristotle's old age, the result of a conversion to a philosophical outlook expressing belief in the occult power of things represented by mercury.[40] In
this work the pseudo Aristotle admitted that we do not know the essential differences between metals and put in their place properties or accidents peculiar to
each. Alchemy, as represented in the *Secreta secretorum,* holds the key to understanding the relationship between accidents and substance (the superficial varia-
tions in nature and the essential underlying principles). In all metals quicksilver is
the substance, the essence, and sulphur the active principle signifying form. No
metal could be complete and perfect until sulphur had been separated from it; and
only gold represented the true, pure intention of nature with regard to metals
purified of sulphur. Furthermore Bonus was able to claim that Aristotle in the

Secreta secretorum recognized that the existence of primal mercury was scientific proof that the Platonic notion of the existence of universal ideals gave existence to forms and this added force to the claims that mercury was the hidden, divine, pure essence in all things that was able to change the form and essence of metals to gold. It goes without saying that Aristotle's authorship of the *Secreta secretorum* was pure myth and that this work of Syriac origins was at best an adaptation of a work from third-century Greek Alexandria. But Bonus succeeded in claiming as apologists for the art of alchemy the two most important philosophers of antiquity.

Twenty years after Bonus had written *The New Pearl of Great Price*, John of Rupescissa also evoked the authority of the Platonic philosophers of ancient Greece to suggest in *De Quintessentia* that the quintessence represented the incorruptibility of heaven and this was something known to the Platonic philosophers of old but which had become forgotten. This enabled Rupescissa to reconcile the myths about the longevity of the patriarchs of the Old Testament, who were supposedly early adepts in the art of alchemy and upholders of the Platonic wisdom on the existence of universals, with the relatively short life span of his plague-dogged contemporaries in the fourteenth century.

4

Alchemy and the Church

I often beheld as a miracle that artificial resurrection and revivification of mercury, how being mortified into a thousand shapes, it assumes againe its owne, and returns to its numericall selfe.

Thomas Browne, *Works*[1]

Alchemists, by demonstrating the potential of the human body to achieve a state of blessedness in the resurrection, a perfect balance the four humours known as the quintessence, brought an optimism that was in direct contrast to the assumptions shown in fourteenth-century pastoral manuals such as *The Prick of Conscience* or *De Contemptu Mundi* and in the spiritual aspirations of many recluses, monks and even secular clergy, that human life was a blighted pilgrimage through a vale of tears in which the pilgrim's eyes needed to be focussed steadily on the next world, the heavenly Jerusalem. This was a radical shift in the perspective of traditional Christian thought which, since the time of St Augustine of Hippo (354–430), had prioritized the spiritual aspirations of the shepherd Abel (representative of the heavenly city of Jerusalem) at the expense of the materialism of his brother, Cain (representing the symbol of the earthly city of Rome).[2] Roger Bacon, called alchemy *instrumentum salutis* and in his *Liber sex scientiarum* and various texts he prepared for Pope Clement IV he gave it a liberating role, allowing humans to free themselves from the pessimistic views of church writers who tied original sin and corruptibility in an unbreakable knot.[3] By doing so he was in accord with the prevailing mood among clerical intellectuals of the thirteenth and fourteenth centuries which dictated that the human body was becoming an object of veneration far removed from the traditional contempt towards the inevitably corrupt cover for the immortal soul. Thirteenth-century theologians had suggested that Adam's immortality was less a result of divine grace and more a state of innocence in which his body was naturally endowed with physical properties to ensure his immortality. Medical and alchemical treatises were used to discuss the effects of eating from the tree of life, which instilled humoral balance and the nourishment of natural heat to ensure that the inevitable consumption of the radical moisture was resisted, and with it corruption and death. Similarly Christ's body was discussed as a natural phenomenon, the result of perfectly balanced complexion that would be illustrated in such medical texts as the *Book of the York Barber Surgeons*.[4] One of the key goals of alchemists, the production of distilled essences that enabled the human body to achieve this state, was in accord with some of the aims of the clerical elites of the thirteenth and fourteenth century, especially around the Papal court. Popes Innocent IV (c. 1195–1254), Clement IV (1199–1268) and Boniface VIII (c. 1235–1303) were clients or commissioners of medical/alchemical treatises that discussed ways of prolonging life, slowing down the ageing process and preserving youth. Boniface VIII, especially, and lay rulers such as Frederick II, were promoters of the 'new sciences', of medicine, alchemy and physiognomy, which all provided strategies for prolonging one's life.[5] The papacy therefore did not oppose dissections for forensic, academic reasons, and by the end of the thirteenth century the first public dissections for medical and juridical purposes occurred under papal approval. The motivation for such endorsement of medicine and alchemy was the notion of the importance and integrity of the body, and the possibility of a smooth and direct passage from life to death and resurrection in which a perfect, young body became the instrument of salvation and resurrection that was in accord with the laws of nature.[6]

In the thirteenth and fourteenth centuries there was an emerging scientific curiosity about nature and a desire to subject the mysteries of faith, such as the role of Mary in the generation of Christ, the role of the Holy Spirit as a substitute for the sperm in the development of the life of Christ, and possible astral influences at the time of Christ's birth, that reveals a departure from the traditional Christian view of nature, which was that it was alive because it had been created by God and its life or spirit was derived from a divine principle above nature; and therefore to reach God it was necessary to turn away from nature. Alchemists perhaps went further than any natural philosophers and physicians in their endorsement of this new interest in penetrating the divine mysteries at the heart of nature. Central to their quest was their belief that God could only be known within nature. To understand God one had to understand the spirit of nature, the philosopher's stone. This was a radical shift in the perspective of St Augustine of Hippo who regarded the compulsions and pleasures of the body, in particular the sexual instincts, as the consequences of the fall of Adam and inherently evil.[7] Such assumptions were implicitly rejected by alchemists' claims that God was present in nature in the form of mercury.

The hermaphroditic mercury consisted of the original maternal water and the spirit or sperm that moved on the face of these waters to form the four elements. Less patriarchal than orthodox Christian teaching on the Trinity, the father and holy Ghost was replaced in alchemical theory by the mother and the spirit of mercury that was believed to have had a pre-existence in this fallen world, and which could not be seen in manifest bodily form unless through the incarnation of mercury in sulphur, the male principle of light and consciousness, the alchemical equivalent of Lucifer. The belief that this incarnation of the divine mercury in matter could only take place through the agency of sulphur also had profound implications for traditional

Christian teaching. Sulphur, because of its combustibility and earthy nature, was a source of corruption in metals in the same way that the Devil was a corruptor of souls; and yet it gave body to the spirit: without sulphur there would be no incarnation of mercury, nor any fire or light. Sulphur was the source of procreation as well as corruption and death. This represented a radical departure from popular religious belief. In the York Corpus Christi Passion plays of the fourteenth century the devil (in alchemical terms sulphur) was a malevolent presence intent on bringing about the destruction of mankind and its redeemer: tricked by God he persuades Pilate to hand over Jesus for crucifixion in the mistaken assumption that this will thwart the divine will. Alchemical texts of this period on the other hand attempt to show that the close relationship, the marriage, between mercury and its opposite, sulphur, resulted in an alchemical crucifixion which was essential to the welfare of mankind and was a fundamental law of nature. The church had always made the conflict between good and evil absolute; but alchemists recognized that there was no such distinction in nature. The two opposites of mercury and sulphur (the sun and moon), which in the orthodox Christian hierarchy stood for Good and Evil, spirit and body, represented for the adept a Gnostic acceptance of the principles of nature where there was no such thing as good and evil. Alchemy was concerned with the widening of consciousness following the dictum of Genesis: 'Ye shall now surely die, for God doth know that in the day ye eat thereof that your eyes shall be opened and ye shall be as Gods knowing good and evil.' In such a philosophy it is knowledge of nature and experience of life that lead to God rather than transcendent faith. Orthodox Christianity emphasized the power of the host, the round white object that could be identified with the purified manifestation of mercury; but alchemy also celebrated the light and warmth of the sun or sulphur, and in this sense its practitioners could not avoid endorsing a more pagan and Gnostic view of the world.

The alchemists' celebration of the power of sulphur was manifested in a heliocentric vision of the universe. The sun, identified with sulphur, was seen as the force that brought metals to a state of perfection in the form of gold and it also brought light and warmth, generating new growth each year. The *Secreta secretorum* meditates on the mysteries of nature in an attempt to understand the rhythm of the seasons from melancholy autumn when the harvest is brought in, through the months of age and death in winter, to the regeneration of spring. This was the time when the alchemist was supposed to begin his great work, when the sun melted the snows that filled the rivers and generated the seeds with its warmth. According to the author this was the time when the earth was covered in pastures and flowers, the birds began to sing, and men, with the rising of blood and sap, feel the urge to mate.[8] Fourteenth-century alchemists saw the passage of the seasons as an alchemical drama of the process of death and rebirth. John Dastin in *Rosarius* compares the heating of mercury by the fires of sulphur to the gradual journey of the sun through the signs of the zodiac. In the spring the heat of the sun is so gentle that it does not burn the young, gentle tender crops; but as it passes from Aries to Gemini to Leo its heat increases.[9] The alchemical understanding of natural processes was essentially circular, encouraged by constant meditation on evaporation and condensation in the alembic; and this is in strong contrast to conventional Christian thinking, summed up by St Augustine's assertion in his *de civitas dei* (*City of God*) that 'the ungodly think in circles', and that saw the journey from life to eternity was a linear progression in which the body and sex were rejected. For the fourteenth-century alchemist meditation on the divine mysteries involved contemplation of the pro-creative forces governing life. John Dastin, in a letter to Cardinal Napoleon Orsini, described how the golden sperm or seed, the spirit of mercury, impregnated the maternal earth, the primeval waters of chaos; and from this intercourse emerged the four elements.[10] For Dastin this primordial act was the result of the assertion of the Divine will (in human terms lust) which could be comprehended by meditating on the sexual processes throughout nature where all birth and growth was the result of the placing of male sperm or spirit in the waters of the female womb. Alchemists celebrated carnal instincts as an integral part of the process of rejuvenation and regeneration from death. Dastin, in his vision, sees the opposites of the sun and moon, fire and water, as sexual poles and saw spring as a time of sexual conjunction of sun and water, a union of mercury and sulphur:

> The sun that sitteth so high a lofte,
> His golden dew droppes shall clearly raingne downe?
> By the mean of mercury that moves first make softe
> Then shall be a glad conjunccion.[11]

The marriage of mercury and sulphur involves a constant interplay of the forces of procreation and death; whereas in funeral monuments and wills of the late four-teenth century death and putrefaction were seen as a terrifying process leading to the kingdom of heaven. Dastin meditated on the circular process by which death and putrefaction brought about an end to the strife between the four elements, a conjunction leading to the renewal of life: 'the grain of wheat falling in the ground cannot grow unless it dies then increase doth begin when it doth putrefy'.[12]

Alchemists' belief that life depended on the balance of the opposites of spirit and body, life and death, led them to focus exclusively on the world of nature. They believed that the study of the relationship between the four humours and the four elements could unravel the mysteries of the *Book of Genesis* and explain why it was that Adam and Eve's bodies before the fall were in a state of equilibrium and har-mony. Instead of accepting the conventional medieval wisdom that the body should be rejected and the soul prepared for eternity, they sought a state of proto-salvation in which the four humours existed in equilibrium in perfect health and youthfulness, a state believed to have been attained by Christ. In the fourteenth century Arnold of Villanova, the author of the *Testamentum*, Petrus Bonus and John of Rupescissa, introduced a new medical purpose into traditional alchemical theories of transmutation to create a universal panacea composed of the quintessence, the Aristotelian mean between matter and spirit, out of which the heavenly spheres were formed. Their confidence that their investigations into nature could unlock religious mysteries extended to a conviction that they could explain scientifically what had always been seen as a matter of faith, the Resurrection. In contrast to conventional religious assumptions about the relationship between this world and the next, they could demonstrate that nothing is ever lost in a natural world in constant process of change and flux. Many alchemists believed that lead was a degenerated form of gold. They claimed to show in their experiments that gold could be broken down to its first matter through a process of distillation, and evaporation, and subjected to a process of disintegration and putrefaction before being resurrected with the aid of mercury. This was described by Dastin in his allegory of a sick king dying of leprosy who is 'restored againe right fresh and well hewed'.[13] Death for the alchemist was a principle of life, merely part of a process of endless revolutions of nature: the king ascends to spirit and then descends deep into the flesh. Roger Bacon, in his notes to the *Secreta secretorum,* began this process of investigating scientifically the principles of salvation that lay in the secret wisdom of nature, suggesting that the Hebrew patriarchs were the founders of the science of alchemy revealed them by God. When Bacon's followers, Dastin and Bonus, used the religious language of the Passion and the Resurrection to depict the death and regeneration of gold and show that the principles of death and resurrection, mortality and eternity, could be found here in the natural world in the interaction of mercury and sulphur, they came close to doing what Socrates did in his dyadic pedagogy for which he was charged with corrupting the youth of Athens claiming that religious myths were allegories of science. They were advancing a discovery of mythological archetypes of the story of creation and redemption that was not specifically Christian and which anticipated the increasing interest in the fifteenth century in classical myths that offered alternative explanations for the workings of the natural world. This controversial and explosive claim is another aspect of the intellectual and religious upheavals of the late fourteenth century.

Alchemists, by seeking God (the spirit) within the body (sulphur), were applying a science of nature entirely new in the West and seeking God in the light of nature for which the light of scripture was an explanatory myth. However to describe the phenomena that they observed in their laboratories they would often resort to the sort of language used by their contemporaries the mystics, and like the fourteenth-century contemplative writers Richard Rolle and Walter Hilton they sought a direct experience of God, but through the experience of observational science rather than the emotions.[14] Alchemists shared in common with the late medieval recluse contempt for the world (the *incipit* to a pseudo Lullian work of alchemy declares that a man who knows a woman cannot make the stone, and Bonus declared that an alchemist needed to lead an eremitic life[15]); this was a vocation of study and contemplation and a search for knowledge through revelation. Alchemists believed that the basis of scientific insight was a life of purity and spiritual discipline, and there were even parallels between their seclusion from the world in laboratories and the recluse's choice of cell or anchorage. In fact many alchemists also pursued a religious vocation as monks or friars. The Franciscan John of Rupescissa, who wrote most of his works while in prison in Avignon where he was placed by the order of Pope Innocent VI 1352–67 and who was burned at the stake in 1362, placed special value on the extraction of the quintessence of antimony by placing this basest of metals in powder form in distilled vinegar until the vinegar turned red and one could see in the glass drops of the blessed wine descending, like red drops of blood, down the pipe of the limbeck. He described this as a blessed secret of secrets because it represented the redemption of corrupt matter containing the basest of metals into a pure spiritual essence.[16] There was in this experiment much symbolism such as the use of vinegar, the appearance of blood like droplets, and the numerical significance of the quintessence and the five wounds of Christ, that pointed towards the Passion, the redemption of the world and men from the leaden waters of chaos that echoed the imagery of the late fourteenth-century English mystics. Rupescissa claimed that in extracting the essence of blood a sweet savour and smell was procured that echoes the ecstatic language used by the Hampole hermit, Richard Rolle, in describing the *calor* and *canor* experienced when meditating on the Passion.[17] Here the fourteenth-century language of science and mysticism converge linking alchemy with divine inspiration. In the *Rosarius*, attributed to John Dastin, there is a reference to the *calor* of the philosopher's stone.[18]

The alchemist's conviction that God/mercury was found in nature led him to the conclusion that this divine principle could also be found within the mind and soul of the artificer (himself a combination of the four elements) and the quest for the philosopher's stone, for the hidden mercury within the earth, became a search for the buried self, the spirit bound up in the *prima materia*, with the object of releasing this spirit from the unconscious to the light of consciousness. In Dastin's vision mercury, the elemental matter, represented the unconscious, the primal force of nature, and the sick king who dies and triumphs over the serpent, to be triumphantly reborn after 40 days, represents gold or consciousness, the evolution of a higher form of self-awareness after an encounter that results in an integration with the darker, intuitive forces within the self. Alchemical writers of the period describe the vessel as a grave and the earth as a place of birth and a mother who receives her dead children back again. Apart from expressing the natural mystery of the circular processes of life ceasing to be and coming into being, visions such as those of Dastin also convey the sense of the grave and death as a psychic condition. The descent of the soul into the physical world where it discovers hidden forces and results in the emergence of the spirit, refreshed and strong as a result of this encounter, expresses the Gnostic's belief that the spirit was bound up and concealed in *prima materia* and released from a maternal grave to the light of consciousness represented by gold. For the alchemist death and burial was the starting point of the *opus* and the end is the realization of a life lived fully and consciously in which flesh and spirit are in harmony. The Resurrection is seen as the transformed life. The dictum of self-knowledge and realization was expressed in the *Emerald Tablet*: 'thus will thou possess the glory and brightness of the whole world and all obscurity will fly from thee'.[19] The moon/mercury represents the soul and the sun consciousness, and the mysterious philosopher's stone, the self, is Christ, the sun. In traditional Christian thought death and burial are the conclusion of a life and signify the beginning of a new life of the spirit. The Resurrection therefore came to be seen as the triumphal realization of a life of destiny and self-awareness, the birth of the inner man represented by the creation of the *homunculus*.

The facility of alchemists to meditate on the natural world and the process of change, decay and regeneration through religious imagery had potential implications for religious practice and belief, and this can be seen in the religious lives of devout laymen at the court of Edward III. Members of this court were accustomed to associating the main principle of alchemical medicine, the redemptive and regenerative power of sulphur and mercury, the red and white, with meditations on the Passion. A dietary containing medicine to be applied to all parts of the body throughout the twelve-months of the year was made by the masters of Salerno for Lady Philippa, queen of England and wife of Edward III, in 1320. Many of the prescribed medicines are alchemical in origin: such as those requiring filings of gold and silver heated in the fire[20] and the application of *sol ammoniac* for the stemming of blood flow.[21] Instructions on the application of ointments and plasters are interspersed with religious reflections and imagery. Christ is depicted as the physician, and a section on stemming blood loss contains a meditation on the crucifixion and spearing of Christ and the flowing of blood and water (the red and white of sulphur and mercury) from his side.[22]

The structure and imagery of this work seems to have influenced Henry Grosmont, the second duke of Lancaster and a close friend of Philippa's husband Edward III. Henry integrated his activities as a courtier, diplomat, military commander, and key figure at the royal court, with an active religious life that is highlighted by his autobiographical account of his inner life as a reformed sinner and penitential follower of Christ. Henry was also interested in alchemical medicine. He instituted regulations in 1356 to prevent the spread of infection in the hospital of St Mary in the Newarke, Leicester, founded by his father the first duke of Lancaster in 1330, announcing his intention of building a leprosarium at the end of town;[23] and he attended medical lectures at the University of Montpellier. He was also at the siege of Algeciras in Granada in 1343 with the English physician, John Ardene, who used alchemical remedies to treat the wounded, dressing cuts with arsenic powder and administering cordials containing gold, silver and pearls; Ardene also treated soldiers suffering from gonnoreah with oil of roses. It was at this siege that gunpowder containing sulphur was used in weapons for the first time. Henry, like Edward III, owned a copy of the *Secreta secretorum*;[24] his alchemical interests are revealed in his *Le Livre de Seyntz Medicines* where he displays an ability to discuss his religious life through images that reveal an intimate knowledge of alchemical theory and practice.[25] As a proud sinner Henry, delivering himself into the hands of the divine physician, must first allow his soul to be dissected to disclose his sins as a lesson to others, in the way bodies of executed criminals were dissected before surgeons and medical students at Montpellier. His sinful heart is compared to the vortex of the sea and approximates to the forces of chaos and darkness that is the basis of all alchemical work. His recovery can only begin with the application of a powerful medicine capable of burning up all his sin and destroying his pride. None is stronger than the substance of the devil himself which is treacle or *theriac*, a powerful laxative obtained from the venom of the serpent, a scorpion (in alchemical terms sulphur or the dragon, the most destructive substance known in matter). With his resistance broken, the poisons in his body expelled and his personality shattered, Henry can convalesce and rebuild himself with the help of the Compassion of the Virgin and the Passion of Christ; and this too is depicted in terms of alchemical medicine. The patient must recover his strength with the help of an invigorating broth known as the Virgin's milk: a capon is placed in a small earthen pot which is closed tightly and placed in a vessel filled with water and placed in a fire. The capon cooks and sweats, exhaling a beneficial broth that is like Christ's blood. In this imagery the Virgin is the earthen vessel in which is distilled her son's blood, the precious medicine warmed by sin and her tears. The sinner's wounds must then be cleansed with the Virgin's tears, compared to the cleansing antiseptic found by picking white grapes growing at the top of the rose tree and ripened by the sun (the rose tree, planted at the end of the grape vine as a sentinel for the early detection of diseases that could affect the grape, was a common image of the crucified Christ) and these grapes are made into a white wine that is distilled in a gentle, slow heat (an alchemical process described two years later by John of Rupescissa) to produce the Virgin's sorrowful tears, an *elixir vitae*. To prevent a reoccurrence of sinful impulses (or in medical terms humoral imbalance and fever) the convalescing sinner should be given rosewater (a remedy recommended by John Ardene for sexually transmitted diseases), which also represents Christ's blood. Red roses blooming at the top of the rose tree, ripened by the Spring Lenten sun, constitute another image of Jesus outstretched on the Cross, and they are placed in a lead container called a helmet and heated in a fire; the precious liquid flows from the petals into a glass vessel, a limbeck. This healing balm is like the blood of the Saviour, a precious distilled elixir, a few drops of which can redeem all sinners; and it is placed on the temple of the patient to lower the temperature that causes the overheating and drying up of the vital spirits, and which is compared to the drying up of the Holy Ghost by sin.[26] All this imagery discloses an intimate knowledge of alchemy, and the central theme is the interplay of the Virgin and Christ, the moon and the sun, mercury and sulphur, the red and white; and what is especially significant is the ease with which Henry, as a devout and scientifically educated layman, was able to move so easily between the two spheres of alchemy and religion.

The practising alchemist, and those like Lancaster who were interested in this new science, therefore had a lot in common with practitioners of the new devotional movements of the fourteenth century: the insights and experiences of recluses such as Richard Rolle, with their emphasis on individuality and an entirely intuitive concept of salvation, could, in their implied rejection of priestly authority, represent a threat to the established church, and there was a subversive element to some of the experiences and visions of alchemists. The circumstances of alchemical meditation were inherently volatile; besides meditating on religious icons and images the alchemist would also stare at the mixtures in his retort as they morphed into various shapes and what he believed to be essences. Such a process, combined with the noxious fumes he inhaled, would encourage hallucinatory experiences and the development of a state of mind in which solid forms of existence would take on a fluid, protean existence, and this influenced alchemical writers' parodying of the most venerated objects of fourteenth-century contemplative piety: the Incarnation, the Crucifixion, the Pieta and the Virgin and Child.[27] By the sixteenth century alchemical symbols that paralleled Christian icons had become commonplace. The central principle of alchemy, mercury, contained a dual nature as the source of all life and through its incarnation as sulphur as a destructive force, and this duality was also perceived in the Christian God of the Old Testament as the angry judge and as the life giving force of the *New Testament* Christ. A number of symbols were used by both alchemists and the church to express this duality and they were usually horned, powerful animals. The white hart was a powerful stag; but trapped by the hunter he became Christ, the servant of man, a divine force confined in a mortal body and the passive redeemer of the *New Testament*. The unicorn, usually associated, and often indistinguishable from the lion to whom it makes obeisance in the *Chymical Wedding* of Rosencreuz,[28] was a fierce animal of unknown origin; in the *Book of Job* it is potentially violent, devastating[29] and according to St Basil even evil, it was trapped by hunters when it was lured to lay its horned head on a virgin's lap and calmed.[30] It too, according to the church fathers, represented the violent terrifying God of the *Old Testament* and the passive redeemer of the *New Testament*[31] and in its union with the Virgin it represented the Holy Ghost. Both animals were related to the horned bull, a fierce, powerful beast which, like Christ, protected its herd.

The horns of these creatures represented power, masculinity, authority and penetration, and yet they were also hollow vessels, female and associated with the chalice. Their duality served the purposes of the alchemists.[32] In the *Tabula smaragdina*
(*The Emerald Tablet*) there is a son of immense strength who comes down to earth
and penetrates everything solid, and in this key alchemical text there is a thinly
disguised allusion to the mother–son incest.[33] These powerful white, horned beasts
symbolized in their free state the powerful, elusive force of mercury, and the potentially destructive power of sulphur, the forces of nature. These horned beasts penetrated the earth, enacting the sexual dynamics of the interplay of mercury and
sulphur, and trapped, they became fixed mercury or *aqua vitae* the servant of the
alchemist and the source of gold. Their horns reminded him of the horns of the
moon and the redemptive chalice.

These symbols had become commonplaces of alchemical illustrations by the
seventeenth century but their origins lay in the late Middle Ages. The way the white
hart and unicorn were used for both religious and alchemical purposes represented
a potentially subversive threat to conventional religion, and this was demonstrated
by George Ripley in the fifteenth century in his meditation on the green lion lying
in the queen's lap with blood flowing from his side.[34] This allusion to the unicorn
wounded by the hunter and caught in the Virgin's lap draws on the hermaphroditic
role of the unicorn/mercury as the passive, feminine maternal principle and the
fierce, masculine penetrator of the earth in a vision of the union of the sun and
moon. Yet Ripley also explicitly alludes to the pieta, the most hallowed icon of lay
piety, in what amounts to a blasphemous parody of incest. This unsettling conjunction of alchemical and religious iconography dates back to the period when Muslim
alchemy was beginning to become popular in the early fourteenth century and this
was during the period when the visions and teachings of the Hampole hermit,
Richard Rolle, were beginning to arouse the enthusiasm of lay followers in such a
way that would alarm the church and merit a response. Ripley's theme of the sexual
union of the sun and moon, the taming of the unicorn in the virgin's lap, was
anticipated in the vision of John Dastin. Dastin describes himself falling asleep and
having a vision in which he is visited by one shining like the sun who shows him a
book of seven seals (like the *Book of Revelation*). The book contains a story of the
incarnation of a pure golden king, conceived in purity in an incestuous marriage of
the moon and the sun, mother and child:

> The sun has chosen without war or strife
> The bright moon when she was at the full
> To be his mother first, and after hys wedded wife.[35]

The product of this incestuous marriage of sun and moon, sulphur and mercury, is a
pure golden king who will die and redeem his corrupt brothers (the six impure metals).

When the circumstances of alchemical experimentation are considered: the breathing in of noxious fumes and the contemplation of the way substances metamorphosized, it is to be expected that some of the results would be surreal and hallucinatory. This can be seen a century later when they were incorporated into mainstream devotional art of Heinrich Bosch, a member of the devout order, the brethren of the common life, who would commemorate the Adoration of the Magi in a triptych showing the six metals to be redeemed by Christ's Incarnation as six corrupt figures paying tributes to a king. The foremost figure, Lead or Saturn, is shown in the form of a distillation pelican. Bosch's art shows how such disturbing iconography was becoming increasingly common knowledge by the end of the middle Ages.[36] It is possible to see these meditations as a surreal response to a period of intellectual ferment and profound social change and it could be argued that such art anticipates the way modernist artists would capture equally profound and changes and dislocations of the early twentieth century. The late medieval English alchemist should therefore be seen as an original artist or thinker who made an important contribution to mainstream cultural and intellectual life and the evidence for this exists in the literature of the court.

But the fourteenth century was a time when throughout Europe, under the Inquisition, and in England under the control of the archbishop of Canterbury, Thomas Arundel, the church exerted strict control over all aspects of religious practice and belief. The teachings of Richard Rolle were subjected to a rigorous programme so that they were adapted for his followers.[37] Under the leadership of Thomas Arundel, archbishop of Canterbury, the activities and writings of recluses, who espoused a new emphasis on direct experience of God's love, were so closely watched that Arundel and his clergy even adapted these teachings so that they conformed to the institutional and communal religion fostered by the church.[38] By 1401, with the passing of the statute *de Heretico comburendo*, this duty had even extended to the burning for heresy anyone convicted of spreading the teachings of the Oxford theologian, Dr John Wyclif. Wyclif and his followers were branded Lollards for encouraging independence from the clergy and the sacraments of the church and for urging the laity to lead a religious life based on a close adherence to the teachings of Holy Scripture. Wyclif's criticism of the doctrine of transubstantiation, relics and pilgrimages, was seen by his followers an assault on the church's role as a guardian of occult power exercised over a superstitious and credulous laity who needed to be given direct access to the real source of power, the scriptures and the revealed word of God. Alchemists similarly were engaged in unlocking what they perceived to be the divine secrets of nature, revealed through knowledge and reason. Arundel was hostile towards any disclosing of occult mysteries to the laity. The Bible to him was a repository of divine secrets, hidden from laymen in the mysterious language of Latin and to be mediated by his clergy to the less educated who had to rely on faith. And yet it is striking that alchemists, whose lives of secluded study and contemplation deviated from the communal aspects of scholastic science and paralleled so closely the lives of hermits, solitaries and even Lollard preachers, received no censorious attention from an increasingly repressive and watchful church. There is no evidence that alchemists were seen in this way; no evidence of any response from the church to their disturbing and shocking visions which cannot be dismissed as marginalized eccentricities. Very few books of natural philosophy were banned by the Holy See or local church officials, and when works of philosophy were submitted to ecclesiastical proscription, such as Aristotle's *Libri de naturali philosophis,* it was not because of any occult magic content but implication of heresy or doctrinal errors. In the library of the papacy there were many manuscripts of alchemical works and the Papal court played a dominant role (together with the imperial court) in the dissemination of the most influential alchemical, occult text of this period, the *Secreta secretorum.* There was no systematic attempt to censure this text through the expurgation of suspicious parts and after his translation of the *Secreta secretorum* in c. 1231 the cleric, Philip of Tripoli, was rewarded with various benefices by the papacy and the text made its way into the academic centres of Europe in the universities of Paris and Oxford.[39]

The explanation partly lies in the common ground between alchemy and religion. Alchemical discourse was suffused with the language of Christianity and the mysteries of Christian faith increasingly came to be depicted and explained by means of chemical analysis and this legitimized the study of alchemy. The scientific approach to questions of faith became crucial for a church embattled with threats posed to orthodox Christian doctrine by the Cathar heresy in Languedoc, the Lollard heresy in England and the advance of Islam in the East. The most crucial contribution alchemists could make to this conflict with the enemies of the church within and without was in buttressing the most important aspect of late medieval religion, the doctrine of transubstantiation. The ceremony of the mass, which took place behind a closed screen accompanied by chanting and the smell of incense and which was communicated in a language understood only by a few clergy, was the church's celebration of the occult forces that were manifested in the transubstantiation of the round disc of the host. The alchemist similarly celebrated the transformative powers of a round object whether it was the moon or the sun. The late fourteenth century was a period when the alchemist's belief in the presence of God in matter in the form of mercury had profound implications for clergy. The explanation may lie in the alchemist's belief in the presence of God in matter in the form of mercury and in the endorsement that he gave to the doctrine of transubstantiation in his theories on transmutation. Opinions on this subject defined orthodoxy and heresy in this period: the daily miracle of the manifestation of Christ on the high altar determined the faith of parish communities and established social cohesion in the parish and parishioners' dependence on the intercessions of ordained clergy. The three most important heresies condemned by the Blackfriars council of May 1382 were concerned with transubstantiation.[40] Wyclif and his followers took a rational, realist view that the essence of the bread and wine on the altar table could not change because of the existence of their archetypes in a supra real dimension. According to Walsingham, Wyclif suggested that although God's power was perfect it was limited in that he was unable to bring it about that on the sacrament of the altar there should be accidents without substances.[41] Petrus Bonus, however, represented Christ's Incarnation as the ultimate transmutation, mirroring the development of the perfect metal; he demonstrated the feasibility of alchemical transmutation against such scholastic arguments by attempting to show, scientifically, that the transition from spirit to body and body to spirit occurred throughout nature in such incidents as the evaporation of smoke from a fire before it assumed fixed form as soot: 'for here a spirit as it were evaporating from the fire assumes a corporeal form'.[42] Dastin similarly argued that the generation of insects or small animals from ordure proved the possibility of transmutation.[43] Metals were believed to be penetrated by an all pervading agent (mercury) which was seen as the philosopher's stone, an agent of transmutation, and the same divine principle underlay the transubstantiation of the host: in both cases there was a physical presence, sulphur and the host, and a spiritual presence, mercury, the redeemer of metals, and Christ, the redeemer of man. The relationship between sulphur, mercury, and the host and Christ, was even suggested by the identical colours with which they were associated: red and white representing sulphur and mercury and the blood and sweat of the saviour. Alchemy, by offering scientific proof of the phenomenon of transubstantiation, of the presence of Christ in the material world, closed the gap between science and religion; knowledge and faith, and provided a rational answer to the charges of Wyclif and his followers that belief in the Sacrament was mere credulity and superstition. Furthermore the simplicity and unity of the doctrine of the original primal divine substance was, according to Petrus Bonus, a truth understood by Greek, Latin and Arab sages and showed that there was in alchemical wisdom a universal language[44] that offered a church embattled by heresy and the advance of Islam under the Ottoman Turks the prospect of a reassertion of the crusading ideal backed by scientific principles. It is perhaps for this reason that alchemy was allowed to develop as a parallel system of beliefs and practices that closely paralleled those of the Christian church. Whereas the church had Moses as its prophet, alchemists had Hermes Trismegistus, with the *Tabula Smaragdina* (*The Emerald Tablet*) the equivalent to the Ten Commandments of Moses; Jerusalem was the heart of Christianity and for the alchemist it was Alexandria and the Nile valley; the twelve gates of alchemy corresponded to the twelve apostles; the equivalent of Christ for the alchemist was mercury; and the alchemist read the signs and wonders of nature in the same way that the clergy would use scripture for exegesis. This way of acquiring knowledge by way of the signs and wonders of nature had been expounded by Arnold of Villanova: the way of the wisdom of Solomon was through hermetic principles; nature was seen like a biblical text resonant with hidden meaning and this would be the way commentators such as John Erghome would view the fourteenth century.

The mystics of fourteenth-century England and the Lollard reformers may have embraced eremitic ideals but they were hostile towards the church in its role of enforcing social cohesion. The alchemist on the other hand was a true loner with no interest in social issues and for this reason he posed less of a threat to ecclesiastical authorities. What he did share in common with contemplative writers was that they all offered their followers a direct experience of God. Richard Rolle, Walter Hilton and Nicholas Love offered guidance on how to achieve a direct religious experience beyond faith that engaged the emotions; but the alchemists offered the faithful a more immediate earthly encounter with the divine through the scientific exploration of nature that engaged the intellect. If mercury represented a transcendental spiritual ideal, then sulphur, its earthly counterpart and partner, like the incarnate Christ, provided a more earthly, emotional even carnal way of approaching God.

5

The Cultural Impact of Alchemy

Full fathom five thy father lies
Of his bones are coral made
Those are pearls that were his eyes
Nothing of him that doth change
But doth suffer a sea-change
Into something rich and strange

William Shakespeare, *The Tempest*[1]

It has been suggested that alchemical authors in the fourteenth century did not influence other writers[2] and that the arcane mysterious language of alchemy had little influence on visionary or prophetic literature.[3] These assertions rest on a narrow definition of an art that attracted some of the greatest minds of the period, drawn to a discipline that shared a relationship with science, astrology, medicine, psychology and mythology. Alchemy offered explanations as to how the universe was formed and provided a key to understanding the workings of the natural world, which included insights into the workings of human nature and society. This was a knowledge that brought power because, traditionally, power was seen as a supernatural manifestation of divine grace mediated through the sacramental host (frequently described as heavenly) or the shrines and bones of the saints. Alchemical wisdom held the key to understanding powers that came from within the earth and within man himself: according to the author of *Secreta secretorum* man is the little world created by God as the wisest of all things in the greater world. These terrestrial forces were seen as a concentration of forces within the heavens radiating down to earth from the seven planets; but the heat and energy of the earth was also seen to exist independently through the operation of the twin poles of mercury and sulphur. According to the *Secreta secretorum* a natural heat (independent of the sun) lay hidden in these two substances which, together with the warmth of the sun, brought the four elements and seven metals to a state of perfection, the quintessence, represented by gold.[4]

The signs and numbers produced by the inhabitants of the earth too were seen as a source of hidden wonders. The Augustinian friar, John Erghome, whose collection of books included a large selection of alchemical and occult texts, wrote a commentary on the prophecies attributed to St John of Bridlington (the fourteenth-century mystic John Thweng).[5] Thweng's poem, inspired by feverish

dreams attributed to the inspiration of the Holy Ghost, revealed to the Augustinian canon in the 1330s, celebrated the virtues of Edward III in contrast to the inef-
fectiveness of Edward II. During the 1350s the vision was revised to comment on
Edward III's siege of Calais and the Black Death of 1349 and to celebrate Edward's
bull like qualities and the destiny of the chosen people of his realm, while lamenting the king's weakness for women and to predict a bright future for his son, the
Black Prince.[6] In the 1360s Thweng, who became prior of Bridlington after the
death of his predecessor from the plague, and whose association with the writing
of the poem probably stems from his subsequent canonization in 1401, made the
poetic vision available to John Erghome, who wrote a commentary on these visions
dedicating it to Humphrey Bohun, earl of Hereford and constable of England, a
member of a group of non-royal nobles who felt excluded from influencing the
king's policies by a clique at the court.[7] Probably composed around 1363 (there are
references to an outbreak of plague which occurred in 1361–62), these commen-
taries interpret the visions attributed to Thweng as a series of inspired prophecies
of the leading political events of the fourteenth century. Erghome, whose inspiration as interpreters of contemporary events were Daniel and St John the Evangelist, the reputed author of the *Book of the Apocalypse*, provided a commentary on
the reigns of Edward II and Edward III that reveals the intellectual life of one for
whom ideas were regarded as the product of alchemical transmutation. The
human soul, according to Erghome, was replete with pregnant thoughts, disclosed
in books, which should be devoured like food because they revealed thoughts hidden in the body and released as if from a prison. Many books, and especially the
Bible, were therefore regarded as sources of occult knowledge and power, and
Erghome saw Latin puns, cognomens and the heraldic emblems of the nobility as
sources of prophetic knowledge holding the key to the political events of his time.
Like the author of *Secreta secretorum,* he regarded knowledge of the occult as a key
to political power: prophecies, names, cognomens, coats of arms, puns, certain
coincidences of accidents, the arrangements of bodies, whether heavenly or geomantic, all were seen to reveal the hidden world of significances and could be the
source of much pleasure for a worldly lord who through such knowledge could
anticipate future events, understand the behaviour of counsellors, and care for the
lives of ordinary men from whom such knowledge is hidden.[8] History, for Erghome,
was played out against a backdrop of occult forces, scriptural precedents, planetary
influences, inspired prophecies and dreams, and symbolism found in heraldry.
John Gower, similarly conveyed, in book seven of *Confessio Amantis* (which para-
phrases sections of the *Secreta secretorum* to provide the first English version of
any portion of this work together with a summary of the principles of alchemy) a
fascination with hidden sources of knowledge, the occult value to be found in the
study of formal relationships between numbers, and secret forces of nature and
their influence on human behaviour. Gower even placed the different nations in

humoral categories according to their ruling planets.[9] The sun, the head planet ruling in the middle of the seven planets orbiting the earth, reigns most over Greece, the source of the wisdom of antiquity, and the planet of England and Germany is the moon (with its associations of water and mercury).[10] But the most fortunate planet was seen to be Jupiter, and according to Gower this planet ruled over Egypt, home of occult learning and alchemy (John Doubelay made a number of references to the alchemical wisdom of Egypt in *Stella alchemiae*).[11] Gower, together with the author of the leading manual for princes in this period, the *Secreta secretorum*, referred to the hidden significance and essence of things and placed no distinction between the physical and the occult and saw the mystical potential of scientific studies. Both authors defined arithmetic as the study of formal relationships and hinted at the occult significance of numbers which they derived from alchemy. Perfection was therefore represented by the number five, occurring in the pentangle, which signified the five senses, the five planets (excluding the sun and moon), the five kinds of beast, the stem, branch leaf, trunk and root of a plant, the five metals and the quintessence. The Cheshire poet, who wrote *Sir Gawain and the Green Knight* and *Pearl* at the court of Richard II, paid homage in his *Cleanness* to the interpreter of signs for King Balthazar as 'wise Daniel in dark knowledge steeped',[12] and he crafted his poems in numerical patterns as carefully as Dante had done.[13] The pearl itself is represented by the number 20, made of four fives (the number of the quintessence) and is also seen as the perfect circle. The poem itself is made up of 12-line stanzas to echo the 12 tiers of the foundations of Jerusalem which are 12 furlongs long. The stanzas together add up to 100, a number of perfect symmetry, offset by an extra stanza to make up 101,[14] the endless knot echoing the year and a day taken by Sir Gawain for his journey to encounter the green knight. On this quest Gawain is protected by an occult symbol on his shield, the pentangle, a sign used by Pythagoras and occult sects because of its association with magic. Gawain's pentangle, described by the author as an alchemical symbol of the quintessence and eternity (the *uroboros* without beginning or end) was composed of

> five pentads, each precious and pure; each joined
> To another, never alone, never ending;
> And finally fixed to the four other points;
> Neither crowded too closely nor cloven asunder;
> Without end at any angle that I can discover.[15]

The power of number to attract sophisticated minds in the late fourteenth-century court was demonstrated by the increasing vogue of the science of geomancy. Petrus Bonus in *Pretiosa Margarita Novella* argued that the same spirituality and power that was found in the heavens could be found in a concentrated form within metals in the earth. The common thread between living things and the physical universe supplied by mercury implied that there was a hidden power or pulse running through the earth which could be more readily understood and tapped than planetary influences. The detection of these terrestrial forces formed the basis of the science of Geomancy (which like alchemy came from the Middle East, from Arab soil divination, and enjoyed great popularity in fourteenth-century England). Crucial decisions of an emotional, medical or professional nature could be made from the interpretations of the significance of the patterns made by random dots formed from a stylus or quill on parchment or a stick in the earth while the eyes were closed and a decision contemplated. This process would be repeated four times to produce four lines of dots, each dot signified a star, each line an element, and each figure the four quarters of the world. The dots would be added, and if they came to an even number two dots would be formed, while an odd number would produce a single dot. The resulting image, consisting of four lines of single or double dots, constituted a geomantic sign or house. Each of the seven classical planets had two geomantic shapes. Four such houses, representing the four elements and the four quarters of the world, constituted the mother houses and a process of sideways addition produced four daughters, four nephews, two witnesses and a judge. Each of these figures or constellations would be associated with the four elements and seven planets and was considered good or evil to a certain degree.[16] Many geomantic signs had alchemical connotations such as *Caput draconis* (the head of the dragon which also means Pendragon the king of Britain when the red and white dragons were unified), *Fortuna major* (the sun), *Conjunctio* (union) and *Albus* (mercury). The sixteen houses would form a shield, like a coat of arms, which constituted a map of the questioner's fate, a history of an individual's illnesses, family, character and destiny. The different signs could mean different things according to their position on the shield; there were twelve houses, six of which were above the horizon and six below. The first house concerned the personality and fate of the questioner; the second rank and fortune; the third family; the fourth fathers and patrons; the fifth judgements; the sixth accidents and pregnancy; the seventh wedlock and sex; the eight death and inheritance; the ninth journeys and faith, the tenth honours; the eleventh friends; and the twelfth enemies, servants and imprisonment.[17] Behind geomancy and the questions posed lay an assumption of the importance of the hidden powers within the earth and the close connection between the earth and the individual questioner closely joined by a common essence (the spirit of mercury). There was no need to wait for the appearance of planets and zodiacal hours in the sky. The fixed signs of the zodiac around the earth, six above the horizon and six below were duplicated in the twelve geomantic houses. When a questioner gave birth to a geomantic chart by the casting of lots he was creating a microcosm of the zodiacal system relevant just to him or herself, a coherent system where the individual was the meeting point of occult influences, providing a tangible link between heaven and earth. Informing the decisions of a man were the deep forces within the unconscious and within the earth. The secrets of fate, destiny and the personality, one's illnesses and friendships, were all linked by the elements shared by man and the earth he inhabited. The key to these mysteries was the power of numbers: four for the four elements and the four quarters of the world; and the numbers one and two, odd and even, which represented the opposites of light and darkness, good and evil, mercury and sulphur.

Geoffrey Chaucer used geomantic figures to give his work the sort of hidden terrestrial pulse and specific location in terms of time and space that James Joyce would impart to *Ulysses*. Chaucer starts from the premise that a man can form a numerical shape on the ground that is full of prophetic significance and attributes the same significance to the shapes of stars. He placed the parting of *Troillus and Criseyde* precisely at sunrise when the cock crowed and observed that, to he that would know, this was when *Fortuna major* (the Pleiades) were below the horizon. This precise information places the event at the time of the writing of *Troillus and Criseyde* on 10 June 1385 when the sun was two degrees below the horizon and mercury was two degrees above at 3.25 am. Chaucer also used geomantic figures in *The Knight's Tale*. Arcite, before meeting his close friend, Palamon, in single combat, prayed at his oratory, decorated with images of *Puella* and *Rubeus* who were associated with his planet, Mars, which was directly overhead. Such an event occurred at the time of the writing of this tale on 4–5 May 1388.[18]

Another aspect of popular culture to be strongly influenced by an interest in the occult and alchemical theories was the interpretation of dreams which was becoming increasingly fashionable in the late fourteenth century. All the leading court writers used dream visions to convey moral, religious and philosophical truths, including William Langland in *Piers Ploughman*, the author of *Pearl*, and Chaucer in *The Parlement of Fowles* and in *The Nun's Priest's Tale*. The standard manual for dream interpretation in this period was a fourteenth-century work known as *Daniel's Book of Dreams*, a description of common forms of dreams and what they signify.[19] In the preface it is asserted that most dreams proceed from humoral disturbances of the body and activities of the previous day. However it is also claimed that during sleep the soul apprehends intimations, shapes and visions of what precedes life and what occurs after death and that these can have prophetic significance. Such powerful knowledge is transmitted in dreams through metaphors and allegories, and this was the medium employed in such visionary alchemical texts as the *Vision of John Dastin* in the early fourteenth century and *Aurora consurgens* in the early fifteenth century. In *Daniel's Book of Dreams* all dreams convey a coded message. Some occur in the form of geomantic signs, so the appearance of a girl (*Puella*) can signify anxiety; a dragon (echoing the dragon's tail in geomancy) could presage a terrible mortality; others convey their message through the inherent quality of the images, so a bow stretching may allude to a new anxiety and bees swarming may signify profit or approaching evil; dreams of gold imminent wealth; and dreams of wolves danger. Behind such interpretations lay assumptions derived from alchemy about the hidden essence of things which were explained in the late thirteenth-century *De mirabilibus mundi* (*On the Miracles of the World*). In this work of Dominican origin, falsely attributed to Albertus Magnus, the basic principle of alchemy, the changing of one substance into another by using the seed of gold to convert baser metals, is applied to the nature in general.[20] The world is shown to be infused with purpose in which the particular shape or colour of things has a meaning and all objects enjoy a particular relationship with one another based on such qualities, so that if something stands in salt it becomes salt and if a timid man stands next to a harlot he acquires her boldness.[21] In *Daniel's Book of Dreams* this principle of sympathetic magic was particularly important in the interpretation of dreams in terms of the sympathy or antipathy of one thing to another and this outlook can also explain the use of heraldic images in the coats of arms of the fourteenth-century nobility. An understanding of the principle of like affecting like, of every natural thing having a natural amity or enmity to some other thing, was a way to appreciate the purpose of nature without which, according to the author of *The Book of Marvels*, a man 'shall go with heaviness of mind, for in these things (natural science) is the marvellousness of all things which are seen'.[22] This positive conception of expertise in the secrets of the natural world was embodied, according to Albertus Magnus, in the art of the three Magi who followed the star of Bethlehem and had the ability to predict and produce marvels in nature from their understanding of the processes of nature. The source of such knowledge was perceived to be the East where, according to William of Auvergne (1180/90–1249), bishop of Paris, in his *de Universo* (*On the World*), the myriad wonders of India and surrounding regions stimulated the practise of natural magic. In the West, according to Geraldus Cambriensis (Gerald of Wales 1146–c. 1249) it was Ireland.[23]

In the reign of Richard II there was awareness among intellectuals that the key to a sense of the wonders in nature lay in an understanding of the marriage of mercury and sulphur. This theme underpins *The Canterbury Tales* and *Sir Gawain and the Green Knight*, two of the greatest works of literature to be written during a period of exceptional literary creativity. Geoffrey Chaucer's post-medieval reputation as an alchemical authority has some factual foundation. The only Canterbury tale with a plot that was the author's invention, *The Canon's Yeoman's Tale*, is about alchemy: its three sections, a prologue, the tale, and an epilogue, cover all aspects of the alchemical art as a self-destructive obsession; a means of duping the gullible; and as a profound, scientific and religious philosophy. In the prologue, the canon's yeoman's account of seven years' service to his master, an Augustinian Canon, poignantly shows the illusionary nature of a quest in which health, wealth and happiness are all sacrificed for an impossible ideal:

> But that science is so fer us biforn,
> We mowen nat, although we hadden it sworn,

It overtake, it slit awey so faste
It wole us maken beggars ate laste.[24]

This is a science that appeals to friars and canons attracted by the study of books
and the prospect of learning 'weird directions verse by verse', and there is a whiff
of the diabolic, seductive power of alchemy and a promise of mysterious powers in
the yeoman's description of alchemists always smelling of brimstone and working
with metals that are violent and liable to split. But above all the canon's yeoman
conveys the bitter sweet nature of a search for something that promises so much
happiness but ends up destroying lives and relationships:

A nay! Lat be; the philosophres stoon,
Elixir clept, we sechen faste echoon;
For hadde we hym, thane were we siker ynow.
For al oure craft, whan we had al ydo,
And al oure sleighte, he wol nat come us to.
He hath ymaad us spenden muchel good,
For sorowe of which almost we waxen wood.[25]

A possible inspiration for this canon can be found in Bernard of Treves. A romantic autobiographical account of Bernard's travels all over Europe, and his periods
of great fortune and poverty, culminating in a spell in Rhodes where he became
an adept, was recorded in *De Chymico miracula*, a work printed as Bernard's in
Basel in 1583. This may be a forgery containing kernels of truth about the fourteenth-century alchemist's life.[26] What is certain is that Bernard was a friend and
correspondent of Charles of Bologna, alchemist at the court of King Charles VI
of France, and that he referred in his letter to two previous writings of his, a
Philosophia and 'my other book sent to you'. Bernard also met with the disapproval of Charles's daughter, Christine de Pisan, who derived the impression
from Bernard that for all his followers he, like all alchemists, was a deceiver or
deceived.[27] Chaucer was also aware of the way the alchemist, through his use of
tinctures and dyes, could also be a master of illusions (in his *Franklin's Tale* the
magic used destroy the dangerous black rocks off the coast of Brittany is an illusion created by high tides) and the *Canon's Yeoman's Tale* describes the deceptions
practised by another canon on a chantry priest. The canon persuades his client
that it is possible to transmute mercury into silver by placing mercury in a heated
crucible into which silver filings are melted and released either from a hollow
wooden coal or a hollow rod stopped with wax which melts as soon as the alchemist stirs the crucible of hot mercury. Chaucer's awareness of such tricks may
have come from personal observation: there is a theory that he was himself a
victim of a hoax perpetrated by a canon of Windsor, but he may have read of such

contemporary practises in the *Stella alchemiae* (1384) which describes the placing of silver filings in a mould.[28]

The Canon's Yeoman's Tale is however much more than a satirical exposure of contemporary alchemical practises and beliefs. Its author exposes the limitations of the well meaning canon's yeoman's understanding of his art when he describes the seven bodies (or metals) of alchemy and assigns to each a ruling planet: gold has the sun, silver the moon, iron mars, lead Saturn, tin Jupiter, and copper Venus; however the canon's yeoman makes an error when he describes quicksilver, or mercury, as a mere metal to which he assigns the planet mercury. However Chaucer does not make the same mistake in his epilogue to the tale when he expounds the mercury sulphur theory of the origin of all life. He acknowledges that although sulphur and mercury are opposites they are one and the same thing, the philosopher's stone, when he explains that quicksilver and its inner sulphur is the dragon, the *alpha et omega* which survives the fire:

> 'There may no man mercurie mortifie
> But it be with brother knowlechyng'-
> Of philosophers fader was, Hermes;
> He seith how that the dragon, doutelees.
> Ne dyeth nat but if he that be slayn
> With his brother, and that is for to sayn,
> By the dragon, Mercurie, and noon oother
> He understood, and brymstoon by his brother,[29]

Alchemy, concludes the author, has driven many men mad because they do not understand its scientific jargon and he cites the genuine alchemists like Arnold of Villanova, who says that mercury cannot be mortified without the use of sulphur, and Hermes Trismegistus, who shows that the dragon can never be slain unless his brother within (sulphur or brimstone) is also killed. This is the reason, Chaucer claims, that many men have been driven mad in pursuit of alchemy for they do not understand its sensitive scientific jargon and its emblems. For the well meaning canon's yeoman mercury was just a metal, the tool for transmuting other metals, and part of the confidence tricksters trade, whereas for Chaucer, as for Petrus Bonus, it was the first matter or chaos, that in which everything exists in a confused state before the conjunction that gave matter its form;[30] and the goal of alchemy is to realize the conjunction or marriage of these primal opposites, mercury and sulphur, drawn according to Hermes from Luno and Sol. One of Chaucer's acknowledged sources among his genuine alchemists was Arnold of Villanova, whose views were recorded by John Dastin in his correspondence with Cardinal Napoleon Orsini,[31] and possibly the *Secreta secretorum* to whom Chaucer added Plato and Senior (al Sadiq).[32] Arnold and Dastin shared Chaucer's scepticism towards most practitioners of alchemy 'illicit purveyors of the art' who in their deluded and literal-minded faith in the four spirits of mercury, arsenic, sal ammonia and sulphur, and their experiments with organic materials, attempted to extract the four elements from blood, eggs, and urine and by distilling them only succeeded in creating a black earth which they projected onto molten bodies, accomplishing nothing because only humans can give birth to humans and 'metals can only be grown from their own seed which is quicksilver, the source of all metals'.[33] For Arnold, Dastin and Chaucer, the foundation of the art of alchemy was the search for the fountainhead of mercury, the secret alchemists deemed dear to Christ; this was the seed of metals and all life found through the reduction of substances to primal matter and when this matter is animated by the ferment, the ashes at the bottom of the cucurbit (the gourd shaped bottom of the alembic used in distillation), containing the soul of the four elements and the four planets Venus, Mars, Saturn and Jupiter, transmutation can take place. This is a mystery that held intense fascination for an artist like Chaucer: 'Now you have achieved the conversion into one another and you have the mixture of the soul body and spirit together and their conversion into one another and you will then have the increase whose usefulness is greater than art or genius is able to perceive.'[34]

Chaucer's vision of the integration of the social and natural worlds through the interplay of sulphur and mercury was given full expression in his *Canterbury Tales* and it is possible to place this epic firmly within an alchemical and medical context. A contemporary work that provides the key to this interpretation is the vernacular uroscopy treatise written for Richard II and Anne of Bohemia.[35] A theme of this work is the existence of an intricate relationship between man and the cosmos, maintained through the interaction of the four elements. Fire, which contains the stars, circulates around the ether; and air, which contains the birds, moves around water; and water, which contains the fishes, and goes around the earth, which contains the beasts. Among the inhabitants of the earth is man, in whom these four elements interact to form the different personalities, who are often in conflict with one another. The health and well-being of the human body and indeed human society is seen to depend on the combination of the two humours of blood and phlegm (or sulphur and mercury). Blood, whose home is the liver and heart, is the source of vital heat and nutriments; and phlegm, from the lungs, cleanses the blood in the veins of impurities produced by the dry cold humours of choler and bile which are trapped and hidden deep within the body in the prisons of the gall and spleen. The conflicts in the body between these friendly and malevolent humours are replicated in human society in the differences between individuals based on the predominance of the different humours. The sanguine man (blood) is well disposed as a warm steadfast and loving man; the phlegmatic man is cold moist slow witted and as unstable as water; the choleric man is hasty as fire, hot, dry, wrathful and subtle of wit; and the melancholic man is dry, cold, envious, guileful, sorrowful and subtle of wit.[36] In this vision of the interaction between the elements in the macrocosm and microcosm health within both spheres is seen to depend on a balance being maintained in the natural and social worlds by the interaction of the red and white (blood and phlegm), sulphur and mercury.

This is a vision realized in *The Canterbury Tales* in the marriage of the moon and the sun, mercury and sulphur in the opening description of the regenerating effect of the sun and water on the drought in early spring. These tales, told on the journey between Southwark and Canterbury, have an ostensibly Christian structure. The pilgrims are brought together after Lent to make their pilgrimages and offerings at the shrine of St Thomas Beckett in Canterbury in an attempt to cure themselves of their ills. The penitential aspect of this work, which includes a long sermon by a parish priest on the Seven Deadly Sins and the author's retraction of his sins and his writings, does not negate the joyous celebration of natural forces which motivate the pilgrims, and it is possible to see behind the structure of *The Canterbury Tales* the alchemical vision revealed in the epilogue to the *Canon's Yeoman's Tale*. The time when the pilgrims meet is spring in the month of April, the time of Aries, traditionally the time for the beginning of the alchemical work and their enthusiasm and energy is a manifestation of the emerging dynamic natural forces of new pagan year. The two forces celebrated in the opening prologue are the warm sun (sulphur) and renewing and regenerating rain (mercury); and it is their union which brings about the phenomenon when 'The drought of March hath perced to the roote' and the sun and water engenders the new life that inspires the mating of the birds and the wander lust of the pilgrims.[37] Chaucer's social vision is one of a post-Black Death people; affluent, afflicted by dietary and humoral disorders that come from overeating and the overstimulation of fiery foods. John Doubelay in the *Stella alchemiae* quoted Egidius's regiment of health in which he advised eating moderately and to 'put away all superfluity because gluttony and surfeiting doth kill more men than the sword'.[38] Most of the pilgrims on the Canterbury road, at the very time when the ascetic eremitic movement was flourishing, are guilty of this: the monk has an excessively oily head, the cook has sores, the product of a diet of rich food, and the Summoner a fiery red face. The author's understanding of human nature is based less on conformity to the Ten Commandments than on the activities of the planets and the humours: the boisterous, aggressive miller is motivated by choler and governed by Mars; the effeminate pardoner is phlegmatic; and the wife of Bath is torn between her Venerian, sanguine impulses for romance and fantasy and her lustful desires for domination, brought about by choler and her other ruling planet, Mars. Melancholy and death is the work of bile and Saturn, and this can be observed in the grasping reeve who rides at the back of the company. In all the satirical descriptions of the pilgrims, however scathing, there is recognition of the importance of vitality, of life, and this sense of energy and vital heat is something that the entire cast of characters share to a greater or lesser degree, and it is on this basis that they are evaluated. Even the pardoner, who capitalizes on human fears of the church and the afterlife, provides in his tale a compelling demonstration of the importance of living according to the forces of nature in the image of an old man searching for death by prodding with his stick his mother, the earth. Throughout *The Canterbury Tales* Chaucer shows that his understanding of human behaviour and conflict is governed by the planets and the occult forces within the earth. The overall vision of *The Canterbury Tales* is not purely moralistic in a Christian sense, nearly all the pilgrims are satirized with a view to showing that the key to happiness is to find a vocation consistent with one's personality and humoral disposition. The prioress, who feeds her dogs roast meat and speaks provincial French, is not mocked for her lack of understanding of the monastic vocation, but pitied because as a person of sanguine, Venerian disposition she is more suited to a life of romance and sexual emotional fulfilment rather than one of service to Christ. The key to happiness in Chaucer's vision is not self-denial or service to an ideal but self-knowledge, an understanding of one's inner nature and allowing oneself to live in conformity to the disposition of the planets and the elements that determine a person's being, and this is very much in accord with the higher ideals of alchemy.

What holds this disparate, truculent band of pilgrims together, whose quarrels are all shown to be originating in the earth within the elements and the humours, is the sunny disposition of the host, who persuades the pilgrims to tell their tales, and the prologue itself which celebrates the warm, regenerative powers of sulphur (the sun the planet of light and consciousness). The vision at the opening of the tales of the beginning of new life in the spring, with the quickening new growth in the plants inspired by the showers of April penetrating the earth and bathing the leaves, and the singing of the birds, echoes the description in *Secreta secretorum* of softly blowing winds, the moisture exhumed to the tree tops and the resounding sound of the nightingale.[39] Throughout *The Canterbury Tales* there is an implied acceptance of the principles of death and renewal that dominates such alchemical texts as the *Secreta secretorum*. It is therefore especially significant that Chaucer includes the phrase *Secreta secretorum* in the epilogue to the *Canon's Yeoman's Tale* to separate his understanding of the natural forces (and this includes above all the marriage of mercury and sulphur) from that of the uninitiated. Chaucer may have paid his dues to the church in his retraction and the parson's sermon; but the genius and vigour of his work owes everything to this 'secret of secrets', the marriage of mercury and sulphur. This conjunction was celebrated in a number of mythic creatures including the dragon, described in the *Canon's Yeoman's Tale;* but it is also possible that Chaucer understood the conjunction of these two substances in terms of the Green lion, which appears in many fifteenth- and sixteenth-century alchemical images devouring the sun and was described in the fifteenth-century *Book of Merlin* as 'the water of life of a greener colour than any man has seen'.[40] In a treatise on the philosopher's stone the 'secret water', or primal mercury, which brings all bodies back to the first matter was known as the blood of the green lion.[41] *Leo viridis* (the green lion) represents the philosopher's stone, the state between male and female, between the sun and moon, or gold and silver alluded to by the legendary alchemist, Maria the Prophetess, and it was described as Venus or copper, which was capable of being transformed into gold or silver in the thirteenth-century alchemical text *Summa perfectionis magisterii* (*Height of the Perfection of Mastery*) of pseudo Geber. The fifteenth-century alchemist George Ripley identified the green lion with the substance drawn from copper in the preface to his *Compound of Alchemy* and in the sixth chapter on Congealation.[42] In his *Bosom Book* Ripley described the process of breaking down and uniting sulphur in terms of the heating of the green lion until it gives off white fumes which condense into a clear liquid. Further heating reduces this to a spongy white mass which is reduced to a strong smelling liquid and this is heated and turned into powder and heated again until it turns black and all the beautiful colours of the rainbow appear over its surface.[43] The same process is suggested in a treatise on the philosopher's stone ascribed to St Dunstan:[44] the green lion is described as secret water by which all bodies may be brought to the first water and all infirmities cured. It has been assumed that Chaucer's lost work, *Book of the Leoun*, refers to the coat of arms of his patron John of Gaunt's ancestors; but it is possible that it may concern the search for this elusive, divine substance.[45]

Chaucer's implicit and subtle attempt to give the penitential, Christian pilgrimage an occult, alchemical dimension was paralleled by his contemporary court poet from Cheshire who did something similar for the chivalric concept of the Christian knights' pledge to overcome evil. Around the same time as the writing of *The Canterbury Tales* (c. 1385) the writer known as the Gawain poet composed an epic poem, *The Tale of Sir Gawain and the Green Knight*, on the adventures of one of king Arthur's knights, Sir Gawain. The Arthurian myth itself had an inherently occult dimension. Merlin, steeped in knowledge of the mysteries of nature, came to be regarded in the fourteenth and fifteenth centuries as an alchemist (a number of alchemical works were ascribed to him) and as guardian and adviser to the young Arthur. He occupied the same role as Aristotle was supposed to have done for Alexander the Great. Merlin's vision of the future of his protégés kingdom, based on a vision of the fighting red and white dragons could easily be interpreted as the conflict and resolution of the opposing forces of sulphur and mercury and the mysterious grail itself. The goal of all the knights of the Round Table could be interpreted as the philosopher's stone and was explicitly identified as the *lapis exsilit* by Wolfram von Eschenbach in his *Parsifal*. More generally the association of alchemy with fertility myths of regeneration traditionally connected with ancient Egypt had their own particular manifestation in the grail stories of the Fisher king. The various adaptors of Geoffrey of Monmouth's account of King Arthur's court brought a chivalric and Christian morality to these myths. Chrétien de Troyes introduced the notion of courtly love and service to a feminine ideal of goodness and purity and Cistercian writers, influenced by the Crusading ethos, suggested that the grail was the cup containing the blood of Christ and made Arthur's knights into a quasi-monastic brotherhood dedicated to the service of Christ.

The Tale of Sir Gawain and the Green Knight ostensibly pays homage to these chivalric and Christian traditions. Gawain is a chivalric and brave knight who accepts the challenge presented at Arthur's court by a gigantic green knight who rides right up to the feasting knights (Westminster Hall in this period had a rammed earth surface to allow the entrance of horses into the palace).[46] Sir Gawain beheads the giant and promises to meet his adversary at his home, the green chapel, within a year and a day and submit to the same treatment. A description of the passage of the four seasons follows which is closely modelled on an account of the varying moods occurring during the passage of a year found in the *Secreta secretorum*. In the course of setting out on his journey Gawain, who dedicates himself to the Virgin Mary, whose image is on the front of his shield, also becomes champion of a married lady. He gallantly resists her sexual advances and receives from her a magic girdle for his protection. Gawain is also the model of the Christian knight who served Christ, and this is commemorated by the symbol of the pentangle representing the five wounds and the five senses as befitting a disciplined, ascetic knight pledged to purity. When setting out to renew his encounter with the green knight Gawain is, as he sees it, preparing to encounter a force of pure evil. Green was traditionally the colour of the Devil, the pursuer of men's souls and was described as such in Pierre Bersuire's fourteenth-century encyclopaedia, a moralization of the natural world: it was the colour used by huntsmen to lure their prey.[47] Gawain rides through a dark wood and comes upon the green chapel, a barrow beside a stream and a green bank, and exclaims:

> Here around midnight,
> The devil his matins sing!
> Dear God, I declare it is desolate here!
> Overgrown with dry grass is this grim oratory.
> It is fitting the fellow whose form is green
> Should here do his devotions in devilish ways
> My five wits feel it is the fiend himself.[48]

Gawain feels the devil himself has tricked him into the most evil place he has ever entered. From the roof of the barrow he hears a barbarous noise of clattering of cliffs as if great sighs were being ground on a grindstone whirring like water in a mill making a great ringing din. It is the green knight preparing his axe.

However, it is possible to see this beheading game in alchemical terms as an illustration of the conjunction of sulphur and mercury and the fixing of mercury.[49] The axe, which decorated the tomb of the famous fifteenth-century alchemist, George Ripley, was a symbol of the dismemberment and passion of mercury, and

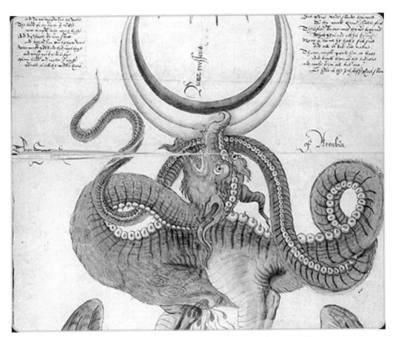

The dragon, sulphur. From the *Ripley Scroll*

an illustration to the early fifteenth-century alchemical treatise, *Aurora consurgens*, shows a version of the beheading game occurring against a backdrop of a green mound (like that behind the green chapel). A blue figure, with blue rays coming from his head like the sun, and carrying an axe over his left shoulder and holding pan pipes in his right hand, hovers over the decapitated figures of a man dressed in red and a woman dressed in white in what appears to be an illustration of the decapitation of sulphur and mercury.[50] The whole tale of *Sir Gawain and the Green Knight* builds up to this climactic conjunction of these two opposing forces, the ride through the dark wood to the green chapel becomes an allegory of an alchemical journey to encounter the mysteries of death and renewal. Gawain in the service of the Virgin, which he bears on his shield, represents mercury, the spirit which must slay the body or Sulphur. The pentangle on his shield of untainted hues of shining gold on red gules identifies him with this divine force without beginning or end, the endless knot or quintessence. The pentangle has purity: 'five pentads each precious and pure' that identifies him with Christ and with gold:

> On his shield thus shaped was that shining, bright knot
> In the richest of red-gold on royal red gules.
> This precious and perfect pentangle learned men
> Revered.[51]

Gawain himself is similarly depicted in terms of perfection, purity and gold:

> as good as pure, unalloyed:
> For virtue without villainy that valiant knight
> Was known,[52]

and he sets off on his journey with his shield

> that shone with bright red,
> With its pentangle depicted in pure, golden hues,[53]

and even his saddle is bright gold with red nails glistening like the sun. His opponent is all in green including his horse, and green was known as the colour of the outside of red sulphur. In *Gemma gemmarum* are the verses:

> Transparent green and fair to view
> I am comixt of every hue
> Yet in me's a red spirit hid[54]

And as such the green knight stands for the spirit of chthonic earth forces, nature and the body. According to an alchemical work attributed to Arnold of Villanova, the Arab philosopher Haly proclaimed: 'the root of all things is green'.[55] The green knight emerges from a green mound and is identified with sexual potency: he is a huge size and bears a holly bush and a phallic club. As befits sulphur he embodies masculinity and when he takes on the form of Gawain's host, Sir Bertilak, he enjoys hunting and obeys the rules of the royal forest 'for that high lord prohibited hunting male deer'[56] for January was well outside the hart hunting season. These scenes which contain graphic descriptions of the carving open of the hinds and of the lust for blood are sexual metaphors and occur while Gawain (as befits mercury) occupies a feminine world in the bed of his host's wife.

All alchemists were aware however that this polarity of mercury and sulphur, spirit and body, was an illusion and that the two forces shared and needed each other's qualities and that they were ultimately one and the same divine force: mercury was not able to exist in any corporeal sense until sulphur gave it body and substance. Gawain therefore shows signs of behaviour appropriate to sulphur and exhibits many signs of corruption. He is sexually compromised by his host's wife (in the form of a kiss) and is given an intimate article of her clothing, a green girdle (representing nature and sexuality) which he thinks will protect him. The green knight behaves in ways more appropriate to mercury. He meekly submits to his beheading in Christ-like fashion, and his body subsequently behaves in a manner reminiscent of the volatile substance when Arthur's knights vainly try to prevent the head regaining the body. Although he is primarily green, there are many references to the golden red tinting of his body; his hose is entwined with gold threads and his bright green glints as gold to suggest sulphur's role in the evolution of gold. He too is a creature without beginning or end: after the beheading he rejoins his head to his body and chooses to meet his adversary within a year and a day. The green knight is another manifestation of the *uroboros* or dragon, the spirit of sulphur or nature and a principle of the endless capacity of nature to renew itself. He appears in bright green in the middle of winter, like the holly bush he bears, and he corrupts Gawain in the same way that sulphur corrupts all metals. However this corruption is fruitful: this marriage of sulphur and mercury engenders a higher form of wisdom for Gawain is deluded in his belief that he is pure and all spirit, and his encounter with the Green knight is an encounter with his dark shadow, his body and above all with his repressed sexuality. The small nick given him by the green knight's axe represents his sin; his corruption through his five senses, and the wisdom Gawain gains as a result of his encounter with the Green knight is the wisdom of the serpent or nature, the realization that good and evil are relative. This encounter with his shadow, with his natural impulses, leads him to a higher state of consciousness or self-knowledge which enables the green knight to proclaim that Gawain has become a 'precious pearl'. The green girdle given to Gawain by Bertilak, or the Green Knight's wife, a token of Gawain's frailty and humanity is subsequently worn by all of Arthur's knights and echoes the garter with which the princess (in the Byzantine myth, popularized in the *Golden Legend* of Jacobus de Voraigne in 1265) leads the dragon that has terrorized Christians, who appease him with offerings of sheep, to the city where George promises to slay it if the inhabitants convert to Christianity.[57] But the Gawain author, drawing on the alchemical tradition that the lance of mercury in the service of the maiden must slay the body or sulphur, introduced a radical and occult interpretation of the St George myth. Perhaps drawing on Eastern European tradition in which 'Green George' was associated with the new life of Spring (and influenced by descriptions of the seasons in *Secreta secretorum*)[58] and the custom of dressing a man in green like a tree on St George's Day on 23 April, he attempts to show the kinship between the Christian knight and the beast who share the same natural impulses. The Gawain author's dragon, the green knight, is a wise spirit of nature (corresponding to the Gnostic view that the son of God took the form of the serpent to teach the first parents discrimination) and Gawain is made to realize that there is no such thing as good and evil in nature, and learns to accept his body, his kinship with the natural world. The author underlines this Gnostic interpretation of the St George myth by concluding his work with the motto of the Order of the Garter 'Evil he who evil thinks'. The Round Table in this tale is seen as a brotherhood dedicated to an encounter with the dark shadow of the self, the integration of body and spirit (sulphur and mercury) and recognition that God, the creature without beginning or end, can only be found in nature and this is the philosopher's stone.

Sir Gawain and the Green Knight survives in a single manuscript[59] along with *Cleanness* and *Patience*. All these works are composed in the same south-east Cheshire dialect and together with *St Erkenwald* they share a coherence of authorial outlook, especially on occult themes drawn from the Bible and the *Book of Revelations* in particular. In *Cleanness* (an epic of Old Testament history showing God's capacity to redeem mankind from chaos and to plunge him back into the abyss) God speaks to Noah of the eternal round of nature and its capacity to regenerate itself:

> Both the sweetness of summer and the Sharp winter winds,
> Both the night, the moon with each new year shall come
> A great cycle unceasing of such you are king

The author is fascinated by the original chaos from which all life emerged, the hell of sulphur. He puts into the mouth of God these words that he delivers to man: 'First I made thee myself and primal matter I used' and sees the Dead Sea as a reminder of this primal state:

> all its clinging, dark days are corrosive and vile.
> There is bitchumen bitter and black; alum too;
> There is sulphur and sandiver; several kinds there.
> From that water, in waxen lumps, wash up great heaps
> of black ashpelt that spice dealers sell.[60]

The poet's emphasis however in *Pearl, Patience, Cleanness* and *Purity* is not on sulphur but on the state of purity and perfection represented by mercury. The symbol the author chose to represent this state, the pearl, was the same as that employed by Petrus Bonus. The pearl is another version of the endless knot, a seamless round without blemish, and in its whiteness combining all the colours of the spectrum. The pearl represents the spiritual purity that emerges from primal chaos, from the filth and disorder of life including bereavement. From the earliest alchemical texts images of death and resurrection prefigured the dissolution of the prime matter and its reconstitution into glorious stones.[61] This same theme is expounded in the *Stella alchemiae*: the stone (the sun and moon) passes through a process of corruption and disintegration: it is buried and washed and turned into moist ash which is whitened and placed in a dark grave for three days until it is quickened and brought back to life so that it can bring good to all men.

Ultimately the pearl is Christ born in the cowshed, and in *Pearl* it represents the triumph over the grief felt by the poet (who adopts the persona of a 'joyless jeweller' at having lost his precious pure child). There is recognition that the pearl and what it represents (spirit and mercury) can never be lost and that it is an agent of transmutation:

> And blessed, your beauteous pearl's become.
> Though fate you feel, has felled your gem,
> It was from naught renewed.[62]

There is in this poem a repudiation of emotion and grief as something which torments the purity of the soul:

> O sir, youre certainly misled
> To say your gem has gone away
> That basks in such a beauteous bed
> As is this garden—
> Forever here she'll frolic, play,
> And laugh; no loss will threaten her—
> But gentle jeweller, since you lose
> Your joy because you lose a gem,
> Your head is much amiss.[63]

And the implication in this work and in *Cleanness* is that only by striving for a state of detachment can this corruption of the spirit by suffering and grief, which also occurs when metals are corrupted by rust, can be avoided:

> If theyre stained with their sins these will show to their grief;
> If theyre sporting a speck or a spat they will lose
> Any sight of the sovereign who sits on high.[64]

Admittance to this court of the lamb, who reigns beyond the pole star, can only be achieved when the soul is refined like base metal into a pure state:

> Those who come to the court of that king must be pure,
> Must be polished perfectly, pure as beryl
> That is sound on all sides, without seams anywhere,
> Without blemish or blot as the beauteous pearl.[65]

Whereas Sir Gawain embraces the natural round and the regenerative principle of life, the later works, *Pearl* (possibly written c. 1400) and *Cleanness*, do not focus on the integration of mercury and sulphur but the purity of mercury/the pearl attained, through death and grief, with the resurrection. In *Pearl* a bereaved jeweller sees his beloved in paradise: she is shining white:

> But whiter still was what she bore
> Upon her breast: a beauteously
> Polished pearl. It was so pure
> A man might meet eternity
> Before he found its like[66]

This pearl is across a silver river and the dreaming jeweller mistakenly believes he can cross this tide to join her, only to be told by his pearl:

> —to forge this way you first
> Must sink beneath clay's canopy.[67]

Only through death can absolute purity and perfection of the pearl be realized. The pearl is a symbol of the process of alchemical transmutation attained through suffering in the fire. This process had been described in one of John Dastin's letters where a body calcined and reduced to ashes is cleansed and whitened. While the ignorant assume sublimation means to go higher, the adept, according to Dastin, knows that sublimation is achieved through the fire making something pure and magnificent out of a corrupt body when one body is changed into another. The water that kills also brings new life when all the colours appear: 'we say that bones are sublimated when they are made delicate and changed into another nature'.[68] The author of *Pearl*, like Bonus, sees the pearl as a symbol of the resurrection; the heavenly Jerusalem of the *Book of Revelations*, a city of gold and pearls; and the conclusion of the great work, the divine plan, is the end of the world, the final release of the spirit/mercury from matter in an idealized vision of society, the body of Christ in the New Jerusalem, the resurrected body in a state of perfect harmony and wholeness represented by the round pearl.

This is a vision that is communicated on the chancel floor of the royal abbey of Westminster, which would be very familiar to both Chaucer and the Gawain poet. The cosmati design on the pavement represents the Divine plan for the universe and shows in the form of circles within circles the rotation of the four elements impressing on basic unchanging primal matter (what Plato called the mother and receptacle of all created things) mercury or the *prima materia*, represented in the central disc of Egyptian onyx, marble-veined and looking like the figure of the earth. Beyond circulates the band of blue sky and the hexagrams and hexagons, the six-sided figures symbolizing God's creation of the world from this formless primal matter. This universal nature, which receives all bodies and new deposits, has her own nature, realizes all impressions which stir, and yet she remains unchanged by them. This is the divine mercury, or in Platonic terms the world soul, is shown in terms of circles and is also represented in the centre of the chancel floor beside the primal central marble circle by a gold disc.

Part 3

The Political Significance of Alchemy

6

The Accession of Edward III

Now our king is rising from the fire and crowned with a diadem. Nourish him until he reaches the perfect age. His father is the sun, his mother the moon.

Letter of John Dastin[1]

The exciting claims made by fourteenth-century alchemists concerning the discovery of the divine, primal substance that was the origin of creation had obvious intellectual attraction for philosophers and artists; but they also attracted the attention of kings and courtiers drawn to the hidden political powers represented by mercury and sulphur. The long reign of Edward III (1326–77) provided alchemists with the opportunity to demonstrate the political significance of their art. Edward's reign coincided with the popularization of Muslim alchemy in such Latin works as the *Pretiosa Margareta Novella* (*The New Pearl of Great Price*) of Petrus Bonus (1330), and in the absorption of alchemical, occult themes in the vernacular literature of the court writers Chaucer, Gower and the Gawain poet. Edward III was a monarch alert to any possibility of celebrating his kingship through ceremony, ritual and imagery and it is likely that he would have been alerted to the potential of alchemical themes and practice at a very early stage in his education. To historians he has always been a somewhat stuffy and remote figure, a symbol of chivalric and military success; but the myths that cohered around him in the late Middle Ages and the Renaissance emphasized his interest in and patronage of alchemy.

Myths concerning Edward III's involvement with alchemists express the fundamental truth about the crucial relationship that existed between the English court and the old Moorish empire in the emergence of alchemy as a political force in the accession of this king. The most persistent myth concerned Edward's patronage of the Majorcan philosopher and theologian, Raymund Lull. This can be traced back to at least the fifteenth century. In the alchemical dialogue *De lapide philosophorum* and *de auro potabile* the fifteenth-century physician Fabri de Dya Fabri, writing for the circle of Pope Felix V 1439–49, reproached kings for having driven their alchemists to the point of despair and extolled Edward III's different attitude 'because in a hermits habit for their art he wandered the earth and howsoever he dealt with Arnold (Villanova) Raymund (Lull) and John Dastin the chroniclers relate with praise'.[2] Edward is described as a benevolent protector who divided up his kingdom between Arnold, Raymund and Dastin. Dastin's possible connections with Edward III will be dealt with later in this chapter. In the sixteenth century a story circulated that Lull came to England to serve the king and transmute metal into gold. In 1555 the Tudor antiquary, Robertis Constantine, affirmed he was shown a coin of very pure gold known as a Raymund noble which was struck of precious metal manipulated by Raymund in the Tower. The coin, showing a rose and a ship propelled by oars, was, according to *Bibliotheque des Philosophes Chimiques*, struck by the king to commemorate his unsuccessful pursuit of the alchemist, Raymund Lull.[3] The myth of Edward's patronage of Lull merits consideration given the number of alchemical texts connected with Edward III bearing Lull's name. Although Lull, an influential theologian who died in North Africa in 1316, had no special interest in alchemy and attributions of his name to alchemical texts did not start until 1378, they do reflect the way Lull's Majorcan origins indicate the importance of this Christian kingdom, formerly part of the Moorish empire, as a source of inspiration of the development of alchemy at Edward's court.

The strongest evidence of the influence of Catalonian and Majorcan alchemists at the court of Edward III to explain the endurance of the legend of Raymund Lull's presence at the Tower of London,[4] is the composition of the *Testamentum*. This comprehensive survey of the theory and practice of alchemy was, according to the colophon of the Catalan Manuscript, written at St Katherine's near the Tower of London at the instigation of one 'A' (possibly signifying alpha or God) for Edward III between 1329 and 1332.[5] The dedication of this Catalan alchemical work from Majorca to Edward III has implications for a corpus of alchemical manuscripts sharing the author of the *Testamentum's* preoccupation with the importance of the quintessence which are ascribed to an alchemist named Raymund and accompanied by colophons of dedication to Edward III. *De 24 Experimentis* (*On the Twenty Four Experiments*) completed in 1330 and containing *Liber mercurum*[6] was supposed to have been written at the church of St Katherine by the Tower in London in 1332 and *Liber naturae et Lumen nostra lapidis* (*Book of Nature and the Light of Our Stone*) was dated at St Katherine's London in 1337.[7] In another pseudo Lullian treatise on transmutation the author claims to have come to England at the invitation of King Edward. The colophon of *Liber de conservatione vitae humanae et quinta essentia* (*Book of the Preservation of Human Life and the Fifth Essence*) reads: 'this book was addressed to the most serene queen Eleanor, wife of the most serene king of the English, Edward (presumably a mistake for Philippa) and completed in London in St Katherine's in 1355'. In this same period the king was a dedicatee of the Pseudo Lullian *de Liber de Secretis Naturae* (*Book on the Secrets of Nature*) which incorporates Rupescissa's *de quintessentiae* and the *Testamentum* and so is post- 1356.[8] The author of another pseudo Lullian work, *Anime transmutationis* (the soul of transmutation) claims to have come over to England at the instigation of King Edward. The *Quatuor libri angelorum testamenti experimentum* (*The Four books of Angels and the Testament of Experiments*) was, according to the colophon, composed at St Katherine's in 1357.[9] Another pseudo Lullian alchemical treatise *Opus Abbreviatum super Solem et Luna* (*Abbreviated Work on the Sun and the Moon*) has a colophon stating that it was written in the same church of St Katherine in London. Another work on the secrets of nature and the fifth essence only survives in an edition of 1547 but its recipes for the extraction of the fifth essence from distilled red and white wine influenced John of Ruspescissa.[10] The *Testamentum* provides proof of interest of Edward III and his court in Majorcan alchemy and lends plausibility to the attribution of these other Catalan works of alchemy from Majorca bearing the name of Raymund to the English king's patronage. One candidate as possible author of these works, Raymund of Tallega from Majorca, was a theologian who was in Montpellier in 1330 and whose writings were burnt by the Inquisition in 1372. Among these works was *Book of Solomon,* no longer extant and an *Invocation of Demons* that may be identical to books bearing these titles in the catalogue of John Erghome's library which he donated to the Augustinian friars of York.[11] One of the texts in the pseudo Lullian canon, *Book of the Secrets of Nature and the Quintessence* addressed to King Robert (Robert the Bruce or Robert of Anjou) teaches the magisterium of resurrecting the dead, described as one of the greatest secrets of life.[12]

The author of the *Testamentum* chose to protect his anonymity, and all that is known is that he was writing at St Katherine's Hospital, that he was a contemporary of John Dastin, Petrus Bonus and a follower of Arnold of Villanova; and we can be certain of his Majorcan identity and the Majorcan origin of the other works dedicated to Edward III. This is important in understanding the way Islamic alchemical traditions took root in the English court and among English scholars studying alchemical medicine. Majorca in the fourteenth century was the centre of alchemical research and experiment, encouraged by such rulers as King Sancho I (1311–24) and the Aragonese princess Sancia of Majorca (1286–1345). In the castle of Almadira, the royal palace of Majorca above the sea at Palma, an alchemical laboratory has been excavated in a room in a place known as the Tower of the Angel which was constructed in the first half of the fourteenth century.[13] During the period between 1281 and 1330 there was considerable trade activity between the isle of Majorca and its kingdom and England, centred on the docks of St Katherine's by the Tower of London. The location of St Katherine's Hospital, at the point where the Thames opens into the sea, suggests alchemical learning reaching the English court from Islamic Spain via the maritime trade routes. The Majorcan navy was diverted to London in 1309 after the conquest of the Gilbertine party of Giascone II.[14] Majorca was also the source of inspiration for English scholars and alchemists because its territories included Montpellier (a possession of Jamie III King of Majorca) the home of the famous medical school patronized by Sancia of Majorca,[15] who renewed the privileges of the practice of medicine of magisters prominent in the medical faculty of Montpellier.[16] The author of the *Testamentum* may have been one of the Majorcans to attend this school (he mentions Montpellier and one of its lecturers, Arnold of Villanova, in his work).[17] A number of physicians and pharmacists from Montpellier were at the English court including Pietro of Montpellier in 1316; and Odo of Odin the pharmacist of Queen Isabella 1328–57).[18] A close friend of the king to come under Catalan, alchemical influence at Montpellier was Henry duke of Lancaster who attended autopsies at the University. His penitential treatise, *Livre des Seyntz Medicines,* which is full of alchemical imagery, was written at the instigation of friends (possibly the king himself).

Another source of alchemical influence at the English court connected with Majorca and the author of the *Testamentum* was the court of Naples. One version of the *Testamentum* was dedicated to Robert of Anjou, king of Naples 1309–43 and heir to the crown of the isle of Sicily, who married Sancia princess of Majorca; like Edward III, he was the dedicatee of a number of alchemical works attributed to Lull including: the *Testamentum, Epistola super alchimium ad regem neopolitem* (*Letter on Alchemy to the King of Napes*) *liber de secreto lapidis philosophii*[19] a *lucidarium* or *Elucidatus Testamenti* written at Montpellier and *De conservendi juventale* which were by Arnold of Villanova, who treated Sancia's father-in-law, Charles II in 1288. The *Tractatus de vinis (Treatise on Wines)*, on the healing properties of wine infused with rosemary and gold leaf as a cure for leprosy and melancholy, was composed for him between 1309 and 1311. The *Testamentum* provides an indication of the mobility between the English and the Angevin courts of the author and other Spanish courtiers in contact with Edward III's court in an account of a series of alchemical experiments in which congealed mercury was made from its menstruale, 'a palpable and inexplicable vision', in the presence of the author and some of Edward III's courtiers including: Bernard de la Brett, a Spanish confidant of the king in 1326, and John of Rhodes who had wandered into a group near Naples.[20] Near this court an alchemical projection was witnessed by two Englishmen, courtiers of Edward III in 1327. Two Englishmen at Sancia's court in Naples were Nicholas Wye, who was described on 26 July 1321 as 'Clericus et familiaris Roberti et Sancia', and a canon of Salisbury. He was described as 'capellus et familiaris domesticus Roberti regi et Sancia regine' on 26 October 1323. He may be identified with Nicola d'Ingelterra who appeared in 1334 as a copyist in Robert of Naples's library. William Alnwick, a Franciscan from Oxford and renowned commentator on Duns Scotus, was at this court from at least 1333. He assisted Sancia in her conflict with the papacy, and acted as Sancia's ambassador in Avignon in 1333.

There is therefore evidence that in the first three decades of the fourteenth century there was intellectual contact between the old Moorish empire, especially Palma and Montpellier in the kingdom of Majorca, Naples and the English court, culminating in the composition of the *Testamentum*, and this suggests that there may have been considerable alchemical learning behind Edward III's accession. Edward's posthumous reputation as a rather boorish, king of moderate intelligence who embarked on a series of wars through a conventional concern for the pursuit of his feudal rights and the acquisition of a chivalric reputation is unfair. Consideration of the role of alchemy in his kingship gives an altogether different picture of a monarch whose policies have an intellectual and philosophical coherence driven by a preoccupation with occult forces. There is a tradition that Edward's first tutor was the Benedictine monk, scholar and bibliophile, Richard Bury (1287–1345), the author of *Philobiblon*, written to encourage clergy in the pursuit of learning. Bury was closely associated with the prince's administration in Cheshire and a member of his household by 1325. The young prince could read, and to a limited extent write, Latin, and he spoke French and English. He certainly grew up in an atmosphere of secrecy and intrigue and appreciated that power often depended on keeping things hidden. His mother's lover, Roger Mortimer, was suspicious of the boy king and had spies placed in the royal household. Edward proceeded by stealth and secretly contacted Pope John XXII and indicated that royal correspondence sent to Avignon that reflected his personal wishes would bear the words *pater sancte* (holy father) written in the king's own hand. Edward assured the pope that only his secretary 'Richard Bury and his close friend William Montagu the first earl of Salisbury (1301–44) would know the secret password.'[21] When Edward made his first journey as king to make an oath of liege homage to the king of France in 1331 he went disguised as a merchant to preserve his honour. In 1326 a copy of the *Secreta secretorum* was prepared for the king by Walter Milemete, a king's clerk and fellow of King's Hall, Cambridge,[22] between the last month of 1326 and March 1327[23] and presented, with illustrations made by a number of different scribes, to the 15-year-old Edward between his proclamation as keeper of the realm on 26 October 1326 and his father's death in September 1327. Milemete wrote that he had copied the book for the king's use along with other supplementary advice on the kingly office so 'that you will have the same advantages as Alexander and if you make use of them when you come to a man's estate you will be eminently successful and in the end attain everlasting life'.[24] Another copy of the *Secreta secretorum* in a French translation was given to Edward as part of a betrothal gift from Philippa of Hainault after August 1326 and before June 1327.[25] Another work following the schema of the *Secreta secretorum*, but which concentrated on political advice with no mention of alchemy and the occult, was *de nobilitatibus sapientiis et prudenciis regem*, which was written by Milemete and presented to Edward III at the beginning of his reign on 25 June 1327 and illuminated between 1326 and 1327.[26] The copying and illustration of the *Secreta secretorum*, a work of Muslim alchemical traditions, for an English king in waiting represents the culmination of the emergence of the alchemy as a political force in the Latin West, something that exists in the earliest known work of Arab alchemy, *Liber de Compositione Alchimiae de Morienus* which Robert of Chester introduced to the Latin world.[27] This work contains the story of a Melkyte, Byzantine Christian, Maryanus, who studied alchemy in Alexandria and discovered the *Book of Hermes*, after which he became a monk in Jerusalem, attracting the attention of a Muslim Caliph in Egypt called Khalid.

The circumstances facilitating the use by the political community in the 1320s of a practical science and a theoretical philosophy of healing and regeneration could not have been more propitious. Edward II lacked the political and military skills of his father, Edward I; his interests, according to Ranulph in his *Polichronicon,* included rustic pursuits, acting and the mechanical arts. He lacked the masculine vigour expected by his subjects and caused scandal in the court with his passive homosexuality and the patronage he bestowed on his favourite, Piers Gaveston, the first earl of Cornwall (c. 1284–1312). Internal rebellion, military humiliation at the hands of the Scots, and the famines of 1315 and 1316, all indicated the malaise of his kingdom. The reputation of the English monarchy fell to its nadir when the rule of the kingdom was usurped by Isabella and her lover, Roger Mortimer, and the king was imprisoned and murdered. His son and heir, Edward III, was king only in name when Walter Milemete began compiling his illuminated copy of *Secreta secretorum,* preparing the 15-year-old for the moment when he would redeem a sick land and its kingship. Friar John Erghome, a collector of occult alchemical texts and works of experimental science, provided a political analysis of the reigns of Edward II and Edward III in his commentary of the poetic vision and prophecies of St John of Bridlington. Erghome suggested that Edward II of Caernarvon failed because he did not have any knowledge or understanding of the forces of nature that a king ought to have. Genealogies of the fifteenth-century Yorkist kings explained the lineage of a king in alchemical terms as the marriage of opposites, mother and father, male and female, the moon and sun, alliances that were like chemical unions.[28] However Erghome also pointed out that a king and his advisers could not afford to be complacent about these hidden forces within the earth that determined the succession of a king and that the picture was complicated by the heavens. Edward III's copy of the *Secreta secretorum* (which has an illustration showing Aristotle pointing out the mysteries of nature to Alexander with the sun in the background generating the plants)[29] provides the prince with the example of kingdom of the Greeks who successfully waged their wars and perpetuated their name around the world through their love of the sciences.[30] The *Secreta secretorum* also offered the young man a scientific explanation to explain his father's disastrous reign. A mother and father may direct their child towards the craft appropriate to his background, but a man's character was determined by the nature of the planets at the time of his conception and his birth, and his real nature may direct him elsewhere. The *Secreta secretorum* illustrated this point with the story of a child born in a weaver's cottage whose figure below the earth was Venus and Mars in Gemini, with Libra above the earth; this configuration dictated that, like Daniel, he would be wise in astrology and the occult and beloved of kings.[31] A converse narrative was provided of a king's son sent by his father to India to study science; but he could not profit from this because his real nature inclined him to a career as a blacksmith. The young Edward would not be able to avoid applying these exempla to his father, born to be king yet drawn irresistibly to rustic pursuits. These questions of the relationship between character and personal destiny and planetary configuration would interest Chaucer in his creation of such complex and contradictory characters as the Wife of Bath.

However, Edward III would have been given many assurances from alchemical advisers that in his case there was no such tragic conflict between the destiny mapped out by his birth and his character. The femininity and sexual degradation of Edward's father meant that special significance was given in his copy of the *Secreta secretorum* to the conservation of heat by encouraging the production of the humours of choler and blood and increasing potency; the point was reinforced by illustrations throughout the manuscript of the sun and the dragon, symbols of sulphur. John Thweng, in his highly symbolic poetic vision, saw Edward's birth in terms of the arrival of the sun bringing an end to winter: begotten in the cold November wind when the sun was in Sagittarius in 1312, he was the sun like *Taurus*, an eagle of the wind bearing the name of his father (in Edward's copy of the *Secreta secretorum* the king is described as an eagle in lordship above all the other birds).[32] John Erghome elaborated on the symbolism of these verses explaining that Edward III was crowned while his father was still alive and he explicitly described the circumstances of Edward II's demise through rectal penetration, which he described as a murder in a dark place. He placed contrasting emphasis on Edward III's identification with sulphur (sun and gold) and maintained that Edward III took the name of the bull, *Taurus*, because he was as brave as a leopard (which he bore on his shield) without weakness;[33] the bull was also taken to signify incorruptible gold because *Taurus* without the T spelt was in Latin *aurum* or gold. This identification of the kingship with the warmth and vigour of sulphur was also encouraged in Edward's copy of the *Secreta secretorum*, which has an illustration showing Aristotle reading to the golden-haired young king (who had adopted the sun in splendour as a badge) with a dragon in the background. In this work it is asserted that the king who is able to harness the four humours and elements and integrate the forces of mercury and sulphur will exhibit the strength and ruthlessness necessary to rule and judge and protect his people. These twin forces of mercury and sulphur are closely identified with the power of the king over his realm. This is signified in the representations throughout the manuscript of the mythic-horned beasts which are not naturally conceived and which integrate the powers of mercury

Occult images in the border of Edward III's copy of the *Secreta secretorum*
(BL Add MS 46680 Folio 3)

and sulphur. They include the dragon, the most obvious symbol of sulphur, but which is also the *uroboros*, the reconciler of opposites including the twin poles of mercury and sulphur, and the two mercurial beasts the white hart (included in the manuscript are images of a hart with huge antlers and a stag hunt,[34] representing the fixation of mercury) and the unicorn, which also in its fierceness and strength represents sulphur and the power of a king who will also be the servant of his subjects. By integrating these mighty opposites (on another page there is an illustration of the lion and the unicorn fighting)[35] the king will become like God unleashing great forces for good and ill; he will become the alchemist who has achieved the philosopher's stone, transforming his kingdom, bringing blessings to the land, and this would include the wealth and prosperity symbolized by the transmutation achieved through reconciliation of opposites represented by the symbolism in this manuscript.

The underlying assumption in the *Secreta secretorum* that the philosopher's stone and the king can be one and the same implies that there is a cosmic order at work when such a king is on the throne. The stone is defined as two stones, red and white, emerging in the Mediterranean sea: 'the white begins to appear upon the water in the falling of the sun and abides upon water until midnight and then beginning to descend downwards, and at sun rising she is at the bottom. The red stone works contrary, for when the son arises she begins to appear, and so to midday, and then begins to descend'.[36] This image of the process of distillation and evaporation is also a meditation on the sun rising falling in unison with the moon, demonstrating the harmony of the natural world. The *Testamentum*, dedicated to the king, emphasizes that God created all things out of mercury, the one substance on earth that in its pure form constitutes the heavenly spheres; this fifth element, the basis of all bodies on earth, is responsible for all generation and growth.[37] The claims made in this work, dedicated to the king, for the great powers to be had from the manipulation of mercury, the fifth element, which would increase the beneficial influence of the planets, must have aroused considerable excitement at Edward's court. In *Secreta secretorum* there is an underlying assumption that it is possible for the philosopher's stone and the king to be one and the same thing: like Christ he is the fulfilment of the divine will and prophecies, a manifestation of the elusive substance of mercury that combines the twin forces of the sun and moon. The dominant illustration inspired by *The Emerald Table*, which occurs throughout Edward's manuscript, is the sun and his mother the moon. The phrase which occurs in *The Emerald Table* and which runs through the *Secreta secretorum* 'that which is above is that which is below' represents not just the power in earth echoing that in the heavens, but the divine power in heaven manifested in the king who rules with justice, the quality of reason revealed in the macrocosm, and symbolized by the appearance in the manuscript of the seal of Solomon, the endless knot with the sun and moon in the middle.[38] The wheels of such a king's justice are compared to the circles of the firmament, establishing the same order and harmony in his realm that exists in the heavens.[39]

However the king was also a man: just as Christ the divine presence could only be manifested on earth through bodily incarnation, so the divine mercury can only manifest itself corporeally through being trapped in the body of sulphur. The philosopher's stone was also defined as the quintessence, this mysterious mercurial fifth essence found when the four habitually competing humours of choler, phlegm, bile and blood are in harmony. This state was believed to have only ever been achieved by Christ, who, in bodily incarnation, gave continuing proof in his words and actions of his divinity. The king too must demonstrate in his rule that he embodies the qualities of sun and moon and the principle of the divine spirit of mercury that existed before creation and is manifested with the help of its body, sulphur. The illustrations in Edward's copy of the *Secreta secretorum* reinforce this connection with numerous illustrations of the sun and moon and an illustration of Alexander/Edward with Aristotle/Edward's alchemist receiving the white stone whose mother is the moon which is mixed with water, and the red stone whose father is the sun mixed with fire.[40] He must furthermore, like Christ, demonstrate in his rule or ministry that he is the philosopher's stone both in terms of his origins as part of a divine plan (mercury) and through his actions as a man (sulphur). To achieve the state of equilibrium and harmony between the four humours he must listen to the advice of his physicians, and there are a number of illustrations showing the king doing this. He must regularly consult the heavens (numerous illustrations depict the king looking towards the sky) and the earth, and to achieve humoral balance he must know when to let blood (an illustration is provided showing the phlebotomizing of the king and another showing physicians examining his urine),[41] take laxatives, ensure when letting blood that the moon is ascending,[42] ascertain what sign the sun is in before taking medicines[43] and show moderation in diet, dress and exercise and beware impediments of the moon such as an eclipse.[44] Extreme moods exhibiting sensuality (excess of blood), melancholy (excess of bile), anger (excess of choler) and lethargy (excess of phlegm) are to be avoided with the help of the culture of the court in the form of soothing music, plays and pleasant sights, fair faces, laughter and fine clothes; exercise should be taken in moderation together with sexual activity and foods that are extremely hot or cold are to be avoided.[45] With the moderating influence of the teaching of alchemical medicine the young Edward could become a king who is worthy of bearing the sign of the quintessence with lordship in the lower and higher regions 'from whom all darkness will flee'.[46] Repeated emphasis is given to the potency that comes with good health, and with masculinity or virility: 'therefore always be manly',[47] and the author promises that the 'conservation of sanity and health is better and more precious than any medicine and they be full necessary to the governance of the world'. Images of the quintessence in the form of the pentangle occur throughout this manuscript (one with roses in the middle, one with the sun and moon in the middle)[48] and there also occurs an image of the *uroboros*,[49] reinforced with repeated references to the importance of the number five, visually demonstrated with an illustration of the five planets (the sun and moon excluded) circling around the earth. Within nature there are five kinds of beast, five kinds of plant, divided into five qualities; within man himself there are five senses and five fingers, and the king's rule must too be governed by the number five: five counsellors ruled by the king as head that rules the body. The king is advised by each counsellor (who must be learned in sciences) individually; he is never ruled by their collective voice and as he represents the intellect that rules the five senses he never reveals his secret purposes to any of his counsellors. Such a king, ruled by intellect, will bring justice to his land 'as if he were their god'[50] and therefore he will become a divine wind bringing storms of anger but also the clouds that bring rain, the grace that clothes the earth in plants and delivers merchants safely to harbour. The identification of the king with rain[51] is especially strong in this work because he becomes the giver of life, the masculine spirit of the king in union with the female spirit of the land; he is like the falling of the original mercury from heaven, illustrated as the falling mercurial sperm, the divine will, and this is represented by a number of illustrations of the moon and the white hart with large antlers,[52] including stag hunts.[53] The rain alluded to is also the divine, mercurial rain of creation, the grail, depicted in the *Ripley Scroll* c. 1460[54] and illustrated shortly after in the fifteenth-century window of St John's Church in Glastonbury depicting the arms of Christ and the two cruets bearing the white and the red.[55] This image also occurs in an illustration in Edward's *Secreta secretorum* depicting the *arma Christi* with the two cruets containing the sweat (mercury) and the blood, the red sulphur. The king is also closely identified with sulphur (represented by illustrations of the sun and the dragon, which occurs alongside illustrations of the royal arms of England) which brings the warmth that together with the rain will fill the granaries of the land. This manuscript, in which such high hopes were placed on the young king, was written in 1326–27 when England was ruled by Isabella and her lover Roger Mortimer, and it is to this period that the visions belong that express in alchemical imagery similar hopes for the regeneration of the kingdom.

One alchemist plausibly directly concerned with the emergence of the young Edward III was the English monk John Dastin, the author of nine letters on the theory and practice of alchemy.[56] He was highly connected: four of his letters were addressed to the powerful cardinal Napoleon Orsini, the legate of the French pope Clement V, the nephew of Pope Nicholas III and the dean of St Andrews in Naples. Orsini was a patron of the Sienese painter Simone Martini, who painted his portrait, and he attended the Neapolitan court of Robert of Anjou, the Wise (1277–1343), the king of Naples, patron of the university of Naples, the painter Giotto and dedicatee of Petrach's *Africa*. At this court alchemical experiments were conducted in the presence of Englishmen. Dastin, in one of his letters to the cardinal, gave a political dimension to alchemical transmutation when he exclaimed: 'For I want you to know reverend father how our king rising from the fire is crowned with a diadem. Nourish him until he reaches the perfect age. His father is the son, his mother the moon. They consider the moon to be an imperfect body and the son to be a perfect one.' This notion of nurturing a young and ripening king, closely identified with the sun, fits the circumstances of the production of the *Secreta secretorum* for the young prince Edward. Dastin alluded to the circumstances of Edward's accession more explicitly in a dream vision known as *The Vision of John Dastin*.[57] The earliest copies of this vision occur in fifteenth- and sixteenth-century manuscripts,[58] but all versions unanimously ascribe it to this obscure English monk, and one dates it to 1328 in Northampton, the time of the Northampton parliament of 4 May when England's political fortunes were perhaps at their lowest ebb: under Roger Mortimer's rule, the English had to accept a humiliating treaty with Robert I (or the Bruce, 1274–1329), king of Scotland, nullifying the achievements of Edward I.[59] This treaty was a long-term consequence of the defeat of the English at the Battle of Bannockburn, an event presaged, according to the alchemist, Robert of York, by a comet seen over York in 1315. The vision employs the process of dreaming to use the obscure myths and images of the alchemical process, possibly for the first time, to express a dangerous and potentially subversive political message. The vision, alchemically speaking, concerns the dissolution of gold back to its original first matter where it is conjoined with mercury, the universal mother and first water, to be regenerated as pure gold (six years earlier Dastin had expounded in a letter, possibly sent to the pope, the importance of quicksilver in redeeming corrupt diseased metals). A parliament is called in the interests of the 'common good' by Mercury, the mother of the six planets, because her children are sick with leprosy, caused by the tainted blood of ancestors. These planets, representing the debased metals, are Saturn (lead) Venus (copper) Jupiter (tin) Mars (iron) and the Moon (silver). The one healthy child is the Sun (gold). The relevance of this to the Northampton parliament of 1328 is clear. Leprosy was a topical subject because rumours that the Scottish King, Robert the Bruce, was suffering from the disease were first mentioned by the Lanercost chronicler in 1341. Bruce had been intermittently ill from 1307 and some deformities of his skull, including a leonine face and missing upper jaw, point to leprosy or sporadic syphilis which was frequently confused with leprosy.[60] Several sixteenth-century manuscripts of alchemical works attributed to Raymund were addressed to a King Robert, and one in particular, a 1547 edition of a work on the secrets of nature and the quintessence which claims to provide an elixir that was a panacea for this disease, a corrosive fifth essence that cleansed flesh and made it grow, was written in response to a request to a King Robert for alchemical information.[61]

A key figure in Dastin's vision is the mother, Mercury, and this could be inter-preted as a reference to Isabella, mother of the young king in waiting, who domi-nated the kingdom under its ailing king. She had a strong interest in alchemical medicine and may have seen its applicability to a kingdom suffering from a malaise caused by lack of strong leadership from the king. It is possible that she may be behind the composition of the Catalan *Testamentum* which was com-posed at St Katherine's hospital. This hospital, which provided a convenient lodg-ing and location for alchemical experimentation for the Catalan author of the *Testamentum,* consisted of a master, three brother priests, three sisters, and ten conversii, and was a royal foundation established by Eleanor, wife of Henry III. In 1330 there was a dispute between Isabella and Philippa of Hainault, wife of Edward III, over the patronage of St Katherine's Hospital. Isabella's defeat in this dispute is testimony to her discredited state following the murder of her husband, Edward II, and would explain the rededication in the colophon to her son, Edward of Woodstock.[62] The omission of any reference to Isabella reflects the scandal sur-rounding her affair with Roger Mortimer and her association with the deposition and murder of her husband, Edward II. Isabella's interest in the medical issues raised in the *Testamentum* is shown in her ownership of works of alchemical medicine including a collection of medical recipes headed 'this book was sent by the king of France to Isabel, queen of England and made by the leches and physi-cians of Montpellier'.[63] Isabel's continuing interest in pharmacological alchemical medicine and its ability to prolong youth and life was shown by her use of an *elixir vitae* recorded by the physician, John Argentine, so that when she was 70 years old and decrepit she availed herself of it with such gratifying results that she was still capable of copulating with young men forty times.[64] Her son Edward III was reputed to have taken a recipe for the quintessence with him on his cam-paigns in Scotland.[65] Isabella was also the recipient of a dietary showing what is good and evil for the brain, eye, breast and heart, which was dependent on the *Tractatus de conferentibus et nocentibus principalibus members nostril corporis* of Arnold of Villanova and headed 'this was written from Montpellier to Queen Isabel of Ynglond, at the preier of ye kyng of Fraunce, hir brother'.[66] Her rival for the patronage of St Katherine's, Queen Philippa, of Hainault was the owner of a prose version of a treatise on the virtues of rosemary written for her by the school of Salerno.[67]

John Erghome implied that Isabella had long schemed for her son's greatness, taking him with her to France and ensuring that if her brother the king of France died without issue, her son would be heir to this realm through her, and then, ensuring that he was also crowned king of England while his father still lived. For this commentator the English bull was created French through his mother. An occult dimension to this maternal scheming is hinted at when Erghome says that all this, the realm of England and the prospects of France, had come to the young man 'through the art of his mother'. The illustrations to Milemete's *De nobilitatibus Sapientiis et prudentiis regum*, written for the young king Edward, stress the key role played by the king's mother, Isabella, in the rebirth of the kingdom. A full-page miniature of her and Edward, seated like a loving husband and wife (Philippa's arms are absent) joined by an angel from heaven, may also hint at the alchemical incestuous theme central to Dastin's vision.[68] An occult dimension to the miniature is provided by the four-leafed clover presented to the couple by the angel. This symbol of good luck, which was supposed to reveal evil spirits to the beholder, represents in alchemical terms the quaternity and the blessings conferred on the kingdom by the cross of Christ.[69] Other occult images in the miniatures include the *uroboros* which occurs alongside the illustration of Edward receiving the royal arms from the Trinity.[70] The prominence of the queen mother in the alchemical celebrations of Edward's accession may help to explain why there were no subsequent recriminations or punishment of Isabella after the coup in 1330 in which Edward removed Mortimer from power. Her offence was not addressed publically: she was simply deprived of the executive authority she had assumed as an unofficial regent and she was granted a generous allowance.

Edward III can be identified in Dastin's vision as sun or gold the child of Mercury 'of seed most cleare and pure'. This highest of all the planets enjoys perfect health because his

> complexion is most temperate
> In heate and cold and in humidity,
> In erth also there is noe debate
> and in him fire so burns that
> of corruption he taketh no sickeness.[71]

Mercury advises her son that he must save his brethren by encountering the dragon and undergoing a death and rebirth. The notion of the king's death and rebirth could apply to the death of Edward II, in all probability murdered by this time, and the rebirth of the kingship, golden and untarnished through the seed of the dead king who, alone of the sons of Mercury/Isabella is 'Of her children of seed most cleere and pure'.[72] The dragon that the sun/gold must encounter is in alchemical terms sulphur, the bodily incarnation, with all its implied pain and suffering, that the pure mercury must undergo; but it could also refer to the inevitable conflict with the actual ruler of England at this time, Isabella's lover, Roger Mortimer, whose considerable pride in his Welsh, Arthurian ancestry (his grandfather, the sixth lord Wigmore, arranged a Round Table feast at Kenilworth) and claims of descent back to the line of Cadwallader gave him a special link with the red dragon. The queen, in the absence of the dead king, Edward II, must become mother and wife to revive the kingship through the seed of her son and cast out the poison of the serpent in order to cleanse the kingdom of the rust of leprosy. Through the death and rebirth of the king there will be a renewal of the monarchy in the form of a young boy king who 'To youth againe he must be renew'd'.[73] The old king, in the form of the sun, descends to the centre of the earth in union with his mother, the moon or Mercury (which in alchemical terms is the dissolution of gold in the primal sea of mercury); but which in terms of the incestuous variation of the pieta and the guarded political allegory of the dream could signify a political union between the mother and her young son. This may have been anticipated by the compilers of the manuscript of the *Secreta secretorum*: an illustration of the unicorn speared with a crowned virgin holding a mirror[74] alludes to the alchemical motif of the tamed unicorn lying in the lap of the Virgin, which was developed in Dastin's vision. The general sense of the vision is clear, a renewal and regeneration of the kingship in the form of a young king who is identified with the full glory of the sun/sulphur: 'Having moe heate in very existence,/ But by cherishing of the fire brought' and with mercury/ the moon 'clothed with a mantle of everlasting whiteness'. The basic elements of this vision seem to have remained with Edward and influenced his insistence on the healing qualities of the royal touch for scrofula: between November 1340 and November 1341 he carried out 355 ritual healings, at least 257 of them in Westminster.[75]

The circumstances of Edward III's accession, the coup against Roger Mortimer, are possibly alluded to more explicitly in an alchemical vision known as the vision of Adam Davy, a marshal of Stratford-atte-bow, which survives in a late fourteenth-century manuscript. In this prophetic vision, which the author claims to have experienced in 1309, he sees King Edward, described as the Prince of Wales. Edward III was never officially Prince of Wales, but when Roger Mortimer mounted an invasion of England with his lover, Isabella, the young Edward fled to Wales and the queen issued a proclamation at Bristol declaring Prince Edward as keeper of the Realm.[76] In the vision the prince is standing before the shrine of Edward the Confessor and attacked by two armed knights. The king returns no stroke and yet remains unscathed, and from his ears two lights, a red and a white, spread across his kingdom.[77] This echoes a description in Edward's copy of the *Secreta secretorum* of the king greeting two horsemen from whom the lights of the philosopher's stone, red and white, shine, and which is also illustrated in the manuscript.[78] The vision corresponds closely to the circumstances of Edward's seizure of power. In late 1330, after Mortimer had insisted on interrogating the king and his followers at Nottingham, the earl of Salisbury, William Montagu, advised the young king to strike before he was struck. On 18 October, the constable of the castle where Isabella and Montagu had locked themselves safely inside showed Montagu and Edward a secret, underground passage into the castle yard, and here Edward joined the conspirators and they made their way up to Mortimer's chamber and struck down the two knights who were guarding the door, laid hold of Mortimer and seized control of the kingdom on Edward's eighteenth birthday.[79] The alchemical works written for Edward III in the early years of his kingship, and the visions concerning his taking control of his kingdom, all celebrate a regeneration of the monarchy and the realm and anticipate that the young king would shed the twin lights of the sun and moon on his kingdom. Certainly Edward's early years as king fulfilled much of this promise, but during his long reign these lights would inevitably diminish.

The coronation service for the young king, which took place in Westminster Abbey, was an enactment of the alchemical drama that saw the fulfilment of divine forces in the exercise of earthly power. The significance of Westminster Abbey in the celebration of Edward III's coronation as the culmination of an alchemical work can perhaps be seen in the persistence of myths concerning the abbey's patronage of Raymund Lull. In the collection of English alchemical works compiled in 1652 by Elias Ashmole there is an alchemical poem called *Hermes Bird*, purporting to be a poem of Lull's translated by the abbot of Westminster, Cremer, who had brought Lull to England (but actually a poem by John Lydgate adapted in the second half of the fifteenth century by an alchemist, probably George Ripley). According to Ashmole, on the instructions of Abbot Cremer in the second decade of the fourteenth century, a painting was executed on an arched wall of Westminster Abbey where now statues of kings and queens sit. The painting showed God in the form of a king (perhaps Solomon) supervising the creation, and blessing three interlocking circles, representing the beginning of the great alchemical work.[80] The painting was also supposed to show a beautiful young man with bright light and many colours shining from his body standing upon the earth.[81]

There is no evidence that there ever was an Abbot Cremer of Westminster Abbey (perhaps the reference was originally to Archbishop of Canterbury Thomas Cranmer, 1489–1556);[82] but this royal church was certainly the focus of alchemical activity that resulted in visual representations of the relationship between the crown and alchemy; and one that survives is the cosmati pavement laid for Henry III in 1268. Interlacing circles represented the divine purpose of the creator, with special emphasis placed on the number sixty, the number of points in a radius of a standard circle. Sixty stone lozenges surround the pavement's central work, each covering an angle of six degrees. Six-sided hexagrams, symbols of God's creation of the world in six days, form the abbey's pavements and the six planets revolving around the earth. The other key number is four, four roundels surround the central circle representing the four elements and four cardinal points of north south east and west; and in the centre is the circle, the reconciliation of the four elements representing the quintessence of Christ and mercury. Edward III was crowned on this central disc of Egyptian onyx marble, containing a gold circle which signified the quintessence, the manifestation of mercury from the four elements, a mathematical and alchemical demonstration of the working of the divine purpose. This would be summed up in the inscription around the centre written by John Flete

The Cosmati pavement, Westminster Abbey

(c. 1398–1466), a monk and almoner of the abbey and author of the four volumes *History of Westminster Abbey*,[83] explaining that the pavement was a representation of the *primum mobile* and the universe of which the central circle is the microcosm. The spot where Edward III was crowned was a squared circle (Dastin described the alchemical process as converting the quadrangle into a round by dividing it into twelve triangles proceeding from the centre to the circumference of the circle).[84] This circle formed from the four corners of the earth was regarded as a magic circle associated with Solomon's hexagram, used to invoke the holy spirit so that when Edward III stood in this circle at his coronation the light of the Holy Ghost descended on him, a point reinforced by the appearance of the seal of Solomon in Edward's copy of the *Secreta secretorum*. When the young Edward stood in this circle at his coronation this light would be seen to descend on him, the culmination of God's work of creation in the six days suggested by the six-sided figures.[85] The motif of the gold circle occurs in various forms in the *Secreta secretorum*,[86] notably in illustrations of God/king presiding over an orb[87] and one of Aristotle pointing out to his pupil the concentric wheels of the heavens.[88] The connection between this alchemical act of creation and the kingship was strengthened by the presence behind the pavement of the coronation throne which had been made to resemble the throne of Solomon. Attempts had been made by Henry III (1216–72) to construct a coronation throne in imitation of Solomon's throne by Henry III (1216–72) who ordered a throne with two bronze leopards either side and steps in front and by Edward I who in 1297 ordered a bronze throne for the stone of Scone, which was completed in 1301 with two gilded leopards either side.

When the throne was empty it was symbolically filled by the large figure on the back showing a king enthroned with his feet on the back of a lion, a representation of Solomon identified by his seal, the hexagram, which is also on the pavement.[89] The intellect behind the complex numerical, astrological and alchemical symbolism of this pavement was probably Roger Bacon, England's foremost scientific thinker. Bacon, possibly acting as Aristotle to Henry II's Alexander, was also the author of a commentary on the *Secreta secretorum*, in which he defined alchemy as a science conceived in metaphors and divinely inspired figurative understanding that could make an important political contribution to the common good of a republic. The coronation of Edward III represents the culmination of a process begun in 1269 by Abbot Richard Ware, who prepared the shrine for reception of the confessor's remains, which shifted the focus of occult power away from Becket's shrine at Canterbury to the crown at Westminster. Edward's identification with his namesake, Edward the Confessor, the last Saxon king, emphasized the point that he was breaking tradition with the line of Norman kings (his subsequent wars with France and encouragement of the use of the English language makes him in many ways the first truly English king) and the alchemical celebration of his coronation before the confessor's shrine suggests a conscious acknowledgement of the alchemical associations of Britain's oldest Celtic name, Albion or *Albus*, the white mercury.

7

Alchemical Themes in the Kingship of Edward III

His glory is like the firstling of his bullock, and his horns are like the horns of unicorns: with them he shall push the people together to the ends of the earth

Deuteronymy[1]

The alchemical texts, and presumably the advice of Edward's physicians and counsellors, stressed how important it was for the young king in waiting to recognize his place in the divine alchemical work and to prove it by attaining, through daily regimen, a humoral balance that would result in just and moderate rule, bringing health and prosperity to the body politic. However the alchemical sources of the early fourteenth century also explicitly maintained that knowledge of the secret of secrets involved an understanding of the hidden forces within the earth, and this in turn would bring earthly power. The most obvious manifestation of this interest in alchemical secrets lay in the belief that controlled experimentation with mercury and sulphur could effect transmutation of base metals into gold. In the fourteenth century there was a great demand for alchemical gold because the shortage of gold and silver coinage had reached crisis proportions. The promise of transmutation was the reason for the employment of many alchemists at the royal courts and an obvious source of trouble when the patience of royal patrons ran out. The myth that Edward III imprisoned an alchemist, Raymund Lull, in the Tower in an attempt to force him to transmute, and then pursued him when he escaped, may originate from Edward's issuing of an order in 1327, a few years after Pope John XII had passed legislation attempting to restrict alchemists from counterfeiting coinage, to have brought to his presence two alchemists, John Rous and Magister William Dalby. In 1350 Edward III had John de Walden thrown into the Tower after providing him with 5,000 gold crowns and 20 pounds of silver 'to work thereon by the art of alchemy for the benefit of the king'. Edward also prevented the imprisonment of an alchemist in 1336 and in 1350 he financed full research.[2]

However there is no evidence that practitioners of alchemy were ever penalized for failing to produce gold and this was because royal patrons were aware of the higher philosophical issues involved and the promise of the benefits of health and the control of powerful forces. Alchemical gold, especially if it was produced through the purification of sulphur into the pure form of mercury, was the one incorruptible pure substance in the fallen world that was a material incarnation of divine spiritual forces, and the *Secreta secretorum* makes it clear that gold represents more than mere money, it is a source of the health, strength and prosperity of a king and his realm. Edward's copy of the *Secreta secretorum* provides insights into the ways alchemists might attempt to steer a monarch away from focussing on the literal act of transmutation by offering them advice on how to hold onto and increase gold through more attainable methods, such as thrift and investment, providing specific, practical advice on how to achieve credibility through the exercise of largesse while finding a balance between avarice and prodigality and therefore avoiding heavy taxation of the king's subjects.[3] The *Secreta secretorum* provides an indication of how alchemists' advice on the multiplication of gold could be no more than commonsense wisdom on how the link between the health and prosperity of a kingdom and its king depended on clarity of intellect, judicious choice of advisers and the exercise of justice. This link was maintained by the number five, the number of the pentangle and the quintessence. Just as the body has five senses the king needs five counsellors which he must rule as the head rules the senses; and the justice with which he rules his body and his kingdom, for example in wise taxation,[4] ensures a healthy regimen in which the body politic is in harmony with the cosmos: 'beneath as above to the conservance of the world',[5] a ratification of the dictum of the *Emerald Table*.

However more was at stake in the alchemist's manipulation and control of mercury and sulphur than the creation of worldly wealth. Alchemical works written in this period, including the *Margarita Preciosa Novellum* and the *Testamentum,* were characterized by the sense of excitement that their authors felt in leaving behind their Arab, Muslim sources and setting out to prove Christ's Incarnation and Divinity in the form of mercury imprisoned in sulphur and providing a Christian, scientific interpretation of the *New Testament* that could be used to provide a motive for a crusade against the infidel, the very civilization that had given them alchemy in the first place. The author of the *Testamentum* moved away from the Arab sources and addressed the Jewish community in Majorca. In a passage on the sublimation of mercury he refers to a Hebrew work *liber de reformacion hebraica* and claims that Hebrews and Arabs are incapable of a correct interpretation of the *New Testament* and that these Jews and pagans ought to pay attention to the theories of the alchemists and 'consider the generation of natural things'.[6] In this he echoed the prejudices of Arnold of Villanova who declared 'it is not credible that certain people know the truth, namely Jews and Pagans'. Showing a knowledge of Hebrew culture, the author of the *Testamentum* specifically refers to the Jewish scholar 'the reprobable Mosse Cohel' and suggests he was influenced by the anti-Semitism of King Sancho's reign[7] and was familiar with Jewish scholars and alchemists such as Menahen, who was in the service of King Pedro IV (r. 1343–87) of Majorca,[8] perhaps with a view to their conversion, by showing them how alchemical experimentation with the sublimation of mercury could affirm the *New Testament* interpretation of the divinity of Christ. His familiarity with alchemical symbolism and theories about the *prima materia* drawn from the *Book of Genesis* suggest a familiarity with Jewish intellectual traditions including cabbala. He was also writing in response to the bull of John XXII providing a potentially hostile pope with scientific proof of the incarnation of Christ (mercury) that could be used in a crusade. The composition of the *Testamentum* for Edward III in 1330, at the time when the king had concluded a pact with the king of Iberia to fight the Moors, helps to explain the persistent legend that Lull, a disciple of Arnold of Villa nova, was brought to London to transmute base metals into gold and make the king rich, the result of which was a gold noble,[9] so long as the king used some of the wealth for the benefit of the church and to finance his crusade against the Turks. Lull reportedly became disillusioned when he realized Edward intended to use the money made by alchemical transmutation to fight France. Edward responded by locking him in the Tower in an attempt to force him to transmute base metal into gold and Lull escaped, feigning leprosy, to flee the country.[10] The facts behind this legend are that Edward's seizure of power from his mother sparked crusade enthusiasm and in March 1330, around the time of the composition of the *Testamentum*, he agreed to a negotiation with the king of Iberia over the possibility of an allied campaign against the Moors of Granada.[11] In the following year Edward agreed to join the French king, Philip VI (1293–1350), on a crusade to the Holy Land. But Edward's commitment to the crusade proved to be little more than an attempt to gain international prestige and he had none of Philip's genuine enthusiasm; this was exposed when he subsequently pursued a hostile foreign policy towards Scotland and France.[12] By the time John XXII was ready to launch a new crusade in July 1333, England and France had adopted hostile positions over Scotland.

Edward's abandonment of his crusading ambitions in the interests of pursuing a policy of conquest of France signalled his intention to use alchemy for the pursuit of power and worldly domination in the way that Alexander the Great was supposed to have done. The mythical alchemist, Aristotle, working with the powerful substances of mercury and sulphur, was handling the very forces of creation, and he could claim to offer a king the possibility of power over the very earth itself. The scale of the meditation on the four elements in the *Secreta secretorum* is literally the four corners of the known world bounded by the rising sun and setting moon, the symbols of sulphur and mercury; and it was the purported recipient of this occult wisdom, Alexander the Great, who applied this learning to mastery of the earth itself. His tutor, Aristotle, promised him that if he took with him on his travels the philosopher's stone then it is 'impossible that any host shall endure against thee, or resist against you but flee hedgingly before you'.[13] Aristotle begins a letter to his pupil setting out on a quest for world domination with the promise that: 'I deliver to you the secrets of this book (described as a sacrament).[14] Read it well and as there is no obstacle between you and it. God has given you great understanding, swiftness of knowledge of literature and science, especially

Image of Alexander/Edward III and Aristotle (BL Add 47680 Folio 51v)

my doctrine, that by yourself you shall rehearse and figuratively understand all that you desire ... and open to you the way to accomplish your purpose and bring your desired end.'[15] The prologue emphasized the importance of a figurative understanding of signs and wonders of the natural world that was central to alchemy and wisdom important for one about to conquer the world. The danger of this 'sciencie sacramentum' (sacramentum of knowledge)[16] falling into the wrong hands of those greedy for power is emphasized: 'I give to you my secrets by signs because of fear that this book come to untrue men's hands and to the power of proud men', and the recipient is warned that to disclose the hidden things and secrets of the earth can bring about divine disapproval and misfortune, unless such things are kept close and used as a mirror for noble conduct. John Dastin, in his letter to the ruler of the Catholic Church, Pope John XXII, boasted that within the philosopher's stone there is a *magisterium* belonging especially to kings and the great of this world and he who possesses it has a never failing treasure. Later in Edward's reign John of Rupescissa issued a similar warning in his book on the quintessence by pointing out that the secret powers of mercury could attract the attention of tyrants.[17] Though the *Secreta secretorum* is described as a mirror for princes the advice is much more than a practical counsel of conventional manuals, and this is underlined by an adjacent illustration of the pentangle,[18] the endless knot, to emphasize that the knowledge necessary for the prince implied occult wisdom of the East, of Egypt. Such knowledge included techniques to retain the natural heat of the king which would ensure strong military leadership and ways to attain humoral balance through diet, medicines, laxatives, and a daily regimen of exercise, and music which would ensure just profitable rule. Secret knowledge of the working of the stars and the forces within the earth could also be used to acquire knowledge of the future; and knowledge of physiognomy would enable a king to read the characters of men in their faces as in a book and enable him to choose wise and loyal counsellors. Such knowledge would enable the reader to establish his soul as king of his body. This alchemical wisdom was seen in the *Secreta secretorum* as potentially the key to domination of the world itself, and it was maintained that the exemplar of one who mastered the occult to such an extent that he both conquered the world and made it a better place was Alexander the Great. According to the prologue of the *Secreta secretorum*, when Alexander had conquered Persia and accomplished his secret purposes[19] he wrote to his tutor, Aristotle, addressing him as worthy doctor and governor of the world. Aristotle replied advising him to govern with goodness and kindness, and Alexander, in following his advice, spread the Greek values of reason throughout his empire. Alexander's alchemical tutor was believed to have ascended to heaven on a pillar of fire because he caused his pupil to live by his counsel, thereby winning cities and conquering many regions of the world, making many peoples his subjects.

There is no doubt that those involved in the preparation of this manuscript intended to encourage Edward III to follow in the footsteps of this great hero by waging war in France; instead of the two greatest powers in antiquity, Macedonian

Greece and Persia, locked in an epic struggle it would be the two most powerful kingdoms in medieval Western Europe, England and France. On a page proclaiming Alexander's achievements in establishing an empire throughout the world there is an illustration of the king of England's arms quartered with those of the French Fleur de Lys; and throughout the manuscript, on pages referring to Alexander's conquests, there are illustrations of Edward's arms with depictions of soldiers in early fourteenth-century armour and illustrations of longbow men and siege machines. Specific military and political advice is often couched in terms of alchemical symbolism: the numbers three, five and seven were the most important;[20] counsellors could number four to signify the four elements and the four corners of the earth, and companies of soldiers should be divided into ten which, as the sum total of one, two, three and four, was the perfect number representing the squaring of the circle (a process described by Dastin as the achievement of the *magisterium* by dividing a quadrangle into twelve triangles, the product of three and four, to achieve the circle).[21] Political and military decisions were only to be taken after consideration of occult factors, and always the role of mercury and the moon was crucial: a journey should not be taken if the moon is opposite to the sun, and before going to battle a king should ensure that the house of the moon is in the middle of heaven with mercury friendly to the house. More practical suggestions, not in the original work, concerning the application of alchemical knowledge to Edward's military campaigns are also provided in the form of illustrations of canons (an innovation in fourteenth-century warfare and hitherto unknown in the West) being rammed with gunpowder made from sulphur.[22] Edward's campaigns were particularly associated with this weapon which employed the destructive power of sulphur. John Barton, archdeacon of Aberdeen, writing in 1371, stated that canons were employed in Edward III's invasion of Scotland, and an inventory of 1338 refers to a small canon in the tower. In 1346 Edward ordered all available saltpetre and sulphur to be brought to him and he employed seven canons at the Battle of Crecy in August 1346.

The identification of Edward III with Alexander the Great, encouraged in this manuscript, may derive from parallels between fourteenth-century myths about the rise of Alexander and the circumstances of Edward's path to the throne. Alexander's origins were believed to have been steeped in the occult. According to the late medieval myths his biological father was not Philip of Macedon, but an Egyptian sorcerer, Nectantibus, who took the form of a dragon to impregnate Olympia while she was sleeping. In his early years Alexander was taught by this sorcerer who abused his occult knowledge, and he then took as a tutor, Aristotle, who was regarded as a legitimate practitioner of alchemy. Edward III's father, like Alexander's, was murdered, and he too assumed power under the dominating influence of a mother whose involvement in the occult took such questionable forms as using *aqua vitae* to sleep with young men in her old age. There was a popular tradition that Edward's decision to invade France was influenced by occult factors surrounding the exile in England of Robert III of Artois (whose wife was half-sister to King Philippe VI of Valois). Robert had fled to England after his confessor, Henry Sagebran had revealed to Philippe a plot by Robert to kill him and his queen, Jeanne de Bourgogne and their son Jean with a death spell. The French king's wrath encouraged Robert to urge Edward to take the title of the king of France.[23] Like his hero, Alexander, Edward consolidated his power with the help of legitimate alchemical instructors, including the compilers of Aristotle's *Secreta secretorum*, the author of the Catalan *Testamentum* and probably the monk John Dastin. Even the legend that Alexander bore horns, the symbol of mercury in the form of the horns of the waning moon, which is referred to in the *Secreta secretorum*, is paralleled by John Erghome's description of Edward as the brave bull with the horned brow who grazes in the fields of France, protecting his people.[24] For Erghome Edward was a hero of epic proportions, a Samson and a David leading God's chosen people. The early years of Edward's reign certainly assumed the proportions of an Alexandrine epic as he embarked on a military campaign that resulted in victory against the Scots at Halidon Hill in 1333 and the naval victory over the French at Sluys in 1340. In 1346 Edward took with him to the siege of Calais the largest and best-equipped army yet to leave English shores which was composed of half the English nobility.[25]

However, at the height of these successes, Edward abandoned the model of Alexander the Great and began to identify himself with King Arthur. Soon after Edward's birth the anonymous Merlin's prophecy of the three kings predicted for him a career of Arthurian conquest. The first indications of his interest in this mythic British king occurred in 1331 when he and his queen visited the grave of Arthur and Guinevere at Glastonbury Abbey and spent Christmas at the abbey. In 1345 he ordered a search to be made for the body of Arthur's supposed ancestor, Joseph of Arimathea. He made his clearest statement that he wished to be regarded as England's once and future king, the returning Arthur, in 1344 when he financed the building project at Windsor Castle, Edward's birthplace and the new focus of his kingdom, replacing Glastonbury and Winchester; this included the construction of a building to house an Arthurian Order of the Round Table that was intended to include 300 knights. During this period Edward hosted a number of Arthurian jousting tourneys. In the first tournament after the Battle of Homildon Hill for which there are records, at Dunstable in January 1334, Edward jousted as the Arthurian knight, Lionel, a name he gave to one of his sons.[26] Between 1327 and 1357 there were 55 royal and aristocratic tournaments; the Windsor tournament of 1344 was the 39th of Edward's reign. Ladies of the court often witnessed these Arthurian pageants with disguises and colourful costumes. Edward III's friend, Henry duke of Lancaster, jousted before him in 1343. After 1347 the king held a series of tournaments at Westminster, Reading Bury St Edmunds, Lichfield,

Windsor, Canterbury and Eltham.[27] There were probably a number of reasons for Edward's decision to emulate a British hero rather than a Greek one. Edward was 32 when he began work on the home of the Order of the Round Table, Alexander at the same age had conquered the known world as far as India; Edward therefore needed a more mature role model with more realistic achievements to emulate. His adoption of a British mythic king was a more patriotic gesture and signified the way alchemical learning was beginning to be disassociated from its Muslim, Arabic roots and acquiring the mythology that it was British in origin and linked to the Grail myths and the cult of King Arthur at Glastonbury. Perhaps Edward had been inspired by his visit to Glastonbury, the site of the red and white springs which encouraged a national mythology that England was the home of alchemy and the grail, the mysterious and elusive mercury that befitted its Celtic name of Albion. The Celtic King Arthur must have seemed, after Edward's visit to the holy places of Glastonbury, a more patriotic alchemical hero than Alexander who was associated with the Muslim world of Egypt. The occult, alchemical credibility of Arthur was well established by the fourteenth century, and there were obvious parallels between Arthur's rise to power and that of Alexander the Great. Arthur, the product of a union between the sleeping Ygrain and Uther Pendragon, who came to her through the agency of Merlin in the form of a dragon, was also the product of a rape orchestrated by magic. He too owed his political success and conquests to the tutelage of one learned in occult, alchemical arts. Merlin defined the alchemical forces governing the land and its kingship in his interpretation of the dream of Vortigern of two fighting dragons, red and white, as a representation of the age-old conflict between mercury and sulphur and the triumph of King Arthur who would reconcile these forces. His successor, Edward III may have similarly seen himself creating a great nation by integrating and harmonizing these two mighty forces within the land.

Edward's adoption of the role of Arthur was complete in 1349 when his plan for the Order of the Round Table was modified into select order of 24 chosen knights, many of whom had fought with distinction in France, into a society known as the Order of the Garter. Each member occupied a stall in St George's Chapel, Windsor, and they met each year to recount their martial exploits. The Order of the Garter has always been seen as a chivalric order, but it had an alchemical, occult dimension: its first historian, Elias Ashmole, was a student of British alchemy. The philosopher's stone was to be found through the conflict with the dragon, and the central symbol of the order, St George and the dragon, is another manifestation of the conflict between St George (mercury) in the service of the Virgin (the patron of the order) and the dragon (sulphur); two opposites who are yet one, reconciled when George kills the dragon and they become integrated; this represents the coming to fruition of Dastin's vision of the king's encounter with the serpent, and this was symbolized by St George's flag, the red cross representing the Crucifixion and also sulphur, on a white background, representing mercury. The alchemical significance of these two colours was discussed by a founding member of the Order of the Garter, Henry duke of Lancaster, who owned a copy of the *Secreta secretorum*,[28] in his *Le Livre de Seyntz Medicines*. Henry prescribed two medicines for a sinful heart, rose water/Christ's blood, distilled by the heat of the sun, and distilled white wine/the tears of the Virgin.[29] It was because George was identified with the red of sulphur as well as the white of mercury that he was seen as a fertility figure associated with the life-giving, regenerative forces of sulphur and the spring, a powerful totem for a chivalric order. This lent particular significance to the first meeting of the order on St George's feast day, 23 April 1349, during the height of the Black Death. These meetings were accompanied by jousts, prompting Henry duke of Lancaster to declare on the St George's Day jousts of 1358 that nothing like it had been seen since the days of King Arthur.[30] This association of the Order and its patron with the regenerative forces of nature suggests parallels with the Knights Templar, a crusading order with a religious ethos. Wolfram von Eschenbach, in his Grail romance, *Parsifal*, made this connection between the Arthurian knights of the Grail, dedicated to the quest for the pure stone called 'lapsit exsilis', and the Templars. The Templars were disbanded in 1313 and charged with numerous heresies, including the worship of an androgynous beast, Bahomet, representing the light and dark image that suggests Gnostic origins to many of their beliefs.[31] The Garter too could be described as an occult order celebrating the chthonic forces of nature, and Edward's sponsorship of this society shows him deliberately distancing himself from the kingship of his father and projecting himself as a monarch who identified himself with the regenerative forces of the Spring, the sun and the vital heat produced by the humours of blood and choler. The young Edward was devoted to St George from the beginning of his reign; his identification with the saint had been encouraged in a full-page illustration in Walter Milemete's *De nobilitatibus Sapientiis et prudentiis Regum* written for Edward c. 1327,[32] showing the saint arming the king and about to hand him the shield of England[33] (the dragon occurs in the border of another miniature showing the king in battle).[34] At the chapel of St Edward the Confessor, in Windsor Castle, rededicated to St George and the Virgin, a stature of St George in armour was placed before the high altar, and when the walls of St Stephen's Chapel in Westminster Palace were redecorated in 1350, St George was painted kneeling before the altar alongside Edward and his sons. On 13 August 1351 George was acclaimed as blessed George, the athlete of Christ, whose name and protection the English armies invoked in war.[35] Edward's interest in the dragon is shown in his ceremonial chamber of St George at Windsor Castle where there hung a red Pendragon banner. According to Jean Froissart (c. 1337–c. 1405), the Hainault chronicler, the banner of St George slaying the dragon was born by Edward's forces in France. One of

Edward's most experienced campaigners, Sir Hugh Hastings (d. 1347), chose to be remembered by a memorial brass showing the spearing of a dragons head. Another fertility symbol that Edward adopted was Taurus the bull described by Erghome as: 'Taurus growing green. Like the evergreen laurel the young king renews the kingship and during his reign the land is fertile, plentiful and bountiful.'[36] This identification with the life-giving and healing properties of sulphur, or the slain dragon, can be seen in Edward's enthusiastic participation in the ceremony of the king's touch for scrofula in which he presented coins bearing the image of St Michael killing the dragon which was hung around the neck of sufferers.

However the chthonic, Gnostic implications of the Order of the Garter run deeper than this into more sinister regions alluded to by the order's symbol, a garter worn by all 24 knights, and the accompanying motto 'shame on he who thinks ill of it'. The official story of the origins of the Garter, recounted by Polydore Virgil in the sixteenth century and accordant with Edward's bluff chivalric image, was that a lady, one of the king's lovers, dropped a garter and Edward picked it up, telling his knights he will found an order around it. The reality corresponds to a much darker event in Edward's life,[37] recounted in 1361 in a rewriting and expansion of Jean Froissart's *Chronicles* covering the years 1325–78 by Jean Le Bel, a chronicler from Liegeois associated with Hainault, the home of Froissart who was born in Valenciennes, and whose patron from 1361–69 was Queen Philippa, the sister of William Count of Hainault. Le Bel was in the service of Sir Jean Hainault, Queen Philippa's uncle and a supporter of Isabella in 1366 and of Edward's seizure of power in 1330. He served Edward III in Scotland in 1328 may have used as a source Jean de Hainault himself, and these events are to some extent corroborated in the *Chronicles* of Jean Froissart. According to Le Bel's chronicle, Edward's Arthurian achievements, inspired by chivalric attitudes towards women, began to be undermined in 1342. In this year the earl of Salisbury, William Montagu, was a prisoner in Paris and the Scots were resurgent in the north of England and besieging the earl's castle. The countess of Salisbury, Catherine Montagu, appealed to the king for help, and while she was entertaining him in her castle he declared his love for her. She rejected his proposal and reassured herself that the king would not dishonour her or his close friend (William Montagu in Thomas Gray's *Scalacronica* was a key figure in the king's seizure of power); but Edward, unable to relinquish his passion, held a 15-day feast in August to celebrate the defeat of the Scots, to which the earl of Salisbury (now released from French captivity) was invited, along with his wife. The king again declared his love for her, and was rejected again; he responded by sending her husband to Brittany with Walter Manny, and on the pretence of visiting the earl's castle to investigate its security he brutally raped the countess leaving her unconscious.[38] The earl, on his return from Brittany in March 1343, rebuked the king for his conduct telling him he should feel *shame* (honteaux). The scandal broke two weeks after Epiphany on the feast of the Round table on 10 January 1344. By this time a partial reconciliation was implied when the earl of Salisbury played a leading role, with his cousin Henry, earl of Derby, at the ceremony in January 1344 organizing a Round Table Feast at Windsor. Shortly after this feast, at a subsequent tournament, the earl of Salisbury, one of the principal tourneyers, suffered wounds from which he died shortly after, and his widow took a vow of chastity. The only account of this incident, written by a royal servant, civil lawyer and chronicler, Adam Murimuth (1274–1347) in *Continuatio Chronicorum*,[39] implied that some sort of betrayal and deception had occurred in this tournament, in which Edward III was one of the principal participants. Rumours subsequently circulated within court circles concerning the rape of the countess and the possible murder of her husband; and in the Bridlington prophecy c. 1350–52 parallels were drawn between Edward's conduct in this affair and that of King David, the warrior king who fell for Bathsheba and orchestrated the death of her husband, his friend, Nathan;[40] ten years later John Erghome, in his commentary, declared Edward to be like David, a sexual sinner and shedder of innocent blood.

Such rumours may explain why the Round Table project described by Adam Murimuth, and building work at Windsor was abandoned: only two jousts took place between the Windsor feast of January 1344 and the beginning of the French campaign in 1346.[41] Tournaments were only revived again in 1348. Edward was unable to sustain his Arthurian image in the wake of this sexual scandal and shake the image of David the sinner; but by 1348 he had recovered his nerve sufficiently to establish the Arthurian Order of the Garter (inspired by a king who was himself the product of rape). There is virtually no notice of this event and there were significant omissions of prominent knights, perhaps refusing to join out of loyalty to the countess and her dead husband. They included Richard Fitzalan the tenth earl of Arundel who had taken the oath to found the Round Table at Windsor, William Bohun earl of Northampton, father of Erghome's patron, Robert Ufford earl of Suffolk, who was not elected until 1349 and Sir Walter Manny, a Hainault knight who was with the earl of Salisbury in Brittany when the countess was raped, was not elected until 1359. The symbol Edward chose for the knights who joined him, the garter, was an intimate and erotic article of female attire used to hold up undergarments of the sort seized from the countess in the attack of 1342; the oath referring to this incident proclaims: 'Shame on he who thinks ill of this'; a less specific, more Gnostic translation would be 'Evil he who evil thinks'. This garter and motto (representing the symbolic taking possession of the countess) was first brandished in 1346 on Edward's Crecy campaign. The alchemical, occult significance of the garter and its motto, given the prominence of the accompanying symbol of the dragon or sulphur and George as a fertility icon is clear. The motto alludes to the garter and the attendant rape only to assert the priority of the power of sulphur and the chthonic impulses in Edward, a king of passion, of choler and blood and one worthy to lead the nation on a campaign of conquest. This is a crude rationalization of alchemical theory, of the relativity of notions of good and evil, of the power of natural impulses, the vernal forces of spring, but it goes deeper than this. If Edward was guilty of violent rape and the murder of a friend he would have had a potentially corroding sin on his conscience; and he took this and made it a source of power and strength: it was a case of what does not kill you makes you stronger (and in an order with such Arthurian pretensions the bond of sexual violence connecting the founder of the order and Britain's first and greatest king would have been immediately apparent). The garter and its motto raises the disturbing possibility that cruelty and ruthlessness brings with it power and achievement of one's wishes, something ratified in the subsequent victories of Poitier (1356), Najera (1367) and especially in the Black Prince's sacking of Limoges in 1370. In a perverse way Edward's crime was exorcized and became empowering through his intransigent challenge to his disapproving court. It operated as a kind of sympathetic magic. This motto was also an oath that he required his 24 garter knights to renew each year. Oaths performed an occult purpose on Edward's French campaigns: they took his knights into a world of fixed determination and resolve. In 1337 bachelor knights among Edward's embassy at Valeciennes wore a patch over one eye until they performed some deed of valour.[42] The oath and motto of the king, which he took with him on his campaigns to Crecy and Calais and brandished on one of his ships, was a much more powerful totem, inspiring fear in any opponents: it proclaimed that this was a man of resolution whose passion and will would not be swayed by any sentiment or remorse.

The alchemical texts of this period had an explanation for such conduct. The *Secreta secretorum* explains how Saturn governs the earth, Jupiter the air, the sun fire, and mercury water. John Dastin, in two treatises dedicated to Cardinal Orsini, explained how behaviour was determined by the link between the humours and the planets: the moon (silver and quicksilver) determined the mercurial unpredictable part of the psyche; Venus (copper) the instincts; Mars and Jupiter (iron and tin) discipline; and a man normally could not resist the influence of these celestial bodies or the elements beneath them which determined the general laws of nature and the natural rhythms of the body. However there were those who were exceptions, those who did not live entirely within the natural world, who made their fates their own and lived by the sign of the sun and acted according to their own individual natures; such men were saints and sinners. Edward probably saw himself as such a man. The circumstances surrounding the founding of the Garter raises a question that is important in any consideration of the occult and that is the nature of evil. Edward, in his crude interpretation of alchemical theory, was announcing that there was no such thing and in a sense his conduct demonstrated the sort of ruthless determination that Machiavelli would endorse. In his *Discorsi sopra la prima deca di tito Livio* (*Discourses on the First Decade of Titius*

Livy) (c. 1513) Machiavelli observed that it was rare to find any individual who had the imagination to be totally good or bad, and gave as an example to avoid, Giovampagolo Baglioni, a tyrant of Perugia, who was totally immoral in the private sphere and yet, because of misplaced moral scruples, he was unable to kill his political enemy, Pope Julius II, when the latter was in his power when he visited Perugia in 1505, unarmed. If Baglioni, according to Machiavelli, had within him the capacity of being honourably evil, the courage to engage in a work of malice, he would have performed a deed that would leave an eternal memory of greatness.[43] Edward, however, took his immoral, private action into the political sphere and succeeded in establishing a reputation as a great and honourable king. And yet, despite the ruthlessness of many late medieval kings, observers of them still retained a notion of evil. Henry duke of Lancaster, who seems to have been compliant in the events surrounding the feast at Windsor and fully supported Edward's Order of the Garter, had plenty on his conscience when he came to write his penitential *Livre de Seyntz Medicines*. Henry meditated on the human hand, the symbol of the five senses and instrument of sin, and focus for the redemption of Jesus Christ through the five wounds. In a possible allusion to Edward's crime and the conquests that followed it, and his own complicity as a founder member of the Garter he wishes 'shame' on any of the company of knights who would not follow the humble infant Jesus and proffer to him a red apple to the value three realms, (in 1354 Edward was attempting to conquer the three realms of England, Scotland and France in fulfilment of Merlin's prophecy of three crowns found in the French *Brut* concerning the boar of Windsor or Edward III).[44] Henry's meditation may well have occurred during chapter meetings while contemplating the seal of the college of St George, three crowns, which was the heraldic device of King Arthur. One famous sinner synonymous with notions of evil in the late Middle Ages was Richard III whose hand, in his earliest and contemporary portrait, was used in a more evasive way to assert his suffering and sacrifices for his crown and people.[45] Richard III's actions and political credibility was compromised by what was widely regarded as the murders he organized of his nephews and friends. It was silence on these actions, his inability to face the consequences of what he had done or to boldly brazen it out like Edward III, that robbed him of both political credibility and vitality of action and led to his association with sin and its wages in ways even such morally compromised figures as Louis XI King of France found unacceptable.

Edward III himself did not escape censure for his private sins. The period between the establishment of the Order of the Round Table and the Order of the Garter 1344–48 is one of increasingly vocal criticisms of Edward's morality. Thomas Bradwardine, the Merton theologian and preacher, addressed Edward III and his court before the Battle of Calais in 1346 warning about the dangers in attempting to find out about the secret forces and knowledge that was God's alone and claiming that demonic forces disorientate humans in their political, military and sexual activities and that the devil could take the form of a beautiful temptress.[46] Chroniclers went further to suggest Edward's sinfulness was beginning to alienate him from God. Henry Knighton, an Augustinian canon of St Mary's Abbey, Leicester, included in his *Chronicles,* stretching from 956 to 1395, an account of Edward's return from Brittany, in which he claimed he was threatened by death for five weeks by a tempest offered by God in response to his sexual misdemeanours. A Latin poem, written in 1346, shows Edward returning from Calais in 1347 in a storm that is a cleansing punishment for the king's sexual licence. The Bridlington prophecies of 1350–52 and the commentary of John Erghome described Edward in the period between 1340 and 1360 as libidinous. Erghome, elaborating on the qualities of Taurus the bull, commented that he would only relinquish the pastures he had won (Edward's French territory) during the mating season, and suggested that Edward after Crecy became a changeable bull: charmed by Diana's empty words he loses all the alchemical sheen associated with Taurus as *Staurus* and *Aurum* and becomes merely a bestial bull: Diana wiggles her backside and the bull throws his testicles at the wild Diana.[47] Diana partly represents Edward's wife who distracted him from his French pastures, but for this Franciscan with alchemical interest, she also stands for the two-horned goddess of the moon or mercury; and Erghome reveals his prejudices in favour of sulphur and the sun to suggest that when the bull succumbs to Diana's secret longings he is becoming feminized (in the late Middle Ages excessive sexuality was believed to drain a man's masculinity) and losing his identity as the sun king. In specific terms Erghome suggested that Edward was becoming like Samson to Delilah and David to Bathsheba, and offered a general condemnation of the morals of the king's household at the time of the siege of Calais. Erghome, like the alchemical writers of this period, made an explicit connection between the health of the king and his land, and this was the secret of the philosopher's stone, the grail; but the sinister corollary to this holistic philosophy was the consequences for the king's people when his morality and spiritual health deteriorated. Erghome goes so far as to attribute the horrors of The Black Death, which arrived in English shores in 1348 and again in 1361 and 1368, to the king's weakness in pursuing Diana in all her forms. It was not the sins of the people that brought about this terrifying divine retribution but the sins of the king.[48] In religious terms the chosen people were being punished because of the sins of David; but the Black Death was a medical, alchemical phenomenon in which the destructive powers of sulphur or the unicorn were unleashed. Edward's defiantly brave decision to hold the inaugural feast of the Order of the Garter on 23 April 1349 in the middle of this terrible epidemic is full of ironies: here was a select society of Grail knights, bearing some similarity to the brotherhood in Eschenbach's *Parsifal,* dedicated to the quest for the Grail or the philosopher's stone, which in the alchemical texts written and copied for Edward III is the pursuit of a morality that acknowledges the close connection between the physical and spiritual health of the monarch and his land; and yet they are plighted to honour an oath proclaiming the king's defiance of this truth. In the following decade Edward continued to defy his critics and carry his challenging motto through military campaigns that culminated in victory at Poitiers in 1356 and the capture of the French king. By 1361, at the Treaty of Bretigny, Edward was at the zenith of his power as ruler of an empire in Northern France that included Gascony and Normandy. However to his critics these successes were achieved in spite of his private sins, not a manifestation of his will, and this treaty, which marks the end of Edward's campaign of conquests and his acting out the role of a martial hero following the footsteps of Alexander and Arthur, was followed by a period of military inertia widely attributed to Edward's licentiousness. Sir Thomas Gray of Heaton in Northumberland and warden of Norham Castle, while a prisoner of the Scots 1355–9, wrote a history of England up to the reign of Edward III, the *Scalacronicon*, in which he suggested that Edward's motive in securing peace at Bretigny was carnal desire; the king subsequently failed to maintain his rights and found pleasure in sensuality. Gray adopted a prophetic tone saying 'God will not allow one to enjoy blessings because of filth of sin just as he prevented Moses from entering the Promised Land' and he implied that pleasure of the flesh and self-inflation prevented Edward's triumphal march into the promised land of Rheims where he could have been crowned king of France.[49]

Edward was aged 50 at the Treaty of Bretigny, and the last phase of his reign was marked by increasing senility and military inertia. For the alchemist this was a predictable natural phenomenon expressed in the primeval, pagan myth of an ageing God or sun in need of renewal, which Dastin had outlined. This archetype would surface again; and now hopes were placed on Edward III's son and heir, the Black Prince. The Bridlington poet, in one of his revisions, predicted that the bull will give way to Gallus, the cockerel, or the Black Prince who will be the new Arthur, the king of France and emperor. Erghome, reflecting on the post Bretigny disenchantment felt by his patron Humphrey de Bohun, drew on his medical knowledge to provide a commentary in which he pointed out that the song of the cockerel or the Black prince will bring hope after days of night, just as the cockerel applied to a fevered brow eases the pain of the sick.[50] Even Edward's friend, Henry duke of Lancaster, celebrating the life-giving power of red sulphur or the resurrected Christ, used this same symbol of the bleeding cock placed on the head of one in a feverish frenzy. Edward's eldest son continued to achieve military success up to the Battle of Najera in 1367; but during this Castilian campaign he became ill, probably from anal fistulas, developed from years of horse riding, and by 1370 he was terminally ill, suffering regular rectal haemorrhages. His demise was accompanied

by an acceptance that the Alexandrine dream was over: Walsingham in his obitu-
ary on the Black Prince reflected that 'as is said of Alexander the Great he attacked
no nation that he did not defeat'.[51] His final end was accompanied by rumours of
occult, malign forces: John Gilbert, bishop of Bangor 1372–75 said: 'I think some
evil spirits are present who are obstructing his speech' and he sprinkled holy water
in the four corners of the home where the prince was lying.[52] The prince died on 8
June 1376, perhaps in the care of John Ardene, a physician with court connections
and the author in this same year of a treatise on fistula.[53] The wound in the region
of the genitals that will not heal recalled the accounts of the romances of Chretien
de Troyes' *Perceval* (c. 1190) and Wolfram von Eschenbach's *Parsival* (1210) of the
Fisher King incapacitated by a wound in the genitals that both reflected and caused
the sterility of his kingdom.

By 1369 the failing health of the Black Prince's father was well known. Edward
III was treated by his physician, John Glaston, for what was probably a series of
strokes that impaired his mental faculties. By 1375 the convention was developed
that the chamberlain of the royal household was entitled to endorse petitions
received at court with roles purporting to be the king's wishes. This suggests
Edward had become a mere cipher and both courtiers and court officials maintained a fiction of strong kingship until his death on 2 June 1377. The king's
wooden effigy, probably a death mask, bore a twisted face associated with a final
stroke. As he lapsed into senility Edward began to resemble the Fisher king of
these grail myths, one who had held onto power too long, presiding over a wasteland subject to plagues (there were serious outbreaks in 1361 and 1369), military
inertia and political unrest culminating in the Good Parliament of 1376. In medical terms this would have been an entirely predictable result of the ageing process:
in his *Secreta secretorum* there is the following warning: 'O high King in all ways
keep and hold study your natural heat for as long as there is temperate heat in
man and natural moisture not passing the heat is tempered and strengthened and
healthy restored.'[54] In the library of Edward III's son, Thomas Woodstock, duke of
Gloucester, were the regimen containing theories about the principles of age and
decay that were based on alchemy. In the encyclopaedias of the natural world
summarizing the science and natural history known to western Europe: *de Proprietatibus rerum* (*On the Properties of Things*) written by Bartholomeus Anglicus
(1203–72) the Franciscan scholar of Paris, who claimed that all metals came from
mercury; and the *Speculum Naturale* of Vincent of Beauvais (c. 1190–1264?), the
Dominican friar who compiled encyclopaedias for Louis XI, are outlined the
theory that the first principle of alchemy, transmutation through heat, occurs
throughout life and is the means by which life is sustained and destroyed. Through
the process of digestion of food, heat produces the four humours. But this heat is
also the means by which the humours are changed and this is the key to the ageing process. The Arab physician, Avicenna, likened it to the burning of oil in a

lamp. The first state of life is *adolescentia,* dominated by cold, wet phlegm, a feminine stage in men. Heat converts this into hot, wet blood, the state of *iuventis* when a man is in his prime. Blood is then turned into hot, dry choler, the state of *senectutis* when the body begins to decline but without loss of power or manhood. However finally choler is converted through heat into a cold, dry, black bile, the humour that predominates in old age when a loss of power and manhood occurs.

There was a political dimension to these theories for they apply to the body politic.[55] As Edward changed from the young Alexander, with his humours perfectly balanced and with an abundance of natural heat and vigour, the country was prosperous and successful. As this heat, the source of all his strength, dries him into senility the land too ages and becomes a withered wasteland awaiting a youthful redeemer. The loss of heat (the very basis of masculinity) also reduces a man to an increasingly feminine, phlegmatic, watery state, and this process it was believed could be accelerated through susceptibility to women. Edward's susceptibility to women would then accelerate the process of feminization. The Black Prince's monthly outbursts of anal bleeding had inevitable associations with menstruation, feminization and divine retribution. Edward's death, a year after his son's, occurred in similar circumstances after he suffered a bowel complaint. A reminder that old age and infirmity had tarnished Edward's image in way that had never happened to the model of his youth, Alexander, occurred in the 1371 scandal at the court over what was seen as the undue influence of Alice Perrors, who had replaced the queen in Edward's bed in the 1360s and who bore him three illegitimate children and had begun to inspire in the old king disgust by what he perceived to be her increasingly malign influence.[56] The king's mistress was seen as a witch who represented Edward's turning away from the legitimate alchemical wisdom represented by Aristotle, the purported author of the *Secreta secretorum,* to the illicit, occult arts that the young Alexander had rejected. She was given a high profile trial in a civil court (such cases prompted Pope Gregory XI to issue a letter in August 1374 asserting the right of the Inquisition to intervene in cases of magic and invoking demons). Alice was banished from the king's court, accused of ensnaring the king, enticing him into an illicit love affair by magic with the assistance of a Dominican friar who pretended to be a physician, but who was in fact an evil magician who made a wax effigy of the king and Alice and used an ancient incantation attributed to the onetime tutor to Alexander, the Egyptian necromancer, Nectantibus.[57] By these means they enticed an old man into an insane love affair, sinful enough in a young man, which sapped his elderly body of all its strength and natural vitality; using magical herbs and incantations the witch Alice was able to engage in wanton sexual coupling with the king so that he spent his last years in senility, doing nothing but hawking and hunting which hastened the end of his life.[58] She also had devised rings that caused forgetfulness and remembrance, just as Moses had done, so that as long as the king wore them he would never forget the harlot. The friar was arrested on the orders of the duke of Lancaster and placed under the guardianship of the Dominicans. Erghome implied that there was an occult, diabolical origin to Edward's libidinous behaviour when he suggested that the bull had been overcome by lechery caused by the devil working on behalf of the king's enemies; and the accusations made against Edward's mistress, Alice Perrors, of witchcraft suggest that the king's ailing health and waning powers were also being linked to diabolic sources.

There was, however, in court circles a perception that the fatal bleeding that created the wasteland may have had older origins than these scandals. Despite the length of the king's reign and long passage of time since the events of 1342 there were some in court circles who attributed the king's decline to his original sin, his rape of the countess of Salisbury. Froissart, who visited Windsor in 1395, continued to adapt his chronicles in book one covering the years 1325–78 while in the English court to allude to this incident:[59] in one version Edward pursues the countess in a game of chess; this shows that the incident was far from forgotten.[60] The Cheshire poet of Richard II's court, the author of *Pearl, Patience* and *Purity,* placed in his *Sir Gawain and the Green Knight,* a tale of sexual desire, chivalry, betrayal and regeneration, a number of clues that would direct his audience to the circumstances surrounding Edward III's founding of the Order of the Garter. The manuscript of this work is dated 1375–1400, and Froissart visited the English Court in 1362–69 and 1395, bringing with him Le Bel's account of the rape with him. The date of the composition of *Sir Gawain and the Green Knight* can only be assigned with certainty to after 1362, when Edward III's son, Lionel, was created duke of Clarence (who is referred to in the text).[61] Internal evidence makes it most likely that it was written around the same time as the other poems in the manuscript, sometime in the 1390s when it would be safe to make some critical allusions to Edward III.[62] The central motif of *Sir Gawain and the Green Knight* is the pentangle, the most frequently occurring symbol in Edward III's copy of the *Secreta secretorum,* and there was a political dimension to this alchemical, occult tale that encouraged readers to apply the concept of the endless knot (the Gawain poet's description of the Pentangle) to the English monarchy which appeared so fragile in the 1370s.

The identification in this poem of Gawain with Edward III, who in miniatures in Walter Milemete's *De nobilitatibus sapientiis et prudencium regem* is shown as the lover knight identified with Christ, receiving his arms in a symbolic representation of good verses evil, and as the knight storming the castle of love, is supplied in the author's provision to the conclusion of his work of the motto of Edward's Order of the Garter, a society of 26 knights bound together with knots of gold. By drawing attention to this motto the poet signified his intention to show in this tale of attempted seduction, sexual temptation and betrayal of the ideals of friendship, chivalry and hospitality, that this would act as a distorted mirror image of Edward's relationship with the earl and countess of Salisbury (who took a vow of chastity after the death of her husband and died (ironically) on the day of the institution of the Order of the Garter on 23 April, 'probably of the Plague'. By drawing attention to this motto the author offered a critical gloss on the rather crude philosophy behind it. Edward may have proclaimed his intention to brazen out a shameful act; but the Gawain poet, by celebrating the regenerative forces of nature represented by the Green Knight, was being careful to avoid celebrating the power of evil for evil's sake, and offering a more subtle, scientific rationale behind this motto and all it implied, to suggest that good and evil, in the eyes of nature, are one and the same thing. This is one of the central principles of alchemy. The Gawain poet was attempting to forestall a crude attempt to celebrate the successes achieved through the display of this motto and to show, through his plot, that Edward did commit a sin, for which in the long run he and his kingdom would pay the consequences. He achieves this by reversing the original attempted seduction by the king of the countess, and has Gawain subjected to three attempts at seduction and temptation by the wife of his host, Bertilak, who comes into Gawain's bedchamber uninvited, and even asks him to take her by force. Gawain succumbs to the sexual test only so far as stealing kisses, which he acknowledges to his host; but when he stealthily accepts her girdle (an echo of the garter worn by Edward and his Garter knights) as a magic talisman, he becomes, according to the Green Knight, guilty of a form of lust by desiring to preserve his life 'for care of thy knokke . . . for ye lufest your lyf'.[63] The Green Knight's assertion that sex and lust are a manifestation of the life urge is at one with St Augustine's claim that the desire to conquer and dominate are all part of the male sexual urge,[64] and this amounts to an acknowledgment of the point Edward made when he took his garter and motto to France to claim his kingdom. Gawain leaves his hostess, wearing her green girdle around his waist, baldric fashion, to protect him in his encounter with her husband, the Green Knight. When he returns back to Camelot he wears the girdle to remind him that his desire for life is a legacy of the frailty of his flesh, and this inspires his excessive self-recrimination of his lustfulness:

the faut and the fayntyse of the flesch crabbed
How tender hit is to entye teches of
fylfth.[65]

All the rest of Arthur's round table knights follow him and wear a green sash baldric wise. Edward and his chosen garter knights similarly wore a blue ribbon with gold beading below the left knee and a sash of dark blue (the colour of the Virgin), which they took with them into battle in France. Edward's garter, and the defiant motto broadcasting the king's shame (the very words used, according to

Le Bel, by the earl of Salisbury to describe Edward's conduct) also acted as a protective totem. However the Gawain poet was also able to demonstrate that Gawain succeeded where Edward had failed by resisting the attempted seduction by the wife of Bertilak and remaining loyal to his host. The slight wound inflicted on his neck by the Green Knight's axe on the day of the Feast of the Circumcision (when Christ's blood was shed in token of man's original sin)[66] was to remind him of his sin in succumbing to lust in the more general sense of attempting to preserve his life; but it also alludes to the fatal wound of the Fisher King, the mortal sinner, Edward III, a point reinforced by the fact that this mock beheading scene occurs in a place called Hautedesert, the wasteland surrounding the Green chapel.

Even if the hints in this work of Edward III's sin may have only been recognized by those courtiers like Froissart who had inside knowledge; in a more general sense this poem suggests that England in the 1370s, under its maimed Fisher king and even sicklier heir apparent, has become a wasteland awaiting the regeneration signified by the alchemical motifs: a beheading that cannot prevent the triumphant emergence of the green man and the coming of spring. Some indication of the expectations surrounding the idea of the regeneration of the kingdom represented by the concept of the green man can be seen in the proliferation of green man carvings in wood and stone in cathedrals and churches throughout England in the late fourteenth century. Lincoln Cathedral has 12 green man misericords dating from the late fourteenth century; a Chester Cathedral misericord of 1396 shows a green man with a crown of oak leaves; in Winchester Cathedral there are wood carvings of heads sprouting vegetation and 20 to 50 full-length green men in the choir stalls dating back to the 1370s. The most poignant example of a green man carving in this period, which in political terms indicates the hopes and expectations placed on the eight-year-old son of the Black Prince, is the ceiling boss showing the green man in the Black prince's chantry in a crypt in Canterbury Cathedral.[67]

8

Richard II the Magus and Boy King

Take Solomon king son of David the gift the lord sent thee, the highest Sabaoth with it thou shalt lock up all demons of the earth, male and female; and with their help thou shalt build up Jerusalem

Testament of Solomon.[1]

If there was one day in the year of the Julian calendar that had occult significance it was New Year's Day, the 1 January (in the Christian calendar the Feast of the Circumcision) when the new year was born from the old, dying year and when the sun began to renew its strength.[2] On this day it was believed magic, supernatural events occurred, such as the encounter between Sir Gawain and the Green Knight (warnings against the practice of witchcraft, the deceptions of sorcery and the exchange of gifts on New Year were issued in such sermon collections as the *Festiall* a work of the Shropshire canon John Mirk c. 1382–90 and *Speculum sacerdotale* c. 1424).[3] The pagan new year was shortly followed by another event in the Church calendar, the Feast of the Epiphany on 6 January, when, according the Gospel of Mathew, three magi (wise men, astronomers or magicians) from the East (probably Persia) were guided by a star that miraculously appeared in the heavens, guiding them to Bethlehem, where a newly born baby was proclaimed to be the king of all men and the son of God. These magi, according to Tertullian writing in the first century AD, were all kings, and they presented the child and his mother, the Virgin Mary, with gifts of gold, frankincense and myrrh. Their bodies were believed to be buried in Cologne Cathedral where Edward III was declared vicar general of the empire in 1338. The key elements in this myth: magicians and kings from the East paying homage to a child, a lamb who would redeem the world and be king of all men, and the presentation of gifts of gold, would acquire alchemical significance in court circles when, on the Feast of Epiphany 6 January 1369 a child was born to the Black Prince and Joan princess of Kent (thereby sharing the sign of Capricorn with Jesus Christ) and baptized John, in St Andrew's Cathedral, Bordeaux, and subsequently christened Richard. Among the little prince's godparents were two aspirant kings visiting the court of the Black Prince: Jamie IV titular king of Majorca (1336–75), and his main supplanter Richard King of Armenia (after whom Richard was named); and it is likely that Pedro, the defeated king of Castile, attended the ceremony too as he was in exile in Bordeaux at the time.[4]

From his earliest year Richard was not allowed to forget the momentous circumstances of his birth; and the significance of the Feast of the Epiphany was emphasized when he acceded to the throne on 22 June 1367 on the eve of the vigil of the Feast of St John the Baptist on 24 June. Chancellor Adam Houghton, bishop of St Davis's, alluded to the Epiphany story in his opening address to parliament in June 1377 when Richard was presented as Prince of Wales; the chancellor urged his listeners to honour the prince as the three kings had honoured the son of God by bringing gifts of gold, frankincense and myrrh. Throughout his reign Richard was encouraged to identify with the three magi who were guided by occult knowledge and even to identify with the object of the magi's devotion, the infant Christ. In 1384 an alchemist John Doubelay, who was probably also a minor crown official, based an alchemical treatise the *Stella alchemiae*, dedicated to the king, on the motif of the star guiding the wise men; this was also the five pointed star, representing the four elements and the quintessence and the five fold star of David formed by the planets at the birth of Christ. In 1393, on The Feast of the Epiphany, Richard was presented with a dromedary ridden by a boy. In 1396 an ambassador of the king of France, Philippe de Mezieres, a French soldier, crusader and writer who had travelled to Jerusalem, addressed Richard in correspondence as a lodestar that always pointed to the Pole Star, or North Star, known as the Star of the Virgin.[5] In the same year Richard was portrayed on the inner panels of a portable altar for his personal use as one of the three kings (the others were St Edmund, king of East Anglia martyred at the hands of the Vikings in 869, and Edward the Confessor) kneeling before the Virgin and the infant Christ, and presented by Richard's patron saint, John the Baptist, whose initials were embroidered on a gown made for the king in Christmas 1386.[6] Each year, on the Feast of the Epiphany, Richard made oblations of gold, frankincense and myrrh, and the names of the three kings: Jasper, Melbese and Balthese were engraved on a ewer in the king's ownership at the time of his deposition. The themes of the Epiphany: power and magic from the East; the role of the king as magician with divine powers and insight; and the importance of the hermit, the Baptist, as herald of the coming of Christ, emerged to define the public image of Richard as *alchemicus rex* throughout his reign.

The coronation service too helped to define the tone of Richard's kingship and emphasized the importance of the king as *alchemicus rex*. The blessing prayer, used at the coronation and subsequent anointings, is replete with adjectives and metaphors capable of alchemical interpretation and which would acquire additional occult resonance during the course of the reign, and especially when Richard attempted to persuade the archbishop of Canterbury to reanoint him with the holy oil of St Thomas of Canterbury in 1397: 'Look down omnipotent God on thy glorious king . . . irrigate and bathe him in thy *potency* . . . Grant him the *dew of heaven* and *fullness of earth* . . . so that while he reigns their may be healthfulness of body . . . unbroken peace in the kingdom . . . grant that the glorious dignity of the royal hall may shine before the eyes of all with the greatest splendour of *kingly power* so that it may seem to glow with brightest ray'.[7] The *De primis regalibus ornamentis Regni Angliae* (c. 1387–89) on the ancient origins and sacramental meaning of the regalia, written c. 1387–89 by a Benedictine monk of Westminster Abbey, William Sudbury, at Richard's request, shows how in this ceremony he had been set apart from ordinary mortals in the archbishop's prayer and blessing and exhorted to follow the example of Solomon and rule in peace and prove worthy 'to reign with the saviour of the world whose likeness he bears in the name of the king'.[8] Richard's divine status was further proclaimed in the coronation ceremony when he was anointed on the head and shoulders behind a gold cloth, and the archbishop of Canterbury placed a crown on his head saying: 'God crown you with the crown of glory'; he was then given a pall depicting four angels, representing the four corners of the earth subject to divine power, and invested with the insignia of dominion: a sword to protect the kingdom; a sceptre rising to a round golden ball with an image of the cross on tip; the rod with a dove on the top for the correction of error; and the ring of his ancestors.[9] These were also the tools of the magician: the sword and rod represented occult power, and the ring was reputed to be the ring given by Edward the Confessor to a beggar who turned out to be John the Evangelist who gave the ring to two English pilgrims to the Holy Land, charging them to return it to the king. This ring was associated with the visionary powers transmitted from St John the Evangelist (in Medieval mythology the vision of the apocalypse and the new Jerusalem was believed to have been experienced by St John the Evangelist on Patmos while slumbering on Christ's bosom) to Edward the Confessor in the exchange of rings.[10] The coronation regalia meant so much to Richard that when he made his will before setting out for Ireland for the last time in 1399 he requested that if his body were snatched from the sight of men by hurricane or tempests he should be laid to rest with his crown and sceptre and with a precious ring on his finger. The impact of this ceremony on Richard was shown in November 1388 when he conferred a gift of a gold ring set with a ruby to the Confessor's shrine, and he recalled the confessor's day when he received the anointing. Richard vowed to leave this ring at the shrine whenever he left the realm.[11] Further alchemical symbolism employed at the coronation included the hollowed out marble column in the middle of the royal palace erected for the coronation banquet; on top of the column was an eagle and from under its feet flowed red and white wines in four directions.[12] It was during this period of the coronation that William Sudbury composed *De regalibus ornamentis* in which he discussed the coronation regalia as the means by which the king takes on a royal dignity above all rules and honours in the world. Sudbury also stressed that this regalia represented the sacred kingship of Edward the Confessor and guaranteed the privileges of the abbey. They became for the king important symbols of the royal prerogative as represented in his portrait in Westminster Abbey. When he entered London with his bride, Anne of Bohemia, he was greeted by angels and the conduits of Cheapside flowed with red and white wine to suggest that his kingship and marriage was the fulfilment of an alchemical conjunction of mercury and sulphur. Similar symbolism was deployed in 1387 after the conclusion of the period of conciliar rule when Richard and his queen entered London and were greeted by the mayor wearing red and white.[13]

Throughout his reign Richard sought the spark of divine powers from these sources evoked by the feast of Epiphany which were also in tune with late fourteenth-century devotional trends. His close identification with John the Baptist, who foretold the coming of Christ and whose feast was celebrated on 7 January after Epiphany, was probably also inspired by the popularity of hermits and recluses in the fourteenth century who were perceived to inhabit realms outside society and therefore had access to a spirituality and powers that were not accessible to those holding positions within traditional power structures of society.[14] Richard chose to be represented in his personal altar alongside the Baptist bearing the lamb, and at times of crisis, for instance before meeting the peasants in 1381, he would consult the Westminster anchorite, John of London. Richard had a keen interest in the history of the British monarchy and he looked for inspiration not to warrior kings, like Edward I or his grandfather Edward III, but to saintly ancestors who conformed to the image of the three magi; and in the *Wilton Diptych* he is represented as one of the three kings alongside St Edmund King and Martyr and Edward the Confessor (who died on 5 January, the eve of Richard's birthday) and who was reputed to be a visionary. This close identification with saintly kings is also related to fourteenth-century religious trends among courtiers who sought consolation and inspiration from saintly holy men, confessors and martyrs, men of special holiness, charisma and insight, who were mediums for divine power.

Richard's fascination with magic, holiness and power is reflected in his love of the objects with which these are associated and the ceremonies of kingship which took on a supernatural significance for him. On Easter Sunday, 1396, he gave to York Minster a gift of the relics of the Holy Innocents enclosed in a silver reliquary: his visit and gift was commemorated by a carving of a white hart. In 1397 he discovered in the tower of London a gold eagle enclosing a stone amphilla of oil used to anoint Edward the Confessor, which the Virgin was supposed to have given to St Thomas of Canterbury and which had been hidden at Poitiers until its discovery by Henry duke of Lancaster. Writing found around the eagle proclaimed that all who wore the eagle around the neck would achieve prosperity and victory, and one king, anointed with this oil, would prove to be the greatest of kings: he would build many churches in the Holy Land and drive out the Pagans from Babylon; and while he bore this eagle on his breast he would prosper; From this time Richard would always wear the eagle around his neck.[15] This legend of the holy oil loomed large in Richard's imagination, perhaps echoing the grail like relics discovered by the British king of the prophecy of the angel, which signified the redemption of the kingdom, a point made when Richard unsuccessfully tried to persuade the archbishop of Canterbury to reanoint him. Richard's fascination with regal objects that had a magical aura for him is shown in the Westminster Abbey Chronicler's account of an evening in January 1385 when Richard took Leo VI of Lusignan, the last king of (little) Armenia (which had been in Turkish hands since 1371) and who had been exiled since 1382 and was mediating between England and France as a necessary preliminary to a crusade, to see the crown jewels in Westminster Abbey. Splendidly arrayed and creeping around by candle light, the kingly pair gazed at the insignia which Richard had worn at this coronation and peered at the abbey's collection of relics. When he entertained visitors in 1398 he proudly took them on a tour of his palace and showed them the various jewels and holy objects in his possession.[16]

The king or magus that Richard most self-consciously attempted to emulate was King Solomon of the *Testament of Solomon* (preserved from around the first century AD and based on traditions not found in the Bible but in a work from around 400 BC which had been invoked by Christ). This Solomon was not only wise but a magician: while working on his temple he was plagued by demons and the archangel, Michael, sent him a ring of magic by which he was able to control the demons and compel them to build the temple.[17] In the *Book of Kings* the Lord appeared to Solomon in a dream saying: 'what shall I give you Solomon', and Solomon replied: 'give thy servant therefore an understanding mind to govern thy people that I may discern between good and evil; for I am able to govern thy great people'. The Lord was pleased Solomon asked this and said: 'because you have not asked for a long life and riches and the life of enemies I shall give you a wise discerning mind so that no-one like you has been seen before you and none like you shall come after you. The Lord also gives him what he has not asked for, riches and honour, so that no king can compare with him'.[18] This was seen in the late middle ages as an alchemical allegory: the alchemist's quest is wisdom and understanding and the incidental benefits included a long life and gold, and the implications were that any king who followed Solomon would achieve all this.

Richard's library did not survive the Lancastrian revolution and evidence for his learning and wisdom is therefore fragmentary, but it does point towards his self-image as a Solomonic magus. Copies of the Bible, the *Roman de la rose* (which contains a section on alchemy) and a *Romance of Gawain* were purchased for him in 1379.[19] Contemporary models for Richard's interest in such things were his two fathers-in-law Charles V, king of France, who had a library of 1,000 books, 10 per cent of which were on alchemy, geomancy, necromancy and related occult matters and Charles IV, king of Bohemia and the Holy Roman emperor, who is depicted as the third magi in an Adoration scene on the ceiling of Karlstein Holy rood chapel in Bohemia.[20] Charles owned a large library of texts on alchemy, astrology, geomancy and related arts and was a dedicatee of one version of the pseudo Lullian *Testamentum novissima*.[21] He became Richard's father-in-law in 1384, and it is pos-sible that John Doubelay, an alchemist who was to write the *Practica et libris Mag-istri Ortolani* in 1386, and who can perhaps be identified with the crown servant involved in a number of transactions in the 1380s,[22] intended his *Stella alchemiae* (*The Star of Alchemy*) as a wedding present to the couple. The influence of Bohe-mian court culture on the couple can be seen in 1393 when, at Richard's command, the wardens of London Bridge, in imitation of the statue of Wenceslaus IV put up in the 1380s on the façade of the bridge tower in the old town of Prague, erected two freestone statutes of Richard II and his queen above the stone gates of London Bridge. Some allusion to the *Vision of John Dastin* may also have been intended, for this vision concerns a marriage of a young, pure king to a queen, identified with the moon, who is of imperial birth. Dedicated, according to the explicit, on 26 April 1384 to Richard II, who is described as a Solomon, the *Stella alchemiae* evokes the symbol of the star to suggest Richard is one of the magi of the Epiphany story and is constructed around the symbol of the pentangle representing the four elements and the quintessence.[23] An allusion to the vision of John Dastin may also be intended in the use of the symbol of the star. In this vision the beautiful king, pure of com-plexion and void of deformity, was 'among the planets in heaven Stellefied'. Doube-lay fuses alchemical and regal symbolism to appeal to the king. The stone will multiply to infinity when it is dissolved in the original water of the Blessed Mary: the four elements are separated, rejoined, and reduced and finally brought together and multiplied to infinity and then you have the 'fugitive servant' or fugitive 'stag', a king reigning over a hundred thousand nations, that is to say the turning of a hun-dred thousand part of every metal into his nature. The stone, therefore, is identified with mercury, the original water, which is female, and with the Virgin; and it is a hermaphrodite, holding within itself the conjunction of sulphur and mercury, the male sun and female moon. The discussion of the process by which the application of heat distils the pure spirit employs the imagery of the royal court. Spirit, distilled through suffering, after a process of death and putrefaction, ascends as a king into heaven, crowned with a diadem. This distilled essence will subjugate all nations and never be destroyed. The *Stella alchemiae* promises to its royal patron that mercury, 'King Mercurius',[24] manifested in such symbols as: the fugitive servant, the fugitive stag (based on the Latin pun *fugitivus cervus* or *fugitivus servus*)[25] and the pearl, will be a source of moral, spiritual and earthly power. The philosopher's stone, or mer-cury, is defined as 'that thing which kings carry in their heads; and through which men are gathered together and kings are slain'.[26] Mercury is closely identified with the king because both are subjected to various forms of humiliation and torture: they are chained, martyred servants of man and victorious conquerors because they are imperishable: resurrected they will be transformed into pure gold. The central motifs of the *Stella alchemiae*: the original maternal water of mercury described as the Blessed Virgin; the notion of the hermaphrodite; and the triumph of the spirit through suffering and resurrection, would surface in Richard's public persona.

Another work confirming Richard's desire to be perceived as a magus, a Solomon, is the only surviving manuscript commissioned by him. It was completed for the king in March 1391 and presented to him at Bristol. This is a book of divination containing various works on the occult arts. Most of the volume is dedicated to a treatise on geomancy which begins with an initialled portrait of Richard.[27] Another portrait of a king bearing a resemblance to Richard occurs in the illustration of the geomantic house of *Fortuna major*.[28] Dedications cannot be used as sole criteria in establishing that kings read and consulted such works; but this book is crucial in establishing that the king's reputation for involvement in the occult was correct: it was especially designed for easy use and the king had another copy made in the fourteenth year of his reign; and this one is more legible and may have been intended for regular use.[29] The prologue explains that the author, who acknowledges a debt to William of Moeberke, the translator of Aristotle from the Greek whose geomancy was written c. 1226, has 'compiled this present book of geomancy in as brief a form as I was able, at the special request of our most excellent Lord Richard, the most noble king of the realms of England and France'. Geomancy is necessary for a king, the author maintains, for the better governance of his people because it harnesses the hidden powers within the earth and the self that govern human destiny. In a preceding work in the volume, *De Quadripartita regis specie*, on the occult principles behind good government, it is maintained that 'nothing is more precious to a king than prudence and foresight ... for in these things he is more ornamented than in gold vestments pearls or precious jewels. These are his kingdoms crown and glory through which foresight he acquires divine aid'.[30] One obvious source of such power is the heavens and a king was expected to consult astrologers; but the tract on geomancy enables a king to unlock these powers within himself: 'since this science of astrology is both great difficulty and is time consuming to learn for which the present life is scarcely sufficient I have compiled this present little book of geomancy, not for my own uses, but for the rules and precepts of established authors; and this art is a way of unlocking the secrets of the heavens without the precise mathematical knowledge required by astrology or dependence on elaborate information of the movement of the heavens'. All that was required was that the king makes marks in wet sand when contemplating a problem or decision (the compiler disapproved of the use of parchment, paper or wax tablets). The prologue to Richard's Geomancy makes a distinction between the influences on the rational soul of the celestial bodies, angelic forms that are the source of celestial wisdom, and the occult powers within the earth, both of which can inform the movement of the hand when forming a geomantic image. Geomancy is a terrestrial astrology based on the forces of odd and even and the four elements, simple mathematical principles

based on the alchemical perspective that the world is governed by the opposites of
mercury and sulphur, which gives rise to 12 anthropomorphized shapes, similar to
the 12 signs of the zodiac, which are used to explain the mysteries of personality
and fate: the hidden forces at work when a decision is being made that involves the
interaction of the four earthly elements and the signs of the zodiac that make up an
individual personality. These forces, if harnessed by a king, should considerably
enhance his will: 'he wol through this little book obtain the naked truth about the
thing sought'.[31]

Richard's Geomancy presupposes that the king was learned in the basic principles of geomancy, for no instructions are provided on how the houses made up of
individual dots are formed. Richard must have depended on this tract heavily (two
copies were made, one for his regular use and another more elaborately illustrated
and elegantly written) for there is no evidence that he had the sort of astrological
expertise of King Charles V of France, for whom as astrological treatise was written
at his request by his friend and counsellor, Nicole Oresme, bishop of Lisieux
(c. 1323–82), the mathematician, physicist and astronomer who provided French
translations of his own works which included *Livre du ciel et du Monde* in which he
proposed a theory of the rotation of the earth, and translations of the works of
Aristotle;[32] but Richard's interest in astrology was attested by ownership of two
hororary quadrants engraved with images of the white hart; his mother, Joan,
owned an astronomical calendar made for her in 1380 by John Somer, a Franciscan
friar; [33] and Richard named his greyhound Mathis, after the fourth-century astronomer, Julius Matheis, who was rediscovered in the West in the eleventh century.
Richard's interest in astrology and geomancy may account for Chaucer's treatise on
the *Astrolabe* in 1391 in which he praises 'the king that is lord of this language', and
in his *Equatorie of Planets* in 1393 Chaucer explains why he was interrupted on his
work on *Canterbury Tales* to write these two technical treatises.[34] This was during
the period that the king ordered the production of the *Liber Judicum Geomancie.*

Another source of hidden knowledge and power was dreams, and included in
Richard's book of divination was a treatise on the interpretation of dreams popular in the late Middle Ages which was attributed to Daniel.[35] The inspiration for
the inclusion of this treatise in the volume may have been Richard's tutor, Sir
Simon Burley, whose library inventory of 1388 included copies of this work in
French. The origins of dreams are explained in terms of disturbances in the body
caused by superfluity of humours: for example dreams dominated by the colour
black were caused by bile, and dreams in which the colour red predominated were
initiated by choler. Dreams were further believed to be influenced by the time of
the day and position of the planets; but special significance was given to those
dreams that provided special insight into the future when the soul, during sleep,
enters a supernatural domain that the individual inhabits before birth and after
death when it is granted knowledge of the future in the form of allegorical dreams.

Some of the dreams and their interpretations would have had resonance for a king: to dream of a shadow on the sun spelt danger to the king; and dreams of whiteness, such as a white horse or white, shining clothes, signified joy and perhaps anticipated some of the imagery of the *Wilton Diptych*.

The theme running through this book of divination is that such occult knowledge acquired through the practices of geomancy, alchemy, physiognomy and interpretation of dreams, is essential for a king who wishes to rule by following the example of Solomon; and this is emphasized in the opening tract, *De Quadripartita Regis Specie*, a tract on good government based on occult principles which is a compendium of the wisdom necessary for a king compiled by one describing himself as 'the most humble servant of the treasury of Ireland during the reign of Richard II'. This was possibly John Thorpe (d. 1401), archdeacon of Suffolk. Thorpe was appointed treasurer of the exchequer in Ireland from 4 October 1394 until 1397,[36] was connected with Richard's physician, Richard Medford of King's Hall[37] and was imprisoned by the Lords appellant in January 1388. The author may however have been a minor official or more loosely the smallest coin of the king's treasure in Ireland. Describing himself as a 'well wisher of an innocent exile whose rehabilitation would be my consolation' he can be considered among Richard's exiled friends in Ireland.[38] *De Quadripartita Regis Specie* contains a compilation of such proverbial wisdom attributed to Solomon as: 'Wisdom is better than rubies and all things that may be desired can not be compared to it'; and 'the lord by wisdom hath founded the earth and by understanding he hath enabled the heavens'. It also contained extracts from the *Secreta secretorum*, including a tract on physiognomy which was advocated as the scientific basis for the selection of counsellors. Instructions were provided to help the king to read men's characters in their faces; the face is described as a book which can be read, and above all the prince must be able to read the significance of the shape and colour of eyes as a physician does.[39] The theme of this tract is that a king who is skilled in the natural sciences will secure the loyalty and obedience of his people (the theme of Michael Pole first earl of Suffolk's first address to the commons as chancellor and his address to Parliament in 1383 in the aftermath of the Peasant's Revolt). It describes itself as a compilation of the counsels of wise men for the use of the king that 'his wisdom might shine forth the more and all his subjects glory in his intellect, bless his rule and become obedient in all things'. The emphasis on obedience, and the fact that the author was in Ireland in the early 1390s, suggests that he may have had close connections with the royal judges exiled by the Lords appellant. The image of Richard II propagated in this volume is summed up in the prologue to the *Libellus Geomancie*: geomancy 'comes from God himself from whose incomparable wisdom a knowledge of natural things is most graciously bestowed on human beings as a distribution from the divine treasury', and he thus becomes one 'who governs by exalting men learned in both laws as well as men at arms; indeed through very long and arduous acquaintance with astronomy has not declined to taste the sweetness of the fruit of the subtle sciences for the prudent government of himself and his people'.[40] Richard's desire to be seen as a subtle man learned in the arcane arts, emphasized in *De Quadripartita* 'O how precious is the wisdom of the king, dressed in the virtue of prudence'[41] was such that three years later he arranged to have inscribed around his tomb a similar epitaph: 'here lies a Homer …a prudent (in contemporary terms sage) ruler' in contrast to the heroic martial qualities stressed in Edward III's tomb epitaph.[42] Richard's image as the wise king was also recognized when he met John Gower on the Thames and requested that he write some new thing for him. The result was the first version of the encyclopaedic *Confessio amantis.*

The image of Richard as a magi, a king who was in touch with the hidden forces of the earth and capable of performing feats of transmutation, was powerfully expressed by Philippe de Meziere, a crusader and adventurer who had been inspired by a visit to the holy sepulchre in Jerusalem in 1347(which according to the St Albans traveller, Sir John Mandeville, was the centre of the world) to found a military Order of the Passion which had as its insignia the lamb of God. The order's patron, John Holand, earl of Huntingdon and first duke of Exeter and the recipient of Meziere's abridgment of the order's rule,[43] was Richard II's half brother through their mother, Joan.[44] Other members of the order who were closely associated with Richard II included: Thomas Mowbray duke of Norfolk, Edward of Rutland duke of Aumale and his father the duke of York the lord Despenser, and the chamber knights Lewis Clifford, and Simon Felbrig. Meziere had associated with alchemists in Naples in 1345 while in the service of the king of Castile and he was on friendly terms with the young king Adrian, and since 1373, he had been in the service of Charles V, the king of France; and in 1396 he had acted as an ambassador to Charles VI. The presence of French alchemists at Richard's court in this period is attested by Leonardo di Maupery, 'gallo familiari Regis Angliae' an alchemist and another great traveller, who annotated a collection of recipes for the production of mercury (the silver of the moon).[45] It was in this capacity as ambassador to Charles VI that Meziere sent the English king a letter, via Robert the hermit, to Richard's palace at Eltham in July 1395 urging a treaty between the two kingdoms to be cemented with a chaste marriage between the recently widowed Richard and Isabella, Charles VI's infant daughter, which he hoped would culminate in a crusade, the proposal for which was presented in terms of a purging of the sins of the militaristic generation of Edward III: 'then fair brother it will be a fit moment that you and I, for the propitiation of the sins of our ancestors, shall undertake a crusade to succour our fellow Christians the Holy Land first won by the precious blood of the lamb'.[46] The argument of Meziere's letter,[47] claiming to be the result of a dream inspired by the dreams of Daniel and the dream of the three kings of Cologne, is largely couched in medical, alchemical metaphors derived from Albertus Magnus's *De Mineralibus.*[48]

The frozen, northern kingdoms of England and France are locked in a futile and destructive conflict; but their present kings will bring to these cold lands an exotic heat from the East.[49] Charles is depicted as a pure balm, found only in Cairo and formed from the heat of the sun (Egypt was the source of traditions of the divinity of kingship) and the ruby (the stone found in Edward the Confessor's ring, Richard's most prized possession); and Richard is shown to be a precious lodestone or magnet, found only in India (the process of the attraction of one element to another was described in alchemical texts as iron following a magnet).[50] The conjunction of these two kings, both descendents of St Louis, a crusading king whose focus was on the East and the recovery of Jerusalem, will thaw their frozen kingdoms. The letter employs the same symbolism as the nativity story and the *Stella alchemiae* and, anticipating Robert Fludd (1574–1637, the English physician and hermetic philosopher who wrote that the world's poles are within man and that the human body could be in harmony with the magnetic poles),[51] claims that Richard, the lodestone and the diamond, has the power to attract men and turn them towards the pole star, the star of the virgin, which will generate chastity and expel poisons from the hearts to his knights.[52] Such a king, Meziere claims, employing the epiphany language to remind the king of his exalted birth, 'may be found worthy to hear the same blessed song of the angels as the shepherds heard, that is to say that in our days glory may be had to God on high and on earth peace to men of good will'.[53] The light shed by the lodestone and the ruby will, according to the author of this letter, illuminate and rebuild the Holy temple of Jerusalem, the Holy Sepulchre and the entire holy city of Jerusalem; and the schism in the church healed. The balm (Charles VI) and the lodestone (Richard II) are furthermore inspired with the spirit of the wine of the vineyards of Engadi.[54] This wine, made in Cyprus, was sold by the Templars to the king of Jerusalem when it became a kingdom and was made from the grapes of vines originally brought from the Holy Land by the Knights of St John. It had been distilled over four years to emerge from a black oil to become a sweet elixir that will intoxicate the two kings and bring about the fulfilment of Meziere's vision. Meziere, who served Peter of Lusignan king of Cyprus from 1361 to 1369, then addresses 'the mighty king of Great Britain' seated at the table preparing for the conquest of the Holy land, and promises him that he, the lodestone or diamond, with the help of the wine of Engadi will have such power 'that the serpents, that is, those who stand in the way of peace, at the scent of the flowers of the vine will cease to exist'.[55] The vineyard, originally owned by the Knights Templar, was last seen by Ludolph, a priest of Suchen in Westphalia between 1336 and 1341 and was described in his notes on Cyprus, *De Terra Sancta et itinere Ihierosol.*[56] Ludolph, who observed that the vineyard was mentioned in Solomon's *Song of Songs*, described the red and white juices of an elixir, and Meziere's vision suggests that Richard was seen as an Arthurian king feasting with his loyal garter knights on an alchemical elixir, a fusion of the red and white to recover the Grail, the New Jerusalem.

The grail imagery helped Meziere to resolve the conflict he felt over his commitment to Christianity and his involvement in occult practices and beliefs that he struggled with throughout his life. During his service before 1345 to Andrew of Hungary, who succeeded Robert (the Wise) of Anjou as king of Naples, he met alchemists at the Neopolitan court and he was attracted by the astrological practices of this court and was only able to throw them off after long fasting and prayer. He describes two forms of occult practice in the letter; the demonic, melancholy sorcery of the cold north, represented by a fountain emitting dark, troubled waters where free will is replaced by astrology; and the good, natural magic of Albertus Magnus which is legitimate, with no rituals or incantations, and which is associated with the sun, the east and the lodestar.[57] In another of Meziere's works *De la Chevalerie de la Passion de Jhesu Crist*[58] he describes Christ as the treacle composed of the venom of the dragon. The embodiment of the practice of this legitimate magic is seen to be Richard II, the diamond, the hardest known stone, used in spells to gain power and combat sorcery and, combined with the lodestone, the greatest source of legitimate power, the philosopher's stone. The lodestone (a magnetic ore) was developed by Chinese to make compasses and was brought to the West by Crusaders in the twelfth century. For medieval scientists and alchemists the magnet provided the link between occult, earthly magic and the heavens. William of Auvergne (c. 1180/90–1241), professor of theology at the University of Paris, and one of first thinkers of the Latin West to engage with Aristotle's works on natural philosophy and the thought of Islamic writers, wrote that there is nothing more strange than the magnet's ability to draw iron;[59] Roger Bacon noted that those in possession of the secret of the mariner's compass were long afraid to reveal it for fear of being suspected of magic. In 1269 Pierre de Maricourt, the French scholar who conducted experiments on magnetism, wrote that the poles of the magnet pointed north and south because the magnet derives its virtues from the poles of the heavens and the earth was part of the magnetic sphere in line with the celestial poles.[60] Nicholas of Poland (or Montpellier), the Silesian who taught at the Dominican school at Montpellier during 1250–70 before he became a healer in Cracow, cited the magnet as proof of the existence of occult virtue,[61] and John of Rupescissa, in the second book of *de quintessentia,* wrote that the claims of the magnet needed to be addressed as an example of the close bond between the stars and earthly things. Richard, the lodestone, was therefore shown by Meziere to be one who commanded the hidden forces in the earth as well as inhabiting a higher astral realm, that of the nine orders of angels of gold which are invisible to ordinary men. The same resolution of the occult and Christianity in a legitimate natural magic can be observed in *Sir Gawain and the Green Knight.* This depiction of an Arthurian court with a young king and court devoted to peace and interested in magic can be seen as a reflection of Richard's court and Gawain, a chaste knight in the Ricardian mould, carries a shield bearing an image of the Virgin on one side and the pentangle on the other.

Meziere's letter cannot be dismissed as courtly rhetoric and flattery: his resolution of Christian and occult themes in a vision of an Arthurian king whose kingdom is old, ill and phlegmatically cold and who, as the incarnation of the philosopher's stone, will transmute his kingdom into the New Jerusalem, was visualized in the following year in Richard's personal altar, the *Wilton Diptych*, which accompanied him on his journeys and was probably housed on a ledge before an image of the Virgin in his private chapel of Mary de la Pew, in Westminster Abbey, refurbished by Richard II c. 1381 after his prayers before a statue of Our Lady in the chapel of Our Lady of the Pew on the Saturday of the Peasant's Revolt, had been answered and the Virgin had restored his kingdom to him. The restored chapel contains much of the imagery of the Diptych: it opens onto the chapel of St John the Baptist, faces the shrine of the Confessor, and traces of the white hart badge can be seen on the east wall of the chapel and the cross of St George on a pillar. Although the images on the Wilton Diptych were intended as objects of devotion and prayer, the Christian iconography is reconciled with more occult, alchemical symbolism in a way that Meziere would have approved. The right-hand panel depicts a desert, the wasteland of the Fisher King, in which a devout King Richard (wearing similar clothes with white hart, pearls and broom cod that he wore to the Anglo-French meeting at Ardes) is ushered by John the Baptist into the company of the infant Christ and the Virgin, who on the left panel occupy an Eastern paradise[62] (the Heavenly Jerusalem envisaged in Meziere's letter) and are surrounded by angels, echoing, the astral realm of the angels in the same letter, who present him with the banner of St George, bearing the colours red and white (sulphur and mercury) topped by an orb showing the island of Great Britain with the white tower of London surrounded by a silver sea. Underlying the obvious heraldic message of the deliverance of the kingdom into the custody of its patron saint, St George, there is an alchemical dimension. The banner displays the white and red of mercury and sulphur, and England with a prominent white tower (the scene of alchemical experiments) emerges from a mercurial sea under the guidance of the mother of God. In seventeenth-century Rome an altarpiece (now lost) showed Richard II and Anne kneeling before the Virgin and offering her the globe and pattern of England with an inscription reading: 'this is your dowry O Holy Virgin therefore rule over it O Mary'.[63] The wilderness from which the Baptist ushers Richard and the lamb is transformed under the Virgin's feet into a flowery meadow guarded by eleven angels (an echo of the maidens who in Arthurian myths were the guardians of the kingdom of Logres). Richard's interest in angels was attested by the presence of eight angels guarding his tomb, the two angels guarding his chapel of Our Lady of the Pew in Westminster Abbey and the shield bearing angels on the roof of Westminster Hall.

Richard's kingdom is symbolized by the orb on top of the banner of St George containing the Tower of London surrounded by a silver sea. This is an image of the philosopher's stone understood as the combined welfare of the realm and its

monarch. The alchemical transmutation of this kingdom is shown by the decora-
tion of the panels. The outside shows the divinely ordained king symbolically
depicted as a white hart on a bed of rosemary, Anne of Bohemia's emblem, chained
and crowned in gold, an alchemical representation of the fixation of mercury in
the service of man, and the incarnate Christ (the antlers evoke the crown of
thorns). This arresting image was probably painted from a live model. In 1393 the
king was given a white hart, which was kept at Windsor, by Sir Stephen Scrope,
Richard's chief justice of Ireland and brother of William Scrope, the earl of Wiltshire, surveyor of the royal forests of Cheshire. The bed of rosemary on which the
crowned hart is resting is also a symbol of mercury and the resurrection. Known
as *flos maris* (sea dew) it represents for the alchemist the *aqua permanens* which is
mercury, a substance that quickens the dead and is the food of the holy[64] and
which, with its sweet smell, evoked the Holy Spirit. Rosemary was also called *Ros
lucidinus*[65] for there is in the moon something that flows from it which nourishes
bodies and this hidden dew, whose mother is the moon, is also mentioned in the
Tabula smaragdina. Rosemary was also used as a love philtre in marriage ceremonies, and for the alchemist its binding power was comparable to the process of
conjunction. If, on the outside panels, mercury and the colour white predominate,
on the inside it is the unburnished and shining burnished gold stippling (a product of the goldsmith's art rather than the painter's) and pearls, which suggest the
process of alchemical distillation and transmutation of mercury into pure gold.
The inclusion of the banner of St George represents a nod in the direction of
Meziere's plans for an Anglo-French crusade to recover Jerusalem (Richard had
collecting boxes set up throughout England in the Spring of 1399 to answer the
call of Pope Boniface IX for a crusade to relieve the East); but this had becoming
increasingly unrealistic after the defeat of the crusading army at Nicopolis in 1396,
and the banner has more relevance as a symbol of the conjunction of mercury and
sulphur and Richard's dream of converting through alchemy his cold wasteland,
the realm of the Fisher King, Edward III, into a warm Eastern kingdom, ruled by
New Troy, his New Jerusalem. The Diptych is best understood as an alchemical
testament having all the essential features of the *Stella alchemiae*: the emphasis on
the feast of the Epiphany, the lodestar or the Virgin, and the notion of the divinity
of mercury in the form of the stag and the pearl.

The symbols and concepts extracted from alchemical and court writings gave
a unique tone to Richard's kingship. His predecessor, Edward III, used alchemical
theories to ratify a reign of military and sexual conquest and to celebrate the life-
giving force of nature and the sun that could be extracted from sulphur. However
the rumours that Richard's father and grandfather had succumbed to venereal
infection probably contributed to the young king's growing distaste for normal
sexual behaviour, and this was graphically illustrated later in his life when, according to the dictionary entitled *Liber de Veritatibus* (c. 1434–58) of that gossipy

Oxford theologian, Thomas Gascoigne (1404-58), the king's uncle, John of Gaunt, when dying of 'a putrefaction of the genitals due to carnal copulation', exposed his rotting member to his nephew.[66] Richard, unhappy with his body, his sexuality, the claims of manhood, and his own mortality, chose to identify himself with the hermaphroditic mercury and the more subtle and chaste feminine force represented by the moon. The compiler of Richard's *Libellus Geomancie* counselled the king on the correct use of the potentially dangerous art of geomancy advising him to concentrate on his innocence and purity, qualities symbolized in the child-like portrait of the king which begins the treatise. This science should not be committed to fools and faithless people and its practitioner should be clear of every mortal sin, clean and pure (qualities that were ideally shared by the alchemist).[67] This innocent, feminine image can also be seen in his portraits in the *Wilton Diptych*, was something Richard deliberately cultivated by associating so closely with his effeminate great grandfather, Edward II (implicitly rejecting his masculine father, the Black Prince, and grandfather Edward III), and in the close, homoerotic relationships he formed with such young courtiers as Robert de Vere, earl of Oxford and Thomas Mowbray earl of Nottingham. All of Richard's portraits show the feminine features described by the monk of Evesham (who may have met him at Westminster), who noted his white, rounded feminine face that sometimes flushed red, accompanied by a stammer.[68] Others described him as beautiful rather than handsome; John Gower, writing near the beginning of the reign, pictured him as 'the most beautiful of all kings, the flower of boys and as beautiful as Absolom'; Usk described him as faire among men as another Absolom.[69] The Carmelite friar, Richard Maidstone (c. 1350–96), asserted in 1392 that no king on earth could compare with Richard for his beauty;[70] and even archbishop Arundel described him as a 'beautiful man'. Other chroniclers were more specific on the question of Richard's sexuality. Henry Walsingham accused him of obscene familiarity with Robert de Vere prior to his creation of duke of Ireland in 1386; the Evesham chronicler alluded to all-night parties with unmentionable acts; and Froissart claimed that the populace of London in 1399 referred to Richard as a 'dirty bugger'. Chaucer may have satirized Richard's femininity and lack of engagement with reality in his portrayal of the effete Absalom with the fan-shaped golden hair, humiliated by having his face thrust into a woman's genitalia. Images of motherhood and virginity in the Diptych and Richard's subsequent marriage to a child bride, the six-year old Princess Isabella, suggest that Richard was locked into a perpetual childhood.[71] The spirit of mercury, manifested in that immortal aspect of monarchy symbolized by gold and pearls, gave an unearthly, unpredictable beauty to Richard's image, manifested in some of the court culture of this period such as the Middle English poem, *Pearl*, and which could be contemplated in the haunting image of the white hart, glowing like a pearl, on the *Wilton Diptych*.

The king's conviction that he was divine was rooted in civil or Roman law, in the notion of the king's two bodies, his immortal, royal line and his mortal body. Richard was a keen student of Roman law and chose to be commemorated in his funeral epitaph as one learned in law. When he entered London in 1392 to be presented a crown by a celestial angel, he would therefore be reminded that it linked two realms, the celestial and the transient, and, according to Richard Maidstone's account of the proceedings in his *Concordia*, he was told 'may he who governs your terrestrial kingdom grant you an eternal heavenly kingdom'. For the Italian jurists the phoenix was a metaphor for the mortality of the individual and the eternity of the species. The phoenix was seen to be the sole representative of its species and a hermaphrodite; it died on its birthday and was reborn.[72] It was therefore used by alchemists as a symbol of mercury and the phoenix served as the title of an alchemical tract which admits to failure in attempting the transmutation of metals and claims that mercury alone can be used in the preparation of the elixir. The *Phoenix* was written in 1399 for King Martin (the humane) of Aragon (1356–1410), who launched a crusade against the Moors in North Africa,[73] by the Frenchman, Jacques Austral, who worked in the laboratory of the Tower of the Angel in Palma supported by stipends from Giovanni I and Martin; in correspondence between Jacques and Martin and in the inventory of Martin's library there is mention of a small book of alchemy in Latin. Jacques also stayed in England during the reign of Richard II.[74] As heir to itself this bird, which emerged from the fire, like the alchemical bird of Hermes, was the first born son and the father, in imitation of the Trinity to which Richard's father, the Black Prince, was especially devoted. The phoenix was without sex and never aged but continually renewed itself like the angels. For Richard, who was obsessed with purity, chastity and angels, the equivalent of the phoenix was the white hart, the mercury of divinely ordained kingship that never dies.

This concept of the eternity of high office or estate was beginning to be commemorated in the funeral monuments of many in high office: the upper tier showing the deceased, resplendent in armour or clerical vestments, and the lower, the decaying cadaver. The funeral monument of Richard's father in Canterbury Cathedral was inscribed with an epitaph dwelling on the contrast between the prince's estate in life and the condition of his mortal remains.[75] Richard's own public image was dominated by his identification with the divine powers associated with transmuted mercury, which he evoked in his attempt to associate himself with the gold and pearls which bestrew his portable altar and the badge of the white hart which is depicted crowned in gold on the outside panels of his personal altar, and the gold and pearls that bedeck the king's image and dominate the inside panel. The unique and exceptionally large full-length portrait of the king in the nave of Westminster Abbey shows him in majesty in gold with a gold frame and background facing the viewer like the triumphant, resurrected Christ, the spirit of transmuted mercury, the crowned R on his robe alluding to the crowned hart on the *Wilton Diptych*;[76]

and the same message was broadcast in the large couched, chained white hart adorning the partition wall of the muniment room of the south transept in Westminster Abbey.[77] Both were images of the evolution of the king's divine essence into perfection, something that could also be witnessed in the cosmati pavement of the abbey, the design of which was also replicated on the floor of Edward the Confessor's shrine.

The public image of Richard II as a Solomonic king and wise man, steeped in the occult arts and especially alchemy, influenced the art, costume and ceremony of his kingship, as he presented an image of a king who was capable of effecting a transmutation of himself and his court into the New Jerusalem. This ideal was pursued by shifting royal expenditure from armaments to jewels, pearls and gold. Richard, in his fascination with precious and semi-precious stones and the goldsmith's art (he took on himself the title of the lodestone and the diamond), showed the same sort of interest as the pharaohs of ancient Egypt in alchemical transmutation and substances that were eternal and pure. During his coronation procession in Cheapside, where the goldsmiths of London were concentrated, young girls showered him with gold leaves and a golden angel presented him with a gold crown.[78] According to the Evesham chronicler, describing the tournament in Smithfield in 1391, Richard had taken to wearing his crown on all public occasions. His reign saw a spectacular increase in expenditure of jewels. In 1386, on the Feast of the Purification of the Virgin, Richard ordered special robes with white harts embroidered with pearls. When he went to Ireland in 1399 he took with him his jewels, including a ring worth 1,000 marks. In 1399, 359 items of jewellery were found in Richard's possession in Cheshire. The inventory included a bejewelled crown with 132 pearls, which was probably the crown of Anne of Bohemia.[79] According to the Evesham chronicler, Richard spent more than £2,000 on a robe lined with precious stones. This emphasis on the almost supernatural aspect of gold and jewellery was captured by the Cheshire poet in *Pearl*, which has a circular, crown-like structure, in a dream vision in which the narrator, a goldsmith or jeweller, contemplates across a river the citizens of the lamb in New Jerusalem, a city of one and a half miles width, like the holy space of Richard's Westminster, with a celestial cleansing river (Richard introduced the first urban sanitation act for London in 1385).[80] Westminster's mythical founder, St Dunstan, was, according to a legend, an alchemist and the patron saint of goldsmiths. The pearl queen in the poem, bearing a resemblance to Anne of Bohemia, wears a crown of pearls, the equivalent of Richard's crown of precious stones and gems worth £2,000. Richard's close friend and instrument in the assertion of the royal prerogative, Thomas Mowbray, duke of Norfolk, who died in exile in Venice in 1399, would have seen in the chapel of the Doge (with whom Richard II corresponded) at San Marco the treasures of gold, altars and vessels and gold leaf books, all adorned with semi-precious stones of sapphire and ruby which had been taken from Byzantium in the ninth century, the realization of a dream of ideal kingship that Mowbray shared with his sovereign. All members of the lamb's household in the poem wear pearls as badges, the equivalent of the white hart of Richard's household. However there was more to the king's interest in alchemy than mere rhetoric and image making, and alchemy had a profound influence on the personal life of the king and his policies.

Alchemical medicine played an important role in the courts of kings in this period, especially the court of Richard's second father-in-law, Charles VI, who was treated for his afflictions with mercury by Thomas of Bologna, the physician and surgeon who attended Charles V on his deathbed, and who also attended Charles VI as astrologer and alchemist. Thomas wrote to Bernard of Treves telling him that he had sent medicine to the king of France shortly after receiving a royal grant on 23 May 1384, which was an elixir or philosopher's stone consisting of gold to which mercury had been added, explaining that the solar, masculine sperm acted as an agent expelling poison with the feminine mercurial sperm. Despite testing the medicine, he fears he has incurred the displeasure of the king's brothers Philip the Bold duke of Burgundy (1363–1404) and Jean duke of Berry (1340–1416) who suspected Thomas of poisoning the king.[81] In his reply Bernard, while recognizing that mercury in its crude form could be poisonous, claimed that quicksilver, as female sperm in a male gold solution, was a gift from God, Christ and the Virgin, efficacious above all other medicines. Charles VI's mental state deteriorated after 1392 and, when riding in the forest of le Mans towards Brittany in the hot midday sun in August, he was afflicted by 'a strange influence from the humours' and, convinced that he was made of glass, he shot one of his servants. Charles brought back with him to Le Mans rumours that he had been drugged and bewitched (it is possible that mercury poisoning contributed to his delusions); and rumours that he was poisoned, or that his illness was brought about by sorcery, reached Richard II. According to a chronicle of the abbey of St Denys written in reign of Charles VI, the French king was also treated with a book called *Smagorad*, the original of which was supposed to have been given by God to Adam to console him for the loss of his son, Abel, and which would enable him to hold the stars in subjection and command the four elements. This was probably the *Tabula Smagdorina (The Emerald Table)*.[82] The images on the tarot cards, many of which such as the burning tower, the moon, the sun, the star, and the king and queen of pentacles, had alchemical connotations, and may have performed meditative functions similar to those in the book of geomancy; and it may be significant that their first recorded use was for the diversion of Charles VI, king of France, in the 1390s during the period of his mental collapse. In the register of the chambers des Compts for the year 1392 there is an entry by Charles Powpart, treasurer to Charles VI: 'To Jacquem Gringonnes, painter, for three packs of cards in gold and diverse colours of several designs to be laid before our said lord king for his diversion.' Figures such as the fool, the wise man, the four cardinal virtues, and prudence, could have been used to lead the king on a journey of self-discovery from insanity to re-integration of the self.[83]

In a more general sense alchemical theories contributed to culinary fashions at the court of Richard II. *The Form of Curry* was compiled for the health of the king's household on the advice of the king's physicians and philosophers in the form of a scroll.[84] This collection of recipes envisaged the body as an alchemical laboratory cooking the humours: the liver was the fire and the stomach the furnace. Cooking is presented as a form of alchemical distillation and transmutation creating sauces or essences by grinding foods into powders, and making broths (the *Stella alchemiae* describes the elixir as a broth) and sauces, reducing foods through the slow application of heat, the 'esy fire', to sauces that contained their true essence or quintessence. Most of the recipes required the use of milk of almonds (which had been brought by the Moors from Southern Spain and was regarded as a sanguine food containing the perfect balance of the four humours).

For Richard the hunting of the hart would have had alchemical significance, reflecting the alchemist's pursuit and fixing of the elusive mercury, and there were direct physical and spiritual benefits to be had from this activity which Richard engaged in every summer in the royal forests of Woodstock and the New Forest. In 1386 he purchased from a London goldsmith a knife to be used in hunting in the woods and a hunting horn of gold enamelled with green tassels of silk.[85] Soon after, at the conclusion of the Merciless Parliament, he hunted for three months. The treatise on hunting, *The Master of the Game*, translated and adapted from the *Livre de Chasse* of Gaston de Foix by his closest friend, Edward Aumale, duke of York, conveys the physical benefits of hunting. The bodily exertion involved in riding hard means that hunters exercise, sweating out evil humours and they eat less and have good digestion whereby 'no wicked humours nor superfluities be engendered, and in the unlikely event that a hunter develops unwholesome humours he will sweat them out, for, as Hippocrates says, "full repletion of meat slayeth more men than any sword or knife"'. The physical exertions and self-discipline involved in a life revolving around organizing the hounds, going to bed early, and hard riding, also distracted the hunter from sinful thoughts and meant that hunters lived longer, having more balanced health and joy in the world and health of the soul after death: 'Wherefore I say that such a hunter is not idle, he can have no evil thoughts, not can he do evil works, wherefore he must go into paradise – when the hounds pass before him then shall he ride after them and shall rout and blow as loud as he may with great joy and pleasure and I assure you he thinketh of not other sin nor of no other evil.' The implication in this work is that for the upper classes pursuit of hunting was a way to achieve nobility of soul and was an important part of the knightly vocation: 'Never saw I a man that loved work and pleasure of hounds and hawks that had not many good qualities in him.' The author of *Sir Gawain and the Green Knight* alludes to this view of the wholesome nature of hunting in Richard's court when he has Sir Gawain being sexually compromised while sleeping in bed while his host hunts; this may be a specific allusion to the point made in Gaston de Foix's original treatise that while a man is idle in bed or in chamber his imagination draws him to lustful thoughts to which the active hunter is immune.

Other medical works were associated with Richard II. His tutor, Simon Burley, owned *Sidrack and Bokkas*. This was an encyclopaedic treatise written in French c. 1246 in the form of a dialogue between a Christian and pagan on medical matters. One medical work written for the king was a treatise on uroscopy, which was translated into the mother tongue for the comprehension and governance of laymen by Master Bartholomew of the Franciscan Order at the request of King Richard and Anne.[86] This commission may have been connected with the king being treated for a stone in his urinary tract which required many payments to physicians for medicine.[87] The treatise demonstrates the practical utility of John Dastin's axiom: 'In water there are many secrets', and expresses an alchemical view that water, in the form of urine, performs the functions of mercury as messenger of God and servant of man. Urine is seen as the result of the purifying activities of water through the blood stream and if properly examined it can reveal the secrets of a man's health (in the way the mercury thermometer still does today), his fate and character.[88] The varying thicknesses and colours of urine in the Jordan (named after the baptismal river) can denote the degree of heat and moisture in a man and his humoral disposition and imbalance that causes illnesses, the degrees of which, like the rising and falling of the ocean tides, can be seen in the passing of urine. The study of urine in the Jordan, which is recommended in the *Secreta secretorum*, is the key to self-knowledge. Richard's ruling humour was probably phlegm (and it is perhaps significant that such praise is levelled at the purity and cleansing functions of this humour and its ruling element in this work). The character of the phlegmatic man is described as unstable as water, cold with pale face and colouring. This accords with contemporary portraits of the king and the possibly satirical portraits of the king by Chaucer in the characters of the Pardoner and Absolom; but the author is at pains to point out that the study of urine was the way to make the best of one's character and humoral disposition by striving for humoral balance: 'And know your complexion be never so evil you may if you turn to good rule turn yourself into a better complexion.'[89]

Alchemical medicine played a significant part in the private world of Richard's anxieties and griefs. His closest friend and reputed lover, Robert de Vere, died in a hunting accident in Louvain in 1391. His body was embalmed (perhaps in *aqua vitae* a process described in Henry of Lancaster's *Le Livre de Seyntz Medicines*)[90] and brought back to England, fulfilling a prediction provided by a triad in Richard's *Book of Geomancy* composed of the witnesses *albus* (white) and *laetitia* (loss) and the judge *carcer* (imprisonment) formed in response to a question posed in the geomancy concerning the return of an absent friend: 'that he will return in a beautiful state'. If Richard ever asked this question he would have seen these triads of white, loss and imprisonment poignantly proclaiming the return of the pale, white body of the bereaved, departed, imprisoned in a coffin, and may have thought of them as he took up de Vere's fingers and gazed for a long time at the preserved body.[91] Alchemical medicine may have played an especially important role in the illness of his beloved wife, Anne of Bohemia. The king's grief at her death in 1394 was so severe he razed to the ground Sheen, the palace most closely associated with her. In 1395 he headed an expedition to Ireland, and two of his knights visited St Patrick's Purgatory in Lough Dergh, perhaps in an attempt to communicate with Richard's dead wife. The two knights went down three or four steps to spend the night in the cave where it was believed the dead would communicate in dreams.[92] They had strange dreams and vivid imaginings but could not remember much the following morning. A court writer from the North West who probably wore the white hart badge composed a poem around the same time that the *Wilton Diptych* was executed whose title may have been taken from the *Preciosa Margarita* of Petrus Bonus. *Pearl* purports to be the meditation of a jeweller (the *Wilton Diptych* in its final form is partly a demonstration of the art of the goldsmith) bereaved by the death of a young girl who has (allowing for scribal confusion) been in this country for possibly 11 years: 'thou lived not two yer in our thede'.[93] This elegy for a young woman, crowned in heaven, was of relevance to the death of Anne which occurred in 1394. Queen Anne was publically mourned by the king at her funeral and at the feast of St Anne in August. Her coronation in heaven as bride of Christ is hinted at in the portrait of the Virgin welcoming Richard in Heaven in the *Wilton Diptych*.[94] The poet envisages the transmutation of the dead after an alchemical process of putrefaction and sublimation into pure spirit, represented by a shining and perfect pearl (Anne was known as the pearl queen and possessed an elaborate pearl crown). The bereaved jeweller/king is comforted by this vision (the *Wilton Diptych* is dominated by a heavenly vision of maidens wearing pearls) and a sight of the New Jerusalem illuminated by gold and pearls. Its king, as the incarnation of the transmuted, pure mercury, is shown bedecked in gold and stippled pearls, which are prominent and three dimensional on the king's crown and collar (throughout his reign Richard showed a love of rich costume and jewellery, especially gold and pearls). The pearl poet's meditation on the death of a virginal girl, described as a pearl queen who wears a pearl on her breast, is in part an allusion to this event. Pearl is described as one who was in this country for only 11 years, the length of Anne's stay in England. After expressing grief at the loss of this pearl:

> From here
> to death the world ends I'll trudge?
> Without my pearl, precious pure,

consolation is offered in the form of alchemical transmutation:

> Though fate you feel has felled your gem,
> It was from nought renewed.

and a vision of her transmutation in heaven:

> Pearl, O pleasure for a prince,
> Enclosed in gold so clear and clean.[95]

Another work by the same poet, St Erkenwald, whose shrine was visited by Richard II in 1392 at the conclusion of his ceremonial entry into the capital, similarly shows the transmutation from flesh to spirit achieved through powerful feeling when the pearl-like tears of the saint rescue the corpse of a pagan citizen of New Troy from limbo so that it can decompose and release its spirit from matter. This is a vision that is echoed in the *Wilton Diptych* which partly served as a consolation for a mourning king as he attended requiem services for Queen Anne in his little chapel of St Mary le Pew adjacent to the Baptist's chapel in Westminster Abbey. Anne is not present in the Diptych in any bodily form; she is remembered in the bed of rosemary (her emblem and a symbol of remembrance) on which the suffering king rests in the form of the crowned and chained white hart, and she is everywhere evoked by pearls which are on the antlers of the white hart and in the daisies at the feet of the Virgin (the old French word marguerite for pearls is a pun on margarite for daisies). If the outside panel suggests memory and grief it also hints at the resurrection. John Dastin in his discussion of the dissolution and calcination of an impure body to clear, white ashes, showed how these ashes constituted a ferment that held the sun and moon; it was the soul formed through suffering, glowing with a whiteness that was the ultimate colouration sought by the alchemist. The white hart lying on rosemary, its bed of grief, bearing a crown of thorns symbolic of pain and humiliation, was a phoenix created out of the suffering of the king, giving birth to a winged soul that effected in its union with the body of the monarch and the spirit of mercury a resurrection into eternal gold. The inside panels endorsed this vision, providing a glimpse of the transmutation and resurrection into a New Jerusalem dominated by pearls which cover the king's gown and gold (in effect the Diptych acts like a mercury backed mirror).[96] In *Pearl* the New Jerusalem is the scene of the marriage of the lamb and the pearl, in which the light of the earthly sun and moon is replaced by the combined radiance of both (the conjunction of sulphur and mercury), a vision of the Resurrection generated by the power of 'the mighty moon'. This is an allusion to what the alchemists referred to as 'our moon'. *Pearl* communicates an alchemical vision of heaven in which the natural light of the sulphuric sun is replaced by the glow of heavenly creation, the pearl or dew of heaven that descended into the abyss, and this vision is endorsed in the *Wilton Diptych*, which similarly shows no natural light but radiance cast by gold and pearls, a heavenly marriage of the lamb and his pearl. This vision of alchemical transcendence was also expressed in the memorial for Anne in the tomb reserved for Richard and his pearl queen in Westminster Abbey, the design of which was agreed before Richard set sail for Ireland in 1399. The king and queen are surrounded by angels, and on the king's robes are white harts, the broom and the rising sun. In an echo of the *Stella alchemiae* the pair are shown under a canopy of stars and the epigraph reads: 'Under the broad stars Anne now lies entombed', and she is implicitly compared to the Virgin Mary for her compassion for the poor who, with her good deeds and beautiful gentleness, offers medicine for the soul.

Even Richard's marriage to the princess Isabella in 1396 may have represented an attempt to perpetuate Anne's life by some form of alchemical transmutation. She had been described as 'our young marguerite, our precious stone, our beautiful white pearl' by Meziere.[97] This six-year-old girl was nothing more than a blank screen onto which the king could project his feelings for Anne. The pearl queen in *Pearl* is a child bride chosen from among many candidates and she is compared to a lily (the fleur de lily occurs on the heraldic shield on the *Wilton Diptych*). When Richard travelled to Ardes to meet his infant queen he made his attendants wear the livery of his dead queen; he wore a hat of hanging pearls, gave his new father-in-law a collar of pearls from the livery of Anne, and at the wedding all the lords and ladies in waiting wore Anne's livery; Richard even presented Isabella with a gift of pearls. It was as if the pearl, symbol of mercury and its eternal resilience, was the means whereby Anne's spirit could be perpetuated by Richard, projecting all his feelings for his dead wife onto this innocent child, so that Jean Creton, the valet-de-chambre to King Charles VI could report in his verse chronicle that when the king left for Ireland in 1399, leaving his child bride in England, he was grief stricken.

A more intimate insight into the private world of Richard II's grief and his anxieties and insecurities can be provided in a reading of the book of geomancy and following the guidelines provided by Italian scholars of the thirteenth century who read and translated Arabic works on medicine, geomancy and astrology. They included: Bartholomew of Parma in *Summa Brevilogium*, written in Bologna in 1288, who divided the geomantic signs into favourable and unfavourable;[98] Peter de Albano (c. 1250–c. 1316), the Padua physician, astrologer who described the different 16 geomantic symbols in his *Geomanzia*; and the famous sixteenth-century magician, Henry Cornelius Agrippa, who provided a similar interpretive map in *His Fourth Book of Occult Philosophy* on geomancy.[99] The 12 images in the book of geomancy bore some similarity to the signs of the zodiac but many were entirely different and had alchemical connotations. Their relative positions in the 12 houses above and below the horizon gave them a meditative power and they served an important medical function, helping the

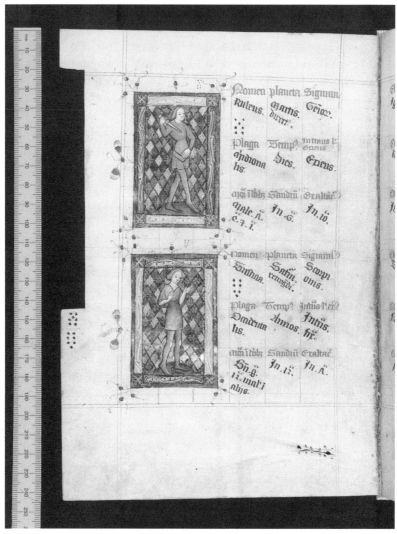

The sinister geomantic images of Rubella and Tristitia with Richard II's
thumb index (Bodley 581 Fo. 20v and 20r)

questioner to make difficult decisions and to engage in sophisticated self-analysis.
Some of the illustrations to houses in the manuscript, such as *puer* (boy) and
Fortuna major (king), conformed to Richard's self-image and others represented
those things he would have feared such as *carcer* (prison), *amissio* (loss) and *populus* (the people), with its implications of public approval and disapproval. The
consultation of witnesses and judges produced by one's own questions and the
self-examination that preceded them and the harnessing of the hidden forces

within the earth and the personality show that the book of geomancy is a key to appreciating Richard's dependence on the occult.

The special significance geomancy had for Richard may have arisen from his identification with the lodestone or magnet. Englebert of Admani in Styria (c. 1250–1331),[100] writing on the marvels of the attractive qualities of the magnetic needle, compared it to the way an inspired geomancer, walking in the quiet of the night, thinking of nothing but the pros and cons of his question and decision, will be lead to the right answer by the configurations formed when his hand is lead by the influence of the pole star, which in Richard's case was his own special star and the star of the Virgin. On two alternative pages of the book of geomancy there is a section entitled *Rosarium Regis Ricardi* (*King Richard's Rosary*): this was a term with many associations for the king signifying prayers to the virgin and the five petalled rose as a symbol of the pentangle. There are two complete readings for questions posed by the king.[101] They take the form of two heraldic shields displaying the four mothers, signs formed from the combination of odd and even numbers of dots made by the questioner, and the four daughters and four nephews, two witnesses and the judge made by sideways addition from the original four mother signs. If shields were normally used in heraldry to broadcast the public image of those of high rank, these geomantic shields reveal an inner world of images formed from the king's anxieties. Some signs themselves were of sinister aspect, such as *tristitia* (loss) and *puella* a yellow beardless boy (rashness and violence) and others could acquire a malevolent character in certain positions on the chart: if *carcer* (imprisonment) occurred in the first house it was recommended that the whole procedure had to be abandoned. These charts of 16 houses encouraged sophisticated analysis of personality and relationships but they could also arouse neurotic anxiety about the future. The key to understanding them now, over 600 years later, is to consider the sort of questions the king would most likely have asked in 1391 when the charts were completed. Questions beyond the standard 25 concerning state matters are provided in the *Flores Questionem et Iudicorum veritatibus Artis Geomancie*, topics taken from everyday geomantic questions in Gerald of Cremona's treatise *Si Quis Per Artem Geomanticem*[102] and in 35 possible questions in the *Rosarium Regis Ricardi* accompanied by an alphabetical table showing which geomantic figures are favourable, unfavourable and neutral.[103] If we assume that one of the most common and urgent questions would relate to the king's relationship with his beloved wife/sister, Anne of Bohemia (one of the triads in Richard's geomancy indicating that this marriage was a successful alchemical conjunction consisted of the witnesses puer and puella – boy and girl – with the judge conjunctio),[104] then the second shield takes on an ambiguous but sinisterly prophetic note, and as events unfolded Richard may have ruefully reflected on the terrifying accuracy of some of the prognostications to be found in the configuration of these images. *Via* in the first house, which relates to the character of the questioner or the object of the question (in this case Anne), is a lunar sign appropriate for Richard and Anne. *Via* also occurs in the seventh house relating to wedlock. In the fourth house is *caput draconis* (head of the dragon) which relates to medicine and the lunar sign *via* which occurs in the seventh house on the negative side of the shield relating to wedlock would imply an illness of a female nature. *Puella* (girl) in the sixth house relates to illness and *Fortuna minor* also occurs on the negative left-hand side. There is therefore a coherence of lunar, watery signs relating to the illness of a young woman and medical treatment, the outcome of which is possibly tragic or at least a long drawn out illness. The two witnesses are *acquisitio* (wealth) and the judge is *populus* (the people) another lunar, neutral sign that reflects its surroundings, good with good and bad with bad. With such an ambiguous chart it would necessary to refer to a reconciler, made by adding the first mother and the judge, in this case *via* in the sixteenth house, another watery sign, the retrograde of *populus*, merely reflecting like the moon. The whole chart is dominated by female signs and a happy marriage is signified with *puella* in the second house, *conjunctio* in the third house (relating to brothers and sisters and therefore an apt reflection of the nature of Richard and Anne's relationship); and in the positive side of the shield it is followed in the fourth house by *Fortuna major* to signify great happiness and fortune; however this happy marriage is blighted by illness and the occurrence of the head of the dragon (medicine) suggests the object of the questions is a woman suffering from an illness perhaps relating to the ovaries; and the prognosis is at best ambiguous. This shield takes the reader into a little understood aspect of late medieval medicine: such geomantic shields may once have performed the same function as a chart on the foot of a hospital bed, holding the fate of the beloved in its schematic configurations. Before 1394 this chart may have been used to diagnose a long standing illness of Anne's and it may have come to hold for Richard special prophetic significance after her death in this year.[105]

If alchemy played a significant role in the king's public image and his private life it also contributed to the politics of his reign. The cult of transmuted king and court amounts to a religious vision and it also had important implications for the tone and policies of Richard's kingship.[106] The mercurial quality of Richard's kingship also resulted in some idealistic policies that enjoyed some measure of support in court circles. A fundamental principle of alchemical change is the capacity of mercury, the eternal and original substance, to renew itself and the substances it comes into contact with (a claim pressed by the Carmelite friar, William Sedacerius (writing in exile around 1378), in an alchemical work called *Sedacina*,[107] and this was applied by Richard II to his claims to perpetual youth. When he came to the throne in 1377 it had been a long time before anyone could remember a young and vital king: Edward III had been sick and indeed senile for years and his eldest son terminally ill from 1370. Richard's appeal was his youth and he referred to it frequently throughout his reign: as late as 1397 in a letter to Albert of Bavaria (1336–1404), the ruler of the counties of Holland, Hainault, and Zeeland in the Low Countries, he referred to his tender years; and his incorruptible youth was central to his claim to regenerate the monarchy and a kingdom blighted by plague, schism, heresy, social unrest and the debts incurred by an unproductive war with France. The alchemical vision of John Dastin, originally applied to the accession of Edward III and circulating during Richard's reign, was especially relevant to a sick, dying king and kingdom waiting for a young redeemer; so too was the circulation of the vision of Adam Davy concerning the alchemical regeneration of the kingdom. By 1396 this vision may have become firmly associated with Edward II with whom Richard II so closely identified. Richard's elaborate coronation ceremony in 1377, described by Walsingham, was full of symbolism that had alchemical resonances. London was transformed into the heavenly city: the conduits in Cheapside ran with red and white wine, and in the middle of the king's palace a hollowed out marble column with a huge winged eagle emitted red and white wines in four directions to represent the four elements and four quarters of the kingdom. A virgin and angels (girls in white of Richard's age) scattered gold coins and offered the king a golden crown, and the bishop of Rochester urged the lords to abandon their vices, including debauchery, and do devotion to the king, who was just a boy and an innocent, and model themselves on the king's innocence and purity; all of this must have encouraged Richard to cultivate an image of the golden youth.

Events early in his reign would have fostered this cult of youth, such as Richard's triumphant meeting with the peasant armies at Smithfield and Blackheath, who bore the banner of St George and proclaimed their loyalty to the king while venting their hatred of the ruling class of higher nobility, both clerical and lay; and Richard continued to stress his youth and surrounded himself with young favourites at the expense of the older generation of barons including his uncles, the surviving sons of Edward III, Thomas Woodstock duke of Gloucester, and Thomas Beauchamp, earl of Warwick. This youthful court is possibly satirized in the depiction of the young Arthurian court in *Sir Gawain and the Green Knight* (Thomas Clifford, knight of the chamber, was one of the 'young knights' granted licence to hunt in the royal forests and closes). Richard's grandfather, Edward III, and his father, the Black Prince, embodied the masculinity identified with sulphur, and for these two renowned warriors kingship was all about fulfilling a role consistent with mature adulthood. Richard's decision to base his kingship on an ideal of youthful immaturity (or potential) was highly unconventional.[108] The Augustinian theologian and natural philosopher, Giles of Rome (d. 1316 in Avignon) in *De Regimine principum*, a treatise on kingship he dedicated to his pupil Philip IV and which was owned by Richard's tutor, Simon Burley,[109] defined youth as *adoloescentia*, the inconstant first state in a man's life, dominated by the element of water and the humour of phlegm, a feminine, warm and wet state (appropriate to mercury). Giles advised that a youth needed to be ruled by more stable, older counsellors with more experience of life;

and it seems Richard consciously set himself against the counsel of this treatise and the advice of his tutors to make a cult of youthful inconstancy, by celebrating this quality of mercury, inconstancy, when he made the symbol of mercury, the white hart, the badge that he distributed to his youthful followers. A sinister warning that Richard could never forget or forgive the humiliations he had suffered as a young man at the hands of older counsellors appears in the *Concordia* written by John of Gaunt's confessor, Richard Maidstone, in 1392: 'All England sees how many ills how many deaths, He has suffered from a tender age, still unavenged'.[110] When he was at the height of his powers, and asserting his prerogative against the older generation of courtiers including: Richard FitzAlan, earl of Arundel; Thomas Woodstock, duke of Gloucester and Thomas Beauchamp, earl of Warwick, all of whom had imposed a continual council on him in 1386, Richard chose to represent himself in the *Wilton Diptych* as a 11-year-old boy to emphasize the rebirth of the monarchy under a golden youth and a symbolic return to the period between his coronation and his triumphant meeting with the peasants, when his youth and kingship was untarnished.[111] Those behind the painting of the Diptych seem to have utilized the vision of John Dastin of a king, a pure youth, who must die and regain his tender youth in an encounter with the dragon:

> To youth againe he must be renewed
> And suffer passion or else all were vain
> The rising againe right fresh and well hewd.

In the case of the Diptych the dragon is alluded to in the banner of St George the dragon slayer. The role of the mother, mercury, in Dastin's vision, the dissolution and rebirth of the golden king in the primal mercury, is suggested in this portable altarpiece by the prominence of the Virgin (mercury was known as the milk of the Virgin), and such images of mercury as the sea, pearls and the white hart. Just as the young king in Dastin's vision is protected by nine angels, so Richard is welcomed into the court of heaven by 11 angels to represent his age at his coronation.

The importance of the role of innocent youth in the redemption of this kingdom into the New Jerusalem was emphasized in the ceremony celebrating the reconciliation of the king with the city of London in 1392. At St Paul's Cathedral a choir of angels enthralled all those who came close to them and observed their youth and indeterminate sex, and 'above all sat a youth, as though like God himself/ A ray of light. Just like the sun, shines in his youth.'[112] The cult of youth was celebrated in the symbol of the innocent lamb, prominent in the *Wilton Diptych* and held by John the Baptist. The role of the king as the lamb, the king of New Jerusalem, was emphasized when Richard was greeted by the citizens of London upon this same royal entry. At the Temple Bar Richard and Anne were confronted by a forest constructed 'like a desert' in which John the Baptist was surrounded in the wilderness by wild beasts, and Richard was greatly comforted by the sight of the Baptist pointing to the lamb of God; the Gawain poet paid homage to the king's role as the redemptive lamb in *Pearl*, which celebrates the triumph of the Lamb in Heavenly Jerusalem. The annual procession and plays of the Corpus Christi guild (both Richard and Anne were members) celebrated the social order held together by Christ's humanity and the divinely established order under King Richard the lamb, victor and victim; the processions in York and Coventry followed the same route as the royal entry; on 18 June 1384 Richard and Anne visited Coventry and watched the Coventry Mystery plays and one of the plays they witnessed was St John the Baptist in the wilderness. Meziere's *Epitre* shows Richard receiving his book from Robert the Hermit with the banner of the lamb which also occurs against a red cross.[113]

Associated with the prepubescent youth alluded to in the *Wilton Diptych* is innocence, and Richard presented himself as a chaste monarch to dissociate himself from his libidinous grandfather, whose sexual sins were believed to have contributed to the malaise of the monarchy; and it is possible that he was even a virgin. His marriage to Anne of Bohemia (endorsed in Dastin's vision of the marriage of the young king to one of imperial birth associated with the moon) occurred when they were both young enough to be considered brother and sister and the marriage produced no children. All the images and symbolic allusions to Anne, such as her funeral monument and the pearls on the *Wilton Diptych*, stress her kinship with the Virgin crowned in heaven. Richard's next marriage, to Princess Isabella, was encouraged by Mezieres as a means of reconciling the state of chastity, which stood second to virginity with matrimony; this would be a chaste marriage with no expectation of children because the couple placed their hopes in the future kingdom of the lamb, the new Jerusalem. Throughout Europe cathedral cities had been built on the model of the four gated city described in the *Book of Revelations* in the shape of a circle squared with a cross.[114] The arrival of Richard II and his new bride in London was probably intended to be a re-enactment of the reception of Edward II and Isabella of France which had been described by Andrew Horn, the city chamberlain, as the entry into New Jerusalem.[115] On his bier in Westminster Abbey Richard had an orb placed, symbol of the realm of England, between the effigies of himself and his queen (Anne) to imply that he left his kingdom to God. Certainly there was no immediate sexual motive behind this pressure involved in this proposed second marriage because Isabella was only six-years-old in 1396. Richard closely identified with another king who was widely regarded as a virgin in a chaste marriage and in the autumn of 1395 he formally impaled the arms of Edward the Confessor, the last Saxon king, with his own in a symbolic marriage. Some complimentary allusions may have been made to Richard II's chastity and innocence by the Cheshire court poet who gave such prominence to the virtue of purity in his poems *Pearl*, *Patience* and *Purity*.[116]

Richard's pursuit of peace, appropriate for his role as the lamb and the magus in the image of Solomon, had important implications for the longstanding, expensive war with France initiated by his grandfather, which had by the 1370s resulted in a stalemate. On the 20th of August 1392, the day before Richard entered London as the returning Christ, he presented himself as a peacemaker in Christendom, answering a call among many of the educated and articulate elite, such as Sir John Clanvowe and John Gower in *Vox clamantis*, who were questioning the justice of war;[117] and he wrote to Charles VI advising him of his intention to negotiate a final peace between the two realms. On 22 August he wrote to the French court, referring to a letter recently brought to him by Robert the Hermit (Robert de Mennot), a Norman knight who had undergone a conversion in the Holy Land and who had returned to Western Europe as an apostle of peace. Negotiations between the two realms were postponed because of the breakdown of Charles VI which lasted until January 1394. By 1395 Charles had recovered sufficiently to entrust a letter to Robert the hermit in which the French king expressed hope in a final peace between the two realms and a united offensive against the Turk. A meeting took place between the two kings at Ardes near Calais on 27 October 1395. This was a high point in Richard's kingship, an occasion similar to the more famous meeting between Henry VIII and the French king on the field of the cloth of gold, with Richard in the role of the prince of peace whose reign, foretold by the magi, was dedicated to the pole star of the Virgin. An anonymous English observer records how Richard turned out in a brand new outfit each day. On the first day he wore a full length gown or red velvet adorned with the white hart and a hat loaded with pearls; on his shoulder he wore a collar incorporating the French king's broom cod. Charles handed over to Richard his daughter, Isabella, and four days of meetings occurred with exchange of gifts and talks of ending the schism and establishing peace. On 4 November Richard married Isabella at Calais and vowed to build a chapel near the spot on which the two kings met, dedicated to Our Lady of Peace. A 28-year truce was proclaimed in January 1396, and Meziere's letter to Richard in the same year was essentially a proposal for a lasting peace between the two realms as a remedy for the Papal Schism, a peace that would enable them to present a united front against the Turkish threat to Christian lands in Eastern Europe.

The schism, exacerbated by the hostilities between these two realms who supported the rival popes, had resulted, according to Meziere, in a wide gaping wound in Christendom, one that could not be healed by the teachings of Avicenna or the physicians of Salerno. The proposed peace is presented in terms of alchemical medicine and the practise of good natural magic. The two kings must make a voyage east to Jerusalem (ultimately this would take the form of a crusade) and pass the two whirlpools of 'Scylla and Charybdis' encountered by Ulysses in Homer's

Odyssey, and these 'two Masters, should fix their eyes ever on the northern star, the Pole Star, that is, the Virgin Mary'.[118] These two whirlpools, identified as the strong restless currents of demonic magic, are the two chivalries of England and France.[119] The medicine is Christ's Passion or *theriac*, the product of the dragon's venom, and Richard is a red rose whose fragrance evokes the memory of the sacrifice of the saviour. Richard also represents the lodestone by adoption of which he becomes the son of God (Christ on the Cross was depicted in the pseudo Arnaldian *Tractatus parobolicus* as a magnet attracting to him all the sins of mankind)[120] and the lodestone was also believed to have the power to staunch the flow of blood. Richard is also described as the diamond into which the lodestone can be transmuted and which is a potent remedy against poisons. Hildegard of Bingen, maintained in *De natura rerum*, an encyclopaedia of natural history, that the lodestone or magnet was also used to treat insanity and attacks of demonic possession (by the time of the writing of this letter Charles was regularly suffering mental breakdowns). Charles VI, according to Mezieres, represented the ruby and a holy balm, obtained from a shrub nourished by the dews of heaven, which with the lodestone will bring the sides of this wound together and establish a conjunction of love between the two realms ruled by two kings descended from St Louis. It was also believed that the lodestone had the power to test chastity and Mezieres promised that the man who has the lodestone must wear it with a heart free from mortal sin, and then: 'our lodestone has wonderfully drawn to itself the iron, that is, the chivalry of both England and France, represented by the goad and its cruel work; and, moreover, this needle, or goad, brought close to our lodestone, Richard, has changed its course through this contact, and looks, as do the sailors to the North Star – to the very sweet Virgin Mary;'[121] with its power of attracting iron, the magnet will transmute the realm of the Black Boar (symbol of Edward III and the Black Prince) and his warmongering knights to that of the precious lodestone, a realm that looks to the Pole star in the North and Jerusalem in the East. Thomas of Cantimpre (1201–72), a Dominican professor of Philosophy and Theology in Louvain, described the ability of adamant to betray the location of the star of the sea, the pole star to guide sailors.[122] Richard's devotion to the Virgin and his service to her as a prince of peace led to the adoption of alchemical symbols that reinforced this role. The marriage with the daughter of Charles VI will transform the child, Isabella, into a 'beautiful white pearl' and 'through her conjugal chastity, not only will the fury of the unicorn be appeased, but the unicorn itself will be taken in the net' an allusion the myth that the unicorn would lay his head in the lap of the virgin and appease his lustful fury.[123] Richard's identification with the savage unicorn, the angry Christ, tamed by the Virgin, was enacted at the Temple Bar in 1392 when the citizens of London sought the king's forgiveness and the restoration of their liberties by showing John the Baptist in a forest surrounded by all manner of wild beasts, including a unicorn. The Baptist pointed his finger and said 'Behold the lamb of God' and Richard observed this closely and his manner grew mild and his anger vanished, especially after Anne, the compassionate mediator, was presented with a tablet with a carving of Christ on the Cross with a sad disciple and distraught mother.[124] Richard also adopted the captured white hart, a hermaphroditic Christ figure, as a symbol representing his taming of the aggressive, martial impulses of the nobility. The Order of the Garter, represented in the Diptych by the cross of St George would then be transformed from an occult order celebrating its founder's military and sexual conquests into a holy order celebrating the king's chastity (which was also commended in the purity of the champion of Arthur's court in *Sir Gawain and the Green Knight*).

As an apostle of peace (the King's dislike of war was attested by Froissart and he frequently expressed his abhorrence at the shedding of Christian blood), Richard closely followed his pious ancestors Edward the Confessor, (whose glorious reign of peace, chastity and visionary powers was described by Aelred of Rievaulx in his life of the confessor which was illustrated in picture cycles in Westminster abbey from 1246) and Louis IX. Louis's crusading ideals were shared among members of Richard II's court. Mezieres offered the king a beguiling vision showing how he, together with Charles VI, would leave his 'the cold lands of the West, that is, in the kingdom of England' to conquer Egypt, Turkey and Syria and eventually the earthly Jerusalem.[125] The currency of these fantasies can be seen in a letter book or formulary, dated 13 October 1395, in which the earl of Rutland gave news of his father, the duke of York, who was in parts of Babylon, and that victories had been achieved near Alexandria and Cairo, and the Sultan of Babylon had been taken prisoner to the honour of the king.[126] The verses of Gildas, probably originally written during the reign of Edward II,[127] were gaining currency in the 1390s and predicted for 'our king now ruling', further identified by marriage to the daughter of the king of France, the subjugation of Egypt, the advance on Babylon and recovery of the world for Christendom.[128]

However, Richard himself focussed more on his ideal of a New Jerusalem, founded on the financial security and prosperity that came with peace. Richard, freed from the necessity of constantly calling parliament, was able to focus on cultural achievements and this is something for which he wished to be remembered. Again Solomon provided the model. King David (commonly identified with Edward III in the second half of the fourteenth century) was a warrior and a sinner who was unable to build a temple of the lord because he had shed blood; and the lord therefore decreed that his son, Solomon, build a temple. Richard established his temples, Westminster Palace and Westminster Abbey, in the holy space of Westminster, the heart of his New Jerusalem. Adelard of Bath had described Solomon's temple as the heavenly Jerusalem, its dimensions determined by the divine harmony of the celestial spheres, and in a similar way the altar floor near Richard's chapel of Our Lady of the Pew and his tomb displayed the representation of the *primum mobile* the divine force of the universe. In 1392 Maidstone described the unobstructed interior space of Westminster Hall where there was a large raised marble throne with lions, evoking the throne of Solomon erected by Henry III. Sometimes the king's chief justice would sin on this throne and at others the king himself, surveying the earthly counterpart to the court of heaven; the roof beams supported 26 angels and the hall was draped in gold. The front of the palace was decorated in 1392, perhaps in an attempt to erase the memory of the humiliations Richard suffered at the hands of the appellants in November 1387 in Westminster Hall, with thirteen statues of the kings of England from Edward the Confessor to Richard II (both virgins and Richard being the last in line like Christ signified the end of time).[129] The abbey contained the relics of Richard's patron saint, Edward the Confessor, and the chapels of St John the Baptist and the Virgin. And it was in the abbey that he chose to be buried alongside his first wife, Anne of Bohemia, his pearl queen. Around the tomb, completed in 1394 and decorated with white harts, runs an epigraph, perhaps completed to mark the King's 1397–98 triumph, the appealing of Gloucester, Arundel and Warwick,[130] that emphasizes the peacetime achievements of a Solomon-like king, steeped in the sort of knowledge contained in Richard's *Book of Divination*, whose wisdom is compared to that of Homer. Homer was regarded as an alchemical prophet in the tradition of Hermes, Moses and Aristotle and who told the story of old Troy which held the seeds of the destiny of Great Britain and New Troy, the home of Richard's temples.[131]

Richard's interest in alchemy may also have contributed to his self-appointed role as defender of Christian orthodoxy. John Wyclif's attacks on organized religion and the established church rested on his attempts to undermine the credibility of the doctrine of transubstantiation. Wyclif was opposed to what he saw as the church's dependence on magic in its emphasis on the importance of the ceremony of the mass and the host as a source of miracles. Orthodox clergy and alchemists had much in common with regard to the focal point of their lives; the parallels between the philosopher's stone/mercury and the host were striking: both were conceived to be white and round and were seen to be one at the same time base matter and divine. Wyclif, in his opposition to the emphasis on magic and popular religion and in his attack on transubstantiation, was by implication attacking alchemical transmutation. Walsingham even reported this heresy using alchemical language asserting that Wyclif taught that when the priest consecrated the four elements at mass they remained bread and wine.[132] In the fourteenth century, thanks to the cult of Corpus Christi, society was also seen as the body of Christ, held together by the celebration of mass. Walsingham saw the Peasant's Revolt representing an attack on this body of Christ: for him it was no coincidence that it took place on Corpus Christi Day. The peasant mob was seen as the limbs of Satan, inspired by Wyclif, an Antichrist figure who's John the Baptist prophet was John Ball.[133] When a knight, Lawrence of St Martin near Salisbury, consumed the host with oysters and wine one Easter, Walsingham maintained that on this night cracks in the ground appeared through which the beast of the abyss would appear.[134] With their brutal naturalism the peasants, in attacking society, were perceived to be attacking Christ's body, denying the divine presence within this social order which was the king; in the same way Wyclif's Lollard followers denied the divine presence in the host. Richard's role in suppressing this rebellion therefore took on symbolic significance as the defender of the body of Christ and he later became a member of the Corpus Christi Guild. His chief justice, who presided over the trial of John Ball, was Sir John Tresilian,[135] later closely associated with the defence of the royal prerogative and perhaps alchemical magic. Walsingham made the host the focal point of the rebellion by describing how the peasants stole the mill stone of St Alban's Abbey (symbol of the host) and broke it into small pieces. Richard II, accompanied by 1,000 archers, and his chief justice, Tresilian (who Walsingham described as possessing the wisdom of the serpent) presided over their trial at the moot hall.[136] Richard may originally had some sympathy with Lollard knights of his chamber; but after he had shaken off the influence of his parents he took a stand as a defender of the church against the Lollards, partly perhaps under archbishop Arundel's influence, but also perhaps because Wyclif and his followers were increasingly critical of the magical element in orthodox religion and Richard was becoming increasingly dependent on jewels, relics and rituals that he believed were a manifestation of divine power. In 1393 he thanked the archbishop for news of a miracle at Becket's tomb and its value in combating Christ's enemies.

Richard's position as defender of orthodox faith was strengthened by alchemical theories endorsing the principle of transmutation as a natural phenomenon and the presence of the divine spirit of mercury in matter: this provided a scientific rationale for the concept of the presence of Christ in the transubstantiated host, with its royal defender represented as the embodiment of the divine mercury in the form of the white hart. This point was made in 1395 by the Dominican friar, Roger Dymock, when he addressed his *Liber contra XII errores et hereses lollardum*, a rebuttal of the twelve errors and heresies in the Lollard manifesto posted on the door of Westminster Hall, to his most glorious, awesome prince, stressing the power given him by God. The presentation copy frontispiece shows Richard sitting on a throne holding a sceptre with two white harts with gold antlers.[137] One of the Lollard errors was to maintain that all trades providing luxuries should be abolished. Dymock responded by citing Aristotle's *Nichomachean Ethics* which maintained that spending on displays of luxury taught people to respect their superiors and disarmed rivals of their power. For Dymock, Richard was a wise king in the tradition of Moses, Solomon, Alexander and Arthur (all believed to be practitioners of a philosophy of alchemy) and he maintained that the key to Richard's wisdom and greatness was displays of royal magnificence and lavish spending, for it was through possession of beautiful buildings and ornate clothing (all things that the Lollards condemned) that Solomon's wisdom was proven. The queen of Sheba hearing of Solomon's wisdom, travelled to his court to impress him with her power by showing him her treasures. When she saw the house that Solomon had built, the food at his tables, the apartments of his servants and their apparel she lost her spirit and said to the king everything I hear concerning your wisdom is true'. For Dymock royal magnificence was a manifestation of the divine aspect of the king which showed he was in touch with occult powers.

9

Richard II and the Occult

*Blessed of the Lord be his land, for the precious things of heaven, for the dew, and for the
deep that coucheth beneath,*

*And for the precious fruits brought forth by the sun, and for the precious things put forth by
the moon,*

The Blessing of Moses, Deuteronymy[1]

The young king's use of alchemical symbolism represented an attempt to elevate
the monarchy to a quasi-religious status, and it aroused considerable opposition
among the generation who had grown up under the rule of Edward III and the
Black Prince. For barons such as Thomas Woodstock, duke of Gloucester and
Richard FitzAlan, the earl of Arundel, traditional kingship was all about fulfilling
the normal roles of a man and this involved fighting wars in defence of the realm,
and begetting children to secure the dynasty. Alchemists were therefore supposed
to facilitate the development of a king into a man of choler and blood, one who
embodied the life affirming, virile qualities of sulphur; and Edward III, until his
decline into feminine senescence, fulfilled this role. Richard, in his insistence on a
never ending and constantly regenerating youth, and his pursuit of policies that
would bring in a period of international peace, represented to many contemporary observers, nothing more than immaturity and an inability to face the respon-
sibilities of mature manhood. According to the Kenilworth chronicler, his Cheshire
body guard would sing over the sleeping king they called 'Dycoun' the sort of
nursery rhyme appropriate for a child: 'Dycun sleep securely, quile we watche, and
dreed nought quile we lyve sestow.'[2] He never appointed older counsellors, developed a military programme like his grandfather and father, or produced children.
Most critics of Richard II focussed on his immaturity. When Richard was 15 Walsingham, reflecting on the dismissal of Richard Scrope as chancellor, commented
that the king had only the wisdom of a small boy;[3] and when lavish gifts were
required for the queen and her Bohemian entourage from abbeys in East Anglia in
1383, Walsingham lamented: 'woe to the land, whose king is a boy'.[4] Throughout
his reign references were made to the king's immaturity: Usk, describing the coronation of Anne, remarked, following Solomon 'woe to thee, O Lord, when thy king
is a child'.[5] When Richard was finally deposed in 1399 much of the criticism of his
reign concentrated on his political immaturity. Archbishop Arundel preached his

deposition sermon based on the text 'A man shall reign over my people'[6] taking the opportunity to contrast Bolingbroke's manliness with Richard's childishness.[7]

Rather than seeing comments on the king's immaturity as a cynical attempt by older courtiers to keep his power in check, it is possible to see them as a reaction to Richard's assertive cult of youth and to see their basis in alchemical, medical theories that the king's behaviour, his narcissism, unpredictability and dishonesty, were symptoms of the behaviour of one governed by the humour of phlegm which predominates in adolescence and generates behaviour more appropriate to a woman. These symptoms had been described by Giles of Rome and in encyclopae-dias owned by Thomas Woodstock, duke of Gloucester. The policy of the king's elder counsellors was to purge the court of youthful royal advisers in the so-called Good Parliament of 1386, and this included William de la Pole, the king's tutor, Simon Burley and his closest friend, Robert de Vere, the earl of Oxford, and to impose on the youthful king a council of older, wiser heads that included his uncle Thomas Woodstock, the duke of Gloucester, Richard FitzAlan, earl of Arundel and Thomas Arundel, the archbishop of Canterbury. Richard was lectured by bishop Arundel and the duke of Gloucester on kingship and the need to recover the domains won by his father and grandfather, lost through bad council. He was also advised to remember the old statutes which said that if a king alienated himself from his people and refused to govern through the advice of the lords his people could depose him. This council virtually ruled England for a year, taking all the decisions involving choice of royal advisers, and finance.

The unease felt by subtle-minded courtiers towards a king whose interest in alchemy took him to mercurial extremes and far from the more conventional identification with the masculine forces of sulphur adopted by Edward III, was expressed by the Gawain poet. Gawain sets out to redeem the honour of Arthur's court and submit to his beheading a year and a day after he has dealt his blow to the Green Knight (perhaps the period involved alludes to the period of conciliar rule). He bears on his shield images of the pentangle and the Virgin Mary and, like Richard, he sees himself as an upholder of the ideals of chastity and purity, quali-ties associated with mercury, in opposition to the chthonic, earthly impulses of sulphur celebrated by the Green Knight. However when Gawain receives his pun-ishment, the slight nick on his neck, he is taught to accept his kinship with the Green Knight. Although he thinks he has resisted sexual temptation, the Green Knight points out that by accepting the erotic article of female attire, the girdle, as a protective talisman, he was lying and attempting to preserve his life, not his hon-our, and this is a form of lust, part of the procreative urge to maintain life and to conquer.[8] Gawain is forced to accept that he has based his self-image on an illu-sory, pure mercurial basis: he has placed women and chastity on a pedestal and denied the masculine side of his personality. The ritual beheading game shows that sulphur and mercury are one and the same: mercury or the spirit cannot exist in this life without sulphur or the body and Gawain is forced, in his encounter with the Green Knight, to recognize and accept his shadow, the chthonic, natural impulses that motivate all life, the changing of the seasons and which brought the world into being. Until he does this he will remain an incomplete personality. The poet's intentions in drawing attention to the imbalance in Richard's dependence on the illusionary purity of the white hart or mercury are subtly demonstrated in the changes he makes to the earlier versions of Gawain's quest. In the post-vulgate cycle *The Suite du Merlin* c. 1245 (later used by Malory) the wedding of Arthur and Guinevere at Camelot is interrupted by a magical event staged by Merlin. A white hart runs through Arthur's hall, followed by pursuing hounds. Merlin informs Arthur that the adventure cannot stop here and Gawain is sent to recover the white hart. The Gawain poet makes much more explicit the association of the hart with the horned beast or Pan, the Greek god with the hindquarters and horns of the goat, by having the Green Knight (or Green Man) as the object of Gawain's quest. The motto at the end of the work, 'evil he who evil thinks', underlines the point that good and evil do not exist in nature that the life force is generated by desire and that these two opposites of spirit and flesh, or mercury and sulphur, must be fully integrated, a point underlined by the colours of the banner of St George, red and white. The poem has political implications for Richard II as well as Edward III: both kings can be seen as incomplete figures: Richard is not simply being praised for his chastity and purity and contrasted to his grandfather who falls into sexual temptation. There are dangerous limitations to a kinship based too exclusively on the principles of the lamb and the virgin: if Edward was all sulphur, Richard is all mercury and he needs something of his grandfather's vigour; like Gawain he must accept that in this life a king cannot be just spirit and pure, he must be a man and all that implies. This political dimension to the literature of Richard II's court can also be seen in Chaucer's *Canterbury Tales*. Richard II's purity and ambiguous sexuality may be hinted at in Chaucer's portrayal of the fair-haired and effeminate Absalom (a name frequently used in association with Richard) who unrealistically places women on a pedestal and the phlegmatic and asexual yellow-haired Pardoner. Both characters lack vital life force and Chaucer is clear in his portrayal of the host (identified with the sun and sulphur) that it is through strong men that society is held together.

Much of the opposition to the king's policies was related to his perceived immaturity and this is how his peace policies, which threatened to undermine all that Edward III and his generation had fought for, were perceived. The letter of Meziere emphasizes the degree to which this policy of peace with France was tied up with alchemical notions of the regenerative power of mercury and Richard's perpetual youth. Its author envisages a new era under the rule of the lamb who will tame the martial impulses of the generation of knights who fought for Edward III: Richard the lodestar and King Charles 'have fixed their eyes and devotion on the precious

Star, that is the Virgin Mary, she has prayed that they should be granted power to restrain the shedding of the blood of their Christian brothers'[9] and professes an alchemical solution a conjunction between the two kingdoms of England and France through a marriage between the six-year-old pearl princess of France and a king devoted to chastity. However there was an aggressive aspect to this letter: the lamb echoes the white hart as a sacred image that stresses Richard's divine anoint-ment and a rationale for royal absolutism. One of the mythic attributes of the stag, according to the author of *Richard the Redeless* (*Richard the Ill Advised*) written by a resident of Bristol in the autumn of 1399 and addressed to Richard II,[10] was the ability to renew itself: as it approached its hundredth year and became feeble it would seek out the wicked serpent, the adder that stings many to death and feed on its venom to become strong again. A similar version of this legend was reported by Richard's cousin, Edward the second duke of York in his *Master of the Game*: the hart when he becomes old beats a serpent with his foot till it is angry and he then eats it and goes to drink water until the venom is mingled in his body and casts out all evil humours 'and maketh his flesh come all anew'.[11] Meziere and Richard may have had in mind the potential opposition of the appellant lords to the proposed Anglo-French alliance and their defeat was envisaged in terms of alchemical medi-cine and magic, a conflict between the white hart and the appellant lords repre-sented by the serpent, a vision that incorporates the essential features of Dastin's vision and the *Wilton Diptych*: 'Most mighty King of Great Britain seated at table for the conquest of the Holy land the carbuncle lodestone or diamond is to be mingled in the wine of Engadi, which will give such power to royal majesty that serpents those who stand in the way of peace at the scent of the flowers of the vine and the scent of wine will cease to exist.'

The proposed alliance with the old enemy was controversial enough but there were further implications of an occult nature that would indicate to many in the court that the monarchy was being taken into an eccentric direction. For alchemists all natural and political events gravitated towards the climax of an alchemical drama, the conclusion of the great work, the return of all matter in the fallen world back to the primal mother, mercury, a realm of pure spirit. According to Petrus Bonus: 'it was through knowledge of this art that the old philosophers knew of the coming of the end of the world when the dead will be resurrected and the body will become unbe-lievably subtilized'. The most important text containing these secrets was the *Book of Revelations*: St John, an exile in Patmos reflecting on the Roman emperor, Nero's domination of Europe, predicted in his vision the destruction of the world and the rebirth of the heavenly 12-gated Jerusalem, and foretold that this would be preceded by plagues which would kill a third of mankind and that the survivors would worship demons and the beast. These events for many were echoed in the second half of the fourteenth century with: the Black Death of 1348/49 which killed at least a third of the population of Western Europe, the outbreak of the Lollard heresy, the Papal

Schism, the Peasants' Revolt, and the march of the Turks eastwards. There arrived a tradition from the *Book of Revelations*, the *Book of Daniel*, *the Sybelline Prophecies* of second-century Alexandria and the *Tiburtine Revelations* of the late seventh century, that these events were the prologue to a reign of peace by a great world emperor who would unite Christendom and establish a rule of saints. After 12 years of rule he would relinquish his crown before the coming of Antichrist who would set out to deceive and rule for the last three and a half years until defeated by the second coming of Christ.[12] There were many predictions of these coming events in the fourteenth century. Arnold of Villanova was arrested for using the *Book of Daniel* to make a prediction in his *Tractatus de tempore adventus Antichristi*, published in Paris in 1300, that the end of the world would come in 1378;[13] in 1354 John of Rupescissa in *Vade Mecum in Tribulacione* predicted the appearance of an Antichrist who will cause the infidels to wage war on the Christians in the east. According to Rupescissa, the clergy would suffer and lose their worldly goods to laymen and tyrants, and in 1367 Christ would elect a new pope who would represent the angel of the apocalypse and a king of France would be made emperor because of his sanctity and, wearing the imperial robes of purple, he would rule the whole of the western world; his sanctity would convince many that he was Christ himself.[14] This prophecy may well have reached and influenced Richard II for John Erghome owned a copy of *Vade Mecum in Tribulacione*. In Langland's *Piers Ploughman*, Piers has a vision of Antichrist. The Corpus Christi plays staged in Chester (and attended by Richard II in 1396) included a play on the coming of Antichrist and the Last Judgement. John Gower in his *Mirour de l'Omme* analyzed the problems of his time as symptomatic of the approach of the last days.[15] For John Wyclif and his followers much of the established church, including the friars and the papacy itself, represented followers of the Antichrist:[16] the author of the Lollard text *Opus arduum*, writing in the 1390s, judged society to be living in the final period of chaotic rule of the papal antichrist. Walsingham saw the Peasant's Revolt as a sign of the approaching end with John Wyclif as a diabolical messiah and John Ball as a John the Baptist figure. For Knighton one of the signs of the approaching end was the Lollards attempts to change the gospels. In 1395 an old prophecy circulated in England 'to the terror and alarm of many people' which predicted an unfavourable conjunction of stars in the autumn bringing eclipses and dreadful signs of natural calamities in the sky – signs of divine wrath as the world approached its end.[17] In a sermon preached at St Paul's Cross, Thomas Wimbledon reported that the end of the world was to occur in 1400.[18]

Richard II was convinced that he was to play a key role in these momentous events and that it was his destiny to be the last emperor. This conviction may have derived from the circumstances of his birth on the Feast of the Epiphany. By 1388 stories about of the birth of his nemesis, the Antichrist, reached the court. Walsingham reported rumours, spread by the knights of St John in Rhodes, of another birth that was a grotesque parody of the birth of the saviour. In the district of Babylon (the ancient city of Old Mesopotamia connected in the *Book of Revelations* and the *Book of Daniel* with the Great Whore of Babylon, decked with pearls and the emergence of Antichrist), after a four-month period of darkness with no stars in the sky and rains of stones and serpents, there occurred, on 25 January, an eruption of the highest mountain in the region, from which flowed white and red lava (which in alchemical terms could signify the conclusion of the great work). This volcanic, sulphurous activity was accompanied by the appearance of words in Latin proclaiming: 'Now has come the hour of my birth and the end and destruction of the world as when the new moon rises and affects this world.'[19] In a remote village in Babylon a grotesque boy was born with eyes like burning lamps who within two months spoke fluently, proclaiming he was the son of God. Saracens forced all in the area to worship this child and the knights of St John concluded that he was the antichrist and that the end of the world was near.

Richard's pursuit of the title of Holy Roman Emperor occurred at the same time as he was attempting to revive the royal prerogative and the *Wilton Diptych* was completed. Richard underlined this point when on 21 July 1398 he despatched an embassy to Cologne sending gifts of silver white harts to the electors. The diptych shows the king in the court of heaven surrounded by the Virgin, Christ and the angels. This picture can be interpreted as a representation of the emperor's rule of the saints, the uniting of Christendom, and establishment of a universal peace under the world emperor and harbinger of the conclusion of the alchemical work in the transformation through mercury of Richard and his kingdom into the kingdom of heaven. This vision was not a heliocentric vision: the light does not come from the sun and in the Gawain poet's *Pearl*, the celestial light in the kingdom of the lamb eclipses that of the sun and the other planets; but when the poet attempts to evoke it he turns to the moon or mercury symbolized by the pearls on Richard's gown:

> Just as the mighty moon will rest
> Before the shining sun is down[20]

•

Admittance to this kingdom is seen in *Cleanness* in terms of the refinement of the pearl, imitating Christ's days on earth: 'As a pearl He's perfectly polished and clean'[21] and through suffering he will

> Be as a pearl through penance, and be purified all—
> And the pearl's appraised the most priceless of gems,
> She so shimmers and shines and her shape is so round,
> So faultless and pure, without filth anywhere[22]

In the cloister and chapter house of Westminster Abbey (which Richard may have seen as his temple of the New Jerusalem) a mural was painted under the patronage of the mayor of London, John of Northampton, and the Westminster recluse, John of London, between 1380 and 1400[23] on the theme of the judgement that showed scenes from the apocalypse, beginning with St John travelling by boat to Patmos, the scene of his visions, and including 24 ancients (echoing the number of the garter knights) falling down before the lamb held by John the Baptist, the symbol of the coming Christ and the last emperor. This scene echoed the procession of 1392 in which the Londoners threw themselves at the feet of the lamb (a scene possibly witnessed by the author of *Pearl*)[24] and Richard for the sake of the Baptist and the Virgin forgave them and said: 'To my palace all of you must come. For there a final end will come.'[25] These messianic and apocalyptic pretensions, accompanied by gestures such as the threat to destroy London and the destruction of Sheen palace must have alarmed many of his subjects.

The close link between Richard's candidacy for the title of Holy Roman Emperor in 1396–97, which involved arranging for the archdeacon of Cologne to go to Rome to entreat Papal support for his candidacy,[26] and his assertion of the royal prerogative was expressed when Walsingham suggested Richard's imperial ambitions were a factor in the royal coup that resulted in the murder, execution and exile of the appellant lords in 1397. Richard sent agents to Cologne, who confirmed that the majority of the seven electors supported his candidacy, but two or three withheld their consent because he could not control his own subjects; this greatly angered him and caused him to turn against his barons.[27] He subsequently explained to the archbishop of Canterbury, Thomas Arundel, that he had arrested the archbishop's brother, the earl of Arundel, to show the Germans that he was master in his own house and attempted to reassure the emperor elect, Wenceslas, whom Richard hoped to replace and who had commiserated with him in regard to rebellions in his realm, that he was able to control his own people. Richard's conviction that he was to be the saintly emperor to precede the Antichrist may have been encouraged by the circulation of the prophetic verses of Gildas in the 1390s predicting for an English king married to the daughter of the king of France that after being offered the crown three times by the pope he would formally accept coronation as the emperor of the world.[28] Prophecies of Merlin (owned by Richard's tutor, Simon Burley) and prophecies concerning the Holy oil in fourteenth-century manuscripts set predictions of British imperial rule against a background of a sacred, apocalyptic world ruler.[29] Two late fourteenth-century manuscripts associated with Norwich Cathedral Priory contain prophecies about the son of an eagle who will die without descendents in the last days; a prophecy of the holy oil of St Thomas of Becket, hidden because of the unworthiness of the English kings until the time when a great future king will be the first to be anointed with the oil; and a prophecy of the lily concerning a son of man who will unite Britain and become a world emperor.[30] The portion of the *Dieulacres Chronicle* written from a Ricardian perspective begins its account of the reign of Richard 'the most excellent king of all kings of the world'. with a series of laudatory prophecies.[31]

Given his conviction that he was the saintly emperor prefiguring the return of Christ, Richard naturally saw the royal prerogative as part of a divine plan and all opponents of it as agents of the Antichrist. These would include the archbishop of Canterbury, Thomas Arundel (conveniently labelled as Antichrist in a Wycliffe sermon for opposing the making available the scriptures in English: 'O men that be on Christ's behalf helpe ye now against Antichrist. For the perilous time is come'), and Henry Bolingbroke, who was seen as a potential opponent of the church. Richard's conviction that he was the last emperor may have contributed to his lack of concern for the succession and helped to fan rumours that he saw himself as the last emperor of the Sybelline prophecies and the prophecies of John of Rupescissa which concerned an apocalyptic last world emperor, a French king, who lays down his crown at Jerusalem when the Antichrist's armies approach to await the coming of Christ.[32] Richard similarly was seen to abdicate his throne in preparation for the coming of Antichrist after a reign of 12 years, the period of Richard's adult rule from 1387 to 1399. Sir William Bagot (d. 1407), the Warwickshire knight who managed to serve the earl of Warwick during the Merciless Parliament of 1386, and to also serve Bolingbroke and Mowbray during the appealing of the appellant lords Arundel, Woodstock and Warwick, and to follow Richard II after the exile of Bolingbroke and yet still survive,[33] recalled in 1399 a conversation with Richard that took place at Lichfield in the Christmas of 1398 in which the king announced that once he had recovered his royal estate and dignity he would renounce his crown and name his cousin (Edward duke of Aumale), as his successor. Bolingbroke and his supporters certainly capitalized on these rumours by circulating the story that Richard cheerfully abdicated his throne. However the Evesham chronicler acknowledged that Richard had said that he would not renounce the 'characters' impressed on his soul, the sanctity of anointing at his coronation was indelible.[34] Such occult language suggests that he saw the coronation as a sacred event that acted as a spell forever separating him from other mortals. Another account of the king's renunciation in the Tower reports that the king, deprived of his visible crown, consoled himself with the thought that the invisible crown could never be snatched from him by a usurper and that the divinely elected kingship could never be abdicated.[35]

Richard's identification with these apocalyptic events went even further and he developed a messianic complex that was so strong that it became a prominent feature of his public image. On the *Wilton Diptych*, executed when Richard was aged 30, approximately the same age as Christ when he began his ministry, he is ushered into the court of heaven before the Virgin by John the Baptist who was integral to this messianic complex. Richard formed his own livery of the Baptist, the only figure in the *Wilton Diptych* actually touching the king, and if the diptych is regarded as an epiphany portrait, the Baptist becomes the prophet foretelling the messiah, the one whom the magi seek; and Richard, represented as the white hart, crowned and chained, presents an image of the suffering redeemer and saviour of his people. This image of the crowned, white hart with the chain around its neck was something with which he closely identified: before setting out for Ireland on 16 April 1399, Richard made his will in Westminster and reflected that since his tender youth he had submitted 'our neck by mercy of the supreme king to the burden of the government of England',[36] suggesting that he identified the office of kingship with a divine martyrdom,[37] an honour of which the English were unworthy. His full frontal portrait in Westminster Abbey, showing him holding the sceptre and orb he received on his coronation (kings were usually shown in profile), is a boldly hierarchic, Christ-like pose in imitation of the godhead in which the king surveys his people.[38] Richard may have seen himself as a defender of the orthodox church in the face of the attacks of antichrist figures such as Wyclif and Gaunt; but by fusing the sacred and the political, and suggesting that obedience was the secular counterpart to orthodoxy, it is possible to suggest that King Richard II, the defender of the church, was suffering under the delusion that he was indeed the messiah of the second coming, the lamb of God, and that he represented for many Christians an even more alarming threat to established religion than the anti-clerical tirades of Wyclif and his followers. Such fears may have been behind Adam Usk's claim that one of the reasons for Richard's deposition was sacrilege. As king he may have ceased to become a servant of God and keeper of the faith and instead asserted himself as an object of the faith.

Richard's messianic delusions may highlight his narcissistic and neurotic dependence on the occult as compensation for his sense of inferiority, and they may have alarmed members of the governing class; but on their own they cannot explain Richard's deposition. However Richard's involvement in the occult also posed a direct, political threat to members of the parliamentary, courtly elite when he used it to assert the royal prerogative in an attempt to crush his opponents. The crucial events in Richard's political life were the parliamentary impeachment of his advisers and the imposition of a continual council on the king, between 1386 and 1387, which compelled him to relinquish much of his political power. The triumph of the appellants exposed the hollowness of royal power. Frustrated by his inability to achieve military success when his Scottish opponents disappeared into the mists, and the continual lectures from his uncles on the pragmatic realities of exerting political power, Richard responded by turning to his twin interests of alchemy and civil law. A group of king's judges, civilian layers trained in King's Hall, Cambridge, where they were schooled in the principles of Roman law with its concomitant theories appropriate to theocratic kingship, made the most remarkable statement on the royal prerogative in the middle ages.[39] They stated that the king's prerogative included the right to choose ministers responsible to him alone and parliament had no right to initiate business or appeal ministers. These royal judges were responsible for elevating the mystique of kingship by placing emphasis on the royal will which acquired mystical, occult status. In August 1386, in Shrewsbury and Nottingham, Richard consulted the king's judges who shared these views on the royal will to establish the extent to which the liberties and prerogatives of the crown had been hampered by the proceedings of parliament in the previous October. Ten questions relating to the attempt to impose a council on the king were put to judges who shared these views on the royal will by Robert de Vere, Alexander Neville and Michael de la Pole.[40] They concluded that any attempt to impose restrictions on the king's prerogative, including his choice of counsellors, was opposition to the royal will, and while the 1352 statute of treason did not allow the possibility of passing sentence of treason on those accused of procuring the appointment of a council, the judges were careful to say they should be punished as traitors.[41] A political dispute had been transmuted: notions of obedience to the royal will had been elevated to a legal and indeed a mystical principle. The intellect behind these pronouncements on the royal prerogative was probably the chief justice of the King's Bench, Sir Robert Tresilian, who many times sat in judgement on a marble throne representing the king's authority in Westminster Hall.[42]

Behind this elevation of obedience to a legal and religious principle lay considerable alchemical learning in which the royal will was identified with mercury, or the white hart. At the heart of alchemical philosophy lay the notion that before creation all was formless chaos, primordial, maternal water that was known as the philosopher's mercury. However mercury was also understood in terms of the divine will or spirit which rained down as sperm on this ocean (a conjunction that was sometimes seen as the philosopher's stone) to create the four elements, out of which emerged the sulphur (the origin of all flesh) and the ordered harmonious universe, a process celebrated in the Cosmati pavement in Westminster Abbey. This conjunction of primal mercury and the spirit or will of God was understood in sexual terms, though not strictly in terms of male or female, but more of a hermaphroditic conception analogous to the workings of the Holy Trinity. However echoes of this primal act of creation occurred in sexual activity throughout the natural world, the union of male sperm and female water generated by lust or the will (something understood by the Gawain poet), which was the only way mortals could comprehend this original manifestation of the divine will in the creation. The will of God could also be seen in the assertion of the will of the king, for human society was seen in similar terms to the natural world. By its very nature society is chaotic, lacking order and form until the will of the king is asserted to create the social order, the body politic (the body of Christ), a conjunction of mercury and sulphur, and this was recognized in the Diptych in the portraits of Richard as a golden, Christ king and as the chained hart with the crown of thorns, the divine spirit of mercury suffering in its bodily incarnation as sulphur as the servant of his people. It is this royal will, or spirit, represented by the badge of the white hart, that Tresilian asserted it was a religious duty of Richard's subjects to obey.

The high ranking officials responsible for imposing the council on the king were justifiably alarmed and arrested Tresilian, who was observing the appealing of Richard's favourites in parliament from the roof of an apothecary's house near the gate of Westminster Abbey. He was subsequently discovered, hiding under a table disguised behind a false beard, and dressed like a beggar and recognized by his distinctive voice.[43] He claimed sanctuary in Westminster Abbey,[44] but Gloucester denied the claim and he was condemned by the Merciless Parliament in 1388 for practising the invocation of demons, and using diabolical names and a demons head in his magical activities.[45] Tresilian was dragged to Tyburn in a hurdle boasting that 'he could not die, so long as he had some thing about him'. Soldiers discovered around his neck clay amulets depicting astrological signs, charms, several diabolic names and a demon's head, which suggests that he saw a connection between this elevation of the royal prerogative and occult sources of power.[46] Physical force was needed to make him ascend the scaffold; his clothes and charms were stripped off, and after hanging his throat was cut as an extra precaution. The lawyer, John Blake, who drafted questions to the judges, was also executed. The other judges: Sir Robert Bealknap, Sir John Lacy, Sir John Holt, Sir Roger Fulthorp, Sir William Burgh and John Cobham, sergeant at law, were arrested and seized in the courts they were sitting in and committed to prison. Originally they were sentenced to death but their sentences were commuted to exile in Ireland.[47] Thomas Rushook (d. 1392), the Dominican confessor of Richard II was also spared the death sentence and exiled to Ireland where he became bishop of Kilmore. So after 1388 there was in Ireland a body of men, expert in law, who had advised the king on the assertion of his prerogative, and this is the context of the composition in Ireland of a tract on kingship, *De Quadripartita regis specie*, written by Richard's treasurer which emphasizes the importance of obedience to the king's will. In the prologue to Richard's *Libellus Geomancie* which follows this text in Bodley 581, Richard himself is praised for his interest in the subtle arts and the two laws. A purge of Richard's other advisers, accused of treason in exerting undue influence over the king and taking advantage of his tender years, occurred in 1387; this resulted in the exile of de Vere and the execution of Simon Burley. The five appellant lords, backed by 500 armed men, entered the Tower and were received by Richard in his chapel. According to the chronicler of Whalley Abbey, the king was deposed for three days but reinstated when Gloucester and Bolingbroke could not agree on his successor. Richard's response was to the events of so-called Merciless Parliament to abandon himself for the next three or four months to hunting. These events permanently damaged Richard (in his later correspondence he referred to the accusation of his friends and advisers in his 'tender years'): they explain his sense of inferiority and the conclusion

that he came to that he could not manage the nobility through the exercise of political skills of compromise and negotiation, and that he needed to find alternative
occult sources of hidden power. This can be seen in his commissioning in 1389–90
Statuta Anglia, a book of statutes from Magna Carta, through the reigns of Edward
I and Edward II to the most recent edicts of his reign on 1 December 1388,[48] proclaiming the rightful succession of English kings from Henry III to Richard II and
attempting to reverse the constraints placed on Edward II. The collection shows
Richard's obsession with the humiliations of his grandfather (nine of the questions
put to the royal judges determined that those imposing the ordinances on Edward
II should be punished as traitors) and his determination to redeem the royal authority achieved through law, and it can be read as a manifesto of the assertion of the
royal prerogative on the same level as the treatises in Richard's *Book of Divination*
(Bodley 581) *Liber judica*. The *Statuta Anglia* begins with an initialled letter R showing the king holding the orb that would feature in the iconic Westminster portrait
as symbol or absolute and divine power.[49] The civil law that maintained the king's
divine authority acquired for Richard the same mystique as the Old Testament,
where kings such as Solomon became the conduit of the divine will. Most of the
other books surviving from Richard's library were similarly concerned with the
sacred office of kingship. They include: a psalter showing the boy king in his regalia
presented to the Christ child; and Chandos Herald's *Life of the Black Prince*, probably written around 1386 under Burley's auspices for the young king, which ends
with a scene in which Edward III and the other nobles swear to uphold the rights of
the young heir.[50]

Richard's recovery of full authority as king, obtained in 1389 when he attained
his majority, was seen in alchemical terms as a regeneration and renewal of the
aura of kingship. In 1390–91 John Gower, in the first version of his *Confessio
amantis*, reflected on the positive mood accompanying Richard's majority: he
employed alchemical imagery to convey the triumph of the golden sun reigning in
the heavens like a bejewelled golden monarch ruling the leaden Saturn, and
pointed out that God had been keeping Richard and his estate safe for this very
moment of triumph. Likening 'my worthy prince' to the sun which has been
masked by cloud he proclaims:

> But how so that it trouble in them,
> The sonne is evere bright and fair?
> Withinne himself and noght empeired:
> Although the wether be despaired
> The led planet is not to wite[51]

One of Richard's most loyal supporters throughout the 1390s was Henry Despenser
(c. 1341–1406), the bishop of Norwich and member of a baronial family that had

provided Edward II's favourites. Despenser, who continued to remain loyal after the king's deposition in 1399, became a royal counsellor after 1388 and owned a collection of prophecies including, 'the Lily, and the Holy Oil of St Thomas Becket', which was full of alchemical imagery and predicted a high imperial destiny for a hero king sanctified by his kingship, a son of man, who bears the holy oil and is identified with distilled gold; this reborn king will ascend to the stars after an assertion of royal power and victory against his internal enemies: 'he will distil gold from trees and stones will shine forth silver . . . he will deserve the highest of blessings and he will fly to the stars'.[52] The assertion of the royal prerogative in the strike against the king's uncles in 1397 was also seen by the king's supporters in alchemical terms. *The Kirkstall Abbey Chronicle*, written in the Cistercian abbey on the River Aire near Leeds before 1399, captures the mood of royalist exaltation by incorporating the language of a royalist newsletter. The chronicler ends an account of parliament, marvelling at the long suffering of the king and rejoicing at the restoration of his power, symbolized by Richard's holding a great court and having his retainers, bearing the white hart, celebrating across London the transmutation of the captured stag, from a figure of martyrdom to that to the resurrected sun. Christ triumphant in the form of the white hart now became the instrument of the royal prerogative: 'Of late the sun had been hidden in a cloud, that is to say when the king's majesty was concealed by the power of others, yet now the king in arms leaps over the hills, tossing the clouds on his horns he shines more brightly than the light of the sun.'[53] This celebration evokes the themes of the resurrection and triumph of King Mercury found in Richard's copy of the *Stella alchemiae:* 'though he is killed and led to hell, the king doth ascend into heaven and comes again to earth crowned with a diadem and shall make most strong battle on the gates of hell and he shall subjugate all nations to him and he shall never be destroyed but remain forever'.[54]

This was a theme to be found in the banner of Richard's father, the Black Prince, the sun shining out of the clouds, and this was modified in Richard's standard, sprinkled with ten suns shining in splendour and lodged cornered by a white hart with golden antlers, an image of the conjunction of sulphur and mercury.[55] The assertion of the royal prerogative in the 1390s amounted in Richard's eyes to the fulfilment of the divine will and underlines his attempts to secure the canonization of his great grandfather, Edward II. The alchemical vision of Adam Davy, concerning the regeneration of the kingdom under the red and white beams of sulphur and mercury, which originally refers to the reigns of Edward II or Edward III, was disseminated in this period.

Richard in the 1390s was attempting to impose on his subjects an autocratic kingship, and it is possible that the inner strength, self-confidence, indeed arrogance, that he needed to assert his will over his powerful barons and seek revenge for his humiliations came from his dependence on mercury which was then believed to be the most powerful substance known to man, the divine principle behind all life which was manifested in the incarnate Christ, in the daily celebration of mass, and in the divinely ordained kingship of Richard himself. Richard made mercury the cornerstone of his kingship through the symbol of the white hart. The hart, as Meziere pointed out, lay embedded in Richard's name (Richart), like the heart (or quicksilver) within the outer body of sulphur which, according to Petrus Bonus, was rendered obsolete by the power of mercury to generate and impart the form of gold on all things.[56] The white hart was first used publically in 1391. During the session of parliament Richard ordered a joust in which the king and his knights challenged all comers. The knights on his side wore on their shields the white hart with gold chain around the neck and crown. The jousts were to last 24 days and were opened by a procession of 24 knights of the garter being lead by 24 ladies in chains of gold from the Tower, through the city to Smithfield, where the jousts were to be held.[57] The sight of the king's knights entering the lists, lead by ladies and wearing the protective symbol of mercury, may have inspired the central motifs of the pentangle and girdle of *Sir Gawain and the Green Knight*. White hart badges began to be frequently used at court, to be worn on the sleeve, on the chest or around the neck as a collar.[58] Richard distributed them among his friends including: Walter Skirlaw (d. 1406), the bishop of Durham and diplomat and adviser to Richard II buried at the king's suggestion in Westminster Abbey, who left a silver cup engraved with the white hart in his will; and Sir John Golafre (d. 1393), a Berkshire knight, esquire of Richard II's chamber and keeper of the king's plate and jewels, who left his white hart broach with rubies and pearls and a gold, enamel cup with crown and hart to the king in 1391.[59] The inventory of jewels and plate handed over to Henry IV in November 1399 included a hart lying under a tree with 27 pearls hanging from the branches and its horns.[60] Accounts of the king's wardrobe in1393 include payment to goldsmiths for two white harts with gold. In 1392 Richard wrote to the doge of Venice saying he had bestowed on a knight the privilege of wearing the white hart badge. White hart banners appeared on the royal barge and were set in stone in Westminster Hall, the ceiling of which supported 26 angels, and flanked the tomb of Edward II. In January 1397 Richard paid for robes for 20 ladies to lead 20 armed men from the Tower of London to Westminster where he received them after the coronation of Isabella on 3 January 1397. The robes designed by the court painter, Thomas Lythington, were of long red silk with white silver harts with crowns of gold and evoked Richard's red gown with white harts on the *Wilton Diptych*.

The white hart badge was used as token of obedience by Richard to rebuild a royal court, creating a peerage loyal to the crown, symbolized by the court of heaven in the *Wilton Diptych* where the eleven angels wear the white hart. This court included the king's half brother, John Holland, K.G., earl of Huntingdon, and first duke of Exeter, who went on a pilgrimage to the Holy Land in 1397;

Edward of Norwich, son and heir of the duke of York, created earl of Rutland in 1390 and duke of Aumale, and according to Creton 'there no man in the world whom Richard loved better'; and Sir William Scrope, earl of Wiltshire knight of the Garter in 1396 and keeper of the forests in Cheshire in 1398, and chief justice in Ireland; who died on a crusade in Prussia fighting with the Teutonic knights against the pagan Lithuanians and Garter members Sir Brian Stapleton, and Sir Lewis Clifford, author of a poem *The Cuckoo and the Nightingale* that equals *Pearl* for sensitivity. These men, and many others, bore the white hart and Richard considered them to be jewels adding lustre to his crown: 'we believe the more we bestow honours on wise and honourable men the more our crown is adorned with gems and precious stones'.[61] A powerful armed affinity was built up around this badge containing the symbol of mercury, the royal will that must be obeyed. From late 1397 Richard granted a growing number of Cheshire knights and squires the livery of the white hart, and established a bodyguard of Cheshire yeomen and archers, 300 strong, divided into seven watches, many of whom would address him in their native English tongue and call him 'Dycoun'. On 19 August 1397 Richard issued a proclamation forbidding any Cheshire archer from enlisting with any other lord or retinue, and on the following day he ordered all lords, knights, esquires and yeomen wearing the livery of the white hart to assemble at Kingston on Thames. In *Richard the Redeless*, a vast army of retainers wearing the badge of the white hart was noted. In 1397 a parliamentary act accorded Cheshire the status of a palatinate, giving it the same sort of autonomy as the principality of Wales, and it was even rumoured that Richard intended to make Chester his capital. A retinue of 750 Cheshire men was on his payroll and the king's entourage included members of almost every Cheshire family of note.

These retainers bearing the badge of the white hart may have provided the primary audience for *Sir Gawain and the Green Knight*.[62] Richard held courts in the north-west in 1387 and 1398–99 and *Sir Gawain and the Green Knight*, copied by a Cheshire scribe, would have made a Christmas, New Year entertainment during the king's sojourn at Lichfield in 1398–99 when heralds were sent across the land proclaiming the jousts and hunts on twelfth night in celebration of the kings birthday; the king's Cheshire retainers, including Sir John Stanley, were all in attendance. The identity of the author of *Sir Gawain and the Green Knight* remains elusive: the name John Massy (a Cheshire name connected with Sir John Stanley) occurs as an anagram in the seventy-sixth stanza of *Pearl*. The base for this affinity was Cheshire in the north-west of England where Richard began recruiting the Cheshire bowmen in 1387 and home of the works of the Gawain poet. According to the chronicler of the *Brut*, the Anglo Norman epic history of Britain extended in 1333 and translated into English in the last quarter of the fourteenth century,[63] Chester Castle was especially loved by Richard, who had white harts added in freestone niches and walls during the Shrewsbury sessions of parliament. Those wearing the white hart badge began to arouse respect and fear. By 1394 Richard retained a corpus of 700 native Cheshire men, knights, esquires and archers, and from this number he retained 300 as a personal bodyguard, most recruited by Sir John Stanley of Hooton, which was used to intimidate the Revenge Parliament of 1397. In this year Richard ordered the sheriff of Cheshire to recruit 2,000 men (the description in *Pearl* of the 144,000 liveried retainers of the Lamb of God each wearing a pearl badge, provided a divine sanction for this large royal *familia*).[64] The issue of the granting of a livery badge (presumably the white hart) as a way of asserting the royal prerogative had been raised in the Merciless Parliament of February 1388 when five appellees were accused of having persuaded the king to give livery badges to a great number of people in order to have the power to perform false treasons. In the Cambridge Parliament of the same year the commons petitioned that all liveries, called badges (signs) of the king, and other lords be abolished. It is significant that an almost occult power was being attributed to some badges and it is likely, given the significance of the stag as a symbol of mercury, that the white hart was in the mind of the petitioners: 'The boldness inspired by their badges makes them unafraid to do those these things and more besides.'[65] Meziere encouraged Richard to pursue his policies of peace and concord with Charles VI in the face of the opposition of his barons by invoking the white hart: 'Remember, and not as in a dream, that your arms, emblems and banners, which bear witness to your power to discomfort and put to flight the enemies of human nature, the enemies from Hell, have long been held in contempt, and still are, in Jerusalem, your spiritual heritage here on earth.'[66] According to the author of *Richard the Redeless* it was the white hart badge in particular that gave Richard's followers feelings of invulnerability:

> For tho that had hertis on hie on her brestis,
> For the more partie I may well avowe,
> They bare them the bolder for ther gay broches
> And busshid with ther brestis and bare adoun the pouere
> Liages that loued you the lesse for ther yuel dedis.[67]

Richard's response to the Cambridge petition was to assert the right of the crown to grant liveries; an ordinance was repeated on 12 May 1390 proclaiming that no person below the rank of bannerette was allowed to distribute a livery badge. This allowed the expansion of a household of loyal, heavily armed royalist retainers, many from Cheshire, something that was criticized by the author of *Richard the Redeless* in 1399, who contended that Richard had been poorly advised and his kingdom mismanaged. This resulted in parliamentary petition of 1397 delivered by Sir Thomas Haxey (d. 1425), the treasurer of York Minster, that complained about the size and cost of the royal household and the multitude of bishops and ladies maintained therein, the culmination of a series of petitions from 1393 to 1397 complaining about the numbers of lesser men knights and esquires wearing the badge of the white hart.[68] The increasing power of the white hart, which by 13 January 1399 covered the roof of St Mary's in Coventry where Richard held court, may have led observers to speculate on the occult significance of the white hart itself, especially when it was born in mind that one of the key figures in Haxey's petition, one of the bishops who had largely been absent from his diocese before 1399 who was the object of these criticisms, was the king's physician, Robert Tideman of Winchcombe (d. 1401), the bishop of Llandaff in 1393 and Worcester in 1395, had been accused of practising magic.[69] This petition was the cue to Richard's assertion of the royal prerogative: he responded to the petition by replying that this was an offence to his majesty which he inherited from his ancestors. It has been suggested that the petition was set up by Richard as an excuse to make his strike (he was now secure enough to avenge the humiliations of 1386–88) and one of the men behind it may have been Robert Tideman.

Richard began his move against the appellants by invoking the aid of St John the Baptist (according to his kinsman, Edward duke of York, in a section on hunting the hart in his *Master of the Game*, the harts have more power to run well from early May until the Nativity of St John the Baptist on 24 June, and from this feast until August they put on new flesh and hair and grow merry).[70] He then followed the procedures used against his friends between November 1387 and February 1388 when the merciless parliament convened and, assembling 300 Cheshire archers bearing the badge of the white hart, he used parliament to appeal Gloucester and Arundel for treason using alchemical symbolism. Their appellants, the earls of Rutland, Nottingham, Salisbury and Despenser and Sir William Scrope, all wore suits of red robes with white borders powdered with letters of gold perhaps to emphasize that this reassertion of the prerogative amounted to an alchemical transmutation, the conclusion of the great work. Parliament was opened by Bishop Stafford of Exeter, who preached a sermon from Ezekiel 37:22: 'There must be one king above all he should be powerful enough to govern his laws properly executed and his subjects obedient.' Thomas Woodstock, duke of Gloucester, was arrested and taken to Calais, where his murder was organized by Richard's long-time favourite, Thomas Mowbray; Richard Fitz Alan, earl of Arundel was beheaded on Tower Hill; Richard Beauchamp, the earl of Warwick, was exiled to the Isle of Wight; and Thomas Arundel, archbishop of Canterbury, was deprived of his see. The *Wilton Diptych* was probably executed in 1396, possibly in January at the time of the Feast of the Epiphany, when Richard was contemplating his revenge against the Appellant lords; and it is a densely allusive testament to these events. There are a number of symbols of alchemical transmutation and resurrection, including the peacocks embroidered on the gown of the martyred King Edmund; but the dominant alchemical symbol is the white hart. The themes of Richard's regeneration, the rebirth of his golden youth and the victory of the white hart over the serpent and its rebirth (which echoes myths about the stag which swallows a snake and consequently loses its antlers and grows a new pair)[71] have a political dimension, celebrating the rebirth of the monarchy, the triumph of the royal prerogative. In 1394 John Trevor, bishop of Armagh, commissioned the translation of *de Armis* of Johannes de Bado Aures at the request of Queen Anne and the section entitled *De Cervo*, on the attributes of the stag, stresses two qualities valued by Richard, prudence and subtlety: 'the hart is able to resist all beasts who come against him and he who bears the hart on his arms is prudent and subtle in war'.[72]

By 1396/7, when the Diptych was completed, these themes would have found endorsement in the *Vision of John Dastin*. Five of Edward III's seven sons were dead; John of Gaunt was terminally ill and the duke of York ineffectual. Richard, the son of the Black Prince, was asserting himself as the sun, like the one pure planet in Dastin's vision, which through his death and rebirth would redeem Edward's monarchy. The idea that mercury or the white hart could be an instrument in the assertion of the royal prerogative was suggested in alchemical texts of the period. Petrus Bonus, in the *Pretiosa Margarita Novellum,* pointed out that quicksilver, the form of gold, has the ability to impose this form of royalty on whatever substance it comes into contact with; in the same way the white hart badge impressed on the common metals of its subjects the form of royalty or gold, and stamped on wax in the form of the seal it could spread the power of the king. The origin of the use of the white hart as symbol of the monarchy may be the appearance of a large, white stag before a wooden castle on the Grand Rue Saint Denis, accompanied by 12 young maidens, protecting the bed of justice in celebration of the marriage of Charles VI and Isabella (the parents of Richard's future bride).[73] On the outside of the diptych the white hart, although crowned, is chained to its crown, which echoes the crown of thorns on the other outside panel and thus implying the martyrdom of the king, the fixation of mercury, and alluding to the martyrdom of those loyal defenders of the royal prerogative from 1386 to 1389: Simon Sudbury, the archbishop of Canterbury, who crowned Richard II and who died at the hands of the peasants in 1381; Simon Burley, executed at the insistence of Thomas Woodstock, duke of Gloucester; Sir Nicholas Brembre, the lord mayor of London in 1377 and 1383–85 who was said to have contemplated abolishing the name of London to replace it with Little Troy and who was executed after the Merciless Parliament;[74] Sir Robert Tresilian, who was also executed after the Merciless Parliament; Michael de la Pole, the earl of Suffolk and chancellor who died in exile in France in 1389; and Robert de Vere, who bore the standard of St George (shown on the inside panel) at the Battle of Radcot Bridge against Bolingbroke[75] and who also died in exile in 1391. At the heart of the Diptych is the notion of revenge for the massacre of these innocents (the abbey where the Diptych was housed was consecrated on Holy Innocents Day) and the objects of this revenge were the lords

The *Wilton Diptych* showing Richard II and the three kings of the Epiphany.
England under the guidance of the Virgin and the alchemical
transformation of the kingdom.

appellant who had denied the essence of Richard's kingship, represented by the
white hart. Inside the panel, with resplendent gold, we have the emergence of the
young king as he was at the time of his coronation (a ceremony that had become a
source of occult power), before the humiliations of 1386–87, receiving his man-
date from Christ and the Virgin. According to Froissart, on Saturday morning in
1381 Richard, before riding out to meet the peasants, went to: 'a small chapel in the
abbey where there is an image of our Lady which performs miracles in which kings
of England have always placed faith'. The king said prayers before this statue; this
may have been the image of the Virgin in the chapel of Our Lady of the Pew.[76]
Richard also visited the shrine of the Virgin at Walsingham in 1383; four years
later he and Anne joined the Lincoln Cathedral confraternity under the patronage
of the Virgin. The accusations of Bishop Arundel and the Appellant Lords of 'tender youth' and immaturity and inability to rule were being turned against political
opponents and made into a source of political strength.

Accompanying the king in the *Wilton Diptych* are eleven angels, all wearing the
white hart, who represent the age of Richard at his coronation, and the 11 blue,
robed knights over whom Richard became commander when he succeeded to his
father's place in the Garter on St George's day 1377, one half of the garter stall
which regularly jousted against the other half. This constituted a secret

brotherhood,[77] inspired by the old crusading orders of the Templars and Hospitalliers and such new orders as the knot of Naples and Meziere's Order of the Passion,[78] tied together by loyalty to the king: Robert de Vere, elected to the Garter in 1384, assured Simon Burley, a member of the Order from 1377, that 'I will never forsake you, are we not companions'.[79] These 11 angels also signify the 11 knights or apostles dedicated to defending the royal prerogative, who would have included such Garter members as: John Holand duke of Exeter, Richard's half brother; his nephew, Thomas Holand, the duke of Surrey; his cousin, Edward duke of Aumale; Sir John Stanley, Richard II's chief Justice and Lord Deputy; William Scrope, earl of Wiltshire; and the royal servants: Edmund Stafford, bishop of Exeter; Robert Tideman, bishop of Worcester; Thomas Merks, bishop of Carlisle; Richard Maudelyn, Richard II's clerk; and William Ferriby, the king's notary. Like Christ's apostles, they were held together by a symbol of their loyalty and devotion to the royal cause, the white hart, which they gave each other as expressions of brotherhood and shared loyalty.[80] Sir John Golafre, a knight of Richard's chamber, left a brooch of the white hart and enamelled cup decorated with a crowned and chained white hart, and a cup decorated with harts, to another chamber knight, Baldwin Beresford. The altar for this order, perhaps completed on the advice of a royal chaplain,[81] would be the diptych itself, in which the angels in the court of heaven wear blue, the colour of the Garter. However one knight is missing in the Diptych: when Richard took command of half the Garter in 1377 he would have had 12 knights under his command, the twelfth being his cousin, Henry Bolingbroke who, on the same day that Richard became a member, succeeded to the stall of Jean de Grailly, the Black Prince's companion in arms. Bolingbroke's absence in the Diptych may point to his identification as the thirteenth apostle, the one remaining threat to Richard's absolute power, the Judas who would soon betray and dethrone him.[82] On this level the diptych stands as a very private, occult document, perhaps representing a vision of the king as he worshipped in the chapel of St Mary le Pew, revealing mysteries about a secret society or brotherhood, one that overlapped that of Meziere's Order of the Passion, and dedicated to upholding the prerogative, the king's will, symbolized by the white hart. The east end of Westminster Abbey, where the Diptych was kept, became the burial place of many of Richard's followers, including: the Garter Knights Sir James Bernes, Sir John Salisbury, Sir John Golafre; the queen's chamberlain Sir Bernard Braen; and John Waltham, the bishop of Salisbury and Lord High Treasurer who was buried in 1395 near St Edmund's chapel in a tomb decorated with a chained and couched white hart.[83]

The alchemical and occult texts owned by the king emphasize the importance of obedience to the royal will which is equated with the divine will. The central theme of the *Quadripartita Regis* is obedience to the king; the theme of Richard's 1395 expedition to Ireland was to secure the obedience of the Irish chieftains. In the proverbs of Solomon in Richard's[84] *Book of Divination* occur such sayings as:

'Fear thou the lord and the king'; 'meddle not with them that are given to change'; 'The wrath of a king is as a roaring of the lion who so provoketh him to anger sinneth against his soul'; and 'the wrath of a king is as a messenger from death but a wise man will pacify it'. This exalted view of the royal prerogative had been expressed as early as 1382 by John Gower in a letter of advice addressed to Richard and included in *Vox clamantis*: 'You are above the laws and your wrath is death you can do what is not allowed'. The secret of wisdom from an alchemical perspective is therefore obedience to the king, and the assertion of the prerogative acquires a magical power. The point was made by Richard when, in February 1397, he recalled from exile in Ireland the judges who in 1387 had expanded the scope of definitions of treason to include derogation of the king's regality, and who had elevated the royal will to a legal and divine principle.

The correspondence and recorded conversations of the king in this period reflects his determination to enforce a royal prerogative that he was convinced was the will of God. The source of Richard's exalted ideas about the prerogative was probably his tutor, Simon Burley, who possessed a copy of Giles of Rome's *De Regimine Principum* which stresses the role in government of the king's will which must be obeyed, and which asserts that all honour and privilege came from the king.[85] Richard said as much in his patents of ennoblement. The revenge parliament of 1397 was opened with a sermon from Edmund Stafford based on Ezek. 37.27 on the absolute and inviolate nature of the king's power. In the same year Richard wrote to Albert of Bavaria, count of Holland, declaring that his arrest of the appellants was based on his Christ-like identity and he attempted to make his chastity and immaturity offensive weapons in the service of God and the royal prerogative by explicitly stating his belief that behind his actions lay a divine and supernatural force. He expressed thanks to the 'highest observer of human minds, in whose hands are not only the hearts but bodies of princes and kings, and who has protected our royal throne and person since the very cradle from the hands of all enemies, and especially those of household intimacy whose contraries are notoriously more destructive than any plague'. Reflecting how, since his 'tender years', 'the nobility and members of his household had traitorously conspired to disinherit our crown and usurp our royal power', leaving him hardly anything beyond the royal name, he proclaimed that 'by the just judgment of God our avenging severity has been meted out to the destruction and ruin of their persons. Through God's providence we have brought together the right hand of our power to bruise these confessed traitors'. Richard expresses confidence that: 'His obedient subjects will obtain a grace to last forever' and warns his opponents the fate of 'punishment be perpetual on their heirs . . . that posterity learn what it is to offend the royal majesty established at howsoever tender years, for he is a child of death who offends the Virgin'.[86] On St George's Day, Richard received a communication from Manuel Palaelogus II, the Byzantine emperor, asking for his assistance against the

Turks. Richard in his reply explained that he could not help because: 'some of his subjects, magnates and nobles, while we were yet of tender age and afterwards, also have made many attempts on the prerogative and royal right of our regal state'. He was therefore resolved to 'stretch forth his arm and tread on the offenders' necks and 'ground them down, even to the roots, establishing a peace that would last forever'.[87] Richard spent time reflecting on the history of English kingship (he was a guest at Berkeley Castle in 1386 when John Trevisa was at work on the *Polichroni-con*) and the state of the prerogative, and he requested the compilation of a history of the English kings from Brutus to Richard II in 1390/91.[88] Sir William Bagot reported that Richard, during Christmas at Lichfield in 1390, had told him he desired to live long enough 'to see the crown held in such high respect and obeyed with lowly humility by all his lieges as had been the case under previous kings, for he considered himself to have been humiliated by his lords and commons, so that it might be chronicled forever that with skill and strength he recovered the royal dignity'. While Richard was imprisoned in the Tower on 21 September Adam Usk, in his capacity as an advocate of the archiepiscopal court and close associate of Thomas Arundel, dined with him as the king reflected sorrowfully on England's reputation for regicide and rebellion: 'By God this is a strange and fickle land which has exiled, slain destroyed and ruined so many kings' and he recounted the names of those who has suffered such a fate. Usk, remembering the trouble of his mind and that all around him there were spies and strangers and reflecting on the fickle fortune of the world, 'departed much moved at heart'.[89]

There is evidence that in his mystical assertion of the royal will or prerogative Richard was prepared to go beyond the badge of the white hart, and that he was prepared to find other occult sources to use in an aggressive way against his political enemies. A precedent had been set by Charles V, king of France, who employed the alchemist, Thomas of Bologna, to make leaden images of soldiers with astrological characters and the name of the English king; these were then buried in the centre of France and in four corners of the realm in an attempt to expel the English.[90] Like his close adviser, chief justice Tresilian, Richard depended on charms and perhaps spells and tended to see politics in terms of sorcery. In November 1397 at Woodstock, Pierre Salmon, secretary of Queen Isabella, recalled a conversation with the king about Charles VI. Richard insisted that the duke of Orleans had brought about the king's illness through necromancy and planned to usurp his brother's throne. Richard allegedly promised to reward Salmon lavishly if he would make a drink for Orleans that would ensure he never harmed the king or anyone else.[91] Walsingham recorded that when Richard was taken prisoner there was discovered among his possessions a cloth festooned with pearls and occult writings and a scroll containing magic arts.[92] When the king's tomb was examined in 1871 fragments of twigs were found and around them was wound a piece of light yellow string, shaped like a reel with black lines around it, which subsequently turned to dust. Rowan tree branches and twigs were tied with red string and placed over doors and windows in Ireland to dispel the power of unfriendly, otherworld or malevolent energies.[93] It is interesting given the Irish origins of Richard's *Book of Divination*, that Richard's supporters turned to an Irish charm which they placed over the body as a precaution against witchcraft. Richard also used oaths as a form of talismanic protection against his enemies.[94] His favourite oaths were by his two most important patron saints, Edward the Confessor and John the Baptist (he had images of St John the Baptist and John the Evangelist in his chapel, and in Christmas 1386 he had a gown embroidered with the name of the Baptist). Richard evoked the names of John the Baptist and Edward the Confessor, whose curse he believed was especially powerful when arresting his uncle, Richard FitzAlan, earl of Arundel.[95] In 1389 Richard invoked the curse of the Confessor on any subject who objected to his granting the lordship of Queensburgh Castle.[96] Richard visited the confessor's shrine at times of crisis, for example during the Peasant's Revolt, and in 1392, after his reconciliation with the Londoners. In 1386, when Richard was faced with the imposition of a council curbing his powers, he requested the abbot of Westminster, Nicholas Littyngton (d. 1386), to deliver to him the sacred ring of Edward the Confessor. An atmosphere of fear of malignant practice of magic certainly prevailed at the court of Richard's second father-in-law, Charles VI, and Richard attributed this monarch's mental collapse to sorcery. In 1393 it was considered that Charles's sister-in-law, the duchess of Visconti, daughter of the duke of Milan (a land regarded at this time as celebrated above all others for sorcerers and poisons), had rendered the king mad by sorcery. The ministers of the court resolved to put a magician against her, one Arnould Guillaume, who was brought from Guienne as a 'subtill adviser to the noble lords'. Arnauld employed against this spell an alchemical text, the *Smagorad* of the patriarch Adam (possibly the *Tabula smaragdina*), but in the meantime the king recovered.

Richard's own use of charms, oaths and ritualistic magic could be seen as a reaction to the humiliations he suffered in his youth. His lack of real political power led him to seek compensation in the alternative hidden truths and earthly powers to be found in the realm of the occult. This can be seen in Richard's increasingly autocratic behaviour from 1389, when he sought to distance himself from ordinary mortals. As early as the coronation ceremony, Chancellor Adam Houghton, the bishop of St David's, proclaimed Richard's Christ-like identity in a sermon, citing St Paul, to urge his subjects to submit themselves to a king sent them in the same way God had sent his only son to act as his vicar general and legate of God on earth;[97] and the archbishop of Canterbury, investing him with the royal pall, said Richard received this from four angels who represented the four corners of the world and who were subject to divine power; no one, the archbishop maintained, could reign in prosperity on earth who had not been granted power from heaven. Richard pushed these ceremonial pronouncements to their extreme political limits to achieve the royal supremacy proclaimed by St Paul. From 1389 he sought to exalt his person and surround himself with a semi-religious mystique to stress the sacral roots of his authority. To this end he encouraged the use of lofty forms of address such as 'prince' or 'your majesty' rather than use the simpler language of lordship used by his predecessor, Edward III.[98] From 1391 counsellors addressed the king as 'his most excellent, most renowned prince'; 'most gracious lord your highness'; and 'royal majesty'. For civil lawyers the prince was a sovereign ruler who acknowledged no earthly superior. Bishop Waltham, the treasurer, writing in 1394, used the language of lordship in his opening address and switched to the phrases your highness, your majesty (a civilian concept [99] originally referring to the power of a ruler but which was acquiring a religious gloss) and your high royal presence. The speaker, Sir John Bushy, addressed Richard in similarly grandiloquent terms in September 1397.

The tone was set for this distancing of Richard from his subjects with the reconciliation between the king and the city of London after a quarrel stemming from the refusal of the mayor and aldermen to accept a large jewel as collateral for a loan of £5,000 from the king's council.[100] Richard responded by confiscating the liberties of the city and from June until mid-September 1392 London was ruled by a royally appointed warden.[101] The mayor and aldermen were only restored to office after the payment of a corporate fine of £10,000 to the king.[102] A pageant was staged to commemorate the royal entry into the city on 21 August which was commemorated in a Latin poem dedicated to Richard II by Richard Maidstone (d. 1393), confessor to John of Gaunt at a time when the duke was a staunch upholder of the monarchy. Beyond the formulaic panegyrics this is a disturbing testimony to the development of Richard's messianic complex. The city was personified as New Troy (the citizens even offered the king a propitiatory gift of a horse) and as the bride; and Richard, riding a white horse, was depicted as the returning Christ and the bridegroom. The king and queen, wearing a red dress to offset her golden hair, were met by 24 aldermen, arrayed in the alchemical colours of red and white. The most important buildings, such as St George's Southhall and Westminster Palace, were decorated in hangings of gold, silver and red. Wine flowed down the conduits, and an angelic boy and girl, hovering on invisible wires, presented the couple with gold goblets.[103] At the end of Chepe Street Richard saw, atop of the little conduit, a *tableau vivant* of the heavenly Jerusalem, arranged with choirs of singing angels and a radiant youth who portrayed God. At the Temple Bar he witnessed a tableau of St John the Baptist prophesying in the wilderness, in which the hermit pointed his finger at Richard, proclaiming him to be the Lamb of God. The keeper appeared before the king approaching the city walls offering him the key and holding the point of his sword down towards his throat saying: 'the humble citizens prostrate themselves at your feet begging you not to destroy their beautiful walls or to tear down the kingdom for they are the king's own to do whatever he pleases with them'. At the Temple bar Anne occupied the role of the

Virgin as she went down on her knees before Richard, sitting in state on the marble throne in Westminster Hall pointing out that never in the history of Britain, even in Arthur's time, had there been a king so honoured. Anne was subsequently praised for interceding with the king on the city's behalf.[104] These events were followed by the feast of the Confessor in the abbot's hall, where Richard sat crowned on the top stall on the south side of the choir with his queen opposite him on the north side.[105]

It was around this time that a massive portrait (perhaps inspired by the portraits of Bohemian kings in Charles IV's castle at Karlstein) was commissioned by Richard and affixed to the back of his choir stall to stress his continuing presence in the capital. The Dominican friar, Roger Dymock, in his dedicatory copy of the *Refutation of the twelve errors of the Lollards,* written during the session of parliament 27 January–15 February 1395, compared Richard to the Emperor Constantine and described him as a wise king whom providence had raised to such a high rank, providing the English people with a king whose diligent, forceful and zealous concern for the divine law ranks him with David, Solomon, Alexander and Arthur. In the same year Mezieres was similarly urging Richard to use his 'genius', the magnetic power of the lodestone with which he was so closely identified, to attract both friends and enemies to enforce the prerogative. At the opening of parliament of September 1397, described by Walsingham, the speaker, Sir John Bushy, imputed to the king and his statutes divine rather than human origins and found 'strange fluttering words hardly suitable to mere mortals', so whenever he addressed the king, who was seated on his throne, he would extend his arms and supplicate with his hands as if he were praying to him, entreating his high excellent most praiseworthy majesty that he might concede those things.[106] Walsingham further suggested that Richard was beginning to take the forms and rituals of kingship literally when he added that the king did not stop these words but rather delighted in them. During the sessions of parliament in which Gloucester was murdered, Richard entered the city with a large retinue wearing the white hart and sat an a high stage where he could deliver judgements, prompting the monk of Evesham to declare that he presided with greater solemnity than any other king of the realm before. After the exile of Bolingbroke, Richard marked the occasion in September 1399 by celebrating the Feast of Edward the Confessor in the following month at Westminster and, according to the *Eulogium* chronicler, the king came to Westminster to celebrate the feast of the Confessor in October of the following year and he had a throne prepared for him on which he sat ostentatiously from dinner to vespers. He would talk to no one but cast his eyes over all and, when he looked at anyone whatever their rank they had to fall on their knees before him.[107] The strike against the appellants and the revival of the laws of treason forbade any criticism of the monarchy and its advisers, and this could justify all forms of extravagance and wrathfulness: to glorify the person of the king meant to glorify the crown. Richard's gem-encrusted crown became visible testimony of the inviolable crown he received from God.

While some of Richard's exalted behaviour and bold political moves can be attributed to an accumulation of financial power and the building up of a strong court, it can perhaps also be explained by the king's growing conviction that the divine will ran through him like fixed mercury; and this would explain why Richard sought a resolution of some political issues in his book of geomancy. The *De Quadripartita regis specie*, which precedes it, gives an impression of a king who is so unsure about who he can depend on that he is advised to send two or three trusted counsellors to act as 'secret agents' in the courts of noblemen, feigning other business with the squires of their households and other officials, to ascertain the character of these lords as a potential royal servants. In such a highly charged, paranoid atmosphere it was natural that the king turns to the next text in the manuscript which offers the possibility of political advice in the form of celestial writing from the hand of the geomancer. According to the prologue to the *Libellus Geomancie*, when the king formed images in the wet sand his soul would rise towards heaven to partake of its angelic form and fiery nature. 'Just as it is not the hand of the hammerer that gives form to the thing he is making, but rather the diligence and talent of the artificer, so neither does the hand calculating in the sand give knowledge of all but rather the power of celestial bodies duly moving the calculating hand'.[108]

To access this power the compiler of Bodley 581 created a text designed especially for the king's own personal use, which made him potentially independent of advisers. It is unique in its simplicity. Other near contemporary books of geomancy, such as the one produced by John duke of Bedford's personal physician[109] or Humphrey duke of Gloucester's geomancy,[110] required a professional practitioner to generate geomantic figures, assign to them to astrological houses, interpret the results based on an understanding of the interactions between figures and houses, and then account for special circumstances. Richard's geomancy however was designed to avoid the disadvantages of face-to-face consultation. Whereas the preceding texts *De Quadripartita Regis Specie* and the preface to *Somniale Danielis* are written in small handwriting and dense Latin, clearly produced for use through a clerical intermediary, the *Libellus Geomancie* was intended for easy use with its large handwriting, short simple sentences, visual illustrations and thumb index with geomantic signs along the left-hand margins of the pages. It has even been suggested that the book has a naive 'pop up' quality that accords with Richard's child-like image.[111] It was also unconventional in its machine-like nature, designed to be used, rather than read in a linear fashion; like a volvelle producing divination by wheels, it performed a form of magic, enabling the king resolve any of the 25 standard questions, most concerned with matters of state, without consulting his subjects. Instead, when he wanted advice, the index would direct him to such relevant topics as choice of friends, money or military matters, dynastic succession or journeys, enabling the king to subject himself to inspired advice, without becoming anyone's subject, to advise himself while still receiving objective advice.[112] The *Book of Geomancy* may have accentuated Richard's tendency towards absolute rule: instead of seeking the advice of counsellors he could summon the witnesses and judges that were descended from the four geomantic signs he would make when faced with difficult choices. Some of his more erratic decisions may have been derived from this method. In 1399 he chose to leave his kingdom in a vulnerable state and go to Ireland, allowing the exiled Bolingbroke the opportunity to invade. There are many combinations of witnesses and judges in the triads in his geomancy that would favourably ratify the King's decision to undertake a journey. These include the judge *populus* (the people) which reflects the favourable prognosticions of the two witnesses, *aquisitio,* suggesting great profit and wealth; and the judgement of the lunar sign associated with travel, *via,* which endorses the prophecies provided by the witnesses *Fortuna major* and *Fortuna minor.*[113] Such judgements would have been endorsed by prophecies circulating linking the conquest of Ireland with an Arthurian high destiny.

When he made important decisions Richard may have believed that the signs he made, whether on paper or parchment, or in the ground by his hand, would have been formed by this same divine will. One reaction to the humiliating court purges of 1387 had been to turn in 1391 to geomancy. By prefixing to the *Libellus Geomancie* excerpts from *Secreta secretorum* the compiler of Richard's *Book of Divination* emphasized the way both works could enforce the royal prerogative. A fundamental concern of *Secreta secretorum* was how a ruler can maintain and increase his power over his subjects, and this is also addressed in the *Libellus Geomancie.* In the preface the compiler cites the saying attributed to Ptolemy, 'A wise man rules the stars', implying that the ruler who is wise enough to have power over the influence of the heavens through the art of geomancy was no longer dependent on movement of the stars in a fixed, zodiacal grid around the earth. Richard instead could exert an active influence by casting lots and this could also enhance his political power. In August 1388 Richard had unsuccessfully attempted to assert the royal prerogative by putting a series of questions to the king's judges. In his two illuminated books of geomancy he would be able to put similar questions to witnesses and judges, all internalized in his own mind, and he could receive the answers he was looking for, and what he believed were the powers to back up his decisions, in the form of an endorsement from the hidden powers within the earth and within himself, ratifying his actions, giving him hidden knowledge of the future and the fates of his enemies. One hundred and thirty four questions concerning the choice of friends, the times to take journeys, could now be determined by placing a 'pricke in the sond'[114] and consulting the triads formed from witnesses and judges derived from the ensuing geomantic shapes; this would give him much more autonomy than he had in 1386, when such questions were decided by the council enforced on him. There would not even be the need to consult his own trusted counsellors, and whereas astrology could not be used without consultation of professionals, geomancy could be pursued without any intermediary advice and was therefore more idiosyncratic.

Richard's dependence on geomancy may also have accentuated his apprehensive nature and the doubts and fears that were inspired by prophecies and omens. In geomantic terms he would have been perceived as an anxious and melancholic personality: his birth sign was Capricorn, an earth sign ruled by Saturn. The compiler of his *Libellus Geomancie* understood this. The image of *Fortuna major* (normally the most fortunate of the twelve houses) is an image of a golden-haired child-like Richard II. It was commonly recognized that Geomancy, concerned as it was with the earth, was especially associated with Saturn and melancholy. Gower in *Confession amantis* described it as:

the craft which that Saturnus fond,
To make prickes in the Sond.[115]

The compiler of Bodl 581, answering objections that geomancy encroached on God's omniscience and man's free will, pointed out that while God can foreknow a decision a man will reach by exercising his rational powers, it is legitimate to use stars to predict acts and impulses of thoughtless men. This is the key to the compiler's assessment of the pitfalls and potentialities of his monarch because he addresses specifically the problems of the melancholic governed by Saturn. The melancholic, if he is thoughtless (in other words if he fails to use geomancy), will be ruled by his physical desires, governed by the heavenly bodies, or Saturn. He will be wrathful and sad, even though he would rather be happy and jovial. Geomancy enables the king to rule that which is ungovernable and above the law, that is himself and his own melancholic humour; and this had political implications, enabling him to predict the actions of those melancholics around him (an early example of an awareness of the melancholic malcontent that would be the inspiration for Renaissance Revenge Tragedy) who, if they are thoughtless and ignorant of geomancy, will act irrationally, governed by short- and long-term assessments of self-interest. The compiler persuades the king that regular use of this book will enable him to dominate the stars and understand the humours influencing others and to dominate them as well as shrugging off their influence over his own actions.[116]

In the section of *Libellus Geomancie* known as *Rosarium Regis Ricardi* there are two geomantic readings in the form of shields made for the king. The nature of the signs on the first shield takes on particular relevance if the question which led to the composition of this chart regarded Richard's political future. Pietro d'Abano (1257–1315), the physician and astronomer who taught medicine at the University of Padua and attempted to reconcile Greek and Arabic medical traditions, maintained in his *Geomanzie* that 'fortune could be predicted by means of character as geomancy teacheth'. The first mother house, which occurs just below the earth's horizon, relates to the questioner's character. In this case in Richard's Rosary it is *laetitia* (joy), which is particularly appropriate for a king. *Fortuna major* in the second house signifies wealth and recovery of good fortune after a period of loss, which could be interpreted as Richard's recovery of authority on 13 May 1389 after attaining his majority, and this reading would be increasingly significant after 1396 when he asserted the royal prerogative. *Puella* in the third house relates to brothers and sisters, which could be interpreted as a reflection of Richard's chaste and happy relationship with Anne of Bohemia. If the mother houses on the right-hand side of the shield suggest great joy and recovery of wealth, the position is complicated by the daughters and nephews on the darker left-hand side. In the sixth house, representing servants and recovery from illness, occurs *Fortuna major*, which could also signify recovery of what is lost; but in the seventh house of wedlock and war occurs *rubeus*, the red-headed and violent-tempered boy associated with the sign of Scorpio, an evil sign signifying violence and deceit, the treachery of adversaries eager to overcome by crafts and subtle wiles and by circumventing the law. This sign could have been interpreted as a reference to Richard's second, unpopular marriage and his eventual deposition. The eighth house relates to inheritances, and here appears the fortuitous sign of *caput draconis*, (the head of the dragon), with Richard's planetary sign of Capricorn, which could be applied to the confiscation of the Lancastrian estates. More unfortunate signs follow; *rubeus* occurs again in the tenth house relating to fame and reputation, and this could have been applied to the king's growing reputation for tyranny and his violent end, either murdered by his subjects or taken captive by his conquerors and put to ignominious death or imprisonment. The eleventh house relates to relatives and friends and contains *carcer* (imprisonment), also connected with Richard's sign of Capricorn, and this could also imply betrayal by kinsmen such as Bolingbroke. However in the twelfth house for sorrows and servants, at the end of the day at sunset just over the horizon, with the rising of the moon, occurs the sign of *Fortuna major*. This offers the hope of deliverance, freedom from suffering and imprisonment due to the loyalty of servants. The witnesses are *via* to the right, a sign of the moon reflecting good with good and bad with bad, and to the left is *laetitia* (loss). However the judgement, *acquisitio*, a sign associated with Jupiter, is unambiguous: good fortune will follow and the sixteenth reconciler is also the lunar sign of *via* reflecting the good fortune of the judgement. A totally unambiguous picture emerges on this shield which mirrors Richard's political life. The original promise of his youth is followed by treachery and betrayal, the humiliation of the purges in 1386–87 and the eventual deposition and imprisonment. However hope surfaces with the rising sun and an appropriate endorsement of

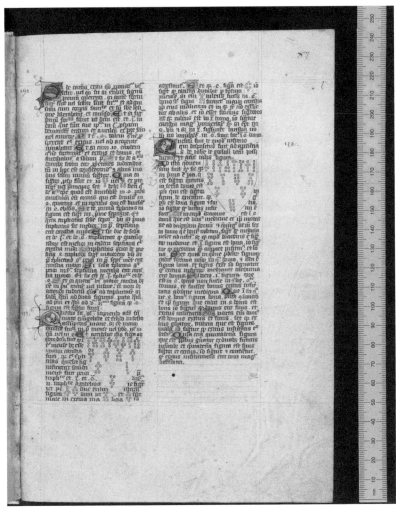

Two geomantic shields from Richard II's rosary showing prognostications with
implications for the health of the queen and the political future of the king
(Bodley 581 Folio 87)

this alchemical regeneration follows with the mercurial moon, possibly the planet
with which Richard most closely identified. In 1391 this shield may have given
Richard the courage to brave the problems ahead; and in 1399, as he lay in prison
awaiting deliverance with the help of loyal favourites, those Garter Knights who
upheld the prerogative, he may have meditated on the many favourable prognostications of deliverance from prison provided by the triads of *Fortuna major* and
the judge *populus* and on this detailed geomantic judgement in his Rosary as he

contemplated the efforts of Holland and Salisbury and Richard Maudelyn, who were planning his release and rebirth on Twelfth Night of 1400, an appropriately momentous date that would resonate with the Epiphany, when Richard would become the risen Christ.

Richard's dependence on the occult may have contributed towards his increasingly neurotic, apprehensive state of mind (according to Froissart he was apprehensive by nature)[117] in which he anxiously looked for supernatural signs of impending doom. The chronicles show Richard troubled by unfavourable prognostications. Walsingham recorded a prophecy current in 1398/99 referring to the pomp of John which would last only two years, and this unsettled the king who had originally been christened John. An anecdote in the *Brut* recounts that there was an astronomer in King Richard's court who understood by his cunning that the king would be slain by a toad. Richard became alarmed when Bolingbroke appeared at a Christmas feast wearing a crown heavily embroidered with toads.[118] According to Walsingham, Richard formed his Cheshire bodyguard on account of the nightmares he experienced after the execution of Richard FitzAlan, the earl of Arundel. As this bodyguard may have formed the primary audience for *Sir Gawain and the Green Knight*, it is significant that there are close parallels between the events surrounding the earl's execution at Cheapside (which was carried out by Earl Marshall Thomas Mowbray in Richard's presence) and the plot of this poem. Arundel, like the Green knight, faced his ordeal with considerable bravado. According to Walsingham, during the procession to the place of execution, between the wild men of Cheshire, his face was no paler than if he had been asked out to dinner. He tested the edge of the executioner's axe and, joking that it seemed sharp enough, he urged his executioner to 'do quickly what you have to do'.[119] His head was struck off with one blow and, according to Froissart, the trunk eerily stood for some time (as long as it took to recite the Lord's Prayer) before finally falling to the ground. A cult developed around his tomb and miracles were reported, the most popular one being the rumour that the head and body had miraculously rejoined. The king experienced a series of nightmares surrounding the beheading (according to the Dieulacres *chronicle* his bodyguard stood outside his chamber armed with huge battleaxes). As soon as he fell asleep the earl's ghost fluttered before his eyes and threatened him with indescribable terrors. These apparitions woke him and made him curse the day that he got to know the earl. Richard's turmoil led him in early October to commission the dukes of Lancaster, Albermarle, Surrey and Norfolk, and the earl of Northumberland, to exhume and make an inspection of the corpse, ten days after its burial. The lords arrived in the middle of the night at the convent of Augustinian friars and reported to the king that they found the head and body stitched together with thread, to allay his fears that they had supernaturally rejoined.[120] Richard ordered the friars to rebury the earl and to leave the grave unmarked. Richard's awareness of the plot of *Sir Gawain and the Green*

Knight is suggested when he moved to Windsor in April 1399 and, according to Froissart, held a grand tournament there on St George's Day with 40 knights and 40 squires all dressed in green who challenged all comers .

The king's anxious dependence on the occult had ramifications in the field of politics as he became more unpredictable and irresolute. One of the key decisions in this period that cost Richard his throne was taken after he consulted his book of geomancy. In 1399 Richard finally took action against his cousin, Bolingbroke, and sent him into exile, confiscating his Lancastrian estates. The background to this decision was that he had been confronted by Bolingbroke and Mowbray, who accused each other of raising the question of the king's deposition. Mowbray had long been a favourite of Richard's, and although he was one of the five appellants of 1388, this had probably been inspired by jealousy of De Vere, and he had subsequently been restored to royal favour and had organized the arrest and execution of Gloucester. It is likely that Mowbray was acting as an agent provocateur for the king, attempting to draw Bolingbroke into a treasonable conversation. The plan did not work for Bolingbroke went straight to his father, John of Gaunt, and then to the king, accusing Mowbray. Richard was now in a dilemma. Froissart pointed out that although Mowbray expected more support from his king, Richard had been advised that he could not be seen to favour Mowbray,[121] and his solution was to order a trial by battle, a recognized judicial procedure in a case where there were two disputants and no witnesses. Often such cases were associated with the practice of magic. In 1355 a chaplain of the bishop Salisbury was threatened with disqualification from a judicial combat against the earl of Salisbury for bearing in his clothes prayers and charms (as Sir Gawain would do before his encounter with the green knight).[122] In 1380 a duel took place between Sir John Annesley and Thomas Catterton Esq. Sir John accused Thomas of treason and the case was tried by laws of combat in the court of chivalry, presided over by Richard II. Thomas was required to swear that he was not aware of any magic practises by which he could gain a victory, and that he was not carrying about his person any herbs or stones or any kind of amulet by which evil doers are accustomed to triumph over their foes.[123] Richard also witnessed a trail by battle in 1384, a duel between and English squire, John Walsh, and a native of Navarre who had accused Walsh of treason against the king and realm. Walsh was victorious and Navarre was drawn and quartered despite the pleas of the queen.[124] On the surface Richard's decision to expose his favourite, Mowbray, to the uncertainties of a trial by battle was bizarre because Bolingbroke was a noted tourneyer with considerable military experience including campaigns with the Teutonic knights in Prussia; but it was reported: 'And because the king had it by divination that the duke of Norfolk should then prevail he rejoiced much eagerly striving after the destruction of the duke of Hereford'.[125] Richard would have been able to find in his book of geomancy a number of triads predicting victory for his friend, including the witnesses *Fortuna major, caput draconis* and *laetitia* (joy associated with Jupiter) and the judge *populus*.[126] The trial was intended to be a very public event, taking place on Gosford Green on the edge of Coventry, and presided over by Richard's nephew, Thomas Holand. Richard was seated on a stage and barracks were erected. The king's favourite, Mowbray, was horsed and ready when Bolingbroke entered with 'the best armour that the duke of Milan had sent him from Lombardy with diverse equipments for seven horses, and when they joined battle it seemed to him that the duke of Hereford would prevail'.[127] At the last moment, therefore, Richard lost confidence in the predictions in his Geomancy and called off the battle, sending both men into exile. The incident cost him much political credibility and forced Bolingbroke to make the bid for his confiscated estates which ultimately culminated in the king's deposition. It is appropriate that Richard's last act of assertion of the prerogative, the attempt to rid himself of the one remaining obstacle to absolute power, may have been influenced by his dependence on the occult. By 1399 Richard's reputation for making important political decisions on occult premises was such that MP's, reflecting on the coup of 1397 that saw the arrest and exile of the barons who had humiliated the king in 1386–87, suggested that certain bishops and friars had told Richard that they had found out by calculation and necromancy that unless 'certain lords of the realm were put to death he himself would be destroyed'. Richard had an astrologer brought in from Paris for private consultations around this time to lend credibility to the rumour.[128]

The two most influential figures in the fusion of politics and alchemy in the fourteenth century, King Arthur and Alexander the Great, emerged as heroic and model leaders against a background of magical practises that were potentially harmful. Arthur's tutor, Merlin, was reputed to be the son of the Devil and the diabolical pollution of his art in the hands of Morgan le Fay was revealed in late fourteenth-century romances such as *Sir Gawain the Green Knight and the Awentures of Arthur*. Arthur himself was a product of a rape orchestrated by Merlin, and Alexander the Great was conceived in similar circumstances when a sorcerer and Egyptian king, Nectantibus, took the form of a dragon to convince Queen Olympia that she would conceive through the god Amun.[129] John Gower, in a work originally dedicated to Richard II, the *Confessio amantis*, told the story of the ironic punishment suffered by Alexander's tutor for his abuse of his magical powers: he was killed by Alexander in fulfilment of the prophecy that Nectantibus would die at his son's hands. Gower depicted Alexander's emergence from the corrupt shadow of his paternal tutor to the light of the legitimate alchemical wisdom of his new tutor, Aristotle, the author of the *Secreta Secretorum*, a work consulted by both Edward III and Richard II.[130]

This is the context of a late fourteenth-century debate on correct and incorrect uses of occult knowledge on which Richard II would be judged and found wanting by chroniclers connected with the Lancastrian cause, who attributed Richard's downfall to his dependence on the occult, and the policies and public image so closely associated with the alchemical texts in his possession and circulating in this period. A passage in one of the Bridlington prophecies from Samuel about Saul, who, because he no longer received answers from the Lord in dreams and prophecies, sought through the witch of Endor, answers from familiars and the dead, was interpreted by John Erghome, around 1370, as a warning about the illicit use and dependence on the occult. This would later be taken as an explicit summation of Richard's fate. According to Erghome, God was with David and Saul was dependent on sorcerers; he expelled them from his kingdom but then sought council from the witch of Endor, who told him that the Lord was with David.[131] On the basis of this advice Saul attacked David and the Philistines and was killed. Richard was seen in the 1390s as a Saul-like figure seeking approbation from the same sources, one for whom the words of the *Testament of Solomon* rang true: 'and the glory of God quite departed from me; and my spirit was darkened, and I became the sport of idols and demons'. In 1399 the author of *Richard the Redeless* expressed in a dream vision the conviction that Richard's fall was due to a dependence on the occult which led him down the path of tyranny. Richard had tried to anticipate the prophecies of Merlin but the author commented: 'there is no clerk can tell what can happen in seven days. Men through trying to forsee the future in the stars have lost their heads till heads be hewn off and hop on the green and the whole world wander in their words.'[132] The monk of Evesham portrayed Richard as an extravagant, rapacious and inconstant tyrant dependent on sorcerers, pseudo prophets, necromancers and young men instead of wise counsellors. Such a king, he argued, was as foolish and dangerous as Saul who sought advice from the witch of Endor, the pythonissa, when Yaweh had deserted him for David.[133] Adam Usk, a canon lawyer quoted chapter and verse of the Decretals which allowed for the deposition of such a king.[134] The same point had been made in the Bridlington prophecies, an erring King Saul, after God had chosen David, came to believe the prophecies of sorcerers: '*Rex Saul erravit, et male fecit volens occidere David, quem Deus elegit, ad regnum Israel et ipse Saul ejus mandatoque fregit sortilegis credens, quando per phitonissam suscitavet Samuelem.*'[135] This had originally been intended as a rebuke for Edward II, and was applied to Richard.[136] A Saul rather than a David, Richard was also seen as a Rehoboam in contrast to his father Solomon. Usk compared him to Rehoboam, who lost the kingdom of Israel by following the counsels of younger men;[137] Thomas Wimbledon, in a sermon in 1397, made an allusion to Rehoboam and the *Kirkstall Chronicle* attributed Richard's fall to his spurning the advice of older counsellors and being misled by younger men in the manner of Edward II, who in his own day had been compared to Rehoboam.[138] In Walsingham's account of the last years of Richard's reign which may have been written by the almoner of St Albans, William Wintershill, the abbot's chaplain, it is alleged that the king showed an unhealthy regard for prophecies, omens and irregular sources of advice.[139]

Describing the events of 1397 he says the kingdom was thrown into confusion by Richard's '*levitas*' (childishness and irresponsibility). Throughout Richard's reign it was young men who dominated the inner court: in the 1380s it was Robert de Vere, whose association with the king sparked rumours of a homosexual relationship (according to Walsingham the king was infatuated with him),[140] and Thomas Mowbray; and in the 1390s it was the chamber knights: Sir Thomas Clifford, Sir John Salisbury and Sir John Clanvowe. Richard is said to have taken to hoarding his treasure and surrounding himself with pseudo prophets who spurred him on to his ambition to become Holy Roman emperor and one of the greatest princes in the world.[141]

What these chroniclers pick up is the way the king's dependence on the occult encouraged his grandiose, unrealistic schemes and exalted self-image. In his obsession with his portrayal in statures and paintings (he is the first king to have a life-like image); his dependence on rituals and symbols, the trappings of power rather than its substance; his absorption in his childhood; his fragile sense of identity, shattered by the humiliations of 1386–88; his inability to forgive or forget wrongs done to him; and above all his dependence on magic; he displays all the characteristic traits of a narcissistic personality out of touch with reality and his subjects.[142] The official indictment of Richard II, prepared by a committee of doctors and lawyers among whom Adam Usk, Bolingbroke's legal expert, was a member, besides accusing the royal favourites of taking advantage of the king's tender age and innocence,[143] stated that the king was tainted by perjuries, unnatural crimes sacrileges and sodomitical acts, lack of reason and incapacity to rule. The term sacrilege implies involvement in occult practices that clouded his reason. They were the same charges issued against another ruler involved in the occult, Frederick II, the Holy Roman emperor who was deposed for tyranny by Papal deposition in 1245. The dedication to the *Libellus Geomancie,* in which Richard is described as one who tasted the sweetness of the fruit of the subtle sciences, therefore took on darker connotations. In fact geomancy in this period was being linked by contemporary observers with such dark, earthy saturnine powers. William Langland, in the B text of *Piers Ploughman* written c. 1377–79, discussed geomancy in these contradictory terms:

> —Geomancie is gynful of speche—
> for sorcerie is the Souereyn book that to that science longeth
> Yet art her Fibicches in sorcerers of fele mennes makynge
> Experimentes of Alkenamye the peple to deceyue,[144]

suggesting that it could be a trap coming dangerously close to alchemical manipulation and deception. For this cleric geomancy was politically dangerous, a threat to the social body, because it encouraged individuals to act totally independently, multiplying the number of people who were laws unto themselves; like alchemists geomancers operated entirely outside society. The implications for those observing Richard II's conduct in the 1390s were clear (by this time all reference to geomancy had been excised from the C text of *Piers Ploughman* and it had been linked by Gower with Saturn): here was a king, a self-styled geomancer, for whom 'the laws were in his mouth'.

Increasing alarm was also being voiced by chroniclers who observed that some of those few trusted advisers close to the king were practitioners in the black arts. Adam Usk claimed that one of Richard's advisers was 'Robert Tideman, sometime monk of Hales, whose counsel I had been, and whom king Richard, after Tideman had been driven forth from his monastery for the evil arts of brewing charms and weaving spells, raised up to be bishop first of Llandaff and then of Worcester.'[145] Richard had granted Tideman the keeping of Beaulieu Abbey during a vacancy and stayed with him in mid-August 1393.[146] It was believed that the monk had gained purchase on the king's affections for his knowledge of medicine and the occult sciences. Richard commended him to the election of the bishopric of Llandaff as 'a most virtuous man of great sense and prudence (a quality greatly admired by Richard II) in both spiritual and temporal matters'.[147] Another learned adviser who was reputed to having a 'noxious influence' on the king was the Dominican Thomas Rushook (d. 1392), appointed the king's confessor in May 1379 and described by Gower as a 'tawny confessor and professor of evil who had long hidden under the wings of the king, a friar black within and without'.[148] He was followed in the king's service as Dominican confessor by Alexander Bache and John Burghill. Both men were heavily criticized, perhaps a measure of their influence.[149] Walsingham, revising his chronicles between 1397 and 1399, suggests that Robert de Vere, through a friar in his service, had worked black magic to gain such an influence over Richard that the king was unable to understand what was good or right.[150] A clerk of Richard's, bearing a striking resemblance to the king, Richard Maudelyn (1371/72–1400), fellow of King's Hall, and a canon of Westminster Abbey, was taken captive with Richard, and he was one of the eight counsellors who Richard asked to be spared if he agreed to abdicate. A scroll containing magical arts was found on his possession and when Bolingbroke became king he presented Maudelyn to Parliament in October 1399 to be examined for dabbling in magical arts.[151] Maudelyn was released after he had sworn before convocation that that it had been given to him by Richard II and he denied any knowledge of its meaning.

The hostility Usk and others at the court felt towards Tideman and other advisers of the king related to the growing conviction that Richard was using alchemy and occult arts, and his exalted sense of the royal prerogative, in a hostile manner to attempt to destroy anyone daring to criticize and oppose him. Another of the charges against Richard was that he said the lives of everyone were his to do with as he pleased, as were his liege lands. On his tomb epitaph he chose to be remembered as one who was prudent (in contemporary terms sage) who 'threw down

whoever violated the royal prerogative'.[152] This extreme assertion of the prerogative echoes the words of the keeper of the city of London in Maidstone's poem. It
was reinforced by Richard's familiarity with the civil law which was being viewed
with increasing concern: in one of the deposition articles Richard is accused of
quoting the civilian adage that the laws were in his mouth — or alternately in his
breast.[153] In short alchemy and the occult backed by the civil law had become
instruments of Richard's tyranny and the words of the *Stella alchemiae* about the
power of mercury, the fugitive stag (or white hart) had become truly prophetic: 'It
is that thing which kings do carry in their heads and through it are men gathered
together and kings are slain.'

.

10

Conclusion: The Lancastrian Reaction

Samuel had died, and all Israel lamented for him. And Saul had put the mediums and the spiritualists out of the land.

Samuel 1.3 [1]

Richard may have had an excessive and eccentric dependence on the occult, but he was not alone in believing that political events could be determined by supernatural forces. The Blackfriars council of 17 May 1382, summoned to condemn Wyclif's writings, was preceded by an earthquake widely regarded as a sign of God's disapproval of the heresiarch's attempt to limit divine and supernatural influences in the material world. In the same year a prophet, pretending to be a physician and astrologer, was arrested and paraded around the city of London for persuading many people that unless they stayed indoors on the eve of Ascension Day a pestilential vapour would descend.[2] In 1384 a Carmelite friar came to the court accusing the duke of Lancaster of plotting against the king's life. He was tortured by a group of knights, including John Holand and Simon Burley, and slow roasted over a fire before being put into shackles for fear he might resort to witchcraft.[3] In 1385 John Brugges, chaplain, and John Wygton, a tailor, were tried in an ecclesiastical court for magic and imprisoned by the bishop of London.[4] The sophistication and intelligence of chroniclers like Walsingham, whose writing was full of quotations from Virgil, and other writers with an education in classical literature, such as Usk, and Froissart, was not incompatible with their conviction that political life was profoundly influenced by the supernatural.[5] Walsingham emphasized that Tresilian, who went to his death wearing protective amulets, was also a shrewd and clever man possessing the wisdom of a serpent. For this chronicler the conjunction of Saturn and Jupiter had caused an earthquake (a manifestation of the hidden powers in the earth) and threatened imminent war between England and France in 1385.[6] Chaucer, in *The Knight's Tale*, provided a meditation on the malignant impact that Saturn had on natural disasters and human misfortunes. Froissart, who recounted the stories about a familiar of Raymond lord of Caresse, called Orton, a shape shifting demon taking the shape of a sow to inform the count of Foix (the author of *livre de Chasse*) of such key events as the Battle of Aljubarrah on 14 August 1385,[7] was deeply affected by Richard's fall and recalled that rumours at Kennington were spreading about the prophecy of Merlin indicating that neither the Black Prince nor any of his issue would succeed to the throne, but that it would pass to the house of Lancaster.[8]

The chroniclers saw Richard's fall as an event played out against a backdrop of omens and prophecies. At his coronation three symbols of royalty foretold his misfortune: he lost a shoe, signifying the rise of the common people; one of his spurs dropped off, signifying the rebellion of the knighthood; and a sudden gust of wind blew off his crown, betokening his eventual deposition.[9] A Cistercian monk of Dieuilacres Abbey in North Staffordshire began a retrospective account of Richard's reign describing him as 'the most noble and excellent king of all the kings of the world', and recorded a series of prophecies about him. The Kirkstall chronicler recounted a series of prodigies which occurred in 1377, and these were taken as presaging the schism and the downfall of the new king. For the Westminster Chronicler, the Merciless Parliament was accompanied by a great storm of snow and hail and flashes of lightening, lasting three days.[10] In September 1387 in Derbyshire, during the purges of Richard's court, it reportedly rained blood over an area the radius of a bow shot,[11] and in August 1388 during Vespers, when Richard was recovering his authority and renewing his coronation oath, two stars were observed shining at Haulton, Cheshire in the southern sky, midway between the heavens and earth, and angels began to float about the air for an hour before returning into heaven, as if to signify Richard's recovery of his authority as king.[12] Also in 1388, a comet was observed for eight successive nights, burning with extraordinary intensity, its tail turned towards the west. A monk of St Denis in the *Chronique du Religieaux de Saint-Denys* reported that astrologers took it as a sure sign of the death of a king and the immanence of revolution.[13] In December of the same year, strange lights were seen in the sky in Leicester and Northamptonshire, and in April a blazing dragon (possibly the Aurora borealis).[14] Adam Usk explained Thomas Arundel's recovery of the see of Canterbury in 1399 as the fulfilment of an ancient prophecy:

> Once the tomb has been uncovered, Bishop Thomas will be gone,
> And upon the earth uprooted, falls the once exalted stone,

which he interpreted as referring to Richard guiltily dreaming about the earl of Arundel's head being rejoined to his body, the exile of Thomas Arundel and the fall of Roger Walden.[15] The prophecy that most forcefully illustrates the way the occult was seen to play a part in political life during this period was the prophecy of Merlin. During autumn 1399 Jean Creton, an eyewitness to the events surrounding Richard's deposition, spoke with an ancient chevalier as they rode during the Lancastrian relocation of Richard from Conway to Chester. The old knight told Creton that Merlin had prophesized the taking and destruction of the king: 'during their lifetimes there shall be a king in Albion who shall reign for some twenty or two years in great honour and great power and he shall be united with Gaul until he shall be undone in the parts of the north in a triangular place' (Conway Castle).[16] Jean Creton, observing the political events of 1399 to 1400, was certainly struck by the way they were seen in occult terms and commented that: 'the English held these prophecies to be true and accorded them great faith for they are so disposed in this country that they believe completely in prophecies, phantasms and sorceries and employ them readily'.[17] Westminster Abbey naturally became a focus for rumours of the supernatural, and after Richard's murder four little bells at the corners of the confessor's shrine rang miraculously at their own accord more loudly than if some person rang them to the great terror and amazement of the abbey.[18]

Animals too could be regarded as a conduit for knowledge of these hidden forces. The name of Richard's lion-faced greyhound, Mathis, was a Greek word meaning astrological learning or foreknowledge. Since the death of his first master, Thomas Holland duke of Exeter in 1397, the hound never left the king's side until the meeting between Richard and Bolingbroke at Conway Castle. On this day Mathis left his master and licked the hand of his supplanter, to which Richard observed 'it is an excellent omen for you'.[19] Bolingbroke, taking this as a sign of his changing fortunes, allowed the dog to sleep on his bed and from that moment the animal ignored Richard as if he were merely a private man, to his great sorrow, and never left Bolingbroke's side. Some prophecies were reworked by Lancastrian supporters to incorporate the omens of animals. The greyhound badge of Henry Bolingbroke was adapted by the author of *Richard the Redeless*, Adam of Usk and the *Dieulacres chronicle* to fit the Bridlington prophecies known as the prophecy of the eagle which was found with the prophecies of Merlin in many manuscripts: Bolingbroke was seen as the greyhound putting to flight the white harts in the dog days.[20] The very fact that the deposition of Richard II was seen in terms of a heraldic conflict between the greyhound and the white hart was an acknowledgment of the degree to which the growth of Richard's power and alleged tyranny was associated with this occult symbol of mercury. Edward duke of York hinted at this in the treatise on hunting which he translated while he was imprisoned for his involvement in the plot to release Richard II on Twelfth Night for Epiphany in 1400 which also involved his sister, Constance Despenser, and his brother-in-law, Thomas Despenser, 1st earl of Gloucester. Much of this manual was devoted to the hunting of the hart and included lengthy original passages written by York, who stressed the regal appearance of the hart with its pearled antlers (reminiscent of the white hart on the diptych) and emphasized that the hart in England was never caught in traps but only hunted and killed by greyhounds.[21]

An indication of the way momentous changes in political fortune were presented in terms of supernatural forces can be seen in the rumours spread between February and March 1388 that someone had made a wax head to work magic. At appropriate times it uttered the following three sentences and spoke no more: 'First the head is lowed, second the head shall be raised and third the feet shall be raised above the head'.[22] This may be a reference to accusations made in the Merciless Parliament that

Tresilian used a demon's head in his magical activities.[23] Chroniclers saw these cryptic utterances as a commentary on the political events of 1387–88: the failed attempt by Tresilian to assert the royal prerogative (which involved the use of magic) and the humiliations of Richard at the hands of the appellants and the Merciless Parliament. It is significant that these events of the reign of Richard II involving the use of the civil law to assert the royal prerogative may be the origin of the most popular and influential myth of occult practices in the sixteenth century, the Faustian legend of the story of the creation of a brazen (brass or bronze) head, a prophetic device that delivered the gnomic pronouncements 'time is, time was and time is gone' that was first attributed to the thirteenth-century Oxford scientist, Robert Grosseteste,[24] and then the alchemist and friar, Roger Bacon. This brazen head was the subject of a sixteenth-century play by Robert Greene, *Friar Bungay*, about occult dabbling that presaged Marlowe's *Doctor Faustus*.

An aura of the supernatural remained around Richard II after his arrest and imprisonment; and even his death; and this resulted in Lancastrian repression of alchemy and anything connected with the occult. Richard's supporters attempted to release him on the carefully chosen date of the Feast of Epiphany. Chroniclers, royalist and Lancastrian, were all agreed that he was a king who represented something special, even supernatural. The author of *Richard the Redeless* reflected that he had been crowned 'with a crown that no king under heaven could have brought better, so was it filled with virtuous stones, with costly pearls to punish wrongs and with red rubies to judge what is right'.[25] The *Dieulacre Chronicle* tells of a king who was a Christ-like innocent, betrayed by another Maccabeus. All were struck by the pathos of his fall from such heights of grandeur and opulence, and the sense that such a fall was the result of powerful forces and exemplified by the turning of fortune's wheel. Echoes of Richard's fall can be seen in *The Fall of Princes* (c. 1431–38) of the Benedictine monk, John Lydgate, and in Thomas Lord Berkeley's English verse translation of Boethius' *Consolations of Philosophy,* made in 1410 by John Walton, canon of Oseney Abbey at the request of Elizabeth, daughter of Thomas the fourth lord Berkeley. Froissart, who was brought up in the household of Edward III and Philippa and had attended Richard's baptism in Bordeaux Cathedral, was inspired to visit the king in 1395. After his death Froissart mused on Richard's fate after 22 years of prosperous rule: 'How fickle are the chances of this world.' Usk bade Richard farewell after his death reflecting that he should have been praised if he had ruled better 'for he was as liberal as Solomon, fair as Absalom, grand as Aharsus, as great a builder as Behrus yet you too were cast down at the height of your glory by the wheel of fortune'. Creton had this to say of the machinations of Mistress Fortune who makes one thing and unmakes another: 'her working is a downright dream'.[26] A royal clerk, William Ferriby, reflected on the mutability of fortune: 'In our times the God of majesty hath in heaven decreed on which we not only heard but seen that the most famous prince of this world, glorious in circumstances of his birth – while they thought themselves firmly on the pinnacle of happiness – have fallen instantly with unexpected rush from the summit of prosperity into an abyss of wretchedness.' In *Giles's Chronicle* it is argued that God chastises those he loves and the author finds in Richard's misfortunes a sign of his election in heaven. Many around Richard were caught in the spell of his monarchy, a dream of power, wealth and glamour. Walsingham's appraisal of the Kingship of Minos of Crete who was unmoved by the unruly mob may have had contemporary resonance for the subjects of Richard II.[27] For Richard gold equated with eternity in the same way that it had for the pharaohs of ancient Egypt (a 1398 inventory of Richard's goldsmiths shows an accumulation of gold) and it was widely perceived that the fall of such a king had the hallmarks of occult intervention.

Richard died in prison in middle to late February 1400, a fate that could possibly be read from an interpretation of the readings of some of the triads comprised of the witnesses *tristitia* and *puella* and the judge *populus*, formed from specific questions posed in Richard's book of geomancy concerning the future of the king. No signs of violence were found on his body when it was examined in the nineteenth century, and the official version was that he had starved himself to death.[28] His mortal remains were secretly buried at Langley priory after an office for the dead and a procession from the Tower to St Paul's, while his tomb at Westminster, containing his effigy and that of his queen, Anne of Bohemia, remained empty. The reluctance of Henry IV to allow the king's two bodies to be joined meant that Richard's disembodied spirit still haunted the minds of many of his supporters. Denied burial with his mortal remains, the aura of his kingship, the spirit of mercury, was still at large with the capacity to harm the new dynasty. Between 1402 and 1404, Maud de Vere, countess of Oxford, distributed badges of the white hart. Rumours that the king was still alive affected admirers like Jean Creton, who wrote to his sovereign in 1402 saying he heard that Richard was alive and prayed that it was so; Creton obsessively returned to visions of the king: 'the representation of your image comes to me so often before the eyes of my heart, for by day and night all my mental imaginings are no other than thoughts of you'.[29] Rumours that Richard was alive and would return to claim his throne were encouraged by the circulation of the early fourteenth-century pseudo Merlin prophecy of the six kings to follow John in a text incorporated into the *Brut*. In the prophecy an ass or lamb (Richard) ruled his land in peace and though he will give his throne to an eagle mole or moldorp (Bolingbroke) it was maintained that the ass would return. Ricardian rumours were at the height in 1413–14 during the illness and death of Henry IV. John Wygleharsh, onetime groom and yeoman of Richard II, applied himself to the support of the Scottish imitator of Richard, Thomas Ward of Trumpington. He and others schemed seven years, spreading rumours in England and Wales that Richard was still alive, and in 1413 they revealed themselves in sanctuary of Westminster Abbey from March to June proclaiming that Richard lived in Scotland during Henry V's accession. The perceived threat to the Lancastrian dynasty posed by imaginative speculations about such political matters as rumours concerning the return of Richard II was linked to the crown's attempts to suppress Lollardy. The 1401 statute *De Haeretica comburendum*, specified burning at the stake for all heretics who did not recant, and the 1406 statute against the Lollards proclaimed: 'many men and women by false assurances and signs falsely publicize that Richard, late king of England, is supposed to be alive'.

The persistence of such rumours contributed to Henry IV's repressive approach to all aspects of the occult. The statute *De Haeretica comburendum* included among heretics those practising magic. In the 1402 parliament there was a proscription against any acts of divination in Wales: it was agreed that no wastrels, minstrels or vagabonds should be sustained in Wales, who make unruly gatherings among common people, which by their divinations, lies and exaltations are a cause of the insurrections and rebellions occupying them now. Henry further attempted to limit the use of the imagination which could encompass the occult arts. He was especially concerned with spells against the king. In November 1400 there were revelations of a plot to smear Henry IV's saddle with a magical ointment that would cause him before he had ridden ten miles to swell up and die instantly, sitting upright in the saddle.[30] The treason laws were applied to compassing or imagining the death of the king, and this applied to the execution of William Clere, a clerk of Canterbury in 1402.

While there are obvious, urgent political reasons why the regime prosecuted heretics and anyone contemplating the death of the king, or a revival of the Ricardian monarchy, there is no obvious explanation why alchemists should have been singled out for special attention; to some extent this may reflect perceived links between alchemy and illicit forms of magic. This stems from the growing suspicion towards alchemy by the beginning of the fifteenth century when it began to assume mystical dimensions.[31] In *Contra alchemista*, composed by the Inquisitor of Aragon, Nicolo Eymeric in 1399, the falsification of coins and metallurgic alchemy is targeted and although he did not attack the religious expression of alchemical discourse his suspicion that alchemy was too magical or even demonical was a new contribution to alchemical debates.[32] This same mentality may have led to the passing of legislation against the practice of alchemy in 1404 during Arundel's second period of tenure as archbishop of Canterbury. Arundel may have seen Lollards (unfairly) as in some way in league with those who sought to disclose occult secrets. Henry IV therefore prosecuted alchemists. His son did also: on 30 April 1414, John Hexham, a London apothecary skilled in making drugs, was brought before the mayor William Crowmer hanged for counterfeiting coin.[33] However Henry V also possessed a treacle box and among the drugs prescribed for the king's army in France was sal ammoniac.[34] The new attention the Lancastrian kings gave to the practice of alchemy has never been explained. Given that this

CONCLUSION: THE LANCASTRIAN REACTION

CONCLUSION: THE LANCASTRIAN REACTION

went against the relative popularity and support that alchemy had enjoyed in the previous century it is possible that the regime had more in mind than counterfeiting and that there was a political dimension relating to Richard II's involvement in the occult. The Lancastrian attitude to the chroniclers' claim that Richard was deposed because of his dependence on the occult brings into the political arena the possibility that Richard's reputation for tyranny and the aloof, formal tone of his kingship can be attributed to his belief that the occult could enable him to control his subjects and access hidden powers. Many sources sympathetic to the king were destroyed, including the *Glastonbury Chronicle*, and the original publication of the Acts of the Great Parliament of September 1397, which contained explicit Ricardian propaganda.[35] Richard may have had a large collection of books of an occult, magical nature, like the collections of his father-in-law Charles V or Friar John Erghome, but they were dispersed. Only a glimpse can be provided of the nature of his library from the inventories of his tutor, Simon Burley, and his uncle, the duke of Gloucester, which included the prophecies of Merlin, Giles of Rome's *De Regimine principum* and the *books of the Apocalypse*. His image often suffered the same fate as that of the pharaoh Akhenaton: his face in the illustration showing Chaucer reading his book in a manuscript of *Troillus and Criseyde* was rubbed out.[36] Some of these erasures seem to have been focussed on images and symbols concerned with occult power. The portrait showing a child-like Richard bearing the sceptre and orb at the beginning of his *Libellus Geomancie* was defaced[37] and in the copy of this geomancy the censor after his deposition erased the word *geomancie* as well as *arena*, the sand in which geomancy was practised.[38] Images of the white hart throughout the country were destroyed: the emblems of the white hart set up on the gates of Warwick cathedral by Richard's half brother, Thomas Holand, duke of Exeter, were erased.

There was a consensus that Richard II's use of the occult to enforce royal tyranny was a significant factor in his deposition; but the persistent association of Richard II with the occult, and Lancastrian attempts to repress this, shows that the occult remained a significant factor in political life. This highlights the question, what constituted a proper, politically sagacious use of the occult? The resolution of this issue is one thing that emerged from the fall of Richard II. The prophecy of Merlin concerning the prestigious 22-year reign of a king of Albion who will be undone in the north, which circulated widely in Richard's reign and occurs in the alchemical collection of John Erghome and in a late fourteenth-century scientific collection of Baconian texts,[39] illustrates the way Richard's supporters depended on the occult. If we accept that Richard II believed in this prophecy then it would have become full of potentially positive and destructive energy, both inspirational and malign in its capacity to inspire and depress the king. Because it was deployed to apply to the present and the future it had the capacity to influence the state of mind of the king and therefore future events. Richard also attempted to manipulate the future and the forces of nature (the *Wilton Diptych* and the poems *Pearl, Patience* and *Purity*, with their emphasis on regeneration and resurrection, illustrate this attempt to use the occult to make reality conform to wishes). Such dependence on the unpredictable, hidden forces of the occult would be expected from those denied actual political power; but it is surprising to see it in a king: it is testimony to Richard's uncertainty, his lack of confidence in his political abilities and the amount of damage done to him by the Appellant lords who deprived him of power from 1386 to 1389. Unlike his grandfather, Edward III who based his power on the support of the magnates with whom he closely identified,[40] Richard created a narrow power base of close friends and courtiers and his impotence in handling powerful nobles was demonstrated on numerous occasions: in 1384 he was a helpless and shocked witness to the torture of the Carmilite friar, John Latimer, accused of plotting against the duke of Lancaster, at the hands of Philip Courtenay, John Holand and Simon Burley; and in the following year the duke of Lancaster appeared before the king in full armour to reproach him for having bad counsellors and pursuing a vendetta of private murder against him when he should be above the law with the power to vouchsafe life and limb with a nod. It was this impotence which helped push Richard towards occult sources of power.

Henry IV on the other hand seized the throne through the use of political skill, intelligence, bravery and force of will and passed this hard won power onto his son; these two men were always in control and the so-called powers of the occult were never for them unpredictable. For them prophecies belonged to the past: they were inert and could only be used retrospectively to justify and rationalize events after they had taken place, in modern parlance used as political propaganda.[41] Henry IV turned to events that had happened in the early 1360s during the reign of Edward III in the guise of the Bridlington prophecies; these did not have the power to elate or harm him and he used them out of context to validate his claims. The Bridlington prophecies, originally written and interpreted to apply to the campaigns of Edward III, were used in conjunction with the canonization of their reputed author, John Thweng, to justify the Lancastrian usurpation. Richard II's attitude to the supernatural was more neurotic: in his identification with the role of the magus all alchemical symbols and myths and prophecies had the power to harm or elate him and could substitute for the application of political skill. The contrast between the two rulers can be seen in their respective treatment of a self-styled prophet, the hermit William Norham. In the spring of 1399 he came to Richard demanding he reinstate the lords he had dispossessed or the king would be overtaken. Richard, intrigued by his ragged appearance, asked him to walk on water to confirm his status as a messenger from God, and when Norham explained that he was not a saint who would perform miracles on request he was committed to the Tower. Richard may have been joking but his credulous, or at least intrigued reaction, contrasts to Bolingbroke's abrupt response to being railed at by Norham: he had him beheaded at York. The two kings' different attitudes towards the occult highlights a debate that is still relevant today. Richard's emotional dependence on magic was adolescent; he lacked Bolingbroke's experience of life and maturity; and by believing totally in the alchemical myths that were such an important part of his public image he took the fatal step of making his life confirm to myths and prophecies. In this he was following (probably consciously) in the footsteps of Jesus of Nazareth and he chose a path of martyrdom and self-aggrandizement that amounted in the eyes of the political community to insanity (one of the reasons for his deposition according to Usk). This messianic complex was to surface a hundred years later with an equally egocentric and unsuccessful king, Richard III.[42] The Lancastrian regime marked a departure from the narcissistic and egocentric monarchy of Richard II, and the cult of personality which involved the raising of the kingship to a supernatural level; such things were replaced by the concept of the state. This had been anticipated by John Gower, whose increasing coolness towards Richard II could be seen in the 1390s, when he reworked his *Confessio amantis* and replaced his prayer to Richard II with a prayer for the state of England.[43]

Nevertheless Henry IV remained an unsettled nervous figure, besotted by rumours concerning the appearance of Richard's ghost. Richard Maudelyn, who bore a close resemblance to the dead king, impersonated him during the Epiphany revolt and he was drawn, hung and beheaded. Two months later Richard's corpse was brought to London and Creton, who believed the king was alive, thought this must be the body of Maudelyn. Such confusions did not help the state of mind of Henry IV who had taken the precaution to be anointed with the miraculous oil presented to Becket that Richard II was supposed to have discovered. Plagued by ill-health and guilt, he became a Macbeth-like king fearful of the supernatural (a charm similar to the one found in Richard II's tomb was also found in Henry's), and it remained for his son, Henry V, to lay to rest Richard's ghost and to demonstrate a more wholly pragmatic use of the occult. This is shown in his decision to rebury his former guardian, Richard II, together with the ruby ring of Edward the Confessor, never returned to Richard after his departure to Ireland in 1399, to join the loosed spirit of his kingly aura with his mortal remains so that Richard would become a legitimate figure in the succession, transmitting the throne to Henry V. The reburial therefore became an act of exorcism, and it is significant that Sir Thomas Erpingham K.G. (1357–1428) the soldier, crusader and servant of Henry IV and Henry V, referred to a frequently consulted occult book to demonstrate that Richard II regarded Henry of Monmouth as his successor.[44] Henry V's response to the threat to the dynasty posed by Richard II's ghost was more pragmatic than his father's, and reflects the growing rational, classical perspective of the governing classes. Henry V's attempt to distance himself from the Plantagenets, and from Richard II in particular, consisted in his establishing his regime on what was perceived to be the more rational, pragmatic and masculine foundations of Roman stoic values. The Lancastrians lack of interest in the Graeco-Egyptian myths that were the foundations of English alchemy may thus be explained by their basing their government on the ethical principles of the ancient Romans. This does not mean that there was no interest in alchemy during Henry Vs reign. The king's brother, Humphrey duke of Gloucester, was profoundly influenced by the growing interest in the hermetic arts (especially the Alexandrine *Corpus Hermetica*) in Italy and alchemical symbolism was employed in his epitaph tomb in 1447.[45] William Worcester, the secretary of Sir John Fastolf and antiquary, owned a copy of *Secreta secretorum* and recorded extracts from the writings of the alchemists Roger Bacon and Albertus Magnus, medical remedies and quotations from the classics that he applied to benefit the health of his master, Sir John Fastolf.[46] Fastolf, in the service of John duke of Bedford in France, was at the forefront of the discovery of the works of such classical authors as Cicero, Seneca and Caesar in the library of the Valois kings. His servants and medical advisers, William Worcester and Stephen Scrope Esq., saw the potential of stoic philosophy (which they translated for Fastolf) in contributing towards the humoral balance that alchemical practitioners sought to achieve. This implies that Worcester and Scrope were taking alchemy to another subtler and domestic dimension in their treatment of Fastolf's old age. But it was not till the emergence of the house of York, under Edward IV, that there was a sophisticated, pragmatic deployment of alchemical myths and symbols to political ends. In the fourteenth century the myths and symbols of alchemy lay hidden within Latin texts, and even when used by King Richard II they remained obscurely buried in arcane, private occult works such as the *Wilton Diptych*. In 1422 the *Secreta secretorum* was translated into the vernacular by James Yonge in the English pale in Ireland,[47] Rupescissa's *De Quintessentiae* was translated into English in this period, and by the second half of the fifteenth century works on alchemy were being written in the vernacular by George Ripley and Thomas Norton, and alchemical myths and symbols under Edward IV became political, and more populist rallying points for Yorkist propaganda.

Edward IV saw himself as a successor to Richard II, who had named as his successor Roger Mortimer (1374–98), the fourth earl of March, Edward IV's maternal ancestor, who was killed in Ireland in 1398 wearing the colours red and white, while acting as Richard's lieutenant. Edward IV in genealogical rolls was depicted as the heir of Richard II: both were identified by the cognomen of *Sol*[48] and Edward adopted Richard's badge of the sun in splendour and when he entered Coventry in 1474 he was greeted by a figure representing Richard II who exclaimed:

> we must bless the time of your nativity
> The right line of royal blood is as it should be.[49]

However in his understanding of alchemy Edward of March was more like Edward III in his masculine approach to alchemy and his identification with the sun and sulphur. Richard in his celebration of mercury and the feminine principles of alchemy, *Luna* and virginity, was flying in the face of orthodox, alchemical theory. The late medieval alchemist admittedly created in his laboratory a feminine world of vessels and water. He entered into the body of mother earth, the monster or dragon, and extracted from the womb of mother earth precious metals, appropriating the female principle for its generative power, usurping the role of maternity, harnessing woman's creative energy. The alchemist's laboratory was like a female body, the earth that provided the warmth and nutrition necessary for the birth of the stone. However, although alchemists saw the primal water, mercury, as the source of life, they feared its potentially destructive power. The female principle was essential for the commencement of the alchemical work and the alchemist needed to cautiously manipulate these unpredictable primal forces governed by the moon. From the male perspective *Luna* rather than *Sol* represented the unconscious, and one of the spiritual functions of alchemy was to apply choler, fire and light (or reason) to chthonic maternal forces to facilitate the development of the self: the first step was to fix mercury. Alchemical allegories and meditations were based on the medical philosophy of the Greek physician, Galen of Pergamum, who taught that women were failed males, lacking the necessary vital heat to reach their full potential. Their instability caused by the restless wandering of their wombs in search of male heat and seed could only be calmed when they were pregnant. Virgins, widows, and especially post menopausal women who no longer menstruated, were regarded as especially dangerous because corrupt noxious humours built up in their bodies and this could have alarming implications for the body politic. Men were supposed to possess in abundance this precious heat that could dispel phlegm and female instability or inertia. The king therefore was seen as a vital source of well-being for the body politic, identified with the sun, with its life giving properties and with the light of reason. Richard II's identification with mercury, the feminine, and his chastity, and possibly virginity, were therefore all potentially disastrous for the kingship and the nation. By the fifteenth century the political crisis of the Wars of the Roses became to be seen as the product of excess phlegm and femininity on the part of King Henry VI (a king who shared much in common with Richard II) and the dangers to the body politic posed by unstable women.[50]

Richard II was therefore regarded in the late Middle Ages as an awkward, unstable presence in English political life, and to modern historians he remains something of an enigma, an effete, unpredictable personality. In one sense Richard II was ahead of his time and would have belonged more comfortably in the late sixteenth century. His reign, which was a cultural watershed in terms of the creation of works of art and literature in the vernacular associated with the court, looks forward to the age of Elizabeth I. Holingshed, in his *Chronicles*, noted in the margin next to his account of Richard II: 'Out of a French pamphlet that belonged to master John Dee' (Elizabeth I's astrologer). This pamphlet was a copy of Creton's *Histoire* that was not available in England because of its pro-Ricardian tone.[51] By the sixteenth century mercury, the moon and virginity were successfully integrated in the person of Queen Elizabeth I, the red-haired queen whose image closely resembles that of Richard II in the *Wilton Diptych*. Despite the projections of counsellors such as William Burghley (learned in the English medieval alchemical traditions) who attempted to stabilize the Virgin Queen by getting her to marry and produce an heir,[52] Elizabeth made a virtue of being identified with the cold, chaste and watery beams of the silver moon rather that the choler and sanguine heat of the golden sun. It is therefore significant that she was so struck by the parallels between her reign and that of Richard II that she is reputed to have exclaimed: 'know you not that I am Richard II'. The queen's observations on the parallels between her reign and that of Richard II were made around the time Shakespeare's *Richard II* was first performed in 1595, during the period of the rebellion of Robert Devereaux, the second earl of Essex.[53]

Shakespeare's perceptive insights into the character of Richard II provides evidence of the existence towards the end of the sixteenth century of a more sympathetic understanding of Richard's complex personality and which was encouraged by his marked similarities to the Virgin Queen. Shakespeare's play also shows a sophisticated understanding of the deeper contradictions in his personality and especially his involvement in and dependence on alchemy and other occult arts. His *Richard II* is a king who wholeheartedly identifies with the medieval notion of the king's two bodies.[54] As the vicar of God he is divine, eternal and masterful; but as a man he is destined, like Christ, to suffer humiliations and to be tortured and renewed like alchemical gold. Shakespeare understood Richard's self-image as *alchemicus rex*: as one who had enjoyed absolute power and faced his mortality; he anticipates Prospero of *The Tempest*, an alchemist and wizard whose art ultimately cannot protect him from the fate shared by all. In the play it is John of Gaunt, the defender of the royal prerogative, who sums up the notion of the philosopher's stone as the land justly ruled by its divinely ordained king by seeming to evoke the very images of the *Wilton Diptych*:

> This royal throne of kings, this sceptred isle.
> This earth of majesty, this seat of Mars,
> This other Eden, demi-paradise, —
> This precious stone set in the silver sea,[55]

Shakespeare's Richard however shows all the frailties of the historical king. His dependence on occult sources of power led him to neglect the realities of politics and the management of the baronage and made him susceptible to bursts of elation and delusions of grandeur. He identifies himself with the sun and on his return from Ireland exclaims:

–when the searching eye of heaven is hid
Behind the globe and lights the lower world,
Then thieves and robbers range abroad unseen –
But when from under the terrestrial ball
He fires the proud tops of the eastern pines
And darts his light through every guilty hole,
Then murders, treasons and detested sins,
The cloak of night being plucked from off their back,
Stand bare and naked, trembling at themselves?[56]

His conviction that he is divinely appointed, and his dependence on the rituals and ceremonies of kingship, makes him blind to the realities of political power:

Not all the water in the rough rude sea
Can wash the balm off from an anointed king.[57]

When faced with the gathering might of Bolingbroke's forces he seeks support from an angelic army (Shakespeare may have seen the angels on the roof of Westminster Palace or in the court of heaven on the *Wilton Diptych*):

God for his Richard hath in heavenly pay
A glorious angel. Then, if angels fight,
Weak men must fall, for heaven still guards the right.[58]

However Richard could just as easily fall into depression and despair when contemplating the disparity between his immortal office and his human frailties. He reflects how death keeps court in his body:

Allowing him a breath, a little scene,
To monarchize, be feared and kill with looks,
Infusing him with self and vain conceit.[59]

There is an echo here of the king who kept court in Westminster on a high throne and required exaggerated deference from all his subjects. Faced with the political and military might of Bolingbroke he resorts to curses and conjuration calling on omnipotent God to muster the clouds on his behalf:

Armies of petilence, and they shall strike
Your children, yet unborn and unbegot.[60]

This imprecation set the seal on the fate of Bolingbroke's heirs in Shakespeare's subsequent history plays: the fateful insanity and civil wars that would befall the usurping house of Lancaster in the fifteenth century. Bolingbroke too would evoke alchemical imagery to convey the impact of his confrontation with Richard in terms of the thunder caused by the clash of the elements of fire and water and the usurper assumed the role of the redeeming rains of heaven (a concept derived from the *Secreta secretorum*):

> Be he the fire, I'll be the yielding water;
> The rage be his, whilst on the earth I rain
> My waters–.[61]

However, in the play, as in life, Richard was too feminine to assume the role to the conquering sulphuric sun. On his return from Ireland he identified himself with the mother of her land

> As a long-parted mother with her child
> Plays fondly with her tears and smiles in meeting,
> So weeping, smiling, greet I thee, my earth.[62]

He is also prone to mercurial mood swings and displays of feminine vanity. On his arrest he requests a mirror and gazes into it:

> —Was this the face
> That like the sun did make beholders wink?[63]

He responds to his deposition and imprisonment with copious displays of weeping, and despite the heliocentric rhetoric that he displays, it is the female element of water with which he primarily identifies. He sums up his fate when he reflects:

> O, that I were a mockery king of snow,
> Standing before the sun of Bolingbroke,[64]

But he never loses sight of the concept of the king's two bodies and the divine origins of his kingship:

> —show us the hand of God
> That hath dismissed us from our stewardship;
> For well we know no hand of blood and bone
> Can gripe the sacred handle of our sceptre.[65]

As God's instrument on earth he closely identifies with the martyred Christ, the unloved, betrayed servant of his people:

—Yet I well remember
The favours of these men. Were they not mine?
Did they not sometime cry "All hail" to me?
So Judas did to Christ, but He in twelve
Found truth in all but one: I, in twelve thousand,
none.[66]

In his final moments before his murder he is the bounded, chained hart of the *Wilton Diptych*; and it is appropriate that in his moment of Christ-like despair, when he believes that he is utterly forsaken, a faithful groom appears to the sound of sweet music and Richard responds:

Yet blessing on his heart that gives it me,
For 'tis a sign of love; and love to Richard
Is a strange brooch in this all-hating world.[67]

This brooch of love is of course the white hart badge, the mercury or the fugitive stag with which Richard so closely identified and which was the cause of his undoing. At his final end to the sound of heavenly music, perhaps the music of the spheres, the white hart remains, the king's only friend, symbolizing his unity with Christ.

Notes

Notes to Foreword

1 *The Works of Sir Thomas Malory*, vol. ii, ed. E. Vinaver in 3 vols (Oxford: Oxford University Press, 1947), p. 484.
2 *The Master of the Game by Edward 2nd Duke of York*, ed. W. M. A. and F. Baillie-Grohman (London: Chatto and Windus, 1909).
3 Ibid., p. 28.
4 Ibid., p. 28.
5 Ibid., pp. 109, 188.
6 Ibid., p. 174.
7 Malory, *Morte d'Arthur*, bk iii (ed. Vinaver), p. 105.
8 *Master of the Game*, p. 28.
9 Ibid., p. 148.
10 Ibid., p. 20.
11 Ibid., prologue.
12 Ibid., pp. 166ff.
13 Ibid., p. 143.
14 Ibid., p. 176.
15 K. B. McFarlane, *The Nobility of Later Medieval England* (Oxford: Clarendon Press, 1973); Jeremy Catto, *The History of the University of Oxford*, vol. 2 (Oxford: Clarendon Press, 1992), and his 'Conscience of Government in the Fifteenth Century', *Transactions of Royal Historical Society* (2007); Maurice Keen, *English Society in the Later Middle Ages 1348–1500* (Harmondsworth: Penguin, 1998); Jonathan Hughes, *Pastors and Visionaries: Religion and Secular Life in Late Medieval Yorkshire* (Woodbridge: Boydell and Brewer, 1988).

Notes to Chapter 1: Introduction: Alchemy and the Occult in England

1 *Boron's Book of Merlin, The English version*, ed. H. B. Wheatley EETS 1871 10, 21, 36, 112, vols i–iv, p. 92.
2 The first to use the term 'occult' in connection with magic was Agrippa; see Richard M. Barber, *The Holy Grail; Imagination and Belief* (London: Allen Lane, 2004).
3 Christopher Hill, *God's Englishman: Oliver Cromwell and the English Revolution* (Harmondsworth: Penguin, 1970).

4 Alan Rudrum, 'These Fragments I Have Shored Against My Ruins. Henry Vaughan. The Alchemy, Philosophy and the Great Rebellion', in *Mystic Metal of Gold: Essays in Alchemy and Renaissance Culture*, ed. S. Linden (New York: AMS Press, 2008), pp. 324ff.

5 Stanton J. Linden, 'Smatterings of the Philosopher's Stone: Sir Thomas Browne and Alchemy', in Linden, *Mystic Metal of Gold*, pp. 354–7.

6 Lyndy Abraham, 'A Biography of the English Alchemist Arthur Dee, Author of *Fasciculus Chemicus* and Son of Dr John Dee', in Linden, *Mystic Metal of Gold*, pp. 91–117.

7 Linden, 'Smatterings of the Philosopher's Stone', pp. 339–65.

8 David Gwynn, 'Richard Eden Cosmographer and Alchemist', *Sixteenth Century Journal* 15 (1984): 13–34.

9 Mar rey Bueno, 'La Mayson pour Distiller des Eaues a Escorial: Alchemy and Medicine at the Court of Philip II, 1556–1598', *Medical History Supplement* 29 (2009): 26-31.

10 BL MS Add 59681.

11 BL MS Sloane 299, pp. 37ff.

12 Vaughan's alchemical and autobiographical writings are in BL MS Sloane 1741.

13 Thomas and William Habington, *The Historie of Edward IV* (London: Thomas Cotes, 1640).

14 Yaakov Masceti, '"This Is the Famous Stone": George Herbert's Poetic Alchemy in "the Elixir"', in Linden, *Mystic Metal of Gold*, pp. 301–25.

15 Rudrum, 'These Fragments', p. 325.

16 Carl Jung, *Psychology and Alchemy* (London: Routledge, 1953); *Mysterium Conjunctionis,* trans. F. C. Hull (Princeton: Princeton University Press, 1970); *Alchemical Studies*, in *The Collected Works*, vol. 13 (Princeton: Princeton University Press, 1970).

17 Elias Ashmole, *Theatrum Chemicum Britannicum* (London, 1652).

18 N. Wilkins, *Nicholas Flamel: Des Livres et de l'Or* (Paris: Imago, 1993); Nicolas Flamel, *His Exposition of the Hieroglyphicall Figures* (1624), ed. Laurinda Dixon (New York: Garland, 1994).

19 H. Summersen, 'Saint George', in Mathew H. C. G. and Harrison B. eds, *The Oxford Dictionary of National Biography*, vol. 20 (London: Oxford University Press, 2004).

20 John Dee, *General and Rare Memorials Pertaining to the Perfect Arte of Navigation* (1577) (Amsterdam, New York: Theatrum Orbis Terrarum DeCapo Press, 1968).

21 Linden, *Mystic Metal of Gold*, p. 260.

22 This crystal, allegedly given him by an angel in 1582, is now in the science museum in south Kensington.

23 MS Digby 119 fols, 182v, 211. On fol. 182v a sixteenth-century hand has added *De spirita occultato* in sulphure.

24 *Diaries of John Dee*, ed. E. Fenton (Charlbury: Oxon Day Books, 1998), p. 87.

25 J. Hughes, 'The Humanity of Thomas Charnock and Elizabethan Alchemist', in *Mystical Metal of Gold: Essays on Alchemy and Renaissance Culture*, ed. S. Lindon (New York, 2007), pp. 3–34.

26 Keith Thomas, *Religion and the Decline of Magic* (London: Penguin, 1984), pp. 321ff.

27 The name Merlinus that occurs in alchemical texts may be a corruption of Merculinus. See Jung, *Mysterium Conjunctionis*, p. 266.

28 R. W. Newman, *The Summa Perfectionis of Pseudo Geber: A Critical Edition* (Leiden: Brill, 1991) fourteenth-century manuscripts, Cambridge, Gonville and Caius MS 181; Bodl. Ashmole MS 1384 and fifteenth-century BL MS Sloane 1091; D. W. Singer, *Catalogue of Latin and Vernacular Alchemical Manuscripts in Great Britain and Ireland Dating from Before the XVI Century*, 3 vols (Brusssels: M. Lamentin, 1928), pp. 94–6.

29 Paravicini Bagliani, 'Storia della scienza e storia della mentalita: Ruggero Baxone. Boniface VIII e la teoria della prolongation vitae', in *Aspeti della letteratura Latina nel secolo XIII*, ed. C. Leonardi and G. Orlandi (Florence: L Nuova Italia, 1986), pp. 243–80. *Opus maius* (1267) ed. J. H. Bridges (Oxford, 1897–1900); English translation Robert Burke, 2 vols (Philadelphia, 1928); S. J. Williams 'Roger Bacon and His Edition of the Pseudo Aristotelian *Secreta secretorum*', *Speculum* 69 (1994). *Species De Retardatione accidentionis senectatis*, ed. R. Steele and F. M. Delarme; *Opera haectenus inedita Rogerii Baconis* (Oxford, 1909–40); *Opera hactenas inedita Rogeri Baconi* (Oxford: Clarendon Press, 1909–10); S. J. Williams, 'Roger Bacon and the Secret of Secrets', in *Roger Bacon and the Sciences Commemorative Essays*, ed. J. Hackett (Leiden: Brill, 1997), pp. 365–93; Most texts of *Speculum Alkymie* are anonymous BL Add 15549 (fifteenth century); English version Sloane MS 2688ff., 87v–91v; Singer, *Catalogue of Alchemical Manuscripts*, vol. 1, pp. 177–90; printed *Opera Omnia*, ed. A. Borgnet (Paris, 1890).

30 G. C. Anawati, 'L'alchimie arabes', in *Histoire des sciences arabes iii technologie alchimie et sciences de la vie*, ed. Roshdi Rashed with Regis Morelon, (Paris: Seuil, 1997).

31 Leah DeVun, *Prophecy, Alchemy and the End of Time: John of Rupescissa in the Late Middle Ages* (New York: Columbia University Press, 2009), p. 50.

32 *The Chronica Maiora* of Thomas Walsingham covers the period 1376–1422; *The St Albans Chronicle: The Chronica Maiora of Thomas Walsingham*, ed. and trans. John Taylor, Wendy R. Childs and Leslie Watkiss (Oxford: Clarendon, 2003–) constitutes the fullest printed text of the *Chronica Maiora* for the years 1392–1422.

33 Bologna Univ. MS 500 (fifteenth century).

34 Bodl. Ashmole MS 1459, fol. 81.

35 Bodl. MS 581 *Phisionomia Aristotellis* fols 3r–5v.

36 Bodl. MS 581 *Sompniale Danielis* fols 6r–7r.

37 Bodl. MS 581 *Liber Judicorum* fols 9v–89v.

Notes to Chapter 2: The Origins of English Alchemy and Sources for the Study of Alchemy in Fourteenth-Century England

1 *Merlin and the Grail: Joseph of Arimathea, Merlin, Perceval: The Trilogy of Arthurian Romances attributed to Robert de Boron*, trans. Nigel Bryant Robert de Boron (Woodbridge: D.S. Brewer, 2001).

2 Peter Marshall, *The Philosopher's Stone* (London: Pan Macmillan, 2001).

3 For a summary of Chinese alchemy and links with Western alchemy, see P. G. Maxwell, *The Chemical Choir: A History of Alchemy* (London: Continuum, 2008), pp. 1–17.

4 The Private Diary of John Dee and Catalogue of his library of manuscripts from the original manuscripts in the Ashmolean Museum at Oxford and Trin. Coll. Camb., ed. James Orchard Halliwell (New York: AMS Press, 1968).

5 Nicholas Vincent, *The Holy Blood: King Henry III and the Westminster Blood Title* (Cambridge: Cambridge University Press, 2001); J. P. Carley, *John of Glastonbury's Chronicle*, pp. 28–30; Antonia Gransden, *English Historical Literature* (London: Routledge and Kegan Paul, 1976–87); J. P. Carley, 'Melkin the Bard and Esoteric Tradition at Glastonbury Abbey', *Downside Review* 99 (1981): 1–17; V. A. Logario, 'The Legend of St Joseph', *Speculum* 46 (1971): 209–31; *Culture and the King: The Social Implications of the Arthurian Legend: Essays in Honour of Valerie M. Logario*, ed. Mark B. Shichtman and James P. Carley (State University of New York Press, 1994); Michell, *New Light on the Ancient Mythology of Glastonbury* (Glastonbury: Gothic Image Publications, 1990), p. 94.

6 Michell, *New Light on Glastonbury*; Carley, 'Melkin the Bard'; *The Chronicle of Glastonbury Abbey: An Edition, Translation and Study of John of Glastonbury's*, Chronica sive antiquitates Glastoniensis, trans. David Townsend, ed. J. P. Carley (Woodbridge: Boydell Press, 1988); J. P. Carley, *Glastonbury Abbey: The Holy House at the Head of the Moors Adventurous* (Glastonbury: Gothic Image Publications, 1996), pp. 1–3.

7 BL Harl 1766.

8 *Boron's Book of Merlin, the English version*, ed. H. B. Wheatley EETS 1871, 10, 21, 36, 112, vols i—iv, p. 92.

9 BL Add MS 15, 549, fol.158.

10 BL Add MS 15,549, fol. 155–60.

11 BL Harl MS 2407, fol. 48v.

12 BL MS Harl 2407, fol. 34–45.

13 BL MS Royal 12 Exv fol. 19.

14 Geoffrey of Monmouth, *The History of the Kings of Britain*, trans. Lewis Thorpe (Harmondsworth: Penguin, 1966).

15 'Moyen Age De Quelques Texts Alchimiques Attribues a Arthur o Merlin', *Merologus* 3 (1995): 227–63; Leslie A. Coote, *Prophecy and Public Affairs in Late Medieval England* (Woodbridge: York Medieval, 2000).

16 In the fifteenth-century poem on the philosopher's stone, the stone is identified with Christ and the union of the red and the white.

17 *The Quest of the Holy Grail*, trans. P. M. Matarosso (New York: Penguin, 1969), p. 92.

18 Garth Fowden, *The Egyptian Hermes: A Historical Approach to the Late Pagan Mind* (Princeton, 1993).

19 Okasha El Daly, *Egyptology: The Missing Millenium. Ancient Egypt in Medieval Arabic Writings* (London: UCL Press, 2005), p. 13.

20 Peter Marshall, *The Philosopher's Stone*, pp. 137–49.

21 Robert Halleux, *Papyrus de Leyde, Papyrus de Stockholm: Fragments de recettes*, vol. 1 of *Les alchimistes greces* (Paris: Societe d'Edition "Les Belles Letters" 1981).

22 Halleux, *Papyrus de Leyde*.

23 Marshall, *the Philosopher's Stone*, pp. 181–6.

24 Crisciani Chiara and Pereira Michele, eds, 'L'Arte del sole e delle Luna', *Alchimie e filosofia nel medioevo: centro italianole studi sell'alto medioevo* (Spaletto: Centro italiano di studi sullalto medioevo, 1996).

25 Eighth-century Baghdad even used petroleum extracts to pave streets in tar. Robert Halleaux, 'The Reception of Arabic Alchemy in the West', in *The Encyclopaedia of Arabic Sciences*, vol. III, ed. Roshdi Rashad and Regis Morelon (London: Routledge, 1996), pp. 886–902.

26 Eric John Holmyard, *Alchemy* (New York, Dover), p. 62; Marshall, *The Philosopher's Stone*, p. 217. Al Hassan Ahmad Y, 'The Arabic Original of Liber de compositione alchimie the Epistle of Maryanus the Hermit and Philosopher to Prince Khalid ibn Yazil', *Arabic Science and Philosophy* 14 (2006): 213–31.

27 Ahmad Y. al-Hassan, 'Science and Technology in Islam', in *The Different Aspects of Islamic Culture*, ed. A. Y. al-Hassan, A. Iskander and Mapul Ahmed (Unesco, 2001), vol. 4; A. Y. al-Hassan, *Studies in al-kimia. Critical Issues in Latin and Arabic Alchemy and Chemistry* (Broscher, 2009).

28 al-Hassan, 'Science and Technology in Islam'.

29 al-Hassan, 'Science and Technology in Islam'.

30 Robert Steele and Dorothy Singer, trans. *The Emerald Table* (1927) in Holmyard, *Alchemy*; G. Fowden, *The Egyptian Hermes*.

31 BL MS Add 47680, fol. 6v.

32 M. A. Manzalaoui, 'The *Secreta secretorum* in English thought in the fourteenth to the seventeenth century' (Oxford D.Phil. thesis, 1954). For a printed edition see *Secreta secretorum: Nine English Versions*, vol. I, ed. M. A. Manzalaoui EETS, 276, 1977.

33 Charles Burnett, 'Ketton, Robert of (fl 1141–57)', in *Oxford Dictionary of National Biography* (Oxford: Oxford University Press, 2004).

34 Charles C. Haskins, 'Michael Scot and Frederick II', *Isis* 4; Singer D. W., 'Michael Scot and Alchemy', *Isis* 13.

35 S. Skinner, *Terrestrial Astrology: Divination by Astrology* (London: Routledge Kegan Paul (1980).

36 W. Montgomery Watt and P. Cachio, *A History of Islamic Spain* (Edinburgh: Edinburgh University Press, 1965); L. P. Harvey, *Islamic Spain* (Chicago: Chicago University Press, 1990). The first reference to the practice of alchemy in the West is in a chronicle of Adame of Breme reporting a fraudulent transmutation of gold to the bishop of Hamburg c. 1050 by a Byzantine Jew called Paul.

37 Camb. Trin. Coll. MS 122.

38 BL Add MS 10764.

39 BL Sloane MS 323 (fourteenth century); Sloane MS 1754; Singer, *Catalolgue of Alchemical Manuscripts*, vol. 1, pp. 100–4.

40 Camb. Trin. Coll. MS 1122, fol. 125 (fourteenth century); Oxford Bodl. Digby 119, fol. 217 (fourteenth century); Oxford Bodl. Lib. E mus 63 (fifteenth century) fols 66–66v; Singer, *Catalogue of Alchemical Manuscripts*, vol. 1, pp. 18–25.

41 Fourteenth-century manuscript Oxford Corpus Christi 125; fifteenth-century Camb. Trin. Coll. 1122; Sixteenth-century Bodl. Ashmole 1416; Singer, *Catalogue of Alchemical Manuscripts*, vol. 1, pp. 1–11; Plessner M., 'The Place of the *Turba Philosophorum* in the Development of Alchemy', *Isis* 45 (1954): 331–8.

42 BL Egerton MS 2676 (fourteenth century); BL Royal MS 5f xiv (fourteenth century). Singer, *Catalogue of Alchemical Manuscripts*.

43 David Abulafia, *A Mediterraenean Emporium: The Catalan Kingdom of* Majorca (Cambridge: Cambridge University Press, 1994).

44 DeVun, *Prophecy, Alchemy and the End of Time*, p. 90.

45 J. Ziegler, 'Alchemy in *Practica summari*. A Footnote to Michael McVaugh's Contribution', *Arxiu de textos Catalans Antics* 23/4 (2005): 265–7.

46 Nicolas Weil-Parot, 'Arnaud de Villeneuve et les relations possibles entre le sceau du lion et l'alchimie', *Arxiu de textos catalans* 23/4 (2004–05): 269–80.

47 Jennifer M. Rampling, 'George Ripley and Alchemical Consensus', Sixth International Conference on History of Chemistry, Leuven, Belgium, 28 Aug–1 Sep, 2007.

48 Ziegler includes no alchemical works in the Arnould canon but Thorndike and Calvet include the *Rosarium philosophorum* among the genuine works. See Antoine Calvet, 'Lalchimie d'Arnaud de Villeneuve', in *Terres medievales*, ed. Bernard Ribemont (Paris: Editions klincksieck, 1993), pp. 21–2.

49 M. Pereira 'Arnoldo de Vilanova e l'alchimia. Un'andigne preliminare', in *Actes de la Troboda Internationale d'Estudi sobre Arnau de Villanova*, vol. 2, ed a.c.di J Perernau (Treballs de la seccio de filosofia i sciencies socials, XIX), Barcelona, Institut d'Estudis Catalans, 1995, pp. 95–174. J. Ziegler, *Medicine and Religion c. 1300 The Case of Arnau de Vilanova* (Oxford: Clarendon Press, 1998); *Religion and Medicine in the Middle Ages*, ed. Peter Biller and Josph Ziegler (Woodbridge: York Medieval Press, 2001).

50 Richard.W. Southern, *Robert Grosseteste: The Growth of an English Mind in Medieval Europe* (Oxford: Clarendon Press, 1986), pp. 147–8, 164–9, 172–3, 221.

51 Glasgow Hunt. MS 116 (fourteenth century).

52 BL Arundel MS 164 (fourteenth century); Robert Halleaux, 'Albert le Grand et l'alchime', *Review des Sciences philosophignes et theologiques* 66 (1982).

53 *The Book of Secrets of Albertus Magnus of the Virtues of Herbs, Stones and Certain Beasts, also a Book of the Marvels of the World*, ed. Michael R. Best and Frank H. Brightman (Oxford: Clarendon Press, 1975).

54 Barbara Obrist, 'Les rapports d'analogie entre philosophie et alchemie medieavales', in *Alchimie et philosophie a la renaissance*: acta du colloque international de Tours 4–7 Decembre 1991/reunies sous la direction de Jean Claude Margolin et Sylvain Matton (Paris: J. Vrin, 1993), p. 49.

55 Merton Coll. MS 320 (fourteenth century).

56 Bodl. Digby MS 119.

57 BL Add MS 1549.

58 BL MS Laud Misc 735, fols 1–135.

59 BL Add MS 30 338, fol. 192.

60 Michela Pereira and Barbara Spaggioni, *Il Testamentum alchemnico attribuito a Raimundo Lullo: edizione del testo latino e catelano dal manuscritto Oxford Corpus Christ Coll. 244* (Firenze: Sismel Edizione del Galluzo, 1999); S. J. Williams, 'Roger Bacon and the Secret of Secrets', in *Roger Bacon and the Sciences: Commemorative Essays*, p. 386.

61 John North, *The Ambassador's Secret: Holbein and the World of the Renaissance* (London: Hambledon, 2002), pp. 154–63, 180. There are Cosmati pavements in St Cecilia's Church in Trastavere and St Maria Maggiore Church, Rome, with images of the dragon and the phoenix.

62 The original design is revealed in an engraving of George Venture. See George Foster, *Patterns of Thought. The Hidden Meaning of the Great Westminster Pavement* (London: Cape, 1991), p. 72; Paul Binski, *Westminster Abbey and the Plantagenets: Kingship and the Representation of Power 1200–1400* (New Haven, London: Yale University Press, 1995).

63 Agostino Paravicini Bagliani, *The Pope's Body*, trans. David .S. Peterson (Chicago: Chicago University Press, 2000), p. 227.

64 Ibid., pp. 18ff.

65 Lynn Thorndike, *A History of Magic and Experimental Science* (New York: Columbia University Press, 1923–58), vol. iii, p. 34.

66 CU Trin. Coll. MS 0.2.18, fol. 104 (fourteenth-century manuscript); CU Trin. MS 1127. There is some doubt about the authenticity of this address to the pope for it occurs in later manuscripts and there are no salutary phrases such as occur in Dastin's letters to Cardinal Orsini. See Thiessen, 'The Letters of John Dastin', *Ambix* 55 (2002): 153–68; and W. Thiessen, 'John Dastin the Alchemist as co-creator', *Ambix* 38 (1991).

67 Ashmole MS 1411, fol. 73; Thorndike, *History of Magic*, vol. iii, pp. 85–9.

68 C. Crisciani 'The Conceptions of Alchemy as Expressed in the *Pretiosa Margarita Novella* of Petrus Bonus of Ferara', *Ambix* 20 (1973): 165–81. For the title *Pretiosa novella margarita* see the fifteenth-century manuscript Bl Harl MS 672, fol. 168v; Thorndike, *History of Magic*, p. 147; Printed edition, *Bibliotheca Chemica curiosa*, ed. Jean-Jacques Manget (Geneva: Chouet, 1702), vol. ii, pp. 29ff.

69 George Molland, 'Dumbleton John', *New DNB* (2004).

70 Frederick Hammond, 'Walter Oddington', *New DNB*.

71 Trin. Coll. Camb. MS 1122 (fourteenth century). For sixteenth-century copies see Bodl. MS Digby 119, fols 142r–149r.

72 John North, 'Robert of York', *New DNB*.

73 Bologna Univ. MS Biblioteca Universita 138 (104), fols 245–53v; Michela Pereira, 'The Alchemical Corpus Attributed to Raymund Lull' (London: *Warbourg Institute Surveys and texts*, XVIII, 1989), pp. 1–118.

74 Crisciani Chiara and Michela Pereira, 'The Black Death and Golden Remedies: Some Remarks on Alchemy and the Plague, in *The Regulation of Evil: Social and Cultural Attitudes to Epidemics in the Late Middle Ages*', ed. Agostino Paravicini Bagliani and Francesco Santi (Firenze: Sismel, 1998).

75 DeVun, *Prophecy, Alchemy and the End of Time*, p. 91; Ziegler, *Medicine and Religion*, pp. 54–8.

76 M. McVaugh, *The Development of Medieval Pharmaceutical Theory in Arnoldi de Villanova* Opera Medica Omnia *11 Aphorismi de Gradibus* (Granada: Universitat de Barcelona, 1975).

77 The earliest surviving manuscripts are BL Harl MS 1147 and Bodl. Ashmole MS 1450. For a printed edition see Manget, vol. ii, pp. 324–6.

78 Fourteenth-century manuscript, Trin. Coll. Camb. MS 0.218.

79 Trin. Coll. Camb. MS 0.218, ed. L Zetzner, *Theatrum Chemicum Britannicum* (Strasbourg, 1679).

80 Trin. Coll. Camb. MS 0.218 (fourteenth-century manuscript); BL Harl 1747; ed. J. Manget, *Bibliotheca Chemica curiosa* (Geneva, 1702).

81 *Rosarium*, ed L. Zetner, *Theatrum Chemicum* (Strasbourg, 1622); Manget, *Bibliotheca Chemica Curiosa*.

82 BL Add MS 47680.

83 MS Ferguson 191, fol. 1. This sixteenth-century manuscript bearing the name Richard Arundel has notes taken out of the book of Petrus Bonus.

84 Bodl. MS Digby 43 (fourteenth century) fols 161–20; Singer, *Catalogue of Alchemical Manuscripts*, pp. 276–9; English versions: Bodl. Lib. E Mus 52ff. 33v–42v; Bodl. Ashmole MS 1450; BL Sloane MS 353 and BL Sloane MS 480. Furnivall, ed., *The Book of the Quintessence or the Fifth Essence: Man's Heaven* (EETS London, 1886); *Liber de consideratione quintae essentiae omnium rerum* (Basel, 1561); *Liber Lucis* In *Il libro della luce*, ed. Andrea Aromatico (Marsilio: Editori, 1997); DeVun, *Prophecy, Alchemy and the End of Time*, pp. 116ff.

85 DeVun, *Prophecy, Alchemy and the End of Time*, pp. 64ff.

86 Chiara Crisciana and Michela Pereira, 'Black Death and Golden Remedies: Some Remarks on Alchemy and the Plague', in *The Regulation of Evil: Social and Cultural Attitudes to Epidemics in the Later Middle Age*, pp. 7–39.

87 Marie Louise Von Franz, *Alchemy: An Introduction to the Symbolism and the Psychology* (Toronto, 1980), p. 181.

88 J. M. Lenhart, *Science in the Franciscan Order: A Historical Sketch* (Froncisian Studies vol. 1, Wagner, 1924; Kessinger, 2003).

89 BL Sloane 3457 (fifteenth century); Singer, *Catalogue of Alchemical Manuscripts*; printed Zetzner, *Theatrum Chemicum Britannicum*, iv, 912–34.

90 John Gower, *Confessio Amantis*, ed. G. C. Macaulay, EETS, Ex ser 81 (London, 1900–1), bk v ll, 2496ff.

91 Geoffrey Chaucer, 'The Canon's Yeoman's Tale', in *The Riverside Chaucer*, ed. L. D. Benson (Oxford: Oxford University Press, 1988), ll 554–1481.

92 By the fourteenth century this was being illustrated in a joust between the Sun and Moon. See BL. The tradition that Chaucer was an alchemist goes back to the fifteenth century and can be seen in a Middle English poem 'Galfridus Chaucer his worke' entitled The verses on the elixir. See G. W. Dunleavy, 'The Chaucer Ascription in Trin. Coll. Dublin MS 0.2.8', *Ambix* xiii (1965).

93 *The Complete Works of the Pearl Poet*, ed. M. Andrew, R. Waldron and C. Peterson (Berkeley: University of California Press, 1993).

94 Lynn Thorndike, *A History of Magic*, vol. iii, pp. 611–27. BL Stowe MS 109ff. 170v–172.

95 Raphael Patai, *The Jewish Alchemists* (Princeton: Princeton University Press, 1994)

96 Carole Rawcliffe, ' "Written in the Book of Life" the Libraries of Medieval English Hoispitals and Almshouses', *The Library* 3 (2002): 127–62.

97 Thorndike, *History of Magic*, vol. iii, ch. 2.

98 In *Fasciculus JW Clark dicatus* privately printed in Cambridge in 1909, MR James has an article on the library of the Austin Friars at York which includes the catalogue of the private library of John Erghome.

99 Cf. Richard II's geomancy in Bodl. 581; Charmasson, *Reserches sur une technique divinatoire: la geomancie dans l'occident medieval* (Geneva-Paris: Librarie Proz, 1980), p. 136.

100 Thorndike, *History of Magic*, vol. ii, pp. 279ff.

101 See D. Pingree, 'The Diffusion of Arabic Magical Texts in Western Europe', in *La Diffusione delle scienze islamich nel medio evo europeo: co vegno internazionale* (Roma, 2–4 ottobre 1984), Roma: Accademia Nazionale dei Lincei, (1987): 57–102.

102 Thorndike, *History of Magic*, vol. ii, p. 965.

103 John Stow, *A Survey of London*, ed. C. L. Kingsford (London, 1908).

104 Thorndike, *History of Magic*, vol. iii, pp. 628–32.

105   W. L. Ogrinc, 'Western Society and Alchemy from 1200-1500', *Journal of Medieval History* 6 (March 1980): 103–32.

Notes to Chapter 3: Alchemy and Science and Philosophy

1   John Doubelay, *Stella alchemiae*, Bodl. Ashmole MS 1459, fol. 99. See also George Ripley, *The Compound of Alchymy*, ed. Stanton J. Linden (Aldershot: Ashgate, 2001), p. 61. 'Water is the secret and life of everything. For in water everything has his beginning.'

2   Joseph Ziegler, 'On the Use of the "New Sciences" (Medicine, Alchemy, and Physiognomy) for Religious Purposes c. 1300' (Max-Planck Institute for the History of Science, 2005).

3   Joseph Campbell, *Creative Mythology* (London: Souvinir), p. 279.

4   BU MS 11201, fol. 7r

5   Dastin's *Desiderabile desiderium* CUL. Trin. MS 1122, fol. 87v; Zetzner, *Theatricum chemicum*, iii, 680–1.

6   Ashmole MS 1459, fols 67, 77. 82.

7   P. M. Kean, *The Pearl an Interpretation* (London: Routledge Kegan Paul, 1967); *Part of the 'Opus Tertium' of Roger Bacon*, ed. A. G. Little (Aberdeen, 1912), p. 83; Vincent Beauvais, *Speculum Naturale* (Strasbourg, c.1481); *Mandeville's Travels*, ed. M.C. Seymour (London: Oxford University Press, 1968); John Maxson Stillman, *The Story of Alchemy and Early Chemistry* (New York: Dover Publications, 1960).

8   John Gower, *Confessio amantis*, bk seven.

9   Jung, *The Archetypes and the Collective Unconscious* (Bollinger Series XX, 1959), vol. 7, p. 160.

10   *Stella alchemiae*, Ashmole MS 1459, fol. 95.

11   Trin. Coll. MS R.14.45.

12   *Turba philosophorum*, ed. A. E. Waite (1896).

13   Robert P. Multhauf, 'The Science of Matter' in *Science in the Middle Ages*, ed. David C. Lindberg (Chicago, 1976), ch. 15.

14   *Theatrum Chemicum.* V (Strasbourg, 1622). Micreris is a corruption of Mercurius due to Arabic transliteration. See Jung, *Alchemical Studies*, p. 329.

15   BL Add MS 47680, fol. 46

16   Preciosa Margarita, *Stella alchemiae*, Ashmole MS 1459, fols 77–8.

17   Ibid.

18   Vision of John Dastin Bodl. MS Laud poet 121; Ashmole, *Theatrum Chemicum Britannicum*.

19   *Practica vera alkemia e libris magistri ortolani* (1386) ed. L. Zetzner, *Theatrum Chemicum*; Thorndike , *History of Magic*, vol. ii, p. 189; vol. iii, p. 633.

20   Thorndike, *History of Magic*, vol. iii, p. 86ff.

21 Ashmole MS 1459, fol. 101.

22 Irma Taavitsainen and Paivi Pahta eds, *Medical and Scientific Writing in Late Medieval England* (Cambridge: Cambridge University Press, 2002), p. 52; CUL MS Ii 6 17, fol. 2.

23 CUL MS Ii 6 17, fols 6–7.

24 John of Rupescissa, Liber de consideratione quinte essentie omnium rerum (Basel, 1561), 145ff. Fourteenth-century manuscript Bodl. lib. E Mus 52. Leah De Vun, *Prophecy, Alchemy, and the End of Time; John of Rupescissa in the Late Middle Ages*, pp. 70–1, 92–3.

25 *Liber de consideratione quinte essentie* 58–9. In Dastin's *Rosarius* there are also many references to *calor*, see fol. 119v.

26 Honorius of Autin (Migne PL CXLI, col. 847).

27 Thiessen, 'The Letters of John Dastin', *Ambix* 55, 160ff. Bodl. Ashmole MS 1384, fols 76r–79r. The letter is virtually a copy of work of Arnold of Villanova BL MS add 10764; BL Harley MS 3703; BL Harley MS 3528.

28 Pietro Bona Bona da Ferrara, *Preziosa Margarita Novella*, ed. Chiara Crisciani (Florence: Nuova Italia Editrice, 1976), p. 153.

29 *Stella alchemiae*, Ashmole MS 1459, fols 77–8.

30 CU MS Trin. 1127.

31 Petrus Bonus, *Pretiosa margarita novella* in *Bibliotheca chemical curiosa*, ed. Jean-Jacques Manget, 2 vols (Geneva, 1702); *The New Pearl of Great Prince*, ed. and trans. A. E. Waite from edition of Janus Lacinius (Aldus, 1546), (Montana), pp. 49–297.

32 Ibid., pp. 49–297.

33 *Testamentum alchemico*, 12–16; DeVun, *Prophecy, Alchemy and the End of Time*, p. 96.

34 DeVun, *Prophecy, Alchemy and the End of Time*, pp. 85ff.

35 Ibid., p. 157.

36 Pietro Bona da Ferrara, *Preziosa Margarita Novella*, ed. Crisciani, p. 183.

37 Robert Halleux, 'Lei ouvrages alchimiques de Jean Rupescissa', *Histoire Litteraine de la France* 41 (Paris, 1981).

38 *The New Pearl of Great Prince*, pp. 68ff. Pietro Bona, *Preziosa Margarita Novella*, ed. Crisciani, p. 10.

39 *The New Pearl of Great Price*, pp. 128–9.

40 Ibid., p. 84.

Notes to Chapter 4: Alchemy and the Church

1 Thomas Browne, *Works*, 1: 59.

2 See Saint Augustine, *De civitas dei* (*Concerning The City of God against the Pagans*) trans. Henry Betterson (Harmondsworth: Penguin, 1984), pp. 5.19, 14.16.

3 Ziegler, 'On the Use of the "New Sciences"', p. 14; W. R. Newman, 'An Overview of Roger Bacon's Alchemy', in *Roger Bacon and the Sciences: Commemorative Essays*, ed. J. Hackett (Leiden: Brill, 1997), pp. 317–36; A. Paravicini-Bagliani, 'Ruggero Bacone, Bonifacio VIII e la teoria della 'Prolongatio vitae', in *Medicina e scienze della natura corte dei papi nel duecento* (Spoleto: Centro italiano di studi sull'alto medioevo, 1991), pp. 329–61 and 'Ruggero Bacone e l'alchimia di lunga vita. Riflessioni sui testi', in *Alchimia e medicina nel Medioevo*, ed. C. Crisciani and A. Paravicini-Bagliani (Firenze: Sismel, 2003), pp. 33–54; E. Grant, *God and Reason in the Middle Ages* (Cambridge: Cambridge University Press, 2001), pp. 13–16, 182–282.

4 BL MS Egerton 2572, fol. 54v.

5 Ziegler, 'On the Use of the "New Sciences"', p. 12; A. Paravicini-Bagliani, *Medicina e scienze della natura*, pp. 55–84; Paravicini-Bagliani, *The Pope's body*, trans. D. S. Peterson (Chicago and London: University of Chicago Press, 1998), pp. 171–211, 225–34.

6 Ziegler, 'On the Use of the "New Sciences"', p. 12; A. Paravicini-Bagliani, 'La papaute du XIIIe siècle et la renaissance de l'anatomie', in *Medicina e scienze della natura*, pp. 269–79 and 'The Corpse in the Middle Ages: The Problem of the Division of the Body', in *The Medieval world*, ed. P. Lineham and J. L Nelson (London: Routledge, 2001), pp. 327–41.

7 Saint Augustine, *Confessions*, trans. R. S. Pine-Coffin (Penguin, 1966), pp. 181–97.

8 BL MS Add 47680, fol. 64v.

9 Thorndike, *History of Magic*, vol iii, p. 92. Rosarius BL Harl MS 3528, fols 171r–175r; Ashmole 1416, fols 119r–127.

10 Thiessen 'Letters of John Dastin', 160ff. Oxford Ashmole MS 1384, fols. 76r–79r.

11 For vision of Ripley, see Bodl. MS poet 121, fols 73–4. Printed in Ashmole, *Theatrum Chemicum Britannicum*, p. 374 ff.

12 Mahmoud Manzalaoui, 'John Dastin and the Pseudo Arisotelian, *Secreta Secretorum*', *Ambix* 9 (1961): 166ff.

13 Bodl. MS poet 121, fols 73–4; Ashmole *Theatrum Chemicum Britannicum*, p. 374ff.

14 For fourteenth-century contemplative experience, see Jonathan Hughes, *Pastors and Visionaries*, p. 269ff.

15 Bona, *Preziosa Margarita Novella*, pp. 182–3.

16 *Book of the Quintessence or the Fifth Essence*, ed. F. J. Furnivall, EETS 16 (1866).

17 Richard Rolle, *Incendium amoris*, ed. Margaret Deanesly (Manchester: Manchester University Press, 1915), pp. 145–9.

18 Ashmole MS 1416, fol. 119v.

19 Jung, *Mysterium Conjunctionis*, pp. 219ff. This phrase was used by James Joyce in *Ulysses* to describe the birth of Stephen Daedelus's self on meeting Leopold

Bloom. The purpose of all Joyce's art was the alchemical transmutation of human experience. See James Campbell, *The Masks of God Creative Mythology* (Penguin, 1968), pp. 280ff.

20 Wellcome MS 404, fols 25–6.

21 Ibid., fol. 19.

22 Wellcome MS 404 written in the first half of the fifteenth century. On fol. 37 of this manuscript there is the dietary of Isabella by the physicians of Montpellier.

23 Carole Rawcliffe, *Leprosy in Medieval England* (Woodbridge: Boydell, 2006), p. 19.

24 The Stonyhurst manuscript of the *Secreta secretorum* contains the shield of Henry of Lancaster on fol. 70.

25 Henry duke of Lancaster, *Le Livre de Seynt Medicines*, ed. E. J. Arnould (Oxford: Anglo Norman Text Society, 1940).

26 *Le Livre de seyntz medicines.*

27 Jung, *Mysterium Conjunctionis*, pp. 274ff.

28 Jung, *Psychology and Alchemy*, pp. 432ff. Rosencreuz, *The Chymical Wedding*, trans. Joscelyn Godwin (Grand Rapids: Phanes Press, 1991), p. 73.

29 See Job 39:9 on the devastating power of God, signified by the unicorn.

30 The myth of the virgin and the unicorn was handed down from Isidore of Seville *Etymologiarum*, xii, 62.

31 Priscillian *Opera*, p. 24; *St Basil Vita*, Migne, PG vol. 120, col. 69, ch. XCI; Jung, *Psychology and Alchemy*, p. 442.

32 Jung, *Mysterium Conjunctionis*, p. 274ff.

33 Jung, *Psychology and Alchemy*, p. 446.

34 See also Dastin's *Rosarius*, Ashmole MS 1416, fo. 119v for a reference to the lion.

35 Bodl. Laud MS poet 121, fols 73–4; Ashmole, *Theatrum Chemicum Britannicum*, p. 374ff.

36 Barbara Obrist, 'Art et nature dans l'alchimie', *Revue d'histoire sciences* 49 (1991); Laurinda Dixon, *Alchemical Imagery in Bosch's Garden of Delights* (Ann Arbor, MI: UMI Research Press, 1981).

37 Hughes, *Pastors and Visionaries*, p. 207ff.

38 Ibid., p. 232ff.

39 Ziegler, 'On the Use of the "New Sciences"', p. 3; S. J. Williams, *The Secret of Secrets: The Scholarly Career of a Pseudo-Arnoldian Text in the Latin Middle Ages* (Ann Arbor: University of Michigan Press, 2003), pp. 155–6.

40 Walsingham, *St Alban's Chronicle*, p. 587.

41 Ibid., p. 587.

42 *The New Pearl of Great Prince*, p. 93.

43 Dastin, *Verbum abbreviatum*; Thorndike, *History of Magic*, p. 95ff.

44 Ibid., p. 111.

Notes to Chapter 5: The Cultural Impact of Alchemy

1   Ariel's Song from Shakespeare's *The Tempest*, Act 1, Scene 2, pp. 395–400.

2   Keane, *The Pearl: An Interpretation*.

3   Coote, *Prophecy and Public Affairs*, pp. 73–4.

4   BL Add MS 47680

5   *Political Poems and Songs Relating to English History*, ed. Thomas Wright, 2 vols, Rolls Series 14 (London: Longman, 1859–61), vol. I, pp. 123–215.

6   Coote, *Prophecy and Public Affairs*, pp. 101ff.

7   Ibid., pp. 138–8, 142.

8   *Political Poems and Songs*, vol. I, pp. 123–215.

9   Gower, *Confessio amanitis*, bk vii.

10 According to John Mandeville, the fourteenth-century traveller, England was ruled by the moon which travels around the world more quickly than other planets; and for this reason the English are great travellers.

11 Ashmole MS 1459, fols 92, 95.

12 *The Complete Works of the Pearl Poet*, ll. p. 161.

13 J. M. Bowers, *The Politics of Pearl: Court Poetry in the Age of Richard II* (Woodbridge: Boydell, 2001), p. 83.

14 Ian Bishop, *Pearl in Its Setting: A Study of the Middle English poem* (Oxford: B. Blackwell, 1968); C. D. Chapman, 'Numerical Symbolism in Dante and the Pearl', *MLN* 54 (1939): 256–9.

15 *Complete Works of the Pearl Poet*, ll. pp. 655–60.

16 John D. North, *Chaucer's Universe*; North, 'Celestial Influence: The Major Premises of Astrology' in P. Zambella (ed.), *Astrology Hallucinati: Stars and the End of the World in Luther's Time* (Berlin: Walter de Guyter, 1986), pp. 45–100; E. Grant, 'Medieval and Renaissance Scholastic Conceptions of the Influence of the Celestial Region in the Terrestial', *Journal of Medieval and Renaissance Studies* 17 (1987); B. Hansen, 'Science and Magic', in *Science in the Middle Ages*, ed. David C. Lindberg (Chicago: Chicago University Press, 1978), pp. 483–506.

17 Henry Cornelius Agrippa (attrib), *His Fourth Book of Occult Philosophy*, trans. Robert Turner (London, 1655).

18 North, *Chaucer's Universe*.

19 *A Medieval Dream Book* printed from the original Latin Manuscript with an English translation by B. S. Cron (London: Gogmagog Press, 1963); E. M. Butler, *The Myth of the Magus* (Cambridge: Cambridge University Press, 1948), pt 1, ch. 2.

20 B. Hansen, 'Science and Magic', in *Science in the Middle Ages*, ed. D .C. Lindberg; *The Book of the Marvels of the World*, ed. M. R. Best and F. H. Brightman. Generally found with *Book of Secrets of Albertus Magnus: On the Virtues of Herbs, Stones and Certain Beasts* (Oxford: Clarendon Press, 1973).

21 Hansen, 'Science and Magic' in *The Book of the Marvels of the World*.

22 Ibid.

23 *Topography of Ireland*, trans. T. Forester (Cambridge, Ontario), distinction II.

24 Chaucer, *Complete Works*, ll. pp. 680–3.

25 Ibid., ll. pp. 863–9.

26 This work may be responsible for the erroneous tradition that Bernard of Treves was a fifteenth-century alchemist, a confusion cleared up in Thorndike's analysis of the correspondence between Bernard and Thomas of Bologna. Thorndike, *History of Magic*, vol. iii, pp. 611–27.

27 Ibid., pp. 611–27.

28 Ashmole MS 1459, fol. 79.

29 Chaucer, *Complete Works*, ll. pp. 1431–9.

30 Bonus, *Pearl*, p. 225.

31 W. Thiesen, 'The Letters of John Dastin', *Ambix*, 55 (2 July 2008): 153–68. The work of Arnold's which Chaucer used; see E. H. Duncan, 'Chaucer and "Arnold of New Town"', *Modern Language Notes* LVII (1942): 31–3.

32 Muhammed ibn Umail called al Sadiq probably referring to the *Tabula chemica* a letter from the Sun to the Waxing Moon. See J. D. North, 'The Canon's Yeoman's Tale', in *Alchemy Revisited: Proceedings of the International Conference on the History of Alchemy at the University of Gronigen 17–10 April 1989*, ed. Z.R.W.M. von Martels (Leiden: Brill, 1990).

33 Arnold's letter addressed to a *Verande pater* with the incipit *theorica et practica* is found in the following medieval manuscripts BL Harley 3703, ff. 25–30; BL Harley MS 3528, ff. 4v–8; BL Add MS 10764, ff. 71–74; BL Add MS 15549, ff. 110–121. The manuscript with Dastins' copy is Bodl. MS Ashmole 1384, ff. 76–79 . The letter is printed by Zetzner, *Theatrum Chemicum*, iii, p. 128. See Singer, *Catalogue of Latin Alchemical Manuscripts*, vol. I, pp. 199–203.

34 Ibid., Oxford, Ashmole, MS 1384, fols 76r–79r.

35 CUL MS Ii 6 17.

36 Ibid., fols 5–7.

37 Chaucer, *Complete Works*, ll. pp. 1–19.

38 Ashmole MS 1459, fol. 90.

39 BL Add MS 47680, fol. 64.v

40 BL MS Add.15, 549, fol. 160. In the margin of the manuscript there is a drawing of the green lion.

41 BL Sloane MS 1744.

42 J. M. Rampling, 'Establishing the Canon: George Ripley and His Alchemical Sources', *Ambix* 55, No 3 (2008); *The Summa Perfectionis of Pseudo Geber a Critical Edition, Translation and Study*, William R. Newman (Leiden: E.J. Brill, 1991).

43 BL MS Sloane MS 3667, fols 124–59.

44 BL Sloane 1744, fol. 193.

45 See epilogue to *The Canterbury Tales* in Chaucer, *Complete Works*, ll. pp. 1090–1.

46 C. Given-Wilson, 'Rulers, Artificers and Shoppers: Richard II's Remodelling of Westminster Hall 1393–1399', in *The Regal Image of Richard II in the* Wilton Diptych, ed. D. Gordon and C. Mann (London: Harvey Millar, 1998), pp. 274–88.

47 D. W. Robertson, 'Why the Devil Wears Green', *Modern Language Notes* (November 1954); Fran and Geoff Doel, *The Green Man* (Stroud: Tempus, 2001); Francis Ingledew, *Sir Gawain and the Green Knight and the Order of the Garter* (Notre Dame: University of Notre Dame Press, 2006), pp. 210–16.

48 *The Complete Works of the Pearl Poet*, ll. pp. 2185–92.

49 The source of the beheading game is an Irish tale Bricrius's Feast, a game of a beheading involving a wizard. For the Celts the ritual sacrifice practised by the Druids involved killing by three strokes.

50 The earliest manuscript containing this image is Zentralbibliothek MS Rhenoviensis 172. It also occurs in Glasgow University library MS Ferguson 6 illus. no. 22.

51 *Complete Works of the Pearl Poet*, ll. pp. 662–5.

52 Ibid., ll. pp. 634–5.

53 Ibid., ll. pp. 619–20.

54 Jung, *Psychology and Alchemy*, p. 116; *Dictionarium quod Gemma gemmarum vocant, nuper castigatorum* (Hagenau, 1518).

55 BL Sloane 2560, fol. 5 (fifteenth century).

56 *Complete Works of the Pearl Poet*, ll. p. 1155.

57 H. Summersen, 'St George', *New DNB*.

58 *Complete Works of the Pearl Poet*, ll. pp. 491–535, 726–32 1998–2005.

59 BL MS Cotton Nero Ax

60 *Cleanness*, in *Complete Works of the Pearl Poet*, ll. pp. 1034–39.

61 Ziegler, 'On the Uses of the "New Sciences"', p. 13.

62 *Pearl*, in *The Complete Works of the Pearl Poet*, ll. pp. 271–4.

63 Ibid., ll. pp. 258–65.

64 *Cleanness*, in *Complete Works of the Pearl Poet*, ll. pp. 551–3.

65 *Cleanness*, ll. pp. 553–5.

66 *Pearl*, in *Complete Works*, ll. pp. 220–3.

67 Ibid., ll. pp. 319–20.

68 Thiessen, 'Letters of John Dastin', p. 1

Notes to Chapter 6: The Accession of Edward III

1 Letter of John Dastin, following Arnold of Villanova in Thiessen, 'Letters of John Datin', pp. 153–68.

2 Bologna Bibliotheca Universita MS 138 (144), fols 245–253v; Pereira, 'The Alchemical Corpus Attributed to Raymund Lull', pp. 1–118.

3 Bibliotheque des philosophes chimiques, Jean Maugin de Richebourg C.Paris: chez Andre Gailleau, M.DCCXLI-MDCCXLIV).

4 R. G. Musto, 'Queen Sancia of Naples 1281–1345 and the Spiritual Franciscans', in *Women of the Medieval World, Essays in honour of John H. Mundy*, ed. J. Kirschner (Oxford: Blackwell, 1985), p. 179.

5 The identity of A is unknown but could refer to God (alpha). Oxford Corpus Christ MS 244. A fifteenth-century manuscript translated from Catalan into Latin in 1443 by Lamberton G. in the priory of St Bartholomews and copied in 1455 by John Kirkby. Edited Michela Pereira, *Testamentum*. For an English version see Bodl. Ashmole MS 1418.

6 Vatican 58 466, fol. 119v. *Annales minorum*, ed. Lucas Waddingus, 25 vols (Rome, 1731–1886), 3rd ed. (Florence, 1931), vol. 4, pp. 477–9.

7 Patai, *The Jewish Alchemists*, p. 128. There are no surviving manuscripts.

8 Corpus Christi Camb. MS 112 and Corpus Christi Oxford 244. Pereira, 'The Alchemical Corpus Attributed to Raymund Lull'.

9 The only manuscripts are sixteenth and seventeenth century. Thorndike, *History of Magic*, vol. iv, pp. 8–16.

10 Patai, *Jewish Alchemists*, p. 178 Thorndike's claim that all these works were forgeries by publishers mistaking the period of Lull's life was made before the discovery that the Catalan *Testamentum*, which shares a common theme with these pseudo-Lullian works, the importance of the quintessence, was composed at St Katherine's in 1332; this lends credibility to these sixteenth-century attributions to a Raymund working at St Katherine's hospital.

11 K. W. Humphrey, 'The Library of John Erghome', *Proceedings of the Leeds Philosophical and Literary Society* 18 (1982); Carley *MP* 77 (1980): 361–9; A. Rigg, 'John of Bridlington Prophecy a New Look' *Speculum* 63 (1988): 596–613.

12 Ibid., pp. 203–10.

13 Pereira, *Testamentum* Intro.

14 Pereira, *Testamentum* intro.

15 R. G. Musto, 'Queen Sancia of Naples 1281–1345 and the Spiritual Franciscans', in *Women of the Medieval World, Essays in Honour of John H. Mundy*, ed. J. Kirschner (Oxford: Blackwell, 1985), p. 179.

16 Michael R. McVaugh, *Medicine before the Plague. Practitioner and Patients in the Crown of Aragon 1285–1345* (Cambridge: Cambridge University Press, 1993), pp. 93–4, 113–14.

17 Ibid., pp. 93–4, 113–14.

18 Ibid.; G. E. Trease, 'The Spicers and Apothecaries of the Royal Household in the Reigns of Henry III Edward I and Edward II', *Nottingham Medieval Studies* 3 (1959): 19–52; H. Talbot and E. A. Hammond, *The Medical Practitioners of Medieval England* (London: Wellcome Historical Medical Library, 1965); Faye Getz,

'Medical Practitioners in Medieval England', *Social History of Medicine* 3 (1990): 245–83.

19 This only exists in sixteenth-century manuscripts. Thorndike, *History of Magic*, vol. iv, pp. 8–16.

20 Ibid.; *CPR Ed II 1311–26*; *CPR Ed III*, 8, 11; *CPR Ed III 1327–29* iii. 12; *CPR Ed III 1329*, 28; Rymer *Foedera*, vol. 11, 160–1 and 23 and 45 for letter from Ed III to Bernard of Brette.

21 Michael Packe, *King Edward III* (London: Routledge and Kegan Paul, 1983), pp. 46–7.

22 *CPR Edward III, 1327–30*, p. 250. Michael Michael, 'The Iconography of Kingship in the Walter of Milemete Treatise', *Journal of Warbourg and Courtald Institute*, 57 (1994): 35–47.

23 Ibid., pp. 35–47

24 Ibid., pp. 35–47. The miniatures are not all in the same hand and those on fol. 32v are of the second quarter of the fourteenth century, see J. J. G. Alexander, 'Painting and Manuscript Illumination for Royal Patrons in the Late Middle Age', in *English Court Culture in the Later Middle Ages*, ed. V. J. Scattergood and J. W. Sherbourne (London: Duckworth, 1983), pp. 141–2.

25 It was included in a manuscript of the *Tresor* of Brunello Latina, Paris Bibliotheque Nationale MS fr 571. See Michael A. Michael, 'A MS Wedding Gift for Philippa of Hainault to Edward III', *Burlington Magazine* LXXVII (1985): 582–99.

26 Oxford Christ Church Coll. MS 92; *The Treatise of Walter de Milemete*, ed. M. R. James (Oxford: Roxburgh Club, 1913); Michael Michael, 'The Iconography of Kingship in the Walter of Milemete Treatise', *Journal of Warbourg and Courtald Institute* 57 (1994): 35–47.

27 Ed. L. Stovenhagen, *A Testament of Alchemy* (Hanover, 1974); See R. Lemay, 'L'authentisite de la preface de Robet de Chester a sur traduction du Morienes' *Chrysopoeia* (1991). For a fourteenth-century manuscript of the dialogue between Khalid and Morienus, see Camb. Trin. Coll. MS 122 and BL Harley MS 3703; Singer, *Catalogue of Alchemical Manuscripts*, vol. 1, 161ff.

28 Hughes, *Arthurian Myths and Alchemy: The Kingship of Edward IV* (Stroud: Sutton, 2003), pp. 142–5.

29 BL Add MS 47680, fol. 49.

30 Ibid., fol. 25v.

31 BL Add MS 47680, fol. 31v, *Secreta secretorum*, fols 31v, 51v and 53v show Edward III surrounded by astrologers pointing to the heavens. The *Secreta* advises the king to do nothing without consulting astrologers and one prominent in this period, John Ashenden, claimed to have predicted the plague in 1349.

32 BL Add MS 47680, fol. 20.

33 John of Bridlington Prophecies in *Political Poems and Songs*, vol. I, p. 139.

34 BL Add MS 47680, fols. 75, 99.

35 BL Add MS 47680, fol. 92.

36 Ibid., fol. 47v.

37 *Testamentum*, ed. Crisciani, pp. 44ff.

38 Ibid, fol. 11v.

39 There is an accompanying illustration showing a king with his advisers pointing to the heavens.

40 BL Add MS 47680, fols. 46, 48a.

41 Ibid., fol. 53.

42 Ibid., fol. 54.

43 Ibid., fol. 55.

44 Ibid., fol. 45.

45 Ibid., fol. 48.

46 Ibid., fol. 47v.

47 Ibid., fol., 57v.

48 Ibid., fols 3, 21, 62 (with roses in the middle), 66, and with the sun and moon 91.

49 Ibid., fol. 51.

50 Ibid., fol. 28.

51 Ibid., fol. 20v.

52 Ibid., fols 1, 4, 8v.

53 Ibid., fols 65, 76, 99.

54 MS Bodl. Roll 1.

55 The same imagery can be seen in the crypt of St Alban's Abbey dating from the fifteenth century.

56 W. L. Thiessen, 'The Letters of John Dastin', *Ambix*, 55 (2 July 2008): 153–68. These letters include: 'A letter to a good man' BL Sloane 3738, fols 23r–35r (fifteenth century); A letter to Pope John XXII; a letter with the title Epistola bona pretiosa BL Sloane MS 288, fols 58v–59r; a letter with the title libellus aures Camb. Trin. Coll. Lib. MS 1122, fols 36v–38v (fourteenth century); a letter with the title verbum abbrebiatum Camb. Trin. Coll. MS 91 6, fols 46–75; a letter addressed to Cardinal Napolean Orsini Dean of St Andrews in Naples with the title *De natura metallorum* BL MS Sloane 2476, fols 4r–9v (fifteenth century); another letter addressed to the same cardinal with the title *Speculum philosophorum* BL MS Sloane 212, fols 57–79; and the letter addressed *O venerable father* Ashmole MS 1384, fols 76r–79.

57 *Visio et super alchemia*, ed. J. J. Manget, *Bibliotheca Chemica curiosa* (Geneva, 1702); CU Trin. Coll. MS 0.2.18 (fourteenth-century manuscript).

58 Bodl. Ashmole MS 1407, fols 10–16; Ashmole MS 1446; Ashmole MS 1450, fols 85–86; Ashmole MS 1480, fols 9v–12; Ashmole MS 1486, fols 74–75.

59 BL Sloane MS 288, fol. 209. A seventeenth-century collection of alchemical tracts 'Magister Johannis Daston visio transcripta 7 Idis Martii AD 1328; scripta apud Northampton'.

60 G. Dawn, *Scottish Dermatological Society* (Edinburgh, 2000); M. H. Kaufman and W. J. Maclenna; G. W. S. Barrow, 'Robert the Bruce', *New DNB*.

61 Patai, *Jewish Alchemists.*

62 Pereira, *Testamentum*, xvii; Picarel, *History of the Foundation of St Katherine by the Tower* (London, 1787); Catherine Jamison, *The History of the Royal Hospital of St Katherine's* (London: Oxford University Press, 1952).

63 Wellcome MS 404, fol. 27v.

64 BL MS Sloane 964, fol. 93.

65 Ibid., fol. 93. W. L. Braekman, *Studies on Alchemy, Diet and Prognostication in Middle English* (Brussel: UFSAL, 1988), p. 64: 'aqua miracula cum qua Regina Iezebella septuaginta, decrepita, guttosa et paralitica—quod viro quadragenario voluit copulari'; and Braekman, *Studies on Alchemy*, esp. ch. 1 'the alchemical Waters: Queen Isabella's Dietary and Its context'; Talbot, 'The Elixir of Youth,' in *Chaucer and Middle English Studies in Honour of Rossel Hope Robbins*, ed. Beryl Rowland (London: Allen Unwin, 1974).

66 BL MS Sloane 100, fols 27v–29; Wellcome MS 404, fols 37ff. This survives in fourteen manuscripts. See Braekman, 'The Alchemical Waters of Saint Giles Text', in *Studies on Alchemy.*

67 Thorndike, *History of Magic*, vol. iii, p. 121.

68 Oxford Corpus Christ MS 92, fol. 4v.

69 M. A. Micheal, 'The Iconography of Kingship', pp. 35–47.

70 Oxford Corpus Christi MS 92, fol. 5r.

71 Bodl. MS poet 121, p. 374ff.; Ashmole, *Theatrum Chemicum Britannicum.*

72 Bodl. MS poet 121; *Theatrum Chemicum Britannicum*, p. 374 ff.

73 Bodl. MS poet 121; *Theatrum Chemicum Britannicum*, p. 374 ff.

74 BL MS Add 47680, fol. 92.

75 Marc Bloch, *The Royal Touch: Sacred Monarchy and Scrofula in England and France*, trans. J. E. Anderson (London: Routledge and Kegan Paul, 1973).

76 W. M. Ormrod, 'Edward III', *New DNB*. Ormrod, *The Reign of Edward III: Crown and Political Society in England 1327–77* (London, New Haven: Yale University Press, 1990), pp. 13–15.

77 See Roy Haines, *King Edward II: Edward of Caernarfon, His Life, His Reign and Its Aftermath* (London: McGill Queens University Press, 2002), where the vision is applied to Edward II's martyrdom.

78 BL MS Add 47680, fol. 48v.

79 King Edward is referred to as the Prince of Wales in this manuscript. The only fourteenth-century king to whom this strictly applies is Edward II and for this reason he has been assumed to be the subject of this vision. However this king has no known association with alchemy and as the vision fits so closely the circumstances of Edward's seizure of power, it is possible that the appellation Prince of Wales is a loose description and may refer to the defeat of the Welsh prince Roger Mortimer. Anne Curry, *The Hundred Years War* (Basingstoke: Macmillan, 1993).

80 BL Egerton MS; Ashmole, *Theatrum Chemicum Britannicum*, p. 210.

81 Ashmole, *Theatrum Britannicum*, p. 200.

82 B. F. Harvey, 'John Flete' in *The New Oxford Dictionary of National Biography*, vol. 20, pp. 134–5; Joel Fredell, 'Alchemical Lydgate', *Studies in Philology*, 107, 4 (2010): 429–64.

83 B. F. Harvey, 'John Flete', in *The New Dictionary of National Biography*, vol. 20, pp. 134–5.

84 Trin. Coll. MS 1122, fol. 88r; Thorndike, *History of Magic,* pp. 85–102.

85 John North, *The Ambassador's Secret*, pp. 154–63, 180.

86 BL Add MS 47680, fol. 11.

87 BL Add MS 47680, fol. 16v.

88 Ibid., fol. 5.2

89 Foster, *Patterns of* Thought, p. 72; P. Warmould, 'The Throne of Solomon in St Edward's Chair', in *Essays in Honour of Erwin Panofsky*, ed. Millard Meiss (New York: New York University Press, 1961), vol. 1, pp. 532–7.

Notes to Chapter 7: Alchemical Themes in the Kingship of Edward III

1   Deuteronymy the blessing of Moses 33:13, 14.

2   Ogrinc, 'Western Society and Alchemy', pp. 103–32.

3   BL Add Ms 47680, fols 13–15v.

4   Ibid., fol. 30v.

5   Ibid., fol. 30.

6   T*estamentum*, ch. Iii, 27.

7   J. Cohen, The Friars and the Jews: The Evolution of Medieval Antisemitism (Ithaca, NY: Cornell University Press, 1982), p. 228.

8   Patai, *Jewish Alchemists*, p. 181.

9   Patai, *Jewish Alchemists*, p. 181.

10 Patai, *The Jewish Alchemists*, p. 180. Pereira, *Testamentum*, intro.; Andrew Ducarel, *History*, pp. 10–11.

11 David Abulasia, *A Mediterranean Emporium: The Catalan Kingdom of* Majorca (Cambridge: Cambridge University Press, 1994); *Foedera*, ii, pp. 45–7.

12 Christopher Tyerman, *England and the Crusades, 1095–1588* (Chicago: Chicago University Press, 2009), p. 246.

13 BL Add MS 47860, fol. 48.

14 Ibid., fol. 11.

15 Ibid., fols 11–11v.

16 Ibid., fol. 11v.

17 Bodl. Lib. MS E.Mus 52 Explicit.

18 BL Add MS 47680, fol. 10v, 3.

19 Ibid., fol. 10.

20 Ibid., fols 34v, 41v–42.

21 Trin. MS 1122, fol. 88r–v.

22 BL Add MS 47680, fol. 45.

23 Grillot de Givry, *Witchcraft, Magic and Alchemy*, trans. J. Courtenay Locke (Dover: Courier Dover Publications, 1931), p. 93.

24 John of Bridlington Prophecies, in *Political Poems and Songs*, vol. I, p. 139.

25 Nigel Saul, *Richard II* (New Haven: Yale University Press, 1997), pp. 8, 142.

26 Malcolm Vale, *War and Chivalry: Warfare and Aristocratic Culture in England, France and Burgundy at the End of the Middle Ages* (London: Duckworth, 1981), pp. 64, 83–4; Ingledew, *Order of the Garter*, p. 98; H. E. Collins, *The Order of the Garter 1348–61: Chivalry and Politics in Late Medieval England* (Oxford: Collins, 2000).

27 Ingledew, *Sir Gwain and the Green Knight and the Order of the Garter*, pp. 93ff.

28 The Holkham manuscript has the shield of Henry of Lancaster on fol. 7a.

29 Henry of Lancaster, *Le Livre de seyntz medicines.*

30 *Eulogium Historiarum sive temporis chronicon de orba usque as annum Domini MCCLXCI a monacho Malmesbrie*, ed. Frank Scott Haydon (London: Rolls Series 9, vols 1-3; 1858–63), p. 227. Ingledew, *Order of the Garter*, p. 129.

31 Jeffrey Burton Russell, *Witchcraft and Magic in the Middle Ages* (New York: Cornell University Press, 1972), p. 194.

32 Christ Church Oxford MS 92.

33 Ibid., fol. 59r.

34 Ibid., fol. 60v.

35 *CPR 1350–54*, p. 127.

36 John of Bridlington Prophecies, in *Political Poems and Songs*, vol. I, p. 139.

37 Ingledew, *Order of the Garter*, pp. 93ff.

38 Froissart despite depicting Edward III as a cornerstone of chivalry addresses the rape and acknowledges that it was a possibility. Ingledew, *Order of the Garter*, p. 67. Another account of the rape occurs in *Chronographia regum Francorum* compiled in early fifteenth century from early materials in St Denis Paris. See *Chronographia Regem Francorum*, ed. Henri Moranville (Kessinger, 1897).

39 Adae Murimuth, *Continuatio Chronicarum* Robertis de Avesbury *De gestis mirabilis Regis Edwardi Terti*, ed. Edward Maunde Thompson (London: HMSO, 1889).

40 Ingledew, *Order of the Garter*, p. 72.

41 Ibid., p. 110.

42 Johan Huizinga, *The Waning of the Middle Ages: A Study of the Forms of Life, Thought and Art in France and the Netherlands in the XIV and XVth Centuries* (Harmondsworth: Penguin, 1951).

43 Machiavelli, *The Discourses*, ed and intro. Bernard Crick using the translation of Leslie J. Walker with revisions of Brian Richardson (Harmondsworth: Penguin, 1971), pp. 27, 54.

44 Ingledew, *Order of the Garter*, p. 198.

45 Jonathan Hughes, *The Religious Life of Richard III: Piety and Prayer in the North of England* (Stroud: Sutton, 1997), p. 155.

46 Ingledew, *Order of the Garter*, p. 27; H. A. Oberman and J. A. Wiesheiph, 'The Sermon Ascribed to Thomas Bradwardine (1346)', *Archives di histoire Doctrinale et Litteraire the Moyen Age* 25 (1958): 295–329; Hilary M. Carey, *Courting Disaster: Astrology at the English Court and University* (London: Macmillan, 1992).

47 John of Bridlington Prophecies, in *Political Poems and Songs*, ch. ii.

48 Ibid., ch. 11.

49 Ingledew, *Order of the Garter*, pp. 67–72.

50 Coote, *Prophecy and Public Affairs*, pp. 141–2.

51 *The Chronica maiora of Thomas Walsingham 1376–1423*, trans. David Preest, intro. James G. Clark (Woodbridge: Boydell, 2005), p. 37.

52 Ibid., p. 37.

53 Account in Walsingham *Chronica maiora*; D. Green, 'Masculinity and Medicine: Thomas Walsingham and the Death of the Black Prince', *Journal of Medieval History* (35 March 2009): 34–51.

54 BL Add MS 47680, fol. 92v.

55 Fletcher, 'Manhood Youth and Politics in the Reign of Richard II 1377–99', Oxford University DPhil, 2003, pp. 110ff.

56 Green, 'Masculinity and Medicine', pp. 34–51.

57 Sophie Page, *Magic in Medieval Manuscripts* (Toronto, 2004), p. 11. BL 2004; for an image of Nectantibus in the early fifteenth century, see BL Royal MS 20 B xx, fol. 7. Images of the sun and moon also occur in this manuscript.

58 Walsingham, *Chronica maiora*, pp. 43–4.

59 Ingledew, *Order of the Garter*, p. 58.

60 Amiens version see Ingledew, *Order of the Garter*, p. 74.

61 Leo Carruthers, 'The Duke of Clarence and the Earls of March: Garter Knights and Sir Gawain and the Green Knight', *Medium Aevum* 70 (2001).

62 Ingledew, *Order of the Garter*, p. 159ff. Christian interpretation sees this poem as a contemporary reflection on the scandal surrounding the founding of the Order of the Garter written in the 1360s. There is no evidence to support such a claim, and it is more likely that allusions to Edward's sexual conduct would be made in a court poem after his death. Moreover *Sir Gawain and the Green Knight* has much in common in terms of alchemical occult themes with another work in this manuscript, *Pearl*, definitely a composition of Richard II's court in the 1390s.

63 Ibid., p. 186.

64 Augustine, *De civitas dei (Concerning the City of God against the Pagans)*, trans. Henry Bettenson (Harmondsworth: Penguin, 1984), 5.19, 14.15, 14.16.

65 Ingledew, *Order of the Garter*, 190.

66 Ibid., p. 202.

67 Fran and Geoff Doel, *The Green Man* (Stroud: Tempus, 2001).

Notes to Chapter 8: Richard II the Magus and Boy King

1   'The Testament of Solomon', trans. D. L. Duling in *The Old Testament Pseudographica Vol 1*, ed. J. H. Charlesworth (New York: Doubleday).

2   In pre-Roman times, new year celebrations and exchange of gifts would take place on Yule commemorating the winter solstice on 21 December; but in 46 BCE Julius Caesar established 1 January (from the Roman god of doors looking backwards and forwards) as the official new year.

3   Ingledew, *Order of the Garter*, p. 208.

4   Saul, *Richard II*, p. 12. *William Thorne's Chronicle of St Augustine's Abbey, Canterbury*, trans. A. H. Davis with preface by A. Hamilton Thompson (Oxford: Basil Blackwell, 1934), p. 531.

5   *Letter to Richard II by Philippe de Mezieres, original text and English version of Epistre au Roi Richart*, intro and trans. G. W. Coopland (Liverpool: Liverpool University Press, 1975).

6   Shelagh Mitchell, 'Richard II, Kingship and the Cult of Saints', in *The Regal Image of Richard II in the* Wilton Diptych, pp. 115–24

7   C. Given-Wilson, 'Richard's Artificers: Richard II's Remodelling of Westminster Hall 1393', in Gordon, *Regal Image*, pp. 33–59.

8   Bower, *Politics of Pearl*, pp. 123–4.

9   *St Alban's Chronicle*, ed. Taylor, Childs and Watkiss, p. 70.

10 Bower, *Politics of Pearl*, p. 87.

11 Saul, *Richard II*, p. 313; J. Perkins, *Westminster Abbey. Its Worship and Ornaments* (Alcuin Club, xxxiv, 1930).

12 *St Alban's Chronicle*, ed. Taylor, Childs and Watkiss, p. 70.

13 *Knighton's Chronicle*, ed. and trans. G. H. Martin (Oxford: Clarendon, 1995), p. 401.

14 Hughes, *Pastors and Visionaries*, pp. 77, 115.

15 *Eulogium Historiarum*, ed. Haydon; *An English Chronicle*, ed W. Marx (Woodbridge: Boydell, 2003). An edition of the chronicle previously known as *Thomas Davies Chronicle* (Camden Soc, 64), p. 22.

16 *Westminster Chronicles 1381–94*, ed. and trans. L. C. Hector and Barbara F. A. Harvey (Oxford: Oxford Medieval Texts, 1982), p. 155. Richard presented Leo VI with an annuity of £1,000 a year until he recovered his kingdom.

17 C. C. McCown, *The Testament of Solomon*, edited from manuscripts at Mount Athos (Leipzig: J.C. Hinrichs 1922).

18 1 Kings 4:29–31.

19 M. V. Clarke. , 'Forfeitures for Treason in 1388', *Transactions of Royal Historical Society'* 4th ser., 14 (1931): 14, 64–94.

20 Olga Pujmenova, 'Portraits of Kings Depicted as Magi in Bohemian Painting', in Gordon, *Regal Image*.

21 Patai, *The Jewish Alchemists*, p. 184.

22 A John Dumbleton was given a commission with the sheriff of Worcester to arrest an outlaw in 1378. In April 1381 he was described as a clerk and in 1388 he was given a king's commission to arrest Robert Haypole, outlaw for debt. *Cal Pat Rolls 1377–81*, p. 305; *Cal Close Rolls, 1385–9*, p. 126.

23 Also known as the *Flos reges* (*Flower of the King*) a copy was sent to the king of Naples Charles III Thorndike, iii, 633. The earliest manuscripts of the *Stella alchemiae* are Bologna universitaria MS 500 (fifteenth century) Wolfenbuttel 3282, Fols 224v–244r and BU 303 (fifteenth century), fols 201r–. The manuscript used here is the sixteenth-century manuscript with the dedication to Richard II. Bodl. Ashmole MS 1459.

24 Ashmole MS 1459, fol. 72.

25 Ibid., fol. 95.

26 Ibid., fol. 66v.

27 Bodl. MS 581, fols 9r–89v; For descriptions see F. Saxl and H. Meier, *Catalogue of Astrological and Mythological Manuscripts of the Late Middle Ages* (London: Warbourg University, 1953), pp. 311–12.

28 Bodl. 581, fol. 9.

29 Ibid., see also BL MS Royal C V 12.

30 Bodl. MS 581, fol. 9.

31 Ibid., fol. 9v.

32 Oxford St Johns Coll. MS 164; Thorndike, *History of Magic*, vol. ii, p. 398.

33 BL MS Royal 2 B8.

34 J. Taylor, 'Richard II's views on Kingship', *Proceedings of the Leeds Philosophica and Literary Society*, vol. xiv, pt v (1971): 189–205; C. Wood, *Chaucer and the Country of the Stars* (Princeton: Princeton University Press, 1970), 103–60.

35 MS Bodl. 561, fols 7r–8v.

36 *CPR 1391–96*, p. 584; *1396–9*, pp. 245, 248; *1399–1401*, p. 382.

37 MS Bodl. 581, fols 3r–5v.

38 Bodl. MS 581, fol. 1r.

39 Ibid., fols 3r–5v.

40 Bodl. MS 581, fols 1r–3r 9r; *Four English Political Tracts in the Later Middle Ages*, ed. J. P. Genet (London Society, 4th ser., 18, 1977), pp. 22–5; Carey, *Courting Disaster*, pp. 102–3.

41 Bodl. MS 581, fol. 2r; Katherine Breen, 'A Different Kind of Book for Richard's Sake: MS Bodl. 581 as Ethical Handbook,' *The Chaucer Review* 25, 2 (2010): 133.

42 M. J. Bennet, 'The Court of Richard II', in B. Hanawalt (ed.), *Chaucer's England Literature in Historical Context* (Minneapolis: University of Minnesota Press, 1992), p. 16.

43 Bodl. Ashmole MS 813.

44 Holand was presented with an abridgment of the order's rule Bodl. Ashmole MS 8, fols 1–3.

45 Pereira, *Testamentum*; MS Paris Bib. Nat. 14005, fols 121v–122; Corbett, *Catalogue des Manuscripts alchemiques Latins,* 2 vols (Paris, 1939) ii, pp. 173–4.

46 M. Keen, 'The *Wilton Diptych*: The Case for a Crusading Context', in Gordon, *Regal Image,* pp. 189–96.

47 BL MS Royal 20 B VI.

48 BL MS Add 16584 (fifteenth century); Ashmole MS 1384 (fifteenth century); Digby MS 119 (fifteenth century); Oriel Coll. MS 28; Singer, *Catalogue of Alchemical Manuscripts*; printed *Opera Omnia,* ed. A. Borgnet (Paris, 1890).

49 Meziere, *Letter to Richard II,* p. 63.

50 CU Trin. MS 1122.

51 Urszula Szulakowska, 'The Alchemical Medicine and Christology of Robert Fludd and Abraham von Franckenberg', in Linden, *Mystic Metal of Gold,* pp. 277–301.

52 Meziere, *Letter to Richard,* p. 21.

53 Ibid., p. 20.

54 Ibid., p. 5.

55 Ibid., p. 50.

56 Mons. De mas Latrie's *Histoire de Isle de Cypre* (Strasbourg, 1468). Claude D. Cobham tr. *Excerpta cypria; Materials for a History of Cyprus Cambridge* (Cambridge: Cambridge University Press, 1908).

57 F. Klassen, 'English Manuscripts of Magic, 1300–1500: A Preliminary Survey in Conjuring Spirits', in *Texts and Traditions of Medieval Ritual Magic,* ed. Claire Fangen (University Park, PA: Pennsylvania State University Press, 1998), pp. 3–31.

58 Arsenal Ms 2251, fol. 27r.

59 Lynne Thorndike, *A History of Magic,* vol. 1, p. 359.

60 John North, *God's Clockmaker* (London: Hambledon, 2001), pp. 158–60.

61 Ibid.; Thorndike, *History of Magic,* vol. 1, p. 769. Nicholas cited the authority of De *mirabilibus mundi* attributed to Albertus Magnus.

62 This iconography of sacred kingship had been anticipated in Richard's psalter in 1377, which shows the king and his regalia presented to the Christ child held in the arms of the Virgin. BL MS Cotton Domition Axvii

63 Michael Bennet, *Richard II and the Revolution of 1399* (Stroud: Sutton, 1999), p. 56.

64 Jung, *Mysterium Conjunctionum,* pp. 484, 492

65 Macrobius, *Saturnalia*; Celia Fisher, 'A Study of the Plants and Flowers in the *Wilton Diptych*', in Gordon, *Regal Image,* pp. 55–63.

66 Thomas Gascoigne, *Liber veritatum* Oxford EETS 15 (London).

67 Bodl. MS 581, fol. 9v.

68 *Historia Vitae et regni*; Saul, *Richard II,* p. 447.

69 *The Chronicle of Adam Usk,* ed. E. M. Thompson (London: Froude, 1904), p. 17.

70 Richard Maidstone, *Concordia the Reconciliation of Richard II with London* (Kalamazoo, 2003), p. 25.

71   K. J. Lewis, 'Becoming a Virgin: Richard II and Edward the Confessor the Gender of Holiness', in *Men women and Saints in Late Medieval Europe*, ed. Samantha J. E. Riches and Sarah Salih (London: Routledge, 2002), pp. 86–100.

72   Kantorowitz, *The Kings Two Bodies*, p. 388.

73   Thorndike, *History of Magic* iii, 637.

74   Pereira, *Testamentum*.

75   D. B. Tyson, 'The Epitaph of Edward the Black Prince', *Medium Aevum* 46 (1977): 98–104; N. Saul, *English Church Monuments in the Middle Ages* (Oxford: Oxford University Press, 2009).

76   Jonathan G. Alexander, 'The Portrait of Richard II in Westminster Abbey', in Gordon, *Regal Image*.

77   P. Binski, *Westminster Abbey and the Plantagenets* (New Haven, CT:Yale University Press, 1995), p. 103.

78   Bowers, *Politics of Pearl*, p. 105.

79   This was probably the crown sent as part of the dowry of Blanche, daughter of Henry IV for her marriage with Ludwig III of Bavaria in 1401.

80   Bower, *Politics of Pearl*, p. 120.

81   Bib. Nat. MS 11201, fol. 7r; Thorndike, *History of Magic*, vol. iii, pp. 611–27.

82   *Chronique de Religieux de saint Denys*, ed. M. L. Bellaquet; Chronicle of Charles VI Lib. xii, pp. 88–97.

83   There is no known origin of the Tarot. The oldest surviving set of Major Arcanum is preserved in the Bibliotheque nationale, Paris, and is believed to be the Tarot of Charles VI painted by Gringomar. The figures are fourteenth century.

84   BL Add MS 5016.

85   Saul, *Richard II*, p. 15.

86   CUL MS Ii 6 17, fol. 2.

87   BL Royal MS 12 Ex xii, fol. 132.

88   CUL MS Ii 6 17, fol. 4

89   Ibid., fol. 15

90   *Le Livre de seyntz Medicines*, p. 187.

91   *Walsingham, St Alban's Chronicle*, p. 295.

92   *Froissart Chronicles*, p. 402.

93   The manuscrit, BL Cotton MS Nero Ax, fol. 45v, implies she lived two years in this country (which would mean the girl is an infant), but this may be a scribal confusion for eleven, the number of years Anne of Bohemia lived in England. Bowers, *Politics of Pearl*, p. 154.

94   Imagery of the pearl as bride in the heavenly Jerusalem occurs in *Aurora consurgens*.

95   *Pearl*, in *The Complete Works of the Pearl Poet*, ll. 1–2.

96   Glass-blown mirrors were an invention of the fourteenth century and in Murano in the sixteenth century they were backed by a mercury–tin amalgam.

97 *Letter to Richard II*, p. 69.

98 Thorndike, *History of Magic*, vol. ii, pp. 86–8.

99 Henry Cornelius Agrippa, *The Fourth Book of Occult Philosophy* (London, 1655). Therese Charmasson, recherches sur une technique divinatoine: la geomancie dans L'occident medieval, pp. 206–7.

100 Thorndike, *History of Magic*, vol. ii, p. 398.

101 Bodl. 581, fols 82v–89v.

102 Ibid., fols 75r–87r; Charmasson, *Recherches sur une Technique Dininatoire*, p. 136.

103 Ibid., fols 87r–89r.

104 BL MS Royal 12 C V, fol. 217; Charmasson, recherches sur une technique divinatoine: la geomancie dans L'occident medieval, pp. 206–7.

105 There is a tradition that Anne died of plague but there is no evidence for this.

106 Wellcome Institute MS 36 (mid-fifteenth century). *De vitae*, fols 76v–111; *Quadripartita de lapide philosophoris*, fols 44v–55v.

107 See Thorndike, *History of Magic*, vol. ii, pp. 628ff. The *Sedacina* is in a fifteenth-century Florence, MS Gaddi relig. 181, 70 fols; The *Quadripartita de lapide philosophia* attributed to G. Sedacerius is in a fifteenth-century manuscript, London Wellcome Institute MS 36, fols 76v–111.

108 See Fletcher, 'Manhood and Richard II' for an alternative view. He argues that the charge of immaturity was something political opponents used to attack Richard who made numerous attempts to prove them wrong.

109 R. H. Jones, *The Royal Policy of Richard II: Absolutism in the Later Middle Ages* (Oxford, 1968).

110 Richard Maidstone, *Concordia*.

111 This number excludes the chancellor, treasurer and keeper of the Privy Seal.

112 Richard Maidstone, *Concordia*, pp. 28–9.

113 BL MS Royal B VI, fols. 2, 35.

114 K. D. Lilley, *City and Cosmos. The Medieval World in Urban Form* (London, 2009).

115 Caroline Barron, *London in the Later Middle Ages: Government and People 1200–1500* (Oxford, 2004).

116 K. J. Lewis, 'Becoming a Virgin King: Richard II and Edward the Confessor Gender and Holiness Men Women and Society', in *Men women and Saints in Late Medieval Europe*, ed. Samantha J. E. Riches and Sarah Salih (London, 2002).

117 *The Major Latin Works of John Gower*, ed. E. W. Stackton (Seattle, 1962).

118 *Letter to Richard II*, p. 61.

119 *Letter to Richard II*, pp. 60–1.

120 Ziegler, 'On the Use of the "New Sciences"', p. 15.

121 *Letter to Richard II*, p. 15.

122 Thorndike, *History of Magic*, vol. 1, pp. 143 and 359.

123 *Letter to Richard II*, p. 69.

124 Richard Maidstone, *Concordia*, pp. 370–85.

125 *Letter to Richard II*, pp. 5, 71.

126 BL Harl MS 3988, fols 39–41. J. R. Phillips, 'Edward II and the Prophets', in *England in the Fourteenth Century: Proceedings of the 1985 Harlaxton Symposium*, ed. W. M. Ormrod (Woodbridge: Boydell, 1986), pp. 194.

127 Phillips, 'Edward II and the Prophets', p. 194.

128 Ibid., p. 194.

129 Christopher Wilson, 'Richard's Artificers and Shoppers: Richard II's Remodelling of Westminster Hall', in Gordon, *Regal Image*, pp. 35–59.

130 P. Lindley, 'Absolutism and Regal Image in Ricardian Sculpture', in Gordon, *Regal Image*, pp. 60–84.

131 In Richard Maidstone's account of Richard's entry into New Troy (London) in 1392, Richard is described as Solomon, *Concordia*, p. 38.

132 Walsingham, *St Alban's Chronicle*, p. 117.

133 Ibid., pp. 125–6; *Knighton's Chronicle 1337–1396*, ed. and trans. G. H. Martin (Oxford: Clarendon Press, 1995).

134 Ibid., p. 117.

135 Walsingham, *St Alban's Chronicle*, p. 551.

136 Ibid., p. 181.

137 Trin. Hall Camb., MS 17.

Notes to Chapter 9: Richard II and the Occult

1 *Deuteronymy* 33:13,14,17.

2 Saul, *Richard II*

3 Walsingham, *St Alban's Chronicle*, p. 186.

4 Ibid., p. 205.

5 *Chronicle of Usk*, ed. Thompson, p. 27.

6 *RP* iii, 423.

7 I Samuel ix, 17.

8 St Augustine in *De civitas dei* 5.19, 14.16, pointed out the link between the procreative impulse and the desire to conquer. See Ingledew, *Sir Gawain and the Green Knight*, pp. 26–7.

9 *Letter to Richard II*, p. 16.

10 The incomplete Richard the Redeless from BL MS Add. 4166 was joined with another fragment from CUL MS LI.4.14 and published as *Mum and the Soothsegger*, ed. Mabel Day and Robert Steele (EETS, os cxcix, Oxford: Oxford University Press, 1936).

11 Edward duke of York, *Master of the Game*, pp. 34, 102.

12 R. H. Emmerson, *Antichrist in the Middle Ages: A Study of Medieval Apocalypticism in Art and Literature* (Seattle: University of Washington Press, 1981).

13 Singer, *Alchemical Manuscripts*, vol. I, p. 143.

14 Coote, *Prophecy and Public Affairs*, p. 137; MS Hatton 56, fols 8r–9r.

15 Emmerson, *Antichrist in the Middle Ages.*

16 Leff Gordon, *Heresy in the Late Middle Ages, The Relation of Heterodoxy to Dissent c 1250–c1450*, 2 vols (Manchester: Manchester University Press, 1967), p. 520.

17 Saul, *Richard II* PRO C115/ K 6684, fol. 184v.

18 C. Penn Szittya, 'Domesday and the Book of the Apocalypse', in *The Apocalypse in the Middle Ages,* ed. R. H. Emmerson and B. McGuin (Ithaca: Cornell University Press, 1992), p. 384.

19 Walsingham, *St Alban's Chronicle*, p. 647.

20 *Pearl* in the *Complete Works of the Pearl Poet*, ll. 1094–5.

21 *Pearl* in the *Complete Works of the Pearl Poet*, ll. 1094–5; *Cleanness*, ll. 1066.

22 *Pearl* in the *Complete Works of the Pearl Poet*, ll. 1094–5; *Cleanness*, ll. 1116–22.

23 P.Binski, *Westminster Abbey and the Plantagenets*, p. 199.

24 Bowers, *Politics of Pearl*, pp. 84–7.

25 Maidstone, *Concordia*, pp. 428–30.

26 PRO E 101/1.

27 *Annales Ricardi secundi et Henrici Quinti*, pp. 199, 202–3.

28 Philips, 'Edward II and the Prophets', p. 194

29 Trin. Coll. MS R 7.23 (early fourteenth century) and Cotton Titus D VII, a manuscript associated with Glastonbury Abbey; Coote, *Prophecy and Public Affairs*, pp. 246, 260.

30 Corpus Christi Coll. MS 138.

31 M. V. Clarke and V. H. Galbraith, 'The Deposition of Richard II in Maude Clarke', in *Fourteenth Century Studies*, ed. L. S. Sutherland and May McKisack (Oxford, 1937), pp. 99–114; *Bull John Rylands Lib* xiv (1930): 131.

32 John of Rupescissa, in *Liber secetorum eventum* (*The Book of Secret Events*) 1349; DeVun, *Prophecy, Alchemy and the End of Time*, p. 12,

33 Bagot was restored his lands by Henry IV after a year's imprisonment.

34 *Chrons Revolution*, p. 155; Saul, *Richard II*, p. 421; Michael Bennet, *Richard II and the Revolution of 1399*, p. 178

35 MS Stowe 68.

36 J. Nichols, *A Collection of the Wills of the Kings and Queens of England* (London: J. Nichols, 1780).

37 James L. Gillespie, 'Chivalry and Kingship', in *The Age of Richard II* (Stroud: Sutton, 1997), p. 122.

38 N. Saul, *The Three Richards Richard I, Richard II and Richard III* (London: Continuum, 2005), pp. 126, 234–5. The identification of the white hart with the crucified Christ can be seen in the wall painting of the life of St Eustace in

Canterbury Cathedral executed c. 1480 showing the white stag with Christ cruci-fied between its antlers.

39 Saul, *Richard II*, p. 174; W. Ullman, *Principles of Government and Politics in the Middle Ages* (New York: Barnes and Noble, 1966), p. 150; A. B. Cobham, *The King's Hall within the University of Cambridge in the Later Middle Ages* (Cambridge: Cambridge University Press, 1969), pp. 239–40.

40 Knighton, *Chronicle*, p. 391; S. B. Crimes, 'Richard II's Questions to the Judges in 1387', *Law Quarterly Review* (1956).

41 *Westminster Chronicle*, p. 201.

42 Wilson, 'Richard's Artificers', pp. 35–58.

43 Knighton, *Chronicle*, p. 499.

44 *Westminster Chronicle*, p. 313.

45 *Thomas Faveant Historia sive narracio de modo et forma Mirabilis Parliamenti*, ed. May McKisak, Camden Miscellany xiv Camden soc Public ser 3 xxxvii (London, 1926), p. 18

46 Ibid., p. 18.

47 *RP* iii 240–1. Knighton, *Chronicle*, p. 503.

48 St John's Coll. MS A.7

49 Bowers, *Politics of Pearl*, p. 110.

50 Bower, *Politics of Pearl*, p. 110; *La Vie du Prince Noir by Chandos Herald*, ed. Diana B. Tyson (Tubingen: M. Niemeyer, 1975).

51 Michael Bennet, *Richard II and the Revolution of 1399* , p. 36; *The English Works of John Gower*, ed. G. C. Macauley, 3 vols (London, 1900–1), pp. 469–74.

52 BL Cotton Vesp EVIII. Coote, *Prophecy and Public Affairs*, pp. 153–5. Despenser's arms also appear on BL Add MS 34114 containing *le Songe Vert*, a dream vision written c. 1395 in which the queen of love orders a grieving king to choose another love, a lily (the princess Isabella).

53 *The Kirkstall Abbey Chronicles*, ed. J. Taylor, Thoresby Society 42 (Leeds, 1952): 42–3, 75. Gillespie, *The Age of Richard II*.

54 Ashmole MS 1459, fol. 96, ch. 12.

55 J. H. and R. V. Pinches, *The Royal Heraldry of England* (London: Heraldry Today, 1974).

56 *Pretiosa Margarita Novella* (*The New Pearl of Great Price*), ed. Waite, p. 197.

57 *An English Chronicle, 1377–1461* (Woodbridge: Boydell, 2003), ed. Marx, p. 12.

58 C. Given-Wilson, *The Royal Household and the King's Affinity: Service, Politics and Finance in England 1360–1413* (New Haven: Yale University Press, 1986).

59 Beltz, *Memorials of the Order of the Garter*; P. Binski, *Westminster Abbey and the Plantagenets*, p.199.

60 M. Campbell, 'White Harts and Coronets. The Jewellery and Plate of Richard II', in Gordon, *Regal Image*, pp. 99–108, 183–4.

61 Bower, *Politics of Pearl*; Michael J. Bennet, *Community Class and Careers* (Cambridge: Cambridge University Press, 2003), p. 248.

62 M. J. Bennet, 'Sir Gawain and the Green Knight', *Journal Medieval History* 5 (1979); Bennet, *Community Class and Careers* (Cambridge, 1983) and M. J. Bennet, *A Companion to Sir Gawain and the Green Knight* (Woodbridge: Boydell, 1997).

63 It was named after the legendary founder of Britain.

64 Bowers, *Politics of Pearl*, pp. 133–48.

65 Given Wilson, *The Royal Household and the King's Affinity*, p. 236.

66 Letter to Richard II, pp. 28–9.

67 *Richard the Redeless II*, 36–40.

68 Ibid., p. 238.

69 Bennet, *Richard II and the Revolution of 1399*, p. 60.

70 *Master of the Game*, p. 35.

71 Jung and Von Franz, *Alchemy an Introduction*, p. 258. *Honorius of Autun* (Mign PL CLXii col. 847)

72 N. Morgan, 'The Significance of the Banner on the *Wilton Diptych*', in Gordon, *Regal Image*.

73 Froissart, *Chonicles*, p. 353.

74 Walsingham, *St Alban's Chronicle*, p. 851.

75 *Westminster Chronicle*, p. 223.

76 Froissart, *Chronicles*, p. 211.

77 John Harvey, 'Wilton Diptych', *Archeologia* xlvii (1961).

78 M. Keen, 'The Wilton Diptych: The Case for a Crusading Context', pp. 189–96.

79 Froissart, *Chronicles*.

80 Caroline Barron, Intro.: 'The Regal Image of Richard II in the *Wilton Diptych*', in Gordon, *Regal Image*, pp. 19–26.

81 N. Morgan, 'The Significance of the Banner in the *Wilton Dipych*', in Gordon, *Regal Image*, pp. 179–80.

82 D. Gordon, *Regal Image of Richard II and the Wilton Diptych*; C. T. Wood, 'Richard II's *Wilton Diptych*', in *Joan of Arc and Richard III: Sex, Saints and Government in the Middle Ages* (Oxford, 1988); J. M. Thielmann, 'Political Canonization and Political Symbolism in Medieval England,' *Journal of British Studies* 79 (1996).

83 G. F. Beltz, *Memorials of the Most Noble Order of the Garter* (London, 1861).

84 Patricia J. Eberle, 'Richard II and the Literary Poets', in *Richard II: The Art of Kingship* (Oxford, 1999), ed. Anthony Goodman and James Gillespie, pp. 59–82; *John Gower the Major Latin Works*, ed. and trans. E. W. Stockton (Seattle: University of Washington Press, 1962).

85 Saul, *Richard II*, p. 386; R. H. Jones, *The Royal Policy of Richard II: Absolutism in the Later Middle Ages* (New York: Barnes and Noble, 1968).

86 Ibid.

87 *Eng Hist Documents* iv, pp. 174–5; Saul, 'Richard II's Ideas on Kingship', in Gordon, *Regal Image*, pp. 27–32.

88 Corpus Christi Camb. MS 251.

89 *Chronicles of the Revolution 1397–1400*, ed Given-Wilson, pp. 169–70; Saul, *Richard II*, p. 420.

90 Thorndike, *History of Magic*, vol. iii, pp. 611–27.

91 Memoirs Pierre Salmon, in *Collections des Chronique Nationale Francai*, ed. J. A. Buchan (Paris, 1826), p. 37.

92 *Annales Ricardi Secundi et Henrici Quarti*, p. 321.

93 *Archologia* xlv (1890): 326; Lora O'Brien, *Witchcraft from an Irish Witch* (Career Press, 2004), p. 178.

94 *Annales Ricardi Secundi et Henrici Quarti*, in *Chronica et Annales*, ed. H. T. Riley, Rolls Series (1866), p. 30.

95 Richard received a dish on which the Baptist's head had allegedly been laid from the vicar of All Saint's Pavement, York, in 1386.

96 CPR *1381–85*, 542; Shelagh Mitchell, 'Richard II, Kingship and the Cult of Saints', in Gordon, *Regal Image*.

97 *Rotuli Parliamentorum* ii, 362.

98 Saul, *Richard II*, p. 249; Saul, 'Richard II and the Vocabulary of Kingship', *English Historical Review* cx, 438 (1995): 864.

99 Cobham, *The King's Hall*, pp. 256–8.

100 Bowers, *Politics of Pearl*, p. 144.

101 Michael Hanrahan, 'Defamation as Political Contest during the Reign of Richard II', *Medium Aevum* 62 (2003).

102 Saul, *Richard II*, p. 259.

103 Knighton, *Chronicle*, p. 547.

104 Maidstone, *Concordia*, pp. 370–5, 440–2.

105 *Westminster Chronicle,* pp. 508–11.

106 Saul, *The Three Richards*, p. 116; 'Annales Ricardi Secundi et Henrici Quarti', p. 218.

107 *The Continuation of the Eulolgium Historiarum*, ed. F. S. Haydon (Rolls Series, London, 1863).

108 Bodl. MS 581, fol. 9v; Breen, 'A Different Kind of Book'.

109 BL MS Royal 12 C 11.

110 BL Arundel MS 66.

111 Breem, 'A Different Kind of Book', p. 137; Christopher Fletcher, 'Manhood and Politics in the Reign of Richard II', *Past and Present* 189 (2005): 3–39.

112 Breem, 'A Different Kind of Book', p. 137; Fletcher, 'Manhood and Politics', pp. 3–39.

113 BL MS Royal 12 C V, fol. 56v.

114 Gower, *Confession amanitis*, 6.1293–4.

115   Ibid., 6.1293–4

116   Bodl. MS 581, fol. 9r; Breen. 'A Different Kind of Book', p. 145.

117   Froissart, *Chronicles*, p. 428.

118   Jones, 'Political Uses of Sorcery in Medieval Europe', *The Historian* 34 (1971–77): 678–87.

119   Walsingham, *St Alban's Chronicle*, p. 300.

120   Ibid., p. 303.

121   Froissart, *Chronicles* ii, p. 665.

122   Ingledew, *Order of the Garter*, p. 208.

123   *St Alban's Chronicle*, p. 102.

124   Walsingham, *St Alban's Chronicle*, p. 733.

125   *Chronicle of Usk*, ed. Thompson, p. 41.

126   BL MS Royal 12 C V, fol. 49

127   Froissart, *Chronicles*.

128   *Of Counsellors and Kings: The 3 Versions of Pierre Salmon's Dialogues*, ed. Anne D. Hedeman (Chicago: University of Illinois Press, 2001); Salmon, *Dialogues*, p. 11. Salmon was adviser to Charles VI.

129   For an image of Nectantibus see the early fifteenth-century manuscript BL Royal 20 Bxx, fol. 7.

130   *Confessio amantis*, ed. Peck, p. 350.

131   John of Bridlington Prophecies, in *Political Poems and Songs*, ed. Wright, vol. 1, p. 117.

132   *Mum and the Soothsegeer*, p.77.

133   *Historia Vitae et Regni Ricardi Secndni*, ed. G. B. Stow, Jr (Philadelphia, 1977), p. 166.

134   *Chron Adam Usk*, ed. C. Given-Wilson, p. 134.

135   *Samuel xxviii*, 7; *Chron Adam Usk*, ed. E. M. Thompson, 2nd edn (London: Froude, 1904), p. 36; John of Bridlington Prophecies, in *Political Poems and Songs*, vol. I, 166.

136   *Political Poems and Songs*, vol. I, 397–8.

137   *Historia Vitae Regis Ricardi Secundi*, ed., Stow (Philadelphia 1997), p. 166; C. Barron, The Tyrany of Richard II, *BIHR*, 41 (1968), 1–2; Hilary Carey, *Courting Disaster*; Jones, 'the Political Uses of Sorcery in Medieval Europe', 670–87. *Chron Usk*, ed. Given Wilson, p. 77.

138   *Political Poems and Songs*, vol. I, pp. 397–8.

139   James C. Clark, 'Thomas Walsingham Reconsidered: Books and Learning at Late-Medieval St Albans', *Speculum* 77 (2002): 844. Walsingham, *Historia Anglicana*; Carey, *Courting Disaster*.

140   Walsingham, *St Alban's Chronicle*, p. 242.

141   *Annales Ricardi secundi*, p. 237.

142 Saul, *Richard II*, p. 459; E. Fromm, *The Anatomy of Human Destructiveness* (London, New York: Holt, Rinehart and Winston, 1973), pp. 201–2.

143 Knighton, *Chronicle*, p. 459.

144 Langland, *Piers Ploughman* B text 10.212–19; Breem, 'a Different Kind of Book', 141.

145 *Chronicle of Adam Usk*, ed. C. Given-Wilson, p. 135.

146 Faye Getz, Medical Practitioners in Medieval Europe, *Social History of Medicine* 3 (1990). pp. 245–83.

147 Bennet, *Richard II and the Revolution of 1399*; Anglo Norman Letters and Petitions, ed. M. D. Legge, Anglo Norman text Soc (1901), pp. 61–2.

148 C. F. R. Palmer, *The Antiquary*, xxii (1890), 114–20.

149 R. G. Davies, Richard II and the Church in the years of Tyranny, *Journal of Medieval History*, (1975), 329–62 ; Bennet, *Richard II and the Revolution of 1399*, p. 44 and n. 76.

150 Saul, *Richard II*, p. 446; Walsingham, *St Alban's Chronicle*, p. 251.

151 *Annales* 301. It was not Richard who handed over Maudelyn for examination as Carey suggests. Saul, *Richard II*, p. 450.

152 Lindley, 'Ricardian Sculpture', in Gordon, *The Regal Image*, pp. 60–84.

153 *Chronicles of the Revolution*, ed. Given-Wilson, pp. 177–8.

Notes to Chapter 10: Conclusion: The Lancastrian Reaction

1 *Samuel* ch. 1, v. 3.

2 Walsingham, *St Alban's Chronicle*, p. 609.

3 *Westminster Chronicle*, ed. L. C Hector and B. Harvey (Oxford: Oxford University Press, 1982), mp. 15.

4 Ibid., mp. 63.

5 C. Given-Wilson reedited Usk's Chronicle because the previous editor Thompson was not sympathetic to Usk's interest in the supernatural. *Chronicle of Adam Usk 1377–1421*, ed. and trans. C. Given-Wilson (Oxford: Clarendon Press, 1997).

6 Walsingham, *St Alban's Chronicle*, p. 753.

7 Ingledew, *Order of the Garter*, p. 213.

8 Froissart, *Chronicles* ii, 709.

9 *Chronicle Adam Usk*, p. 116.

10 *Westminster Chronicle*, p. 233.

11 Ibid., p. 235.

12 Ibid., p. 345.

13 *Chronique du Religieux de Saint Denys*, ed. M. C. Bellaquet (Paris: Crapelet, 1837).

14 Knighton, *Chronicle*, p. 430.

15 *Chronicle of Usk*, p. 87.

16 French edition English translation by J. Wells, *Archeolol.* 20 (1824).

17 Ibid., pp. 374, 169–70.

18 *Chronicle of Adam Usk*, p. 116.

19 Froissart, *Chronicles*, p. 146.

20 BL Cotton Faus A viii, fol. 116r; *Chronicle Usk*, ed. Thompson, p. 42; J. M. Thiel-mann, 'Political Canonization and Political Symbolism in Medieval England', *Journal of British Studies* 79 (1996): 255.

21 Edward duke of York, *Master of the Game*, p. 30.

22 Knighton, *Chronicle*, p. 431.

23 J. B. Russell, *Witchcraft and Magic in the Middle Ages*, p. 207.

24 Southern, *Robert Grosseteste*, p. 75. The source of this legend was a Life of Grossteste written in 1502 by Richard a monk of the Benedictine abbey of Bordney.

25 *Richard the Redeless II*, pp. 36–40.

26 *French Metrical History*, p. 110

27 *Incerti Scriptoris*, ed. Giles, p. 12; *Traison et Mort*, app. H, p. 277; Clark 'Thomas Walsingham Reconsidered', p. 859.

28 *Chronicle Usk*, ed. Thompson, p. 69.

29 *French Metrical History*, pp. 87–95; Paul Strohm, *England's Empty Throne* (New Haven: Yale University Press, 1995), p. 109.

30 Select Cases in the Court of the King's Bench under Richard II, p. 111

31 A. Boureau, 'Conclusion', *Micrologus* 3 (1995): 347–53.

32 Ziegler, 'On the Use of the "New Sciences"', p. 15.

33 Faye Getz, 'Healing and Society in Medieval England: A Middle English Translation of Pharmaceutical Writings of Gilbertus Anglicus (Wisconsin: University of Wisconsin Press, 1991); G. E. Trease and J. H. Hodson 'The Inventory of John Hexham a Fifteenth Century Apothecary', *Medical History* 9 (1965): 76.

34 Talbot and Hammond, *The Medical Practitioners of Medieval England*, pp. 42–3; G. Watson, *Theriac and Mithridetium* (London, 1966).

35 *Chronicles*, ed. J. Taylor, *Thoresby Society* 42 (1952): 42–57.

36 Corpus Christi Coll., Camb. MS 61.

37 Bodl. MS 581, fol. 9.

38 BL MS Royal C 5 5, fol. 4r.

39 Oxford Digby MS 28; Coote, *Prophecy and Public Affairs*, p. 147.

40 Saul, *Richard II*, pp. 336–434.

41 Strohm, *England's Empty Throne*, pp 1–31.

42 Saul, *The Three Richards*, pp. 67–83; Hughes, *The Religious Life of Richard III*, pp. 153, 163.

43 Bennet, *Richard II and the Revolution of 1399*, p. 54.

44 *Vita et Gesta Henrici Quinti*, ed. T. Hearne (Oxford, 1727).

45 BL MS Add 34360. Humphrey owned the Stonyhurst manuscript of Henry duke of Lancaster's *Le Livre de Seyntz Medicines* and Gilbert Kymer's *Regimen sanitatis* and a geomancy; see BL MS Arundel 66, fol. 269.

46 BL MS Sloane 4.

47 For the full text of three English translations of the fifteenth century, see Ashmole MS 396.

48 BL MS Add 18268 A

49 Simon Walker, 'Remembering Richard: History and Memory in Lancastrian England', in Simon Walker, *Political Culture in Late Medieval England*, ed. Mike Braddick (Manchester: Manchester University Press, 2006).

50 Jonathan Hughes, 'Alchemy and Late Medieval Sexuality', in *Medieval Virginities*, ed. A. Bernau, R. Evans and S. Salih (Cardiff, 2003), pp. 140–66.

51 The pamphlet is in Lambeth Palace Library. See Peter J. French, *John Dee: The World of an Elizabethan Magus* (London: Routledge and Kegan Paul, 1972), p. 204.

52 Jonathan Hughes, 'The Humanity of Thomas Charnock and Elizabethan Alchemist', in *Mystical Metal of Gold: Essays on Alchemy and Renaissance Culture.*

53 Samuel Shoenbaum, 'Richard II and the Realities of Power', in *Critical Essays on Shakespeare's Richard II,* ed. Kirby Farrell (New York: G.K. Hall, 1999), pp. 41–57.

54 Kantorowitz, *The King's Two Bodies.*

55 Shakespeare, *Richard II*, Act 2, Sc. 1, ll. 44–6.

56 Ibid., Act 3, Sc. 2, l. 43.

57 Ibid., Act 3, Sc. 2, ll. 54–5.

58 Ibid., Act 3, Sc. 2, ll. 60–1.

59 Ibid., Act 3, Sc. 2, ll. 163–6.

60 Ibid., Act 3, Sc. 3, ll. 87–9.

61 Ibid., Act 3, Sc. 3, ll. 55–61.

62 Ibid., Act 3, Sc. 2, ll. 8–11.

63 Ibid., Act 4, Sc. 1, ll. 284.

64 Ibid., Act 4, Sc. 1, ll. 260–3.

65 Ibid., Act 3, Sc. 3, ll. 77.

66 Ibid., Act 4, Sc. 1, ll. 168–71.

67 Ibid., Act 5, Sc. 5, ll. 64–6.

Bibliography

MANUSCRIPTS

BL Add MS 338 *Regimen Sanitatis* of Salerno, a dietary written for a *rex Anglorum*

BL Add MS 5016 *The Form of Curry* dedicated to Richard II

BL Add MS 10764 Alchemical letter of Arnold of Villanova

BL Add MS 15547 *Alchemical dialogue father to son*

BL Add MS 15549 Arnold's letter addressed to a *Verande pater* with the incipit *theorica et practica Bacon Speculum alchemiae*

BL Add MS 15549 *Book of Merlin*

BL Add MS 15549 *Speculum Alkymie*

BL Add MS 16584 Albertus Magnus *De Mineralibus*

BL Add MS 18268 A Genealogical roll of Edward IV with alchemical cognomens

BL Add MS 34114 *le Songe Vert*, a dream vision written c. 1395

BL Add MS 34360 Alchemical epitaph to Humphrey duke of Gloucester's tomb

BL Add MS 47680 *Secreta secretorum* Milemete's copy presented to Edward II

BL Add MS 47680 *Secreta secretorum* presented to Edward III

BL Arsenal MS 2251 Meziere's *Chevalerie de la passion*

BL Arundel 164 *De occulta naturae* attributed to Albertus magnus

BL Arundel MS 66 Humphrey duke of Gloucester's Geomancy

BL Cotton Domition MS Axvii Richard II's psalter

BL Cotton MS Vesp EVIII. Bishop Despenser's collection of prophecies

BL Cotton Nero MS A x *Sir Gawain and the Green Knight and Pearl*

BL Egerton MS 2572 *Book of the York Barber Surgeons*

BL Egerton MS 2676 Fourteenth-century copy of *Secreta secretorum*

BL Harl MS 1147 *Vision of John Dastin*. The earliest surviving manuscript

BL Harl MS 1766 Lydgate's *Fall of Princes* with illustration of Arthur's tomb

BL Harl MS 2407 *Gemma Salutaris* or *laudabile sancta*

BL Harl MS 3528 Arnold's letter addressed to a *Verande pater* with the incipit *theorica et practica* Alchemical letter of Arnold of Villanova

BL Harl MS 3528 Dastin's *Rosarius*

BL Harl MS 3703 Khalid and Morienus

BL Harl MS 3988 Prophetic verses of Gildas

BL Laud Misc MS 735 Roger Bacon's annotated copy of the *Secreta secretorum*

BL Laud Misc MS 735 *Secreta secretorum*

BL MS 10764 Jabir *Summa perfecti magisteri*

BL MS Add 59681 John Dee's Memorials pertaining to the art of navigation

BL Royal MS 2 B8 Astronomical calendar owned by Joan, mother of 'Richard II'

BL Royal MS 12 C 11 Geomancy of John duke of Bedford

BL Royal MS 12 C V Richard II's Book of Geomancy

BL Royal MS 12 Ex v *Looking glass of alchemists*

BL Royal MS 12 Ex xii Treatment for stone in Richard II

BL Royal MS 20 B VI Philippe de Mezieres, *Epistre au Roi Richart*

BL Royal MS 20 Bxx fol 7. For an image of Nectantibus

BL Royal MS 5f xiv Fourteenth-century copy of *Secreta secretorum*

BL Sloane MS 4 William Worcester medical treatises

BL Sloane MS 100 Dietary of Isabella

BL Sloane MS 212 Letter of John Dastin addressed to Cardinal Orsini

BL Sloane MS 288 A seventeenth-century collection of alchemical tracts 'Magister Johannis Daston visio transcripta 7 Idis Martii AD 1328; scripta apud Northampton'

BL Sloane MS 299 William Cecil, Lord Burley collection of alchemical works, including those of George Ripley

BL Sloane MS 323 *Tabula smaragdina*

BL Sloane MS 353 English versions of Rupescissa's *Liber de Consideratione Quinti Essentia*

BL Sloane MS 480 English versions of Rupescissa's Li *Liber de Consideratione Quinti Essentia*

BL Sloane MS 964 John Argentine's medical notes regarding Isabella

BL Sloane MS 1091 *The Summa Perfectionis of Pseudo Geber*

BL Sloane MS 1741 Thomas Vaughan's alchemical and autobiographical writings

BL Sloane MS 1744 *Treatise on the Philosophers stone*

BL Sloane MS 1754 Rhazes *Lumen Luminaium*

BL Sloane MS 2476 A letter addressed to Cardinal Napolean Orsini Dean of St Andrews in Naples with the title *De natura metallorum*

BL Sloane MS 2476 John Dastin's letter addressed to Cardinal Napolean Orsini with the title *De natura metallorum*

BL Sloane MS 2560 Alchemical work attributed to Arnold of Villanova

BL Sloane MS 3457 *Ortensius commentary Emerald Table*

BL Sloane MS 3667 George Ripley *Bosom Book*

BL Sloane MS 3738 John Dastin 'A letter to a good man' (fifteenth century)

BL Stow MS 109 *Thomas of Bologna letter to Bernard of Treves*

Bodley Ashmole MS 1384 *Dastin's copy of letter of Arnold of Villa nova*

Bodley Ashmole MS 1407 *Dastin's vision*

Bodley Ashmole MS 1407 *Vision of John Dastin*

Bodley Ashmole MS 1416 Dastin's *Rosarius*

Bodley Ashmole MS 1416 *Turba philosophor*um

Bodley Ashmole MS 1418 English version of *Testamentum*

Bodley Ashmole MS 1418 fourteenth-century manuscript of *the dialogue between Khalid and Morienus*

Bodley Ashmole MS 1450 English version of Rupescissa's *Book of the Quintessence*

Bodley Ashmole MS 1450; English versions of Rupescissa's *Liber de Consideratione Quinti Essentia*

Bodley Ashmole MS 1459 John Doubelay, *Stella Alchemiae* dedicated to Richard II

Bodley Ashmole MS 1459 *Stella Alchemia*

Bodley Ashmole MS 813 Meziere's abridgment of rules of order of the Passion

Bodley Ashmole MS 813 *Rules of the Order of the Passion*

Bodley Digby MS 111 Icocedron

Bodley Digby MS 119 Albertus Magnus *De mineralibus*

Bodley Digby MS 119 *Tabula smaragdina* owned by John Dee

Bodley e mus MS 52 English version Rupescissa's *Book of Quintessence*

Bodley Laud poet MS 121; *Vision of John Dastin*

Bodley Lib E Mus MS 52 X English versions of Rupescissa's *Liber de Consideratione Quinti Essentia*

Bodley Lib E mus MS 63 *Tabula smaragdina*

Bodley MS 581 Richard II's *Libellus Geomancie*

Bodley MS Digby 43 *Liber de Consideratione Quinti Essentia* and in *Liber Lucis (The Book of Light)* (fourteenth century)

Bodley Roll 1 *Ripley Scroll*

BodleyAshmole 1450 *English version book of quintessence*

BodleyAshmole MS 1480 *Dastin's vision*

Bologna Universita MS 138 Fabri da Dya Fabri *De lapide Philosophorum and de auro potabile*

Bologna Universita MS 500 *Stella alchemiae*

Cambridge CUL MS Ii 6. 17 *Commentarium urinarum* presented Richard II

Cambridge CUL Trinity MS 1127 *Dastin's letter to Pope John XXII*

Cambridge Caius MS 181; *The Summa Perfectionis of Pseudo Geber*

Cambridge Corpus Christi Camb MS 112 Pseudo Lullian *de Liber de Secretis Naturae (Book on the Secrets of Nature)*

Cambridge Corpus Christi Coll MS 138 *Prophecy of the Lily*

Cambridge Corpus Christi College, MS 61. Chaucer *Troillus and Criseyde* (with illustration of Richard II)

Cambridge Corpus Christi Oxford MS 244 *Testamentum*

Cambridge, Gonville and Caius MS 181; *The Summa Perfectionis of Pseudo Geber*

Cambridge Trinity Coll MS 0218 *libellum aureus*; Dastin vision *artem alchemiae*

Cambridge Trinity Coll l0218 Dastin *epistola ad episcopum Iohanne xxii*

Cambridge Trinity Coll *Turba Philosophorum*

Cambridge Trinity Coll Lib MS 1122 a letter by Dastin addressed to Cardinal Napolean Orsini Dean of St Andrews in Naples with the title *De natura metallorum* (fourteenth century)

Cambridge Trinity Coll MS 122 *Dialogue Kalid and Morienus*

Cambridge Trinity Coll MS 1122 Dastin's *Desiderabile desiderium, Tabula smaragdina*

Cambridge Trinity Coll MS R14. 45 Pseudo Albertus Magnus *Semita recta*

Cambridge Trinity College MS O.2.18 *Dastin visio et super alchemiae*

Cambridge Trinity College MS 0.218 *Dastin's Letter to John xxii*

Cambridge Trinity College MS 122 *Kalid and Morienus*

Florence MS Gaddi relig. 181 70 fols; The *Sedacina*

Glasgow University Ferguson MS 191, Norton's *Ordinal of Alchemy*

Glasgow University library MS Ferguson 6 *Aurora Consurgens*

London Wellcome Inst MS 36 G. Sedacerius *Quadripartita et lapide philosophia*

Oxford Christ Church MS 92 Walter Milemete's *de nobilitate*

Oxford Corpus Christi MS 92 Dastin's vision
Oxford Corpus Christi MS 125 *Turba philosophorum*
Oxford Digby MS 28 *Prophecy of Merlin*
Oxford Digby MS 119 *De leone viridi artis et nature potestate artis et naturae; Tabula smaragdina*
Wellcome MS 404 the dietary of Isabella by the physicians of Montpellier
Wolfenbuttel 3282 MS 1487 *Stella Alchemiae*

PRINTED SOURCES

Agrippa, Henry Cornelius (attrib), *His Fourth Book of Occult Philosophy*, tranl. Robert Turner (London, 1655).
Anglo Norman Letters and Petitions, ed. M. D. Legge, Anglo Norman Text Soc. (1901).
Annales minorum, ed. Lucas Waddingus 25 vols (Rome, 1731–1886), 3rd edn (Florence, 1931).
'L'Annales Ricardi Secondi et Henrici Quarti' in *Chronica et Annales,* ed. H. T. Riley (Rolls Series, 1866).
L'Arte del sole e delle Luna: Alchimia e filosofia nel medioevo, eds, Crisciani Chiara et Pereira Michele, Spoleto: Centro Italianole Studi sull'Alto Medioevo (1996).
Ashmole, Elias *Theatrum Chemicum Britannicum* (London, 1652).
Augustine, Saint *Confessions* trans. R. S. Pine-Coffin (Penguin, 1966).
— *De civitas dei (Concerning the City of God against the Pagans)* trans. Henry Bettenson (Harmondsworth: Penguin, 1984).
Bacon, Roger *Opera haectenus inedita Baconis Rogerii* (Oxford, 1909–40).
— *Opera haectenas inedita Rogeri Baconi* (Oxford: Clarendon Press, 1909–10).
— *Opera Omnia*, ed. A. Borgnet (Paris, 1890).
— *Opus maius* (1267), ed. J. H. Bridges (Oxford, 1897–1900); English translation Robert Burke 2 vols (Philadelphi, 1928).
— *Part of the Opus Tertium of Roger Bacon*, ed. A. G. Little (Aberdeen, 1912).
Bibliotheca Chemica Curiosa, ed. Jean-Jaques Manget (Geneva: Chouet, 1702).
Bibliotheque des philosophes chimiques, Jean Maugin de Richebourg (A. Paris: chez Andre Gailleau, M.DCCXLI-MDCCXLIV).
Bolton, G. F. *Memorials of the Order of the Garter* (London, 1841).
Book of the Quintessence or the Fifth Essence: Man's Heaven, ed. F. H. Furnivall (London: EETS, 1886).
Boron's Book of Merlin, the English Version, ed. H. B. Wheatley (London: EETS, 1871), pp. 10, 21, 36, 112.
Browne Sir Thomas The Works of 4 vols, ed. Keynes Geoffrey (London: Faber and Faber, 1964).
Chaucer, Geoffrey *The Canterbury Tales* in *The Riverside Chaucer*, ed. L. D. Benson (Oxford, 1988).
— *Troillus and Criseyde* in *The Riverside Chaucer*, ed. L. D. Benson (Oxford, 1988).
The Chronica maiora of Thomas Walsingham 1376–1423, trans. David Preest with introduction by James G. Clark (Woodbridge: Boydell, 2005), p. 37.
Chronicle of Adam Usk, ed. C. Given-Wilson (Oxford: Clarendon Press, 1997).
The Chronicle of Adam Usk, ed. E. M. Thompson (London: Froude, 1904).

The Chronicle of Glastonbury Abbey: an edition, translation and study of John of Glastonbury's, Chronica sive antiquitates Glastoniensis, trans. David Townsend, ed. James P. Curley (Wood-bridge: Boydell Press, 1988).

Chronicle of Henry Knighton, ed. and trans. G .H. Marks (Oxford, 1995).

Chronicles, ed. J. Taylor (Leeds Publications of the Thoresby Society 42, 1952).

Chronique du Religieux de Saint Denys, ed. M. C. Bellaquet (Paris: Crapelet, 1837).

Chronographia Regem Francorum Chronographia regum Francorum, compiled in early fifteenth century from early materials in St Denis Paris, ed. Henri Moranville (Kessinger, 1897).

The Complete Works of Pearl the Poet, ed. M. Andrew, R. Waldron and R. W. C. Peterson (Berkeley: The University of California Press, 1993).

The Continuation of the Eulolgium Historiarum, ed. F. S. Haydon (Rolls Series, 1863).

Dee, John *General and Rare Memorials pertaining to the Perfect Arte of Navigation (1577)* (New York: Amsterdam Theatrum Orbis Terrarum DeCapo Press, 1968).

Diaries of John Dee, ed. E. Fenton (Charlbury: Oxon Day Books, 1998).

Dictionarium quod Gemma gemmarum vocant, nuper castigatorum (Hagenau, 1518).

Edward 2nd duke of York *The Master of the Game*, ed. W. M. A. and F. Baillie-Grohman (London, 1909).

The Emerald Tablet of Hermes, trans. Steele Robert and Dorothy Singer (1927).

An English Chronicle 1377–1461, ed. W. Marx (Woodbridge: Boydell, 2003) An Edition of the chronicle previously known as *Thomas Davies Chronicle* (Camden Soc, 64) p. 22.

Eulogium Historiarum sive temporis chronicon de orba usque as annum Domini MCCLXCI a monacho Malmesbrie, ed. Frank Scott Haydon (London, Rolls Ser., 48).

Four English Political Tracts in the Later Middle Ages, ed. J. P. Genet (London Society 4th ser. 18 1977).

Gascoigne, Thomas *Liber veritatum* Oxford EETS 15 (London).

Geoffrey of Monmouth, *The History of the Kings of Britain*, trans. Lewis Thorpe (Harmonds-worth: Penguin, 1966).

Gower, John *Confessio Amantis*, ed. G. C. Macaulay, EETS, Ex ser 81.

Habbington,Thomas and William Habbington *The Historie of Edward IV* (London: Thames Cotes, 1640).

Henry duke of Lancaster, *Le Livre de Seynt Medicines*, ed. E. J. Arnould (Oxford: Anglo Norman Text Society, 1940).

Historia Vitae Regis Ricardi Secundi, ed. Stow, Jr (Philadelphia, 1997).

Honorius of Autin (Migne PL CXLI, col 847).

Incerti Scriptoris Chronicon Angliae de Regnis Trium Regum Lancastrensium: Henrici IV; Henrici V; et Henrici VI, ed. J. A. Giles (1848).

Isidore of Seville *Etymologiarum*, xii, 62.

John of Bridlington Prophecies, ed. Wright, in *Political Poems and Songs relating to English History* (London, 1858).

John Gower the Major Latin Works, ed. and trans. E. W. Stockton (Seattle, 1962).

John of Rupescissa, *Liber de consideratione quinte essentie omnium rerum* (Basel, 1561).

John of Rupescissa, *Liber secetorum eventum (The Book of Secret Events)* 1349.

The Kirkstall Abbey Chronicles, ed. J. Taylor (Leeds Publications of the Thoresby Society 42, 1952).

Knighton's Chronicle, ed. and trans. G. H. Martin (Oxford: Clarendon, 1995) p. 401.

La Vie du Prince Noir by Chandos Herald, ed. Diana B. Tyson (Tubingen: M. Niemeyer, 1975).

Letter to Richard II by Philippe de Mezieres, original text and English version of Epistre au Roi Richart, intro. and trans. G. W. Coopland (Liverpool: Liverpool University Press, 1975).

Liber Lucis in *Il libro della luce*, ed. Andrea Aromatico (Marsilio: Editori, 1997).

McCown, C. C. *The Testament of Solomon*, edited from the manuscripts at Mt. Athos (Leipzig, 1922).

Machiavelli, *The Discourses*, ed. with intro. by Bernard Crick using the translation of Leslie J. Walker with revisions Brian Richardson (Harmondworth: Penguin, 1971).

Macrobius Saturnalia, ed. and trans. Robert A. Kustler (Harvard University Press, 2011).

Maidstone, Richard *Concordia the Reconciliation of Richard II with London* (Kalamazoo, 2003).

Mandeville's Travels, ed. M. C. Seymour (London: Oxford University Press, 1968).

Medica Omnia 11 Aphorismi de Gradibus (Granada, 1975).

A Medieval Dream Book, printed from the original Latin Manuscript with an English translation by B. S. Cron (London: Gogmagog Press, 1963).

Melville, Herman *Moby Dick* (Harmondsworth: Penguin, 1972).

Memoirs Pierre Salmon, in *Collections des Chronique Nationale Francai*, ed. J. A. Buchan (Pari, 1826) p. 37.

Merlin and the Grail: Joseph of Arimathea, Merlin, Perceval: the Trilogy of Arthurian Romances attributed to Robert de Boron, trans. Nigel Bryant Robert de Boron (Woodbridge: D.S. Brewer, 2001).

Milemete Walter de The Treatise of, ed. M. R. James (Oxford: Roxburgh Club, 1913).

Mons. De mas Latrie *Histoire de Isle de Cypre* (Strasbourg, 1468).

Murimuth, Adae *Continuatio Chronicarum Robertis de Avesbury De gestis mirabilis Regis Edwardi Terti*, ed. Edward Maunde Thompson (London: HMSO, 1889).

The New Pearl of Great Prince, ed. and trans. A. E. Waite from edition of Janus Lacinius (Montana: Aldus 1546).

Newman, R. W. *The Summa Perfectionis of Pseudo Geber A Critical Edition* (E.J. Brill, 1991).

Nichols, J. *A Collection of the Wills of the Kings and Queens of England* (London: J. Nichols, 1780).

Pereira, Michela and Spaggioni, Barbara *Il Testamentum alchemnico attributo a Raimundo Lullo: edizione del testo latino e catelano dal manuscritto Oxford Corpus Christ College 244* (Firenze: Sismel Edizione del Galluzo, 1999).

Petrus, Bonus *Pretiosa margarita novella* in *Bibliotheca chemical curiosa*, ed. Jean-Jacques Manget 2 vols (Geneva, 1702).

Piers the Plowman. The B Text, ed. W. W. Skeat (The Early English Text Society, 1972).

Pietro Bona da Ferrara, *Preziosa Margarita Novella*, ed. Chiara Crisciani (Florence: Nova Italia Editrice, 1976).

Political Poems and Songs relating to English History, ed. Thomas Wright, 2 vols, RS 14 (London: Longman, 1859–61).

Practica vera alkemia e libris magistri ortolani (1386), ed. L. Zetzner. *Theatrum Chemicum* (Strasbourg, 1659).

Preziosa Margarita Novella (The New Pearl of Great Price) edizione del volgarizzamento, introduzione e note, ed. Chiara Crisciani (Florence: Nuova Italia Editrice 1976).

Priscillian *Opera*.

The Private Diary of John Dee and Catalogue of his library of manuscripts from the original manuscripts in the Ashmolean Museum at Oxford and Trinity College, Cambridge, ed. James Orchard Halliwell (New York: AMS Press, 1968).

The Quest of the Holy Grail, trans. P. M. Matarosso (New York: Penguin, 1969).

Richard the Redeless and Mum and the Sothsegger, ed. Mabel Day and Robert Steele, EETS, OS, 149 (London: Oxford University Press, 1936).

Richard the Redeless and Mum and the Sothsegger, ed. Robert Steele (Kalamazoo, MI: Medieval Institute Publications, 2000).

Ripley, George *The Compound of Alchymy* ed. Stanton J. Linden (Aldershot: Ashgate, 2001).

Roger Bacon, Species De Retardatione accidentionis senectatis, ed. R. Steele and F.M. Delarme.

Rolle, Richard *Incendium amoris,* ed. Margaret Deanesly (Manchester: Manchester University Press, 1915).

Rosarium ed. L. Zetner, *Theatrum Chemicum* (Strasbourg, 1622).

Rosencreuz, *The Chymical Wedding*, trans. Joscelyn Godwin (Grand Rapids: Phanes Press, 1991).

Rymer, Thomas *Foedera*, vol. 11 (London, 1704–34).

The St Albans chronicle: the chronica maiora of Thomas Walsingham, ed. and trans. John Taylor, Wendy R. Childs and Leslie Watkiss (Oxford: Clarendon, 2003) constitutes the fullest printed text of the *Chronica Maiora* for the years 1392–1422.

St Basil *Vita*, Migne, PG vol. 120.

Salmon, Pierre *Dialogues* in Of *Counsellors and Kings: the 3 Versions of Pierre Salmon's Dialogues*, ed. Anne D. Hedeman (Chicago: University of Illinois Press, 2001).

Saxl, F. and. Meier, H. *Catalogue of Astrological and Mythological Manuscripts of the Late Middle Ages* (London, 1953).

Secretum Secretorum: Nine English Versions. ed. M. A. Manzalaoui. Vol. 1. EETS o.s. 276. (London: Oxford University Press, 1977).

Select Cases in the Court of the King's Bench under Richard II.

Singer, D. W. *Catalogue of Latin and Vernacular Alchemical Manuscripts in Great Britain and Ireland Dating from before the XVI Century* (Brusssels, 1928).

Solomon *The Testament of Solomon* trans. D. C. Duling in *The Old Testament Pseudepigrapha Vol. 1* (New York: Doubleday, 1983).

Stow, John *A Survey of London*, ed. C. L. Kingsoford (1909).

The Summa Perfectionis of Pseudo Geber a critical edition, translation and study, ed. William R. Newman (Leiden: E.J. Brill, 1991).

Thomas Faveant Historia sive narracio de modo et forma Mirabilis Parliamenti, ed. May McKisak Camden Miscellany xiv Camden soc. Public ser. 3 xxxvii (London, 1926).

Topography of Ireland, trans. T. Forester (Cambridge, Ontario), distinction II.

Tresor of Brunello Latina.

Vincent, Nicholas *The Holy Blood: King Henry III and the Westminster blood title* (Cambridge: Cambridge University Press, 2001).

Vita et Gesta Henrici Quinti, ed. T. Hearne (Oxford, 1727).

Westminster Chronicles 1381–94, ed. and trans. L. C. Hector and Barbara F. A. Harvey (Oxford: Oxford Medieval Texts, 1982).

William Thorne's Chronicle of St Augustine's Abbey, Canterbury, trans. A. H. Davis with preface by A. Hamilton Thompson (Oxford: Basil Blackwell, 1934) p. 531.

The Works of Sir Thomas Malory, ed. E. Vinaver in 3 vols (Oxford: Oxford University Press, 1947).

Zetzner L. *Theatrum Chemicum Britannicum* (Strasbourg, 1679).

SELECTED SECONDARY SOURCES

Abraham, Lyndy 'A Biography of the English Alchemist Arthur Dee, Author of *Fasciculus Chemicus* and Son of Dr John Dee', in *Mystic Metal of Gold: Essays in Alchemy and Renaissance Culture*, ed. S. Linden (New York, 2008).

Abulasia, David *A Mediterraenean Emporium: the Catalan Kingdom of Majorca* (Cambridge: Cambridge University Press, 1994).

al Hassan A. Y. 'The Arabic Original of *Liber de compositione alchimie* the Epistle of Maryanus the Hermit and philosopher to Prince Kalid ibn Yazil', *Arabic Science and Philosophy* 14 (2006).

— *Studies in al-kimia. Critical Issues in Latin and Arabic Alchemy and Chemistry* (Broscher, 2009).

al Hassan, A. Y., Iskander A and Ahmed Mapul eds. *Different Aspects of Islamic Culture* (Unesco, 2001).

Alchemy Revisited: Proceedings of the International conference on the history of alchemy, University of Gronigen 17–19 April, 1989, ed. Z. R. W. M. von Martels (Leiden: Brill, 1990).

Alexander, J. J. G. 'Painting and Manuscript Illumination for Royal Patrons in the Late Middle Age', in *English Court Culture in the Later Middle Ages*, ed. V. J. Scattergood and J. W. Sherbourne (London: Duckworth, 1983).

Alexander, Jonathan G. 'The Portrait of Richard II in Westminster Abbey', in *The Regal Image of Richard II and the Wilton Diptych*, ed. Gordon, D. (Harvey Miller Publishers, 1998).

Anawati, G. C. 'L'alchimie arabes', in *Histoire des sciences arabes iii technologie alchimie et sciences de la vie*, ed. Roshdi Rashed avec la collab. de Regis Morelon (Paris: Seuil, 1997).

Bagliani, Agostino Paravicini *The Pope's Body*, trans. David .S. Peterson (Chicago: Chicago University Press, 2000).

Bagliani, Paravicini 'Storia della scienza e storia della mentalita: Ruggero Baxone. Boniface VIII e la teoria della prolongation vitae', in *Aspeti della letteratura Latina nel secolo XIII*, ed. C. Leonardi and G. Orlandi (Florence: L Nuova Italia, 1986), pp. 243–80.

Barber, Richard M. *the Holy Grail; Imagination and Belief* (London: Allen Lane, 2004).

Barron, Caroline 'Introduction' in *The Regal Image of Richard II and the Wilton Diptych*, ed. Gordon, D. (Harvey Miller Publishers, 1998).

— *London in the Later Middle Ages: Government and People 1200–1500* (Oxford, 2004).

Beltz, G. F. *Memorials of the Most Noble Order of the Garter* (London, 1861).

Bennet, Michael J. 'Sir Gawain and the Green Knight', *Journal Medieval History* 5 (1979).

— *Community Class and Careers* (Cambridge: Cambridge University Press, 2003).

— 'The Court of Richard II', ed. B. Hanawalt *Chaucer's England Literature in Historical Context*, (Minneapolis: University of Minnesota Press, 1992).

— *A Companion to Sir Gawain and the Green Knight* (Woodbridge, 1997).

— *Richard II and the Revolution of 1399* (Stroud: Sutton Publishing, 1999).

Bennet, Michael *Richard II and the Revolution of 1399* (Sutton, 1999).

Biller, Peter and Josph Ziegler ed. *Religion and Medicine in the Middle Ages*, (Woodbridge: York Medieval Press, 2001).

Binski, Paul, *Westminster Abbey and The Plantagenets: Kingship and the Representation of Power 1200–1400* (New Haven, London: Yale University Press, 1995).

Bishop, Ian *Pearl in Its Setting: A Study of the Middle English poem* (Oxford: B. Blackwell, 1968).

Bloch, Marc *The Royal Touch: Sacred Monarchy and Scrofula in England and France*, trans. J. E. Anderson (London: Routledge and Kegan Paul, 1973).

Boureau, A 'Conclusion', *Micrologus* 3 (1995).

Bowers, J. M. *The Politics of Pearl: Court Poetry in the Age of Richard II* (Woodbridge: Boydell, 2001).

Braekman, W.L *Studies on Alchemy, diet and Prognostication in Middle English* (Brussel: UFSAL, 1988).

Breem, Katharine, 'A Different Kind of Book for Richard's Sake: MS Bodley 581 a Ethical Handbook', *The Chaucer Review* 45, 2 (2010) pp. 119–168.

Bueno Mar Rey 'La Mayson pouer Distiller des Eauerat Escorial: Alchemy and Medicine at the Court of Philip II' 1551–1598' *Medical History* Suppl. 12 (2009) pp. 26–39.

Burford, E. J. *The Orrible Synne A Look at London lechery from Roman to Cromwellian times* (London: Calder and Boyners, 1973).

Burnett, Charles 'Robert of Ketton' in *Oxford Dictionary of National Biography* (Oxford: Oxford University Press, 2004).

Butler, E. M. *The Myth of the Magus* (Cambridge: Cambridge University Press, 1948).

Calvet, Antoine 'Lalchimie d'Arnaud de Villeneuve', in *Terres medievales*, ed. Ribemont Bernard (Paris: Editions Klincksieck, 1993) pp. 21–22.

Campbell, Joseph *The Masks of God, Vol. 4: Creative Mythology* (New York, Arkana: Penguin, 1968).

Campbell, M. 'White Harts and Coronets. The Jewellery and Plate of Richard II', in *The Regal Image of Richard II and the Wilton Diptych*, ed. Gordon, D. (Harvey Miller Publishers 1998).

Carey, Hilary M. *Courting Disaster: Astrology at the English Court and University* (London: Macmillan, 1992).

Carley, J. P. *Glastonbury Abbey: The Holy House at the Head of the Moors Adventurous.* (New York: St. Martin's Press, 1969).

— 'Melkin the Bard and Esoteric Tradition at Glastonbury Abbey', *Downside Review* 99 (1981).

— *Glastonbury Abbey: The Holy House at the Head of the Moors Adventurous* (Glastonbury: Gothic Image Publications, 1996).

— *Glastonbury Abbey and the Arthurian Tradition* (Woodbridge: Boydell, 2001).

Carley, J. P. and David Townsend *Chronicle of Glastonbury Abbey An Edition, Translation And Study of John of Glastonbury's Cronica Sive Antiquitates* (Eastbourne, 2009).

Carruthers, Leo 'the Duke of Clarence and the earls of March: Garter Knights and Sir Gawain and the Green Knight', *Medium Aevum* 70 (2001).

Catto Jeremy, *The History of the University of Oxford*, vol. 2 (Oxford: Clarendon, 1992),

— 'Conscience of Government in the Fifteenth Century', *Transactions of Royal Historical Society* (2007).

Chapman, C. D. 'Numerical Symbolism in Dante and the Pearl,' *MLN* 54 (1939).

Charmasson, *Reserches sur une technique divinatoire: la geomancie dans l'occident medieval* (Geneva-Paris: Librarie Droz, 1980).

Clarke, M. V. and Galbraith, V. H. The Deposition of Richard II in Maude Clarke, *Fourteenth Century Studies* ed. L.S. Sutherland and May McIsack (Oxford, 1937) and *Bull John Rylands Lib* xiv (1930) p. 131.

Clarke, M. V. 'Forfeitures for Treason in 1388', *Transactions of Royal Historical Society,* 4th ser, 14 (1931).

Cobham, A. B. *The King's Hall within the University of Cambridge in the Later Middle Ages* (Cambridge: Cambridge University Press, 1969).

Cobham, Claude D. trans. *Excerpta cypria; materials for a history of Cyprus* (Cambridge: Cambridge University Press, 1908).

Cohen, J. *The Friars and the Jews the Evolution of Medieval Antisemitism* (1982).

Collins, H. E. *The Order of the Garter 1348–61 Chivalry and Politics in Late Medieval England* (Oxford: Collins, 2000).

Coote, Leslie A. *Prophecy and Public Affairs in Late Medieval England* (Woodbridge: York Medieval, 2000).

Corbett, *Catalogue des Manuscrits alchemiques Latins,* 2 vols (Paris, 1939), ii, pp. 173–4.

Crimes, S. B. 'Ricard II's questions to the Judges in 1387', *Law Quarterly Review* (1956).

Crisciani, C. 'The Conceptions of alchemy as expressed in the *Pretiosa Margarita Novella* of Petrus Bonus of Ferara', *Ambix* 20 (1873) pp. 165–81.

Crisciani Chiara and Pereira, Michela, 'Black Death and Golden Remedies: Some Remarks on Alchemy and the Plague', ed. Agostino Paravicini Bagliani and Francesco Santi *The Regulation of Evil: Social and Cultural Attitudes to Epidemics in the Later Middle Age* (Florence, 1998) pp. 165–81.

Crisciani Chiara and Pereira, Michela, 'The Black Death and Golden Remedies: Some Remarks on Alchemy and the Plague', eds Apostino Paravicini Bigliani et Francesco Sancti *The Regulation of Evil: Social and Cultural Attitudes to Epidemics in the Late Middle Ages,* (Firenze: Sismel, 1998).

Crisciani Chiara and Pereira, Michele eds, '*L'Arte del sole e delle Luna*'. *Alchimie e filosofia nel medioevo: centro italianole studi sell'alto medioevo* (Spoletto: Centro Italiano di Studi Sulliato Medioevo, 1996).

Culture and the King: The Social Implications of the Arthurian Legend: Essays in Honour of Valerie M. Logario, ed. Mark B. Shichtman and James P. Carley (New York: State University of New York Press, 1994).

Curry, Anne *The Hundred Years War* (Basingstoke: Macmillan, 1993).

Davies, R. G. Richard II and the Church in the years of Tyrrany, *Journal of Medieval History* 1 (1975) pp. 329–62.

Dawn, G. *Scottish Dermatological Society* (Edinburgh, 2000).

DeVun, Leah *Prophecy, Alchemy and the End of Time John of Rupescissa in the Late Middle Ages* (New York: Columbia University Press, 2009.)

Dictionarium quod Gemma gemmarum vocant, nuper castigatorum (Hagenau, 1518).

Dixon, Laurinda *Alchemical Imagery in Bosch's Garden of Delights* (Ann Arbor, MI: UMI Research Press, 1981).

— *Nicolas Flamel, His Exposition of the Hieroglyphicall Figures (1624)* (New York: Garland, 1994).

Doel, Fran and Geoff *The Green Man* (Stroud: Tempus, 2001).

Ducarel, Andrew C. *The History of the Royal Hospital and Collegiate Church of St Katharine, near the Tower of London* (London, 1790).

Duncan, E. H. 'Chaucer and "Arnold of New Town"', *Modern Language Notes*, LVII (1942) pp. 31–3.

Dunleavy, G. W. 'The Chaucer Ascription in Trinity College Dublin MS 0.2.8' *Ambix* xiii (1965).

Eberle, Patricia J 'Richard II and the Literary Poets', in *Richard II: The Art of Kingship*, eds Anthony Goodman and James Gillespie (Oxford, 1999).

El Daly, Okasha *Egyptology: the Missing Millenium. Ancient Egypt in Medieval Arabic Writings* (London: UCL Press, 2005) p. 13.

Emmerson R. H, *Antichrist in the Middle Ages: A Study of Medieal Apocalypticism in Art and Literature* (Seattle: University of Washington Press, 1981).

Emmerson R. H. and McGuin B. eds, *The Apocalypse in the Middle Ages* (Ithaca: Cornell University Press, 1992).

Fisher, Celia, 'A Study of the Plants and Flowers in the Wilton Diptych', in *The Regal Image of Richard II and the Wilton Diptych*, ed. Gordon, D. (Harvey Miller Publishers 1998).

Fletcher, Christopher, 'Manhood youth and Politics in the Reign of Richard II' (137799) Oxford University D.Phil. (2003).

— 'Manhood and Politics in the Reign of Richard II', *Past and Present* 189 (2005) pp. 3–39.

Flint, Valerie I. J. *The Rise of Magic in Early Medieval Europe* (Clarendon: Oxford University Press, 1994).

Foster, George *Patterns of Thought. The Hidden Meaning of the Great Westminster Pavement* (London: Cape, 1991).

Fowden, Garth *The Egyptian Hermes: A Historical Approach to the Late Pagan Mind* (Princeton, 1993).

French, Peter J. *Metrical History*, Trans. J. Welli *Archeologia* 20 (1824).

— *John Dee: the world of an Elizabethan magus* (London: Routledge and Kegan Paul, 1972).

Froissart, Jean, *Jean Froissart Chronicles,* trans. Geoffrey Brereton (Harmondsworth, London: Penguin 1968).

Fromm, E. *The Anatomy of Human Destructiveness* (New York: Holt Rinehart and Winston, 1973).

Getz, Faye, 'Medical Practitioners in Medieval England', *Social History of Medicine*, 3 (1990).

— 'Healing and Society in Medieval England: A Middle English translation of Pharmaceutical Writings of Gilbertus Anglicus' (Wisconsin: University of Wisconsin Press, 1991).

Gillespie, James L. *The Age of Richard II* (Stroud: Sutton, 1997).

Given-Wilson, C *The Royal Household and the King's Affinity: Service Politics and France in England 1360–1413* (New Haven: Yale University Press, 1986).

— 'Richard's Artificers: Richard II's remodelling of Westminster Hall 1393', in *The Regal Image of Richard II and the Wilton Diptych*, ed. Gordon, D. (Harvey Miller Publishers 1998).

Givry, Grillot de *Witchcraft, Magic and Alchemy*, trans. J. Courtenay Locke (Dover: Courier Dover Publications, 1931).

Goodman Anthony and James Gillespie eds, *Richard II: The Art of Kingship* (Oxford, 1999).

Gordon D. and Mann and C. eds, *The Regal Image of Richard II in the Wilton Diptych* (London: Harvey Miller Publishers, 1998).

Gransden, Antonia *English Historical Literature* (London: Routledge and Kegan Paul, 1976–87).

Grant, E. 'Medieval and Renaissance Scholastic Conceptions of the Influence of the Celestial Region in the Terrestial', *Journal of Medieval and Renaissance Studies* 17 (1987) pp. 1–23.

— *God and Reason in the Middle Ages* (Cambridge: Cambridge University Press, 2001).

Green, D. 'Masculinity and Medicine: Thomas Walsingham and the Death of the Black Prince', *Journal of Medieval History* 35 (March 2009).

Gwynn, David 'Richard Eden Cosmographer and Alchemist', *Sixteenth Century Journal* 15 (1984).

Haines, Roy *King Edward II: Edward of Caernarfon, His Life, His Reign and Its Aftermath* (London: McGill Queens University Press, 2002).

Halleaux, Robert, 'Lei ouvrages alchimiques de Jean Rupescissa', *Histoire Litteraine de la France* 41 (Paris, 1981).

— *Papyrus de Leyde, Papyrus de Stockholm: Fragments de recettes*, vol 1 of *Les alchimistes greces* (Paris: Societe d'Edition "Les Belles Letters" 1981).

— 'Albert le Grand et l'alchime', *Review des Sciences philosophignes et theologiques*, 66 (1982).

— 'The Reception of Arabic Alchemy in the West', in *The Encyclopaedia of Arabic Sciences*, vol. III, ed. Roshdi Rashad and Regis Moreton (Routledge, 1996) pp. 886–902.

Hammond, Frederick 'Walter Oddington', *New DNB*.

Hanrahan, Michael 'Defamation as Political Contest during the Reign of Richard II', *Medium Aevum*, 72 (2003) pp. 71–88.

Hansen, B. 'Science and Magic', in *Science in the Middle Ages*, ed. David C. Lindberg (Chicago: Chicago University Press, 1978).

Harvey, B. F. 'John Flete', in *The New Oxford Dictionary of National Biography*, vol. 20.

Harvey, John 'Wilton Diptych', *Archeologia*, xLvii (1961).

Harvey, L. P. *Islamic Spain* (Chicago: Chicago University Press, 1990).

Haskins, Charles C. 'Michael Scot and Frederick II', *Isis* 4. (1921/22).

Hill, Christopher *God's Englishman: Oliver Cromwell and the English Revolution* (Harmondsworth: Penguin, 1970).

Holmyard, Eric John *Alchemy* (New York: Dover).

Horden, Peregrine, *Hospitals and Healing from Antiquity to the Later Middle Ages* (Ashgate, 2008).

Hughes Jonathan, *Pastors and Visionaries: Religion and Secular Life in Late Medieval Yorkshire* (Woodbridge: Boydell and Brewer, 1988).

— *The Religious Life of Richard III: Piety and Prayer in the North of England* (Stroud: Sutton, 1997).

— 'Alchemy and Late Medieval Sexuality', in *Medieval Virginities*, ed. A. Bernau, R. Evans and S. Salih (Cardiff, 2003).

— *Arthurian Myths and Alchemy: the Kingship of Edward IV* (Stroud: Sutton, 2003).

— 'The humanity of Thomas Charnock and Elizabethan Alchemist', in *Mystical Metal of Gold: Essays on Alchemy and Renaissance Culture*, ed. S. Linden (New York, 2007).

Huizinga, Johan *The Waning of the Middle Ages: A Study of the Forms of Life, Thought and Art in France and the Netherlands in the XIV and XVth centuries* (Harmondsworth: Penguin, 1951).

Humphrey, K. W. 'The Library of John Erghome', *Proceedings of the Leeds Philosophical and Literary Society* 18 (1982).

Ingledew, Francis *Sir Gawain and the Green Knight and the Order of the Garter* (Notre Dame: University of Notre Dame Press, 2006).

James M. R Catalogue of the library of the Austin Friars at York *Fasciculus JW Clark dicatus*, (Cambridge, 1909).

Jamison, Catherine *the History of the Royal Hospital of St Katherine's* (London: Oxford University Press, 1952).

Jones, R. H. *The Royal Policy of Richard II: Absolutism in the late Middle Ages* (New York: Barnes and Noble, 1968).

Jones, W. R. 'Political Uses of Sorcery in Medieval Europe', *The Historian*, 34 (1972) pp. 670–87.

Jung, Carl, *Psychology and Alchemy* (London: Routledge, 1953).

— *Alchemical Studies in The Collected Works* vol. 13 (Princeton, 1970).

— *Mysterium Conjunctionis*, trans. F. C. Hull (Princeton, 1970).

— *The Archetypes of Collective Unconscious* (Collected works vol. 9, 2nd edn. Princeton, NJ: Bollinger, 1981) p. 160.

Kantorowicz, H. Ernest, *The King's Two Bodies: A Study in Mediaeval Political Theology* (Princeton, NJ: Princeton University Press 1997).

Kaufman M. H. and Maclenna W. J. G. W. S. Barrow, 'Robert the Bruce', *New DNB*.

Kean, P. M. *The Pearl an Interpretation* (London: Routledge Kegan Paul, 1967).

Keen, M. *English Society in the Later Middle Ages 1348–1500* (Harmondsworth: Penguin, 1998).

—'The Wilton Diptych: the Case for a Crusading Context', in *The Regal Image of Richard II and the Wilton Diptych*, ed. Gordon, D. (Harvey Miller Publishers, 1998).

Klassen, F. *English Manuscripts of Magic, 1300–1500 A Preliminary Survey in Conjuring Spirits' in Texts and Traditions of Medieval Ritual Magic*, ed. Claire Fangen (Pennsylvania State University Press, 1998).

Lagoras V. A. 'The Legend of St Joseph', *Speculum* 46 (1971).

Leff, Gordon *Heresy in the Late Middle Ages, The Relation of Heterodoxy to Dissent c 1250–c1450*, 2 vols (Manchester: Manchester University Press, 1967).

Lemay, R. 'L'authentisite de la preface de Robet de Chester a sur traduction du Morienes' *Chrysopoeia* (1991).

Lenhart, J. M. *Science in the Franciscan Order* (Wagner, 1924; Kessinger, 2003).

Lewis, K. J. 'Becoming a Virgin: Richard II and Edward the Confessor the Gender of Holiness', in *Men women and Saints in Late Medieval Europe*, eds Samantha Riches, J. E. Riches and Sarah Salih (London: Routledge, 2002).

Linden, Stanton J. *Mystical Metal of Gold Essays on Alchemy and Renaissance culture* (NewYork: AMS Press, 2008).

— 'Smatterings of the Philosopher's Stone: Sir Thomas Browne and Alchemy', in *Mystic Metal of Gold: Essays in Alchemy and Renaissance Culture*, ed. S. Linden (New York: AMS Press 2008).

Lindley, P. 'Absolutism and Regal Image in Ricardian Sculpture', in *The Regal Image of Richard II and the Wilton Diptych*, ed. Gordon, D. (Harvey Miller Publishers, 1998).

McFarlane, K. B. *The Nobility of Later Medieval England* (Oxford: Clarendon Press, 1973).

McVaugh, M. *The Development of Medieval Pharmaceutical Theory in Arnoldi de Villanova Opera*.

— 'The Nature and Limits of Medical Certitude at Early Fourteenth-Century Montpllier' *Osiris* 6 (1990).

— *Medicine before the Plague. Practitioner and Patients in the Crown of Aragon 1285–1345* (Cambridge: Cambridge University Press, 1993).

Manzalaoui, M. A. 'The Secreta secretorum in English thought in the fourteenth to the seventeenth century' (Oxford, D.Phil. thesis, 1954).

Manzalaoui, Mahmoud 'John Dastin and the Pseudo Arisotelian', *Secreta Secretorum*, *Ambix*, 9 (1961).

Marshall, Peter, *The Philosopher's Stone* (London: Pan Macmillan, 2001).

Masceti, Yaakov 'This is the famous stone': George Herbert's Poetic Alchemy in 'the Elixir', in *Mystic Metal of Gold: Essays in Alchemy and Renaissance Culture*, ed. S. Linden (New York, 2008).

Maxwell, P. G. *The Chemical Choir: A History of Alchemy* (London: Continuum, 2008).

The Medieval world, ed. P. Lineham and J. L Nelson (London: Routledge, 2001).

Melville, Herman *Moby Dick* (Harmondsworth, 1972).

Michael A. Michael, 'A MS Wedding Gift for Philippa of Hainault to Edward III', *Burlington Magazine* LXXVII (1985).

Michael, Michael 'The Iconography of Kingship in the Walter of Milemete Treatise', *Journal of Warbourg and Courtald Institute* 57 (1994) 35–47.

Michell, John *New Light on the Ancient Mythology of Glastonbury* (Glastonbury: Gothic Image Publication, 1990).

Mitchell, Shelagh 'Richard II, Kingship and the Cult of Saints', in *The Regal Image of Richard II and the Wilton Diptych*, ed. Gordon, D. (Harvey Miller Publishers 1998).

Molland, George 'Dumbleton John', *New DNB* (2004).

Mons. De mas Latrie *Histoire de Isle de Cypre* (Strasbourg, 1468).

Montgomery Watt W. and. Cachio, P. *A History of Islamic Spain* (Edinburgh: Edinburgh University Press, 1965).

Morgan, N. 'The Significance of the Banner on the Wilton Diptych', in *The Regal Image of Richard II and the Wilton Diptych*, ed. Gordon, D. (Harvey Miller Publishers 1998).

Moyen Age De Quelques Texts Alchimiques Attribues a Arthur o Merlin' *Merologus* 3 (1995).

Multhauf, Robert P. 'The Science of Matter' in *Science in the Middle Ages* ed. David C. Lindberg (Chicago, 1976).

Musto, R.G. 'Queen Sancia of Naples 1281–1345 and the Spiritual Franciscans', in *Women of he Medieval World, Essays in honour of John H. Mundy*, ed. J. Kirschner (Oxford: Blackwell, 1985).

Newman, W. R. 'An Overview of Roger Bacon's Alchemy', in *Roger Bacon and the Sciences: Commemorative Essays*, ed. J. Hackett (Leiden: Brill, 1997).

North, J. D. *Chaucer's Universe*; North, 'Celestial Influence: the Major Premises of Astrology', in P. Zambella ed. *Astrology hallucinati Stars and the End of the world in Luther's Time* (Berlin, 1986).

— 'The Canon's Yeoman's Tale', in *Alchemy Revisited: Proceedings of the International conference on the history of alchemy* at the University of Gronigen 17–19 April 1989, ed. Z. R. W. M. von Martels (Leiden: Brill, 1990).

— 'Robert of York', *New DNB*.

— *God's Clockmaker* (London: Hambledon, 2001).

— *The Ambassador's Secret Holbein and the World of the Renaissance* (London: Hambledon, 2002).

Oberman, H. A. and. Wiesheiph, J. A. 'The Sermon Ascribed to Thomas Bradwardine (1346)', *Archives di histoire Doctrinale et Litteraire the Moyen Age*, 25 (1958).

O'Brien, Lora *Witchcraft from an Irish Witch* (Career Press, 2004).

Obrist, Barbara 'Art et nature dans l'alchimie', *Revue d'histoire sciences* 49 (1991).

— 'Les rapports d'analogie entre philosophie et alchemie medieavales', in *Alchimie et philosophie a la renaissance*: acta du colloque international de Tours 4–7 Decembre 1991 reunies sous la direction de Jean Claude Margolin et Sylvain Matton (Paris: J. Vrin, 1993).

Ogrinc, W. L. 'Western Society and Alchemy from 1200–1500', *Journal of Medieval History* 6 (March 1980).

Ormrod, W. M 'Edward III', *New DNB*.

Ormrod, W. Mark *The Reign of Edward III:Crown and Political Society in England 1327–77* (London, New Haven: Yale University Press, 1990).

Packe, Michael *King Edward III* (London: Routledge and Keagan Paul, 1983).

Page, Sophie *Magic in Medieval Manuscripts* (Toronto, 2004).

Palmer, C. F. R. *The Antiquary*, xxii (1890).

Paravicini-Bagliani, A. *Medicina e scienze della natura corte dei papi nel duecento* (Spoleto: Centro italiano di studi sull'alto medioevo, 1991).

— *The Pope's Body*, trans. D. S. Peterson (Chicago and London: University of Chicago Press, 1998).

— 'La papaute du XIIIe siècle et la renaissance de l'anatomie', in *Medicina e scienze*.

— 'Ruggero Bacone, Bonifacio VIII e la teoria della 'Prolongatio vitae', in *Medicina e scienze della natura*, pp. 329–61.

Patai, Raphael *The Jewish Alchemists* (Princeton: Princeton University Press, 1994).

Penn Szittya, C. 'Domesday and the Book of the Apocalypse', in *The Apocalypse in the Middle Ages*, ed. R. H. Emmerson and B. McGuin (Ithaca, 1992).

Pereira, M. 'Arnoldo de Vilanova e l'alchimia. Un'andigne preliminare', in *Actes de la Troboda Internatione d' Estulis sobra Arnan de Villanovo* Vol. 2. ed. a.c. di. J. Perernau (Treballs de la seccio de filosofia i ciencies socials, XIX) Barcelona: Institut d'Estudis Catalans, 1995.

Pereira, Michela 'The Alchemical Corpus Attributed to Raymund Lull' (London: Warbourg Institute Surveys and texts, XVIII, 1989).

Pereira, Michela and Spaggioni, Barbara *Il Testamentum alchemnico attributo a Raimundo Lullo: edizione del testo latino e catelano dal manuscritto Oxford Corpus Christ College 244* (Firenze: Sismel Edizione del Galluzo, 1999).

Perkins, J. *Westminster Abbey. Its Worship and Ornaments* (Alcuin Club, xxxiv, 1930).

Phillips, J. R. 'Edward II and the Prophets', in *England in the Fourteenth Century*, ed. W. M. Ormrod (Proceedings of the Haarlaxton Syposium, Woodbrige: Boydell, 1986).

Picarel, *History of the foundation of St Katherine by the Tower* (London, 1787).

Pinches, J. H. and R.V. *The Royal Heraldry of England* (London: Heraldry Today 1974).

Pingree, D. 'The Diffusion of Arabic magical texts in Western Europe', in *La Diffusione delle scienze islamich nel medio evo europeo* (Rome: Accademia Nazionale dei Lincei, 1987).

Plessner, M. 'The Place of the Turka Philosophorum in the Development of Alchemy', *Isis*, 45 (1954).

Pujmenova, Olga 'Portraits of kings depicted as magi in Bohemian Painting', in *The Regal Image of Richard II and the Wilton Diptych*, ed. Gordon, D. (Harvey Miller Publishers, 1998).

Rampling, Jennifer M. 'George Ripley and Alchemical Consensus', *Sixth International Conference on History of Chemistry*, Leuven, Belgium 28 Aug–1 Sep, 2007.

Rampling, Jennifer M. 'Establishing the Canon: George Ripley and his Alchemical Sources', *Ambix* 55 No. 3 (2008) pp. 189–208.

Rawcliffe, Carole ' "Written in the Book of Life" the Libraries of Medieval English Hoispitals and Almshouses', *The Library* 3 (2002) pp. 127–62.

— *Leprosy in Medieval England* (Woodbridge: Boydell, 2006).

Rigg, A. 'John of Bridlington Prophecy a New Look' *Speculum* 63 (1988).

Robertson, D. W. 'Why the devil wears green', *Modern Language Notes* (Nov. 1954).

Rudrum, Alan 'These Fragments I have shored against my ruins: Henry Vaughan, Alchemical Philosophy, and the Great Rebellion' in *Mystic Metal of Gold: Essays in Alchemy and Renaissance Culture*, ed. S. Linden (New York, 2008).

Ruggero, Bacone'e l'alchimia di lunga vita. Riflessioni sui testi', in *Alchimia e medicina nel Medioevo*, ed. C. Crisciani and A. Paravicini-Bagliani (Firenze: Sismel, 2003) pp. 33–54.

Russell, Jeffrey Burton *Witchcraft and Magic in the Middle Ages* (New York: Cornell University Press, 1972).

St Alban's Chronicle, The Chronica Maiora of Thomas Walsingham, tranl. David Preest with introduction and notes by James G. Clark (Woodbridge: Boydell, 2005).

Saul, N. 'Richard II and the Vocabulary of Kingship', *English Historical Review* (1995) cx 854–77.

— *Richard II* (New Haven: Yale University Press, 1997).

— 'Richard II's ideas on Kingship', in *The Regal Image of Richard II and the Wilton Diptych*, ed. Gordon, D. (Harvey Miller Publishers, 1998).

— *The Three Richards Richard I, Richard II and Richard III* (London: Continuum, 2005).

— *English Church Monuments in the Middle Ages* (Oxford, 2009).

Saxl, F. and Meier, H. *Catalogue of Astrological and Mythological Manuscripts of the Late Middle Ages* (London: Warbourg Institute, 1953).

Shoenbaum, Samuel 'Richard II and the Realities of Power', in *Critical Essays on Shakespeare's Richard II,* ed. Kirby Farrell (New York: G. K. Hall, 1999).

Singer, D. W. 'Michael Scot and Alchemy', *Isis* 13.

— *Catalogue of Alchemical Manuscripts*; printed *Opera Omnia* ed. A. Borgnet (Paris, 1890).

— *Catalogue of Latin and Vernacular Alchemical Manuscripts in Great Britain and Ireland Dating from before the XVI Century* (Brusssels: M. Lamertin, 1928).

Skinner, S. *Terrestrial Astrology: Divination by Astrology* (London, Routledge Kegan Paul (1980).

Southern, W. Richard. W. *Robert Grosseteste the Growth of an English Mind in Medieval Europe* (Oxford: Clarendon Press, 1986).

Stillman, John Maxson *The Story of Alchemy and Early Chemistry* (New York, Dover Publications, 1960).

Strohm, Paul *England's Empty Throne* (New Haven: Yale University Press, 1995).

Summersen, H. 'Saint George', in *The Oxford Dictionary of National Biography* vol 20, eds Mathew H.C.G. and Harrison B. (London: Oxford University Press, 2004).

Szulakowska, Urszula 'The Alchemical Medicine and Christology of Robert Fludd and Abraham von Franckenberg', in *Mystic Metal of Gold: Essays in Alchemy and Renaissance Culture*, ed. S. Linden (New York, 2008).

Taavitsainen, Irma and Pahta Paivi eds, *Medical and Scientific Writing in Late Medieval England* (Cambridge: Cambridge University Press, 2002).

Talbot, H. 'The Elixir of Youth', in *Chaucer and Middle English Studies in Honour of Rossel Hope. Robbins*, ed., Beryl Rowland (London: Allen Unwin, 1974).

Talbot, H. and Hammond, E. A. *The Medical Practitioners of Medieval England* (London: Wellcome Historical Library, 1965).

Taylor, J. 'Richard II's views on Kingship', *Proceedings of the Leeds Philosophica and Literary Society* vol xiv pt v (1971).

Therese, Lilley *City and Cosmos. The Medieval World in Urban Form* (London, 2009).

Thielmann, J. M., 'Political Canonization and Political Symbolism in Medieval England, *Journal of British Studies* 29 (1996) pp. 241–66.

Thiessen, W. L. 'John Dastin the Alchemist as co-creator', *Ambix* 38 (1991).

— 'The Letters of John Dastin', *Ambix*, 55 (2 July 2008).

Thomas, Keith *Religion and the Decline of Magic* (London: Penguin, 1984),

Thorndike, Lynn *A History of Magic and Experimental Science* (New York: Columbia University Press, 1923–58).

Trease, G. E. 'The Spicers and Apothecaries of the Royal Household in the reigns of Henry III Edward I and Edward II', *Nottingham Medieval Studies* 3 (1959).

Tyerman, Christopher *England and the Crusades, 1095–1588* (Chicago: Chicago University Press, 2009) p. 246.

Tyson, D. B. 'The Epitaph of Edward the Black Prince', *Medium Aevum* 46 (1977).

Ullman, W. *Principles of Government and Politics in the Middle Ages* (New York: Barnes and Noble, 1966).

Urszula, Szulakowska 'The Alchemical Medicine and Christology of Robert Fludd and Abraham von Franckenberg', in *Mystic Metal of Gold: Essays in Alchemy and Renaissance Culture*, ed. S. Linden (New York, 2008).

Vale, Malcolm *War and Chivalry: Warfare and Aristocratic Culture in England, France and Burgundy at the End of the Middle Ages* (London: Duckworth, 1981).

Vincent, Nicholas *The Holy Blood: King Henry III and the Westminster Blood Title* (Cambridge: Cambridge University Press, 2001).

Von Franz, Marie Louise *Alchemy: An Introduction to the Symbolism and the Psychology* (Toronto, 1980).

Walker, Simon 'Remembering Richard: History and Memory in Lancastrian England', in Simon Walker, *Political Culture in Late Medieval England*, ed. Mike Braddick (Manchester: Manchester University Press, 2006).

Warmould, P. 'The Throne of Solomon in St Edward's Chair', in *Essays in Honour of Erwin Panofsky ed., Millard Meiss* (New York: New York University Press, 1961).

Watson, G. *Theriac and Mithridetium* (London, 1966).

Wedding Gift for Philippa of Hainault to Edward III', *Burlington Magazine* LXXVII (1985).

Weil-Parot, Nicolas 'Arnaud de Villeneuve et les relations possibles entre le sceau du lion et l'alchimie' *Arxiu de textos catalans* 23/4 (2004–5).

Wilkins, N. *Nicholas Flamel: Des Livres et de l'Or* (Paris: Imago, 1993).

Williams, S. J. 'Roger Bacon and his edition of the pseudo Aristotelian *Secreta secretorum*', *Speculum* 69 (1994).

— 'Roger Bacon and the Secret of Secrets', in *Roger Bacon and the Sciences Commemorative Essays*, ed. J. Hackett (Leiden: Brill, 1997).

— *The Secret of Secrets: The scholarly career of a Pseudo-Arnoldian text in the latin middle ages* (Ann Arbor, University of Michigan Press, 2003).

Wilson, Christopher 'Richard's Artificers and Shoppers: Richard II's Remodelling of Westminster Hall', in *The Regal Image of Richard II and the Wilton Diptych*, ed. Gordon, D. (Harvey Miller Publishers, 1998).

Wood, C. *Chaucer and the Country of the Stars* (Princeton: Princeton University Press, 1970).

Wood, C. T. 'Richard II's Wilton Diptych', in *Joan of Arc and Richard III: Sex, Saints and Government in the Middle Ages* (Oxford, 1988).

The Works of Sir Thomas Browne, ed. Geoffrey Keynes, 4 vols (London: Faber and Faber, 1964).

Zambelli, Paolo (ed.) *Astrologi Hallucinati: Stars and the End of the World in Luther's Time* (Berlin: Walter de Gruyter, 1986).

Ziegler, J. 'Alchemy in *Practica summari*. A Footnote to Michael McVaugh's Contribution', *Arxiu de textos Catalans antics* 23/4 (2005).

Ziegler, Joseph *Medicine and Religion c. 1300 the case of Arnau de Vilanova* (Oxford: Clarendon Press, 1998).

— 'On the Use of the "New Sciences" (Medicine, Alchemy, and Physiognomy) for Religious Purposes c. 1300' (Max-Plancck Instit. Für Wissenschaftsgeschichte (2005)).

Index